D0915372

Crime and Justice

Crime and Justice

An Annual Review of Research

Edited by Michael Tonry and Norval Morris
with the Support of The National Institute of Justice

VOLUME 7

The University of Chicago Press, Chicago and London

This volume was prepared under grant 83-IJ-CX-0040 awarded to the
Castine Research Corporation by the National Institute of Justice, U.S.
Department of Justice, under the Omnibus Crime Control and Safe Streets
Act of 1968 as amended. Points of view or opinions expressed in this volume
are those of the editors or authors and do not necessarily represent the
official position or policies of the U.S. Department of Justice. Additional
support was provided by The German Marshall Fund of the United States
under grant 1-31536.

The University of Chicago Press, Chicago 60637
The University of Chicago Press, Ltd., London

© 1986 by The University of Chicago
All rights reserved. Published 1986
Printed in the United States of America
91 90 89 88 87 86   5 4 3 2 1

ISSN: 0192-3234
ISBN: 0-226-80801-7

LCN: 80-642217

364.05
C929
v. 7

Contents

Introduction

The essays in this volume focus on what is the central purpose of *Crime and Justice:* statements of what is known, not what is believed; of what has been established by measurement, not what has been accepted by tradition. To some this will appear as pettifogging preoccupation with detail, irrelevant to the broad and accepted sweep of well-tried methods of preventing crime, catching and punishing criminals, and deterring those who are inclined to criminality. And, since the products of such studies so often cast doubt on established practice, they tend, if not to be rejected outright, to diminish the moral fervor of those charged with the various tasks of enforcing the criminal law.

In the physical sciences, few are dismayed when the findings of the scientific method, the controlled experiment, the critical testing of a causal theory, prove counterintuitive; in the social sciences, and particularly in the study of crime and its treatment, research results that run counter to common sense risk immediate rejection. Criminology, in some ways, is still at the flat-earth stage, with unexamined common sense, allied to prejudice and illusion, dominating established knowledge.

Research projects testing by methodologically acceptable means the efficacy of diverse methods of preventing crime, of policing neighborhoods, of catching, convicting, and sentencing criminals, are scarce; budgets to those ends are scant. As a rhetorical matter everyone asks, What works? As a matter to be enquired into seriously, by controlled experiment, by substantial funds being directed to that end, the question is neglected.

Is this because research in the social sciences is more difficult than in the physical sciences? Or is it that ethical obstacles inhibit research into human behavior? Taking into account the present stage of knowledge in those sciences concerned with the behavior of man, it is true that there are larger practical and ethical difficulties in experimental research here than in many studies in the physical sciences; but that is not the whole story. Medicine has come in the last century to an insistence on controlled experiments to test competing treatments and fundamental research to test causal theories. Here, though, the study of mental illness lags, in terms of scientific validity and effort, well behind that of physical illness, and this may reaffirm the larger difficulty of research into the inner worlds of man than into the world he inhabits.

In criminology, this contrast between what is relied on and what is known is sharp and apparent. The war story takes precedence over the statistic; experience is preferred to counterintuitive fact. Consider, for example, some strongly held beliefs about police practices: the intensity of police patrol reduces crime; two-person police cars are more effective than those with one occupant and better protect the police; increasing the speed of police response to emergency calls improves "clearance" rates. All those propositions have been tested and shown to be either false or imprecise, but the conventional wisdom continues to affirm them, and there are powerful media and political pressures that will preserve their domination of police patrol practices, particularly in the inner city.

One can present similar sad scenarios for the work of the prosecutor, the judge, and the correctional official—to say nothing of the defense counsel, about whom myths reign unchallenged. Yet in the long run, and sometimes in the shorter run when, following Maynard Keynes's precept, we may not all be dead, tested knowledge does influence practice. This is the central role of *Crime and Justice*. The policy of our editorial board, generously supported and encouraged by the National Institute of Justice, is to bring to the attention of the practitioner and the scholar what is known, not merely believed, and in other than jargon to present the basis on which that claim is made. We do not delude ourselves that there will be a rush to the immediate acceptance of such tentative truths (since all truths, other than those revealed, are tentative) as we can produce, but we do believe that this critical search for validity is the obligation of this series.

For those with a taste for "bottom line" solutions and large generalizations, the essays in this series must be disappointing, and this volume will be no exception. But for those who realize that marginal advances in practice are the building blocks of efficiency and decency, this volume is a substantial contribution.

And, so, the menu for this volume. David P. Farrington reviews the evidence on the relations between age and crime. Rolf Loeber and Magda Stouthamer-Loeber, in an essay of remarkable range and precision, review research on the familial correlates of juvenile behavior problems and delinquency and on the promising results of training in parenting skills and other programs targeted on conduct problem children. Peter W. Greenwood reviews evidence on the criminality of young people, on the identification of chronic juvenile offenders, and on the processing of juvenile offenders in both juvenile and adult criminal courts. Michael R. Gottfredson assesses the substantive findings of two decades' experience with victimization surveys. Philip J. Cook explicates an "opportunity" perspective for understanding crime and demonstrates why analyses of incapacitative and rehabilitative crime control strategies must account for their effect on the attractiveness of opportunities for crime. Ironically, by reducing the number of active offenders and decreasing victimization probabilities, such crime control efforts may cause prospective victims to undertake fewer self-protection efforts and thereby create more attractive criminal opportunities that may entice new people into offending and thereby undermine the effects of crime control efforts. Finally, Peter Reuter and Mark Kleiman use economic analysis to assess the effectiveness of current strategies for dealing with drug trafficking. On the basis of the limited effect that current strategies have on retail drug prices and, by implication, on drug availability, they conclude that current efforts to pressure source countries to forbid or control production, to interdict importation, and to prosecute high-level traffickers are unlikely substantially to diminish supplies of marijuana and cocaine.

Philip J. Cook

The Demand and Supply of Criminal Opportunities

ABSTRACT

Criminal opportunity theory provides a framework for examining the
interaction between potential offenders and potential victims. Criminals'
behavior influences the nature and amount of self-protective measures
taken by potential victims, and changes in self-protection make criminal
opportunities more or less attractive. Criminal opportunity theory has
precursors in criminological theory, preeminently in the work of Cloward
and Ohlin, but in these theories opportunities are mediated through social
learning. Criminal opportunity theory employs the economic theory of
markets to describe and predict how criminals and victims interact.
Evidence is available that potential victims take more self-protection
measures when the perceived risk of victimization is greater and that
prospective criminals are likelier to attack relatively more vulnerable
targets. Little research is available on whether increases in self-protection
reduce the total volume of crime or merely displace crime to more
vulnerable targets; the extent of displacement probably differs among
offenses. The market perspective has several benefits to the investigation
of interaction between potential victims and offenders: it assembles
different topics encompassed by criminal opportunity theory into a
coherent whole, it is expressed in a form that facilitates borrowing from
economic theory, and it generates new and important insights for policy
evaluation and criminological theory. One central insight is that law
enforcement strategies may alter the quality of opportunities and thereby
precipitate additional crime. Effective incapacitation or rehabilitation
policies, for example, may reduce the number of offenders in circulation
and thereby reduce the perceived risk of victimization. This may cause
individuals to reduce their self-protection efforts, making them more
attractive targets than before and thereby stimulating increased crime
rates on the part of those criminals who remain active.

Philip J. Cook is Professor of Public Policy Studies and Economics at Duke University.

The core propositions that make up what I want to call "criminal opportunity theory" can be stated in a few sentences.[1] Criminals tend to be somewhat selective in choosing a crime target and are most attracted to targets that appear to offer a high payoff with little effort or risk of legal consequences. The large differences in victimization rates for different target groups can be understood in terms of their relative attractiveness to criminals. Potential victims respond to the crime threat by engaging in self-protection efforts, the intensity of which tends to increase with the probability of victimization. These efforts do modify victimization patterns to some extent. The quality of criminal opportunities (as modified by private protection) tends to have a positive influence on the overall volume of crime as well as on its distribution. Indeed, the interaction between potential offenders (responding to the net payoff to crime) and potential victims (taking actions to modify the payoff to crime in response to the crime threat) is akin to the interaction between buyers and sellers in a marketplace. "Equilibrium" in the "crime market" will be modified by actions of the criminal justice system.

These propositions, and some pertinent evidence, have been developed piecemeal during the last two decades by a number of criminologists and economists. The work that has generated the greatest interest for policymakers focuses on "situational prevention" methods for reducing crime, including increased surveillance, target hardening, and environmental management (Clarke 1983). Perhaps more profound are the policy implications of the equilibrium analysis of the market for crime opportunities (Ehrlich 1981), particularly in the context of predicting the aggregate effects of efforts to reform or restrain individual offenders; the market process may create incentives for remaining criminals to "fill in" where reformed or incapacitated criminals have left off. The theoretical framework is also relevant to the purely scientific concerns of criminology since it provides guidance in understanding (and predicting) crime patterns and trends (Cohen and Felson 1979) and patterns in private accommodation to the threat of criminal victimization (Clotfelter 1977; Skogan and Maxfield 1981).

It should be noted that this concern with the nature and quality of criminal opportunity has precursors in the criminology literature. For

---

[1] Cohen, Felson, and Land (1980) employ the term "opportunity theory" for a related set of propositions.

example, consider this statement by Cloward and Ohlin (1960) in their seminal work *Delinquency and Opportunity:* "Much of the criminological literature assumes . . . that one may explain a criminal act simply by accounting for the individual's readiness to employ illegal alternatives of which his culture, through its norms, has already made him generally aware. Such explanations are quite unsatisfactory, however, for they ignore a host of questions regarding the *relative availability* of illegal alternatives to various potential criminals" (p. 145). But Cloward and Ohlin, and other sociologists working in their tradition (Bordua 1961), were oriented by a different set of concerns than are contributors to modern criminal opportunity theory. For Cloward and Ohlin, criminal opportunities influence criminal behavior indirectly, by their influence on the development and maintenance of a delinquent subculture. This subculture creates an environment for the acquisition of relevant skills and values and for support of the performance of the criminal role once it is learned (1960, p. 148). Thus the social learning process is at the heart of this perspective. The modern perspective, in contrast, emphasizes individual choice guided by the perceived costs and benefits of criminal activity (Cook 1980; Clarke 1983).

Criminal opportunity theory does not necessarily discount the importance of the process by which some youths acquire values and skills that tend to foster criminal activity; surely this process is important to explaining interpersonal differences in participation in criminal activity. Rather, modern day opportunity theory is oriented by questions that are more productively addressed within a choice framework than within a social learning framework.

This essay is not an exhaustive review of the relevant literature. I have attempted to discuss all the important ideas, however, even if all the available empirical evidence is not cited. (A good companion piece for this essay is Clarke [1983], which provides a more thorough review of the evidence relevant to situational crime prevention.) My primary concern is to bring together the different strands of criminal opportunity theory, with emphasis on the nature and implications of the interaction between criminals and potential crime targets. As may already be obvious, my perspective is that of an economist, diluted perhaps by a greater-than-average appreciation for the contributions of other social scientists.

Subsequent sections cover a lot of territory. A roadmap may help.

The major regions are

Patterns of Victimization,
Private Efforts to Prevent Victimization,
Influences of Criminal Opportunities on Aggregate Crime Rates,
Implications for Incapacitation and Rehabilitation, and
Encouraging Self-Protection.

Section I considers the implications of the intrinsically greater attractiveness to criminal predators of some potential crime targets than others. Potential victims respond to their perception of this threat by protecting themselves in various ways—for example, by reducing their exposure to crime. Observed patterns of victimization of different categories of people and commercial places can be interpreted as reflecting the net result of intrinsic attractiveness and exposure. This framework also yields a highly satisfactory explanation for divergences between the high levels of fear of crime reported by some groups, notably women and the elderly, and these groups' relatively low victimization rates.

A more complete characterization of private efforts to defend against crime is presented in Section II. The social and economic cost of private defense efforts is enormous, probably exceeding total expenditures by the criminal justice system. There is solid evidence that decisions to engage in self-protection activities are influenced by the crime rate. There is not much systematic evidence, but plenty of casual observation, on the effectiveness of such efforts.

It is possible that target exposure and attractiveness influence the distribution of victimization but have little effect on the total volume of criminal activity. Self-protection efforts by some potential targets may simply displace crime to other, unprotected targets. Some evidence on this issue is reviewed in Section III. One of the more interesting unanswered questions is whether the proliferation of targets of a particular sort in the same geographic area will increase the volume of crime committed against this type of target. For example, if the number of branch banking offices in a small city increases, is there any reason to expect that the number of bank robberies in this city will increase, or will the same rate of bank robberies simply be spread more thinly among the available targets?

If crime rates are influenced by the quality and quantity of criminal opportunities, and vice versa, then the aggregate crime rate is determined by the interaction between the public, as "providers" of crime opportunities, and potential criminals. This interaction is closely analogous to a market process in which price and quantity are determined by the interaction between supply and demand. It turns out that this market analogy yields some very important insights into the influence of the criminal justice system on crime rates. In particular, it can be demonstrated that rehabilitating or incapacitating criminals will have less than the expected influence on crime rates in the long run to the extent that potential criminals are responsive to opportunities and that the public's provision of opportunities is responsive to the crime rate. The results of this analysis are presented in Section IV.

Section V presents some thoughts on encouraging self-protection. In Austria, people who leave their cars unlocked in public areas may be ticketed and fined. This approach to the problem of auto theft may be justifiable if it is less socially burdensome to deter car owners from being careless than it is to deter teenagers from stealing unlocked cars. But this crime problem may not be analogous to other types of crime and other means of self-protection. This section offers some suggestions on the general shape of public policy to encourage self-protection activities. A brief concluding statement, Section VI, follows.

I. Patterns of Victimization

It is common knowledge that victimization rates for crimes of theft and violence differ widely among different groups of people. Young men are much more likely to get into serious fights than, say, elderly women. Inner-city residents are more likely to be burglarized than residents of rural communities. Cab drivers, convenience store clerks, and gas station attendants are more likely to be robbed than college professors. Perhaps it is precisely because such patterns are so obvious that criminologists have not deemed them a fit subject for systematic study and theory development, until quite recently (Gottfredson 1981). But with the advent of large-scale victimization surveys (Ennis 1967), and in particular the National Crime Survey and its antecedents, a wealth of data has become available for creating a detailed picture of victimization patterns, particularly along socioeconomic, demographic, and geographic dimensions (see, e.g., Hindelang, Gottfredson, and Garofalo 1978, chaps. 1, 5). This new capability to describe has been coupled with an effort to explain. In part, the motivation for developing an explanation of victimization patterns is the hope that understanding the *distribution* of crime will generate new insights into the determinants of the *volume* of crime, as discussed in Section III below. But the distribution question is of interest in its own right.

Hindelang et al. (1978) conclude their extensive exploration of victimization patterns and related issues with a chapter entitled "Toward a Theory of Personal Victimization." Their perspective is that individuals operate in an environment that is characterized by broad differences in victimization risks—"there are high-risk times, places, and people" (p. 245)—and that victimization patterns are the result of differential exposure to such risky circumstances. Differential exposure is in turn the result of differences in life-style. Briefly, "life-style refers to routine daily activities, both vocational activities . . . and leisure activities" (p. 241). In this model, life-style is viewed as the result of individual adaptations to "role expectations" and to "structural constraints" such as economic, familial, educational, and legal status. Life-style determines exposure to crime, both directly and through personal associations. Hindelang and his colleagues add that, for a given "exposure," the probability of victimization will depend on the "desirability" and "vincibility" of the individual as a potential crime target (p. 264).

This life-style model can be used to rationalize some demographic patterns of victimization when considered in conjunction with what is known or assumed to be true about life-styles characteristic of different demographic groups. A direct test of this model, however, requires information about life-styles of victims and nonvictims (Hindelang et al. 1978, p. 241). Recognition of the potential importance of routine activities in explaining victimization has motivated a series of proposals to include questions on this topic in the National Crime Survey (beginning with Penick and Owens [1976, p. 98]). The British Crime Survey (Hough and Mayhew 1983) and the Northwestern University Crime Survey (Skogan 1978) are notable as early attempts to gather an empirical basis for the study of victimization patterns.

One important element that is lacking from the life-style model is a "feedback loop" by which the individual's exposure to risky circumstances is influenced by his concern with being victimized (Garofalo 1985). If we view individual behavior as resulting from choices based on anticipated consequences (the economist's perspective) rather than as the predetermined consequence of role expectations and social constraints, then it is natural to postulate such a feedback loop—individuals will choose to limit their exposure to a degree that is influenced by their anticipation of being victimized when exposed. A simple model developed by Balkin (1979) incorporates this type of feedback. His model provides some useful insights, particularly with respect to the "fear-crime" conundrum: why some groups that appear to have a relatively low victimization rate, notably, women and the elderly, report a relatively high level of fear of crime.

Balkin's model postulates three functional relationships, each of which is written in linear form (with positive parameters a, b, and e) for the sake of simplicity (1979, p. 345). They are fear of crime:

$$F = eR,$$

exposure to crime:

$$X = a - bF,$$

and observed victimization rate:

$$C = RX \quad \text{or} \quad R = \frac{C}{X}.$$

The key variable here is R, which is defined (in the third equation) as the ratio of the observed victimization rate to exposure. Exposure has a time dimension; for example, exposure to robbery may be measured as the time spent walking alone in public places. For the crime of robbery, R can be thought of as the robbery victimization rate per man-year of exposure. Thus the observed victimization rate (C) for a particular group may give a misleading indication of the relative risk of victimization that confronts these individuals when they are exposed (R) if that group's exposure is exceptionally high or low.

The logical relationship between the observed victimization rate (C) and fear (F) is the reduced form of these three equations:

$$C = \frac{a}{e}F - \frac{b}{e}F^2.$$

Thus, depending on which part of this quadratic relationship is relevant, the victimization rate may be either positively or negatively correlated with fear. Elderly people and women are attractive targets for muggers because of their physical vulnerability; their relatively low victimization rates may result from their being more careful (and therefore less exposed) than prime age males, in part because they know they are attractive targets. Arguably, then, "fear of crime is a rational response to the actual incidence of crime, and . . . where discrepancies appear it is because of faulty 'objective' measures of crime incorrectly calibrating the real risk" (Balkin 1979, p. 343).

This type of explanation for the fear-crime conundrum is satisfying because it does not require irrationality or misperception on the public's part. It should be noted that one element of Balkin's perspective did occur to Hindelang et al., who admit that "a definite possibility exists that a high level of fear *produces* a low risk of victimization" (1978, p. 189). They did not, however, develop this possibility or incorporate it into their life-style model.

The word "exposure" is perhaps inadequate to convey the full range of actions and attributes that influence victimization patterns. What is needed is a list of the determinants of victimization risk for common crimes of theft and violence (Cohen, Kluegel, and Land [1981] and Sparks [1981], among others, offer lists of this sort). Gottfredson (1981, p. 716) suggests that we take the criminal's perspective as a basis for generating such a list; individuals, households, or businesses that are attractive targets for criminals will suffer high rates of victimization. A "normal" criminal presumably is looking for a high payoff in exchange for a minimum of effort or risk. This statement suggests that several specific attributes of potential targets will be salient to the criminal. For the sake of brevity, I limit discussion of these attributes to the example of robbery victimization.[2]

1. *Propinquity.* Robbers want to economize on time spent searching for a suitable target. Robbers are more likely to encounter a suitable target if it is located near the robber's normal hangouts rather than elsewhere. Hence individuals' victimization proneness will be relatively high if they spend time in neighborhoods, schools, or other places frequented by active robbers. Commercial places located in or easily accessible from such areas will tend to suffer a high victimization rate.

2. *Payoff.* Robbers are mostly in it for the money. Individuals who appear to be carrying a lot of money and valuables will be more attractive targets than others. Generally, commercial places offer a higher payoff than individuals. Banks are the most attractive targets of all in this respect.

3. *Vulnerability.* Robbers want to complete the theft successfully and to avoid circumstances in which they may encounter effective

---

[2] For a more complete discussion of the robbery process from this perspective, see Cook (1983*b*). On the basis of his interviews with a number of convicted robbers, Conklin (1972) concluded that, "in considering whom to rob, the offender usually considers the amount of money available, the vulnerability of the victim, the risk he faces during the robbery, and the likelihood that the victim will resist" (p. 88). Each of these concerns is included in my list.

resistance by the victim or intervention by bystanders. Potential targets that appear capable and willing to defend themselves will be less victimization prone than others. Women, elderly people, and some drunks will be relatively vulnerable, especially when they are alone and in an otherwise deserted public place. Commercial places that hire guards, dogs, and other means of protection will thereby reduce their vulnerability to robbery.

4. *Access to Law Enforcement.*   Robbers want to minimize the probability and severity of punishment. One reason vulnerable victims are attractive to robbers is that a robbery that can be completed quickly and easily is relatively unlikely to result in an on-scene arrest. Another class of potential victims that is attractive in this respect includes drug dealers, men soliciting prostitutes, and others who are unlikely to report a robbery to the police or to cooperate with a court proceeding. Finally, commercial places that install alarms and automatic cameras may thereby deter some robbers.

Similar considerations apply to other crimes of theft and violence.[3] In the case of assault and most criminal homicides, the payoff is not financial but rather, typically, the assailants' satisfaction in hurting those who have threatened, insulted, or otherwise angered them. Wolfgang's (1958) notion of "victim precipitation" applies in many such cases. Propinquity, vulnerability, and access to law enforcement are arguably important in violent crime victimizations as well as in thefts.

What predictions follow from this discussion of victim proneness? One could easily generate a list of propositions of the form, Other things being equal, more lucrative targets will have higher victimization rates than less lucrative targets. Such a list is not very useful, however, because "other things" are unlikely to be equal. In particular, more lucrative targets will typically take pains to reduce their propinquity and vulnerability, and the net effect is not predictable without further information—we cannot safely predict that banks will experience a higher robbery rate than gas stations or skid row bums. Thus we expect that individuals, households, and commercial places that are inherently attractive to criminals in some respects will attempt to compensate by reducing their attractiveness in other respects. Observed patterns of victimization may then be interpreted as reflecting the net effect of the

---

[3] For some interesting specifics about what makes one house a more attractive target for burglary than another, see Repetto (1974); and for reviews of his and others' findings, see Rubenstein (1980) and Clarke (1983).

various attributes. A theory of victimization proneness, if it is to have empirical content, must incorporate the compensating self-protecting actions of targets. A complete model of this sort has not been formulated, but some research on self-protection decisions and effectiveness is available. The next section reviews this work.

Before turning to the issue of self-protection, however, it is appropriate to consider a generalization of the victim-proneness question. Predatory crimes of all categories—robbery, burglary, murder, et cetera—can be committed by using any one of several "techniques." For the violent crimes of robbery and murder, the successful assailant has adopted a technique characterized by sufficient power to overcome the victim's natural tendency to resist. From the criminal's viewpoint, the minimum necessary power will depend on the vulnerability of the intended victim. Thus a successful robbery of a crowded tavern may require a technique that includes shotguns and several perpetrators working together; a successful mugging of an elderly woman may be easily accomplished by a single unarmed youth. In Cook (1976), a study of noncommercial robbery, I concluded on the basis of victimization survey data that "the offenders' propensity to choose relatively well-defended victims (males, groups of two or more, adults) increases consistently with the deadliness of the offender's weapon and number of offenders involved" (p. 181). I found a related result in a study of weapon use in assaultive criminal homicide in which both the killer and the victim were male. The likelihood that a gun (as opposed to a less lethal weapon) would be the murder weapon depended on the relative ages of the killer and victim: in almost every case in which an elderly male (aged sixty years and over) killed a youthful male (aged eighteen to thirty-nine), the weapon was a gun, whereas when the relative ages were reversed, a gun was used less than half the time (Cook 1981, p. 257). Age, of course, correlates highly with physical strength.

The relationship between target vulnerability and criminal technique could also be explored for crimes of auto theft, burglary, rape, and so forth. The point is that an exploration of victim vulnerability (and hence victimization proneness) must focus on the question of vulnerability with respect to what technique. This question leads naturally to a framework for interpreting the technological details of victimization patterns.

II. Private Efforts to Prevent Victimization

One important point made in the preceding discussion is that "exposure" to crime is not simply a by-product of life-style or routine activities; rather, exposure is to some extent a matter of choice, influenced by the individual's perception of the likelihood of victimization. Exposure and victimization interact. It is natural to refer to private efforts to limit exposure that are motivated by the threat of crime as self-protection. Self-protection activities can be roughly classified into three categories: actions to make successful commission of a crime difficult, such as storing valuables in safes and avoiding deserted public places at night; actions to increase the apparent risk that a criminal will be arrested and punished, such as installing alarms and placing identification numbers or other markers on merchandise; and actions to minimize the loss if a victimization occurs, such as keeping a minimum of cash or valuables on hand and keeping weapons available for defense against attack. This last category includes actions that may discourage criminals by reducing the apparent payoff to them. Kakalik and Wildhorn (1977, pp. 49–50) provide more examples of self-protection services and equipment employed by businesses:

Security services purchased by clients include guard service, investigative service, patrol, and armored-car delivery. Security equipment may be categorized as being deterrent equipment or systems for monitoring and detection. Each may be broken down into subcategories. For example, deterrent equipment includes devices that make initial penetration difficult or discouraging, fences and gates, electronically controlled doors, burglar-resistive file cabinets and safes, and bank equipment such as vaults, safes, deposit boxes, night depositories, teller windows, drive-in windows, and remote-teller communications. Deterrent equipment also includes lighting equipment, such as high-intensity lamps and area floodlighting systems. Monitoring and detection systems include central station alarm services, local and proprietary alarms, closed circuit television, and other detection and surveillance devices.

A recent report on the private security industry (Cunningham and Taylor 1984) found that gross expenditures for private protection were nearly $22 billion in 1980, exceeding by a substantial margin the public expenditure for police protection. "Private security personnel also significantly outnumber sworn law enforcement personnel and non-military government guards by nearly 2 to 1. Total private security employment in 1982 is conservatively estimated at 1.1 million persons (excluding Federal civil and military security workers)" (Cunningham and Taylor 1984, p. 3).[4] Cunningham and Taylor also make an intriguing observation concerning the more rapid growth of private, than public, protection in recent years: "Such expanded use of private security and increased citizen involvement signals an increasing return to the private sector for protection against crime. The growth and expansion of modern police reflected a shift from private policing and security initiatives of the early 19th century. Now the pendulum appears to be swinging back" (pp. 3–4). Current projections call for continuing rapid increase in private resources devoted to private protection against crime.

These data on protection-related employment and expenditures do not give a complete accounting of private protection activities. We know that the threat of crime creates a pervasive distortion in the way we live, but we lack the data to quantify the social costs of such self-protection activities as children avoiding school rest rooms for fear of being robbed, middle-class families accepting the inconvenience and cultural sterility of living in the suburbs partly for the sake of a safer neighborhood and school, and urban residents avoiding public places and public transportation for fear of being exposed to crime.

While it is obvious that self-protection activities such as those discussed above are motivated by a concern over crime, it is not so clear that the level of self-protection activities is responsive to changes in the crime rate. More precisely, the question is whether an increase in the probability of victimization will induce a change in self-protection expenditures and actions. Several economists have published empirical findings that suggest a positive answer.

First, data from a 1968 survey of small businesses conducted by the Small Business Administration demonstrate that the fraction of businesses reporting various protective devices (such as burglar alarms, reinforcing devices, firearms, and subscription to protective services) is higher in ghetto areas than in nonghetto central cities and higher in central cities than in suburban locations (Kakalik and Wildhorn 1977, p. 28). Bartel's (1975) multivariate analysis of the same survey data extends these results; she found that, other things being equal, the likelihood of a business employing a guard or subscribing to a protective service increases with the victimization rates and average losses of similarly situated businesses.

---

[4] Earlier accounts of the size of the private protection business are in Kakalik and Wildhorn (1972), National Advisory Committee on Criminal Justice Standards and Goals (1976), and Clotfelter and Seeley (1979).

Clotfelter (1978) studied household behavior using a 1971 survey of households in the Washington, D.C., metropolitan area. He found that the likelihood that a household would take certain protective measures was a positive function of the rate of robbery and burglary victimizations in the household's section of the city or suburb (p. 396), holding constant certain other characteristics of the household. The following protective measures were significantly positively related to the neighborhood crime rate: "installed additional locks," "obtained watch dog," "put bars on windows," "usually lock house when at home," "carry something for protection," "ever stay at home because of crime," and "ever take taxis because of crime" (p. 397).

McDonald and Balkin (1983) used the Northwestern Crime Survey of Chicago, San Francisco, and Philadelphia residents to assess the relationship between the frequency of "going out at night" and the respondent's rating of the safety of his neighborhood (see also Skogan and Maxfield 1981). They found that respondents who rated their neighborhoods "very safe at night" went out at night about 1.4 times per week more often than those who rated their neighborhoods "very unsafe at night" (controlling for various characteristics of respondents and their households).

These studies demonstrate that targets located in high crime areas tend to put a relatively high level of effort into self-protection. But location is just one dimension of exposure to crime. In the typology presented in the previous section, another dimension is the payoff. Lucrative targets have greater intrinsic exposure to victimization and may adapt to this risk by adopting special protection measures. An obvious example is the use of guards and armored trucks to ship bullion or large quantities of currency. Precious jewelry is displayed by retailers in locked cases, whereas costume jewelry is often displayed on open racks. And so forth. The examples are numerous and easily generated from personal experience.

Are self-protection measures effective? Again, personal experience and common sense suggest that many of the measures taken by individuals, households, and businesses on a routine basis are effective. Clarke (1983) provides a thorough review of the published literature on this subject. A few examples will suffice here. Chaiken, Lawless, and Stevenson (1974) reported that a wave of bus robberies in New York City ended abruptly when an exact fare system was adopted. Hannan's (1982) careful study of 236 banking offices in the Philadelphia area found that the presence of bank guards was an important deterrent to bank robbery, although the presence of an automatic camera had no discernible effect. Schneider's (1976) evaluation of the Portland Burglary Prevention Program found that homes displaying stickers (indicating that possessions had been engraved with an identification number and could be traced) were less likely to be burglarized than were their stickerless neighbors. Rubenstein (1980) reviewed a number of evaluations of efforts to reduce the quality of criminal opportunities inherent in the "built environment," including target hardening, improved lighting and monitoring by cameras and guards, and design changes aimed at improving residents' and users' ability to detect suspicious behavior. Good locks and strong doors help prevent burglary; other environmental design strategies are more problematic.[5] To give a related example, ignition locks have proven highly effective in reducing auto theft.

III. Influences of Criminal Opportunities on Aggregate Crime Rates

The conclusions from earlier sections can be summarized in a few sentences. Differential exposure to crime helps explain observed victimization patterns. Targets that offer criminals a high payoff in exchange for relatively little effort or risk will suffer relatively high victimization rates. Knowing this, individuals, households, and businesses that are in intrinsically high-risk positions tend to exhibit greater caution and spend more on self-protection than do other potential targets. To the extent that these self-protection efforts are effective, they serve to modify victimization patterns.

An obvious question at this point is whether this "exposure theory" of victimization patterns has implications for the overall volume of crime. This question is often posed in the context of evaluating specific self-protection actions (Repetto 1976). Take, for example, a burglary-prevention program of the type evaluated by Schneider (1976). Suppose that the police enroll half the houses in a particular neighborhood in an Operation Identification program to inscribe identification numbers on household belongings and that an evaluation later demonstrates that homes displaying an "Operation ID" sticker experience a lower burglary victimization rate than do their stickerless neighbors. It seems likely that at least part of this difference in victimization rates is the

---

[5] For the conceptual context motivating this approach to crime prevention, see Newman (1972) and Jeffrey (1977).

result of displacement—burglars may be nearly as active in this neighborhood after the program is instituted but have a tendency to avoid protected homes. Thus the reduction in burglaries against protected homes is achieved at the cost of some increase in burglaries against unprotected homes. Displacement may be partial (in which case the total volume of burglaries will fall) or complete.

The logically extreme viewpoint on the displacement issue is that displacement is always in some sense complete. In this view, the rate at which a criminal commits crimes is not influenced by the overall quality or availability of criminal opportunities. Although criminals may exercise some care in choosing their targets, they will not be deterred by the disappearance of some attractive targets or encouraged by the appearance of more lucrative targets. Private protection activities have no effect on the volume of crime no matter how comprehensively they are adopted. It should be noted that any theory of crime determination that does not consider the opportunities available to criminals is implicitly accepting this viewpoint.

Perhaps the most notable recent proponents of the view that opportunities do influence the volume as well as the distribution of crime are Cohen and his associates. Cohen and Felson (1979) discuss the creation of criminal opportunities in terms close to those of the life-style model (Hindelang et al. 1978), focusing on the "routine activities of everyday life": "We take criminal inclination as given and examine the manner in which the spatio-temporal organization of social activities helps people to translate their criminal inclinations into action" (Cohen and Felson 1979, p. 589). More specifically, they link the dramatic increase in crime rates since 1960 to changes in the routine activity structure of American society and to a corresponding increase in target suitability and decrease in the presence of "guardians" such as neighbors, friends, and family (p. 598). The decrease in the presence of guardians is in part a result of a trend toward increased female participation in the labor force and an increase in the number of "nonstandard households"; that is, the daytime presence of adult caretakers in homes and neighborhoods has diminished in the postwar period, and, as a result, the volume of crime has increased. Of course it is possible that other forms of self-protection have been substituted for this personal guardianship. In any event, Cohen and Felson report the results of a multiple regression analysis of national crime rates for 1947–74, which demonstrate a positive association of FBI Index Crime rates with a "residential population density ratio" (the fraction of households in which the wife works or there is no married couple).[6] Further regression results for this ratio are presented in Cohen et al. (1980) for the crimes of robbery, burglary, and auto theft. Cohen and his associates also stress another dimension of criminal opportunity—the ready availability of valuable merchandise that can be easily stolen and fenced.

Results such as these suggest that the volume of crime, and not just its distribution, is influenced by the general quality and quantity of criminal opportunities. This conclusion is in complete accord with the modern economic theory of crime first propounded by Becker (1968) and developed by Ehrlich (1970, 1974) and many others (e.g., Cook 1980). In Ehrlich's (1974) formulation, the supply of offenses is a function of the relative "wage rate" to licit and illicit activities. An increase in the net return (payoff per unit of effort) to crime will stimulate participation in criminal activity. Ehrlich (1974) postulates that the payoffs to crimes such as robbery, burglary, and larceny "depend, primarily, on the level of transferrable assets in the community, that is, on opportunities provided by potential victims of crime. . . . The relative variation in the average potential illegal payoff . . . may be approximated by the relative variation in, say, the median value of transferrable goods and assets or family income" (p. 87). A number of other economists have also employed proxies for the payoff to property crime in estimating multivariate supply-of-offenses equations (for a partial list, see Nagin [1978, pp. 100–104]). Most use a measure of household income for this purpose, but Vandaele's (1973) study of auto theft employs a more specific variable—the average price of new cars. It should be noted that none of these authors considers the issue of how self-protection efforts may compensate in part for the increase in value of the available property.

Thus the hypothesis that property crime is stimulated by an increase in the accessibility and value of potential loot has been subject to a number of empirical tests, with generally positive results. Formulating tests of the criminal opportunity theory on the basis of aggregate data is more difficult for violent crime rates, but there is some evidence that is worth recounting. In 1975, Massachusetts implemented the Bartley-Fox gun law, which made the illicit carrying of a firearm punishable by a one-year mandatory prison term. A number of evaluations of this

---

[6] Chapman (1976) anticipated Cohen and his colleagues by incorporating a measure of female labor force participation in his study of intercounty differences in burglary rates in California.

legal change have reported substantial evidence that it deterred some gun assaults, robberies, and homicides. Pierce and Bowers (1981) found that, while gun assaults fell, the total number of armed assaults apparently increased as a result of Bartley-Fox. Their explanation fits the criminal opportunity perspective perfectly: "With fewer guns being carried into assault-prone situations, potential assaulters may feel less restrained, and hence the increase in nongun assaults could more than offset the decrease in gun assaults" (p. 123). A better-established finding in the violent crime area is the dramatic reduction in airline hijacking effected by the introduction of airport security measures (Landes 1978).

One interesting and unresearched question is the effect of "target proliferation" on the volume of crime against this type of target. For example, will the proliferation of branch banking offices in a small city tend to generate an increased volume of bank robberies in that city? It seems reasonable to suppose that every would-be bank robber can easily locate a suitable office to rob when there are, say, ten such offices in the city, and it is hard to see why his opportunity is improved if that number doubles. In Cook (1979, p. 768), I suggested one possible mechanism—I justified the inclusion of the "number of stores per capita" in a multiple regression analysis of per capita city robbery rates as follows:

> The extent to which store owners defend themselves against robbery (e.g., by minimizing the amount of cash kept on hand, hiring guards, and so on) depends in part on the probability that the store will be robbed. The robbery victimization rate *per store* will be lower in cities with a high density of stores, other things (including the robbery rate per capita) being equal. Therefore the arguable effect of an increase in store density is to dilute the robbery rate, thus reducing the incentive to self-protect and thereby increasing the attractiveness of stores as robbery targets.

My estimation results did not provide much support for this hypothesis, but that does not settle the issue.

There are other circumstances in which it is perhaps more plausible that target proliferation will induce an increase in the volume of crime. For example, the volume of street muggings may be stimulated by an increase in the density of suitable targets—people walking alone in deserted places, drunks flashing rolls of money, and so forth—because an increase in the density of such targets will increase the probability of contact between them and potential robbers. This situation is akin to a hunter-prey situation, in which an increase in the density of prey increases the likelihood of success for the hunter (Neher 1978).

It is often the case that robbers and burglars do not know the precise attributes of a potential target. For example, a house burglar will ordinarily be unsure about the value of the goods in a house, or what sort of alarms or other protections it has, or even whether there is someone at home. If there is an upward trend in the fraction of homes that contain more-or-less unprotected valuable goods, then burglars will perceive an increase in the probability of success in any one "job." An interesting case in point is household possession of firearms. Firearms are valuable loot to a burglar, so cities with a relatively high level of firearm ownership offer burglars relatively lucrative hunting grounds. On the other hand, it is possible that a burglar is more likely to be shot in such cities. There is one bit of evidence suggesting that the net effect of high gun ownership rates is to increase the volume of burglary. In Cook (1983a), I reported a multiple regression analysis of burglary rates for large cities in the mid-1970s, finding that the burglary rate is strongly positively related to the density of gun ownership when other crime-related characteristics of the city are taken into account.

In summary, an increase in the net payoff per unit of effort on the part of the criminal will, other things being equal, increase the overall volume of property crime. Denial of this proposition is tantamount to claiming that potential criminals as a group are unresponsive to economic incentives—that they are fundamentally different from everyone else, if indeed there is anyone who can be excluded from the "potential criminal" category. However, in practice it can be difficult to judge when a particular trend in the activities of potential victims actually generates a substantial change in the net payoff to crime: increases in household wealth may generate more lucrative crime targets, but households may simultaneously adopt more effective means of protecting their possessions; increases in female labor force participation and related trends may result in reduced guarding of property by owners, family members, and friends, but other means of protection may be substituted for this personal guardianship; and the implications of target proliferation for the net payoff to crime are sometimes unclear, as in the example above of the proliferation of branch banking offices.

Despite these difficulties in the empirical implementation of the theory, the theory itself—that the quality of criminal opportunities influences the crime rate—seems right and serves as an important addition to traditional criminological frameworks for understanding crime rates and patterns (Cohen and Land 1983).

IV. Implications for Incapacitation and Rehabilitation

If potential victims adapt their self-protection efforts to the probability of victimization (Sec. II above) and potential criminals adapt their rate of predation to the overall quality of criminal opportunities (Sec. III), then the actual volume of crime is determined by an interactive process involving these two groups—potential victims and criminals. This perspective provides some important insights concerning the effectiveness of criminal justice system activities, particularly punishments oriented toward incapacitation and rehabilitation.[7]

The interaction between potential criminals and victims is akin to a market process in which the interaction of suppliers and demanders establishes a price and a rate of transactions for a commodity. A market is said to be in equilibrium when the plans of suppliers and demanders are consistent at the going price. For the crime market, we could speak either of the supply and demand for criminal opportunities or of the supply and demand for offenses; the latter is the common usage in the literature. What is needed, then, is to define the "supply of offenses," the "demand for offenses," "price," and "equilibrium." With this apparatus in place, the economic theory of markets can be applied to the determination of crime rates.

Following Ehrlich (1981), we can define the "price" analogue as the "net return per offense." For a property crime, this is equivalent to the average dollar payoff net of the cost to the offender of legal punishment (discounted by the probability of arrest and conviction). As this price increases, the suppliers' desired quantity of offenses will also increase as new criminals enter the market, existing criminals become more active, or both. The "demand for offenses" is a strange-sounding term, but the concept is readily understood as the flip side of the demand for safety; as the threat of victimization increases, potential victims demand more self-protection, with the result that the net payoff to crime falls. Hence the demand for offenses is a negatively sloped relationship between the rate of offenses and the net payoff to offenses, reflecting the level of self-protection adopted by potential victims at each offense rate. Equilibrium in this crime market occurs when the net payoff is

---

[7] This insight was first suggested by van den Haag (1975, 1983) and was further developed by Cook (1977) and Ehrlich (1981, 1982).

compatible with the offense rate for both potential victims and offenders.

What does this theoretical apparatus have to do with assessing the effectiveness of crime control activities? The most important implication is that there is a built-in bias in traditional evaluations of the effectiveness of policies to stop particular offenders from committing crime (by means of incapacitation and rehabilitation). The nature of this bias is explained in the following example.

Suppose that a county with an average "stock" of 100 equally active burglars implements a miraculously effective rehabilitation program, thereby reducing this active population to an average of 80. Under normal assumptions—those implicit in most evaluations of rehabilitation and incapacitation programs—the burglary rate will then fall by 20 percent. But this prediction is overly optimistic. The market perspective suggests that this initial 20 percent fall in the burglary rate will result in a series of adaptations first by potential victims and then by burglars that will cause some of those rehabilitated burglars to be replaced. For example, in response to the new, safer environment, some stores and households will start keeping more valuables on hand, and some will reduce costly self-protection efforts. The result will be an increase in the average net payoff to burglary. With burglary now more profitable, new burglars will be lured into the market, and old burglars may become more active. The ultimate result is that a new equilibrium is established, characterized by a lower rate of burglary than before the rehabilitation program was instituted, but not one 20 percent lower.

This example is illustrated by figure 1 (adapted from Cook [1977, p. 170]). This figure represents the rehabilitation program as a downward shift in the burglary supply schedule. The original equilibrium is at 100 (with net payoff denoted P_1). The new equilibrium is at eighty-four (with a higher net payoff, P_2).

The "replacement effect" in this example equals four—the difference between the new equilibrium burglary rate (eighty-four) and the rate that would have resulted in the absence of adaptation by potential burglars and victims (eighty). A little experimentation with this diagram illustrates the following theorem: the magnitude of the replacement effect increases if the supply schedule is made steeper (more responsive to net payoff) or if the demand schedule is made less steep (more responsive to the victimization rate). The magnitude of the replacement effect, then, is determined by the degree of responsiveness to the relevant incentives on the part of the two groups. In particular, if

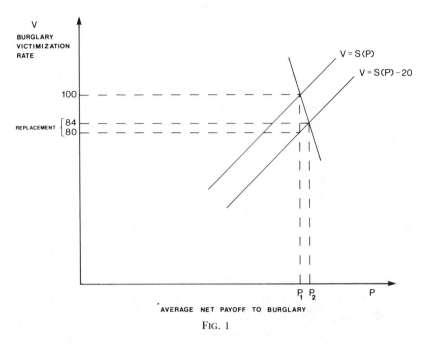

FIG. 1

either group is completely unresponsive to incentives, then there is no replacement effect, and the assumptions that govern most evaluations of rehabilitation- and incapacitation-oriented programs (Cohen 1983) are correct. But responsiveness is surely the norm. It is conventional but probably incorrect to assert that violent criminals such as rapists are insensitive to incentives. The question is whether the degree of caution adopted by women has any influence on the rape rate. It seems that women's propensity to hitchhike, jog alone, and date strangers will in fact influence their overall victimization rate. If so, and if the degree of caution exhibited by women is responsive to the probability of victimization, then the replacement effect for rape will be nontrivial.

The market model for crime developed above has a different and more transparent application that deserves mention. As Ehrlich (1981) notes, "There are, in fact, explicit markets for voluntary exchanges in all illicit goods and services, including goods that are acquired through the commission of crimes against property and person" (p. 309). Thus the net payoff to auto theft will be determined in part by the demand for "hot" cars and parts; the net payoff to burglary and shoplifting will be determined partly by the demand for stolen merchandise. If some thieves are rendered inactive by, say, imprisonment, the net payoff to theft will increase not only because of the resulting reduction in caution by property owners but also because black market prices will rise in response to increased scarcity. This additional market process will enhance the replacement effect.

It should be emphasized that this market theory of criminal opportunities only offers a framework for assessing the preventive effects of incapacitative or rehabilitative punishment modes. The framework encourages consideration of a possible replacement effect, but there is no presumption that this effect will be large. Its importance will no doubt differ, depending on the type of crime and the characteristics of the criminal. My intuition is that there will be little or no replacement if child abusers or drunk drivers are reformed or restrained and that replacement will be near complete in the case of street-level sellers of illicit commodities. Careful analysis of specific crimes is needed to extend our intuition.

In conclusion, I would assert that this theory of interaction between potential victims and offenders, in which crime rates are determined by a process akin to that which holds in a market, has three great virtues: it assembles the different strands of thought encompassed by criminal opportunity theory into a coherent whole; it is expressed in a form that facilitates borrowing from the highly developed economic theory of markets; and it generates new and important insights for policy evaluation and criminological theory. One task that remains in developing this theory is to integrate it fully with models of the interaction between criminals and the criminal justice system. This work has been started by Ehrlich (1981) but tends to be too technical for review here. The next section is concerned with a different problem—the normative implications of criminal opportunity theory.

V. Encouraging Self-Protection

The private response to the threat of criminal victimization has a profound influence on the volume, distribution, and nature of criminal activity. Since private self-protection efforts affect matters of such intense public concern, it is important to consider the appropriate basis for developing a coherent public policy with respect to protection activities.

Some types of self-protection may pose a hazard to the community, as with the private possession of firearms or the employment of inadequately trained guards. The former has long been subject to regulation by all levels of government (Cook and Blose 1981), and the latter is generating concern that may result in increasingly stringent regulations (National Advisory Committee on Criminal Justice Standards and Goals 1976). Most forms of self-protection do not pose such obvious problems, and the collective interest is more difficult to specify.

To introduce some of the relevant normative considerations, consider the crime of auto theft. Individuals protect themselves against auto theft by a variety of actions, including locking the doors, installing alarms, parking in locked or guarded garages or parking lots, and buying less expensive cars than they might otherwise. To the extent that the overall volume of theft is reduced by self-protection efforts, the public benefits in a variety of ways—insurance rates are lower, teenagers are less likely to go joyriding, and there is some savings in criminal justice system resources. Since some of the benefits of self-protection are thus enjoyed collectively rather than only by car owners, it is arguable that the natural incentive to self-protect should be supplemented by government action. The form of this argument should be familiar to anyone who has studied economics—the public benefit of my locking my car exceeds the benefit to me personally, so there will be a tendency for me to put less effort into protecting my car than I "should" from the collective viewpoint. This tendency to undersupply protection effort is of course exacerbated if my car is insured and, as is usually the case, if my insurance premium does not accurately reflect the degree of care I take (Ehrlich and Becker 1972).

In practice, the principal government regulation designed to prevent auto theft is the requirement that new cars be equipped with steering wheel ignition locks. Justifying this regulation requires an argument that the steering wheel lock is worthwhile from a collective perspective even though it was apparently not deemed worthwhile by individual car buyers. There are of course other legal requirements that could be imposed, including a requirement that people lock their car doors or be subject to a fine, as in some European countries. In any event, the motivation for any such requirement is that the collective benefit exceeds the intrinsic private benefit.

There may be some private protection actions for which the reverse is true—that the collective benefit is less than the privately perceived benefit. This circumstance may arise either because the self-protection action has direct social costs (acquiring a firearm for self-protection, middle-class flight to the suburbs) or because its main effect is to displace rather than to deter crime. The rationale for government regulation discouraging such private protection action corresponds to the rationale for promoting it in the case of auto theft, but finding a workable, politically acceptable mechanism is usually difficult.

VI. Conclusion

The last two decades have been characterized by a vast increase in the attention paid to crime victims by criminologists and policymakers. Nevertheless, the role of victims and potential victims in determining the volume and distribution of crime has been largely neglected, at least until quite recently. Traditionally, explanations for observed patterns of crime have focused on criminals or, in policy discussion, on the interaction between criminals and the criminal justice system. Yet at least for predatory crime there is a victim for every crime, and the victim's attributes and behavior influence the likelihood and nature of the crime. One can imagine a radical reformulation that is complementary to the traditional approach to explaining crime patterns, one focusing entirely on victims and viewing perpetrators as a "given" that needs no particular explanation or characterization. The point of this essay is that such a reformulation would be no more incomplete than traditional formulations are. A complete theory of the volume and distribution of crime requires a complete characterization of both potential criminals and potential victims and of the nature of their interaction. Those who claim that the behavior of one group or the other is unimportant in some particular context may be correct, but such a claim warrants careful scrutiny. The postulates of criminal opportunity theory offer a systematic guide for a productive broadening of our inquiry into the causes of crime.

REFERENCES

Balkin, Steven. 1979. "Victimization Rates, Safety, and Fear of Crime." *Social Problems* 26(3):343–57.
Bartel, Ann P. 1975. "Analysis of Firm Demand for Protection against Crime." *Journal of Legal Studies* 4(2):443–78.
Becker, Gary S. 1968. "Crime and Punishment: An Economic Approach." *Journal of Political Economy* 76(2):169–217.
Bordua, David J. 1961. "Delinquent Sub-cultures: Sociological Interpretations of Gang Delinquency." *Annals of the American Academy of Political and Social Science* 338:119–36.

Chaiken, Jan M., M. W. Lawless, and K. A. Stevenson. 1974. "The Impact of Police Activity on Subway Crime." *Urban Analysis* 3:173–205.

Chapman, Jeffrey I. 1976. "An Economic Model of Crime and the Police— Some Empirical Results." *Journal of Research in Crime and Delinquency* 13(1):48–63.

Clarke, Ronald V. 1983. "Situational Crime Prevention: Its Theoretical Basis and Practical Scope." In *Crime and Justice: An Annual Review of Research*, vol. 4, edited by Michael Tonry and Norval Morris. Chicago: University of Chicago Press.

Clotfelter, Charles T. 1977. "Urban Crime and Household Protective Measures." *Review of Economics and Statistics* 59(4):499–503.

———. 1978. "Private Security and the Public Safety." *Journal of Urban Economics* 5(3):388–402.

Clotfelter, Charles T., and R. D. Seeley. 1979. "The Private Costs of Crime." In *The Costs of Crime*, edited by Charles M. Gray. Beverly Hills, Calif.: Sage.

Cloward, Richard A., and Lloyd E. Ohlin. 1960. *Delinquency and Opportunity: A Theory of Delinquent Gangs*. Glencoe, Ill.: Free Press.

Cohen, Jacqueline. 1983. "Incapacitation as a Strategy for Crime Control: Possibilities and Pitfalls." In *Crime and Justice: An Annual Review of Research*, vol. 5, edited by Michael Tonry and Norval Morris. Chicago: University of Chicago Press.

Cohen, Lawrence E., and Marcus Felson. 1979. "Social Change and Crime Rate Trends: A Routine Activity Approach." *American Sociological Review* 44:588–608.

Cohen, Lawrence E., Marcus Felson, and Kenneth Land. 1980. "Property Crime Rates in the United States: A Macrodynamic Analysis, 1947–1977; with Ex Ante Forecasts for the Mid-1980s." *American Journal of Sociology* 86(1):90–118.

Cohen, Lawrence E., James R. Kluegel, and Kenneth Land. 1981. "Social Inequality and Predatory Criminal Victimization: An Exposition and Test of a Formal Theory." *American Sociological Review* 46:505–24.

Cohen, Lawrence E., and Kenneth Land. 1983. "Sociological Positivism and the Explanation of Criminality: A Synthesis of Social Control and Criminal Opportunity Theories." Mimeographed. Austin: University of Texas, Texas Population Research Center.

Conklin, John E. 1972. *Robbery and the Criminal Justice System*. Philadelphia: J. B. Lippincott.

Cook, Philip J. 1976. "A Strategic Choice Analysis of Robbery." In *Sample Surveys of the Victims of Crime*, edited by Wesley Skogan. Cambridge, Mass.: Ballinger.

———. 1977. "Punishment and Crime: A Critique of Current Findings Concerning the Preventive Effects of Punishment." *Law and Contemporary Problems* 41(1):164–204.

———. 1979. "The Effect of Gun Availability on Robbery and Robbery Murder: A Cross Sectional Study of Fifty Cities." In *Policy Studies Review Annual*, vol. 3, edited by R. H. Haveman and B. B. Zellner. Beverly Hills, Calif.: Sage.

————. 1980. "Research in Criminal Deterrence: Laying the Groundwork for the Second Decade." In *Crime and Justice: An Annual Review of Research*, vol. 2, edited by Norval Morris and Michael Tonry. Chicago: University of Chicago Press.

————. 1981. "The Role of Firearms in Violent Crimes." In *Criminal Violence*, edited by M. E. Wolfgang and N. A. Weiner. Beverly Hills, Calif.: Sage.

————. 1983*a*. "Does Gun Ownership Deter Burglary?" Mimeographed. Durham, N.C.: Duke University, Institute of Policy Sciences.

————. 1983*b*. *Robbery in the United States: An Analysis of Recent Trends and Patterns*. Washington, D.C.: National Institute of Justice.

Cook, Philip J., and James Blose. 1981. "State Programs for Screening Handgun Buyers." *Annals of the American Academy of Political and Social Science* 455:80–91.

Cunningham, William C., and Todd H. Taylor. 1984. *The Growing Role of Private Security*. Washington, D.C.: National Institute of Justice.

Ehrlich, Isaac. 1970. *Participation in Illegitimate Activities: An Economic Analysis*. Ph.D. dissertation, Columbia University.

————. 1974. "Participation in Illegitimate Activities: An Economic Analysis." In *Essays in the Economics of Crime and Punishment*, edited by Gary S. Becker and William M. Landes. New York: National Bureau of Economic Research.

————. 1981. "On the Usefulness of Controlling Individuals: An Economic Analysis of Rehabilitation, Incapacitation, and Deterrence." *American Economic Review* 71(3):307–22.

————. 1982. "The Market for Offences and the Public Enforcement of Laws: An Equilibrium Analysis." *British Journal of Social Psychology* 21:107–20.

Ehrlich, Isaac, and Gary S. Becker. 1972. "Market Insurance, Self-Insurance, and Self-Protection." *Journal of Political Economy* 80:632–48.

Ennis, Philip. 1967. *Criminal Victimization in the United States—a Report of a National Survey*. Research Report to the President's Commission on Law Enforcement and Administration of Justice. Field Survey no. 2. Washington, D.C.: U.S. Government Printing Office.

Garofalo, James. 1985. "Lifestyles and Victimization: An Update." In *Reorienting the Justice System: From Crime Policy to Victim Policy*, edited by Ezzat A. Fattah. London: Macmillan.

Gottfredson, Michael R. 1981. "On the Etiology of Criminal Victimization." *Journal of Criminal Law and Criminology* 72(2):714–26.

Hannan, Timothy H. 1982. "Bank Robberies and Bank Security Precautions." *Journal of Legal Studies* 11(1):83–92.

Hindelang, Michael, Michael Gottfredson, and James Garofalo. 1978. *Victims of Personal Crime: An Empirical Foundation for a Theory of Personal Victimization*. Cambridge, Mass.: Ballinger.

Hough, J. Michael, and Patricia Mayhew. 1983. *The British Crime Survey: First Report*. London: H.M. Stationery Office.

Jeffrey, C. Ray. 1977. *Crime Prevention through Environmental Design*. 2d ed. Beverly Hills, Calif.: Sage.

Kakalik, James S., and Sorrel Wildhorn. 1972. *The Private Security Industry—Its Nature and Extent*. 4 vols. Santa Monica, Calif.: Rand.

————. 1977. *The Private Police: Security and Danger.* New York: Crane, Russak.

Landes, William M. 1978. "An Economic Study of U.S. Aircraft Hijacking, 1961–1976." *Journal of Law and Economics* 21:1–32.

McDonald, John F., and Steven Balkin. 1983. "Citizen Demand for Exposure to Street Crime." *Urban Studies* 20:419–29.

Nagin, Daniel. 1978. "General Deterrence: A Review of the Empirical Evidence." In *Deterrence and Incapacitation: Estimating the Effects of Criminal Sanctions on Crime Rates,* edited by A. Blumstein, J. Cohen, and D. Nagin. Washington, D.C.: National Academy of Sciences.

National Advisory Committee on Criminal Justice Standards and Goals. 1976. *Private Security: Report of the Task Force on Private Security.* Washington, D.C.: Law Enforcement Assistance Administration.

Neher, Philip A. 1978. "The Pure Theory of the Muggery." *American Economic Review* 68:437–45.

Newman, Oscar. 1972. *Defensible Space: Crime Prevention through Urban Design.* New York: Macmillan.

Penick, Bettye K. E., and Maurice E. B. Owens III, eds. 1976. *Surveying Crime.* Washington, D.C.: National Academy of Sciences.

Pierce, Glenn L., and William J. Bowers. 1981. "The Bartley-Fox Gun Law's Short-Term Impact on Crime in Boston." *Annals of the American Academy of Political and Social Science* 455:120–37.

Repetto, Thomas A. 1974. *Residential Crime.* Cambridge, Mass.: Ballinger.

————. 1976. "Crime Prevention and the Displacement Phenomenon." *Crime and Delinquency* 22:166–77.

Rubenstein, Herb. 1980. *The Link between Crime and the Built Environment: The Current State of Knowledge.* Vol. 1. Washington, D.C.: National Institute of Justice.

Schneider, Anne L. 1976. "Victimization Surveys and Criminal Justice System Evaluation." In *Sample Surveys of the Victims of Crime,* edited by Wesley Skogan. Cambridge, Mass.: Ballinger.

Skogan, Wesley G. 1978. "The Center for Urban Affairs Random Digit Dialing Survey—Reactions to Crime Project." Evanston, Ill.: Northwestern University, Center for Urban Affairs.

Skogan, Wesley G., and M. G. Maxfield. 1981. *Coping with Crime: Individual and Neighborhood Reactions.* Beverly Hills, Calif.: Sage.

Sparks, Richard F. 1981. "Multiple Victimization: Evidence, Theory, and Future Research." In *Victims of Crime: A Review of Research Issues and Methods.* Washington, D.C.: National Institute of Justice.

Vandaele, Walter. 1973. "The Economics of Crime: An Econometric Investigation of Auto Theft in the United States." In *American Statistical Association, 1973 Proceedings of the Business and Economic Section.* Washington, D.C.: American Statistical Association.

van den Haag, Ernest. 1975. *Punishing Criminals.* New York: Basic.

————. 1983. "How Not to Cut Crime: Rehabilitating Criminals Cannot Cut Crime." *Policy Review* 26:53–58.

Wolfgang, Marvin E. 1958. *Patterns in Criminal Homicide.* Philadelphia: University of Pennsylvania Press.

Rolf Loeber and Magda Stouthamer-Loeber

Family Factors as Correlates and Predictors of Juvenile Conduct Problems and Delinquency

ABSTRACT

A meta-analysis was performed of concurrent and longitudinal studies on the relation of family factors to juvenile conduct problems and delinquency. Analyses of longitudinal data show that socialization variables, such as lack of parental supervision, parental rejection, and parent-child involvement, are among the most powerful predictors of juvenile conduct problems and delinquency. Medium-strength predictors include background variables such as parents' marital relations and parental criminality. Weaker predictors are lack of parental discipline, parental health, and parental absence. The effect of these factors seems to be about the same for boys and for girls. Analyses of concurrent studies comparing delinquents with nondelinquents, and aggressive children with nonaggressive children, largely parallel these findings. Data from concurrent normal samples, however, show less importance for parental child socialization practices and relatively more importance for the child's rejection of the parent and the parent's rejection of the child. A small proportion of families produces a disproportionate number of delinquents. The presence of one child with delinquency, aggression, or covert conduct problems increases the probability that other children in the family will exhibit those behaviors. Deficiencies in parenting skills are

Rolf Loeber and Magda Stouthamer-Loeber are Assistant Professors at the University of Pittsburgh, School of Medicine, Western Psychiatric Institute and Clinic. The authors are greatly indebted to Linette Postell, Danette Waller, and Pat Wilson for their assistance. Michael Tonry and Celia Eatman transformed our Anglo-Dutch into Anglo-American. David P. Farrington, Ted Jacob, Chris Thomas, and James Q. Wilson provided valuable comments.

associated with the seriousness of the child's delinquency. Treatment studies demonstrate that systematic changes in parenting behaviors can lessen the frequency of a child's conduct problems and that of siblings and, to a lesser extent, reduce involvement in delinquent activities.

Juvenile conduct problems have been systematically studied since the early part of the century, when clinicians such as Healy (1915) began to describe in detail the home conditions that accompanied delinquency. Only with the advent of systematic data collection by Burt (1930) and the Gluecks (Glueck and Glueck 1934, 1940) was juvenile delinquency related in a quantifiable manner to numerous aspects of family life. These latter efforts were breakthroughs, although, in retrospect, the quality of measurement of family conditions left much to be desired.

I. Introduction

This essay summarizes what is known from social science research about the relations between family life and delinquent, aggressive, and criminal behavior. A substantial literature has accumulated on these subjects. However, it has not been fully integrated because it results from efforts by researchers in different disciplines—especially sociology and developmental psychology—using different methods and pursuing somewhat different aims (Sutherland and Cressey 1960, 1966; Hirschi 1969; Elliott, Ageton, and Canter 1979; Patterson 1982a, 1982b). The situation is little changed from what it was nineteen years ago, when Rodman and Grams (1967) wrote that "due to a severe lack of interdisciplinary communication . . . few attempts have been made to consider both the sociological and psychiatric-psychological aspects of the family's role in delinquency" (p. 195). This lack of integration is also true of a third group of studies, of a type called by McCord (1984) "eclectic empiricism," that lack elaborate theoretical frameworks (Powers and Witmer 1951; Robins 1966; McCord, McCord, and Zola 1969; West 1969; Rutter, Tizard, and Whitmore 1970; West and Farrington 1973, 1977). We attempt such an integration here to see whether there is substantial similarity in findings. Our general approach is to pull together all accessible reports on relevant research, to isolate the relations of interest, and, using statistical methods described below, to determine for each study the strength of association or correlation between variables of interest.

Briefly to anticipate our conclusions, there is substantial consistency in the findings of research by investigators using different methods and bringing different perspectives to bear. A number of parenting, household, and sibling characteristics are correlated with juvenile problem behavior. If such characteristics can be identified and ameliorated, it should be possible to reduce children's behavior problems; results of parent training programs are encouraging and suggest that this possibility can be realized.

Section I of this essay introduces ways of addressing the causal relations between family variables and juvenile conduct problems and delinquency. It also presents the aims of this study, explains the meta-analyses used, and describes four "heuristic paradigms" or sets of hypotheses formulated to organize the data. Sections II–V discuss research bearing on, respectively, the *neglect paradigm:* the neglect of children by the parents; the *conflict paradigm:* unusual levels of conflict between parents and children; the *deviant behaviors and attitudes paradigm:* the influence of parents' deviant behavior and attitudes on children; and the *disruption paradigm:* disruptions to family functioning such as death, illness, or divorce. Section VI discusses the cumulative effects of multiple deficits in families on children's behavior. Section VII presents research on the effect of sibling relations on juvenile conduct problems and delinquency. Section VIII reviews research on shifts in child conduct problems and parental behavior over time. Section IX discusses the operation and effects of programs designed to teach parenting skills, and Section X summarizes the meta-analyses and suggests research and policy implications.

A. The Causal Role of Family Factors

It is tempting to reduce the role of the family in juvenile conduct problems and delinquency to simplistic causal statements such as, Poor parental child-rearing practices cause children to grow up as delinquents, or, Delinquent parents produce delinquent children. Others may claim, Some children are temperamentally so difficult that they tax even the most competent parent, who will be powerless in witnessing a child develop into a delinquent. However, there is often a lack of hard empirical evidence supporting statements that either the parents or the child is the prime cause of delinquency.

Discussions of the causes of crime often contrast hereditary influences and social influences. Hereditary influences are often difficult to measure directly. A genetic cause is sometimes postulated when parents of delinquent or behavior problem children are or have been delinquent themselves or manifest other forms of antisocial behavior or psychopathology such as alcoholism or substance abuse. Hereditary influences may also be used to account for temperamental differences among children that are expressed in their activity levels, psychophysiology, intelligence, impulsivity, and willingness to take risks. By contrast, social influences such as children's exposure to poor child-rearing practices, marital conflict, loss of a parent, or learning delinquent skills from siblings or peers are thought to mold children's behavior. It is difficult to disentangle cause from effect when studying interactions between family factors and child behavior problems and delinquency. There are, however, a number of ways in which causal hypotheses, whether based on hereditary factors, social factors, or both, can be tested. The following examples are partly based on Rutter (1981).

First, causally related variables are often correlated with each other. Thus, if family factors "cause" juvenile conduct problems and delinquency, they also tend to be correlated with each other. It can be expected, when comparing delinquent with nondelinquent youngsters, that family handicaps are more likely to be present in the former group than in the latter. However, in either instance, causal inferences may be weak, for two reasons: it is possible that the effects are actually "caused" or dependent on the presence of other variables that have not been taken into account, and it is often difficult to know what caused what. For example, in the case of parents' conflict with youngsters, it often is hard to disentangle whether the conflict "caused" the misbehavior (favoring the social explanation) or whether the misbehavior "caused" the conflict (favoring the heredity explanation).

Second, it is important to recognize that causal variables precede outcomes rather than the reverse. For factors to gain causal status, they must *predict* later juvenile conduct problems and delinquency. However, the critical question is whether they predict later outcomes independently from other possible causal variables.

Third, when family influences have a causal status, they are likely to affect more than one child in the same family; this can favor either a hereditary or a social explanation.

Fourth, if several family conditions individually predict delinquency in offspring, then the presence of multiple familial handicaps is probably related to an increased probability that youngsters will become delinquent. This favors the social explanation, although, depending on which familial handicaps are included, the hereditary explanation cannot be totally excluded.

Fifth, if family handicaps have a causal status, then one can expect a direct relation between the handicaps and deviant child behavior. The higher the degree of handicaps, the higher the degree of deviant behavior in youngsters.

Sixth, some youngsters, although not displaying deviant behavior at a given time, develop such behavior later. When such a change in child behavior takes place *after* an increase in familial handicaps, this strengthens the inference that familial handicaps have a causal status. The same can be said when improvements in family handicaps are followed by a *decrease* in the child's problem behavior. The temporal covariation between changes in family functioning and child behavior favors a social explanation and would be difficult to account for on the basis of hereditary factors alone.

Seventh, some familial handicaps can be systematically changed. An example would be parent training programs to improve child-rearing practices. Causal inferences about these social factors can be made, especially when the training is based on the random assignment of families to experimental and control groups, so that hereditary or other factors are equally distributed among subjects in each group. When the training is followed by improved child behavior in the experimental but not in the control group, then it is likely that child-rearing practices have a causal status in the emergence or maintenance of juvenile conduct problems and delinquency. It is important to note, however, that factors associated with the *emergence* of children's problems are not necessarily the same as those associated with their *maintenance*. In addition, parent training may incorporate corrective techniques that are not common to emergence or maintenance of problem behavior. Failure to change children's problem behavior is not necessarily evidence that hereditary influences are predominant. Some children develop multiple problem behaviors over time that are difficult to eradicate fully, even for the most skilled parent. Further, in the more serious cases, the child will have developed behaviors primarily aimed at undermining adults' attempts to bring about change in the child's behavior.

B. Aims of the Essay

The causal issues are addressed below in the course of reviewing data from numerous concurrent and longitudinal studies. Emphasis is placed primarily on social factors because biological factors have recently been reviewed by Mednick and Volavka (1980) in this series.

Studies included in this review were selected on the following grounds. First, studies are included of both juvenile conduct problems and delinquency because there is increasing evidence of continuity of behavioral problems over time. Research has consistently shown that patterned conduct problems, such as aggression, truancy, and lying, are predictive of delinquency (Loeber 1982; Loeber and Dishion 1983; Loeber and Stouthamer-Loeber 1986). Developmental studies tend to show that the majority of chronic delinquents have displayed high rates of conduct problems when young (Loeber 1986; Loeber and Stouthamer-Loeber 1986). Second, only studies of children from age six on are considered. Although some studies have linked conduct problems during the preschool years to later problems (e.g., Kraus 1973; Richman, Stevenson, and Graham 1982; Fischer et al. 1984), this has not been consistently found (see, e.g., Kagan and Moss 1962; Mac-Farlane, Allen, and Honzik 1962; Bronson 1966). In addition, inclusion of the vast research on conduct problems in preschool-aged children would increase this review to an unmanageable size. Third, the focus is on behavioral manifestations rather than on cognitive or moral aspects of conduct problems and delinquency. Fourth, we emphasize external rather than internal controls in association with conduct problems. Finally, for reasons of space, the substantial literature dealing exclusively with multivariate analyses and with juvenile substance use is rarely mentioned.

Most studies of self-reported or official delinquency concern boys only. Presumably this is because boys have much higher delinquency rates than girls do. In studies using mixed-sex samples, the results are not always presented separately for boys and girls. Combining the data on boys and girls may not be wise since it is clear that girls and boys often engage in different kinds of delinquency (Canter 1982b). Moreover, we know from the child development literature that parents deal differently with boys than with girls (Maccoby and Jacklin 1974; Fagot 1978).

The preponderance of studies concern white children. Even though blacks represent only 11.7 percent of the population of the United States (U.S. Bureau of Census 1984), 26 percent of juvenile arrests involve blacks (Federal Bureau of Investigation 1984). Our lack of knowledge about this segment of the population of problem children is a serious handicap.

Many of the large survey studies rely exclusively on information from children regarding both their own and their parents' behavior. This weakens the conclusions somewhat since the children's perceptions of their own behavior may color their descriptions of their parents' behavior. In addition, several studies report quite divergent re-

DELINQUENT   NONDELINQUENT

	DELINQUENT	NONDELINQUENT	
PRESENCE OF PREDICTOR	VALID POSITIVES (a)	FALSE POSITIVES (b)	a+b
ABSENCE OF PREDICTOR	FALSE NEGATIVES (d)	VALID NEGATIVES (c)	d+c
	a+d	b+c	(TOTAL)

FIG. 1.—Elements of a 2 × 2 prediction table

sults depending on whether children or their parents were respondents (see, e.g., Zucker and Barron 1971; Olson et al. 1983; Rittenhaus and Miller 1984; Tims and Masland 1985). Moreover, studies varied as to the number of questions to children or parents used to measure parent behaviors (Glueck and Glueck 1950; Nye 1958; Dentler and Monroe 1961; Gold 1963; Hirschi 1969; Jensen 1972; Hindelang 1973; Belson 1975; Zill 1978; Offord et al. 1979; Wilkinson 1980; Wilson 1980). Studies relying entirely on old case records have not been included because of the multiple levels of inference involved.

C. The Meta-Analyses

To integrate the results of many studies, we have reduced the variety of outcome statistics. In the case of categorical variables, we used an index that could summarize the relevant information from a 2 × 2 table. Figure 1 shows such a table and indicates the number of individuals correctly thought to be at risk (the valid positives in cell a) and the individuals correctly though *not* to be at risk (the valid negatives in cell c). The proportion of the valid positives and valid negatives compared with the errors in the prediction table (false positives and false negatives) is an overall indicator of how well one can identify, for example, the delinquent and nondelinquent youngsters on the basis of such family factors as poor parental supervision.

However, chance alone will account for a share of the correct predictions. Therefore, a measure of association needs to correct for chance. Moreover, as explained in Appendix A in detail, a discrepancy between the base rate and the selection ratio makes it impossible to identify correctly a proportion of subjects. (The base rate is the proportion of individuals who are delinquent in a population, while the selection ratio is the proportion of individuals who are thought to be at risk.) Ideally, an index of association should correct for maximum values within a 2 × 2 table. For that reason, we chose an index called Relative Improvement over Chance (RIOC) that corrects for chance and for maximum restrictions and that summarizes how well a categorical variable concurrently or predictively distinguishes between delinquent or nondelinquent youth (Loeber and Dishion 1983).

The index has a fixed range from 0 to 100. A value of 100 signifies perfect association for cross-sectional data and perfect predictability for predictive data. Values less than 100 indicate the improvement over chance expressed as a percentage of the possible improvement over chance given the selection ratio and the base rate. A negative value indicates an association at a level of less than chance. In studies in which variables had more than two categories, the categories were dichotomized so as to optimize the fit between base rate and selection ratio. Statistics that could not be converted to RIOC, such as t- and F-values, have been expressed in terms of a standard effect size estimate, called Cohen's d (Cohen 1977; Miller and Berman 1983). The advantage of using d is that studies with different sample sizes can be compared, whereas the significance levels of t and F are dependent on the sample size. Following Miller and Berman (1983), d is calculated as the difference between two group means divided by the pooled within-group standard deviation. In other words, the difference between the means of two groups is expressed in standard deviation units. For example, d = .10 means that the difference is one-tenth of a standard deviation. If either the group mean or the standard deviation is not reported in comparisons of two groups, d can be estimated (see App. B).

In the tables that follow, those instances in which the original statistic did not reach significance are noted. Whenever results were reported to be nonsignificant and the data necessary to calculate RIOC or d were missing, RIOC or d was conservatively estimated as zero. Some studies did not allow for conversion to either of the two statistics and are reported with their original statistics.

A final summary indicator is the percentage of analyses with statistically significant results. This gives an overall assessment of the relation between variables across studies, but it should be carefully interpreted since some studies have so small a number of subjects as to preclude statistical significance unless correlations are very high.

We separately discuss concurrent studies using comparison groups, concurrent studies with normal samples, and prospective studies, which virtually all concerned normal samples. Normal samples are study samples that were not selected on the basis of the absence or presence of delinquency or conduct problems but that contain a cross section of children on either dimension. The distinction between studies using comparison groups and studies using normal samples is necessary because studies with comparison groups, usually consisting of contrasting groups of official delinquents and nondelinquents or aggressive and nonaggressive children, tend to produce larger effect sizes than do studies based on normal samples.

Sometimes the terms used by different researchers should be interpreted with caution. For instance, two of the studies on aggression use broad definitions. In Bandura and Walters's (1959) study, the subjects were primarily official delinquents. Also in the work by Eron and his colleagues (Eron, Walder, and Lefkowitz 1971), theft and other nonaggressive antisocial behaviors were included as aggression.

At the end of each section we summarize the evidence in order to extract the general direction found in a diversity of studies. The summary tables incorporate each analysis mentioned. This means that some studies are more frequently represented than others because they may measure more variables, measure them separately for boys and for girls, or measure them separately for father and for mother. As long as each analysis offers new information, we treat it as a separate test even though different analyses within the same study may not be independent of each other.[1]

Finally, we occasionally categorize certain aspects of family functioning involving direct parent-child contacts under the heading *socialization variables*. These variables are contrasted with *background variables*, such

[1] In order to verify whether our summarization strategy would lead to the same conclusions if we had used studies as the unit of analysis, we also calculated summary scores using the mean RIOC or *d* for each study. The mean rank-order correlation between the two sets of summary scores calculated per table (separately for concurrent and predictive studies and for RIOC and *d*) was .91. The rank-order correlation across tables was .80 for RIOC and .70 for *d*. Since the correlations between the two sets of summary scores were high, we felt justified in reporting here only the summary scores based on the individual analyses.

as marital conflict, parental illness, family size, and parental absence, that probably indirectly affect parent-child interactions.

D. Four Paradigms of Family Influences

It would be marvelous if child conduct problems and delinquency could be explained by means of one theory or model. It is more likely that multiple causes and various developmental paths lead to the same outcome (McCord et al. 1969; McCord 1979; Loeber 1986). We propose four heuristic paradigms of family functioning—neglect, conflict, deviancy, and disruption—that help organize our understanding of child conduct problems.[2]

1. *The Neglect Paradigm.* This paradigm refers to a family pattern in which parents spend insufficient time positively interacting with their children and are often unaware of the mischief that their children get into. Parents may be neglectful about trivial conduct problems, such as excessive arguing, bullying, and minor thefts, and may learn of more serious acts only from neighbors or the police. Even then, parents may neglect to monitor their children's whereabouts, their choice of friends, and their activities. This neglect may extend to other siblings, and siblings without adequate parental supervision may serve as models and encourage each other in engaging in problem behaviors. Superficially, the parents may appear to be "permissive." Limited time together and limited awareness of the child's problem behaviors can severely curtail the parents' opportunity to impose discipline. The neglect paradigm is not limited to the assumption that the parents withdraw from the child; the lack of involvement may be mutual. Subsequently, children may "do their own thing," with little or no parental guidance and ample opportunity to become alienated from the parents (Bronfenbrenner 1974).

2. *The Conflict Paradigm.* This paradigm refers to a family pattern in which parents and children become enmeshed in escalations of conflict. The conflict may often result from the child's chronic disobedience at home, which eventually may spill over to situations outside the home (Sutherland and Cressey 1966; Patterson 1982*b*). Typically, the parents are aware of the child's disobedience and conduct problems but are

[2] The paradigms are influenced by the authors' collaboration with G. R. Patterson and his colleagues at the Social Learning Center, who cannot, however, be held responsible for the present formulation, which also is much influenced by Nye (1958), Sutherland and Cressey (1966), Hirschi (1969), McCord et al. (1969), West and Farrington (1973, 1977), Norland et al. (1979), Griest and Wells (1983), Wilson and Herrnstein (1985), Wahler and Dumas (1986*a*).

unable adequately to set limits or impose discipline that would curtail the problem behavior in a nonaggressive manner. Parents who use frequent, but ineffective, low-level aggressive modes of child rearing, or physical punishment, tend to evoke similar behaviors in youngsters.

Inadequate disciplining can have several effects. It may not terminate the problem behavior when it occurs, and it probably will not prevent recurrence of the behavior. Parents often do not apply discipline consistently for fear that the child's conduct problems will escalate. Attempts by parents to implement controls, where controls have been absent, may result in youngsters becoming more evasive or outright obnoxious. Moreover, inadequate disciplining can fuel aggressive conflicts between siblings; parents may fail to intervene until escalations have already taken place. In extreme forms of inadequate disciplining, the parents may no longer play a parenting role with the conduct problem child; the latter replaces the parents as the dominant force in the household. Parents and children may begin to see each other as enemies, may have a low opinion of each other, and may reject each other. This may fuel further conflict and discipline encounters.

3. *The Deviant Behaviors and Attitudes Paradigm.* Parents may act in several deviant ways that directly influence children to do the same. For example, parents may have engaged in delinquent activity themselves. Or parents may genetically predispose children to become delinquent. Alternatively, children may witness parental lawbreaking or hear about it and imitate these acts.

Some parents, although not actually engaging in deviant behaviors, may display attitudes condoning or encouraging deviant acts by their children. Or they may fail to label serious child misbehavior as deviant. Other parents may not tolerate deviant behavior inside the home but condone it outside (Sutherland and Cressey 1966). For example, parents may urge their children to be "tough" and to use force in social disputes with peers rather than relying on nonviolent methods of problem solving.

Parents may also transmit deviant attitudes concerning other people's property. They may condone the youngster's bringing stolen property, or property of doubtful provenance, into the home (Reid 1975). One might expect such parents to protect children once the police or others draw the parents' attention to the child's behavior. Thus parents with deviant values are likely to shelter their children from the negative consequences of their misbehavior and are less likely than other parents to try to eliminate the problem.

The deviant parents' values are likely to affect all children in the family (although differences may exist for boys and girls). In these families, younger children may learn problem conduct, such as aggressive behavior, theft, or substance use, from the values that the parents hold and from their older siblings.

4. *The Disruption Paradigm.*   Neglect and conflict may arise when unusual events disrupt normal family behavior patterns. Chronic conflict between spouses and breakup of the marriage may directly or indirectly affect the children's behavior. Family members affected by these stresses may be irritable and prone to aggressive outbursts (Patterson 1983). Children may respond in kind or may learn to avoid the irritable parent. This pattern reduces the likelihood that the parents will teach positive social skills to their children or that they will deal with the child's problem behaviors effectively. Once, however, the stress in the parents' lives is reduced or resolved, the parents' behavior toward their children and the children's conduct problems may revert to the prestress level.

E. How the Familial Handicaps Can Interlock

In our experience, families with child conduct problems often experience several handicaps concurrently or at different times. We offer three examples, although more are possible.

1. *Parents' Deviant Values Followed by Family Conflict.*   Parents may initially overlook trivial conduct problems because they see them as age appropriate. In some children, these problems may not subside but rather progress to more serious antisocial acts. At that point, either the parents may be ineffective in dealing with the problems, or the children may disregard or overcome the parents' interventions, resulting in escalations of conflict. This then may pit spouses against each other, especially if they blame one another for the child's problems or if one spouse undermines the controls attempted by the other.

2. *Family Conflict Followed by Neglect.*   Problem behavior by children may persist over a long period and may result in the parent's disliking the child and lacking the persistence needed to discipline the child effectively. When the oppositional behavior becomes chronic, the child rather than the parents is in control. Intense strife between siblings and between parents and children may further erode family members' affection for each other. Parents may learn to avoid conflict by abdicating their parental responsibility to control the problem behavior. Ultimately, these families may fit the neglect paradigm, the only difference

being that parents may continue helplessly to disapprove the problem behaviors.

3. *Family Disruption Followed by Neglect or Conflict.* In a third scenario, when disruptions such as chronic marital discord take place, parents' relationships with their children can suffer. The parents may become more coercive in their child-rearing practices, and the conflicts may spread to the children, or the parents may become so absorbed in trying to cope with the stress in their own lives that they supervise their children less and spend less time with them.

These examples illustrate the need to study and understand unfavorable family influences both in terms of their *outcomes*, including juvenile conduct problems and delinquency, and in terms of the *processes* within families over time that lead to these outcomes.

II. The Neglect Paradigm
This section brings together evidence from studies measuring parental neglect, particularly lack of parental involvement with children, the degree of children's involvement with parents, and the quality of parental supervision.

A. *Lack of Involvement*
Table 1 shows eleven studies in which parental involvement with their children was measured. Of the twenty-nine analyses presented, twenty-two showed a significant relation between lack of parental involvement and delinquency and aggression. Indices of lack of involvement ranged from the absence of outings with parents to neglect, indifference, ignoring, and less cooperation. Most often children reported on parental attitudes or global behaviors. However, some studies (Alexander 1973; Reid and Hendriks 1973; Hautzinger 1985) reported on the amount of positive and negative interactions between parents and children as observed in the home or in a laboratory. The median RIOC for studies using comparison groups of delinquents and nondelinquents was 61.5 percent, with a range of 32.4–87.1 percent. The median d was .55, ranging from 0 to 1.70. The values for the official delinquency studies were slightly higher than for aggression studies. No RIOCs or d's were reported for studies using normal samples.

Lack of involvement of the father with the children generally has a stronger relation to delinquency and aggression than does the mother's lack of involvement (Bandura and Walters 1959; Gold 1963; Medinnus 1965; Cortes and Gatti 1972; Hautzinger 1985); it should be noted, however, that fathers were rarely the respondents in these studies. This was not true for two of the three observation studies (Alexander 1973; Reid and Hendriks 1973), in which the mother's lack of involvement was more strongly related to child problem behavior.

Only one study related parental involvement to later delinquency. Wadsworth (1979), in a follow-up study of over 5,000 children, found that teachers' ratings of parental lack of interest in their son's primary school education was significantly related to later delinquency (RIOC = 31 percent).

The traditional role of mothers as housewives and full-time child minders has changed since large numbers of mothers have entered the work force. It is a popular opinion, supported at times in the scientific literature (e.g., Hirschi 1983), that mothers' working contributes to their children's chances of becoming delinquent. However, the evidence is far from clear. Some studies have found that working mothers had a higher percentage of delinquent children than nonworking mothers (e.g., in Glueck and Glueck [1950], RIOC = 17 percent); others found no difference (e.g., Pulkkinen 1983) or even that working mothers had less delinquent children (e.g., in West and Farrington [1973], RIOC = −12 percent). It seems that, if other factors, such as socioeconomic status (Wadsworth 1979) or parent and child characteristics (Robins 1966), are taken into account, the relation between working mothers and delinquency disappears. Thus that mothers work need not have an adverse effect on the child's probability of becoming delinquent.

Children's involvement with their parents, although not strictly a measure of parental neglect, offers another indication of the amount of time and the activities that parents share with their children. Child-parent involvement, such as the amount of intimate communication, confiding, sharing of activities, and seeking help, has often been used to measure children's attachment to parents. As can be seen from table 2, delinquency and aggression were associated with less child-parent involvement in the eleven studies listed. Only four of the forty analyses turned out to be nonsignificant. The median RIOC for comparison group studies was 49.3 percent, with a range of 28.4–74.7 percent. The median d was .58, with a range from .21 to 1.44. For studies using normal samples, RIOC was 18.3 percent, with a range between 15 and 26.4 percent. Only two values for d were reported (.40 and .60). It is clear that children's lack of involvement with the parents was more strongly related to delinquency and aggression in the comparison group studies than to self-reported delinquency in the studies using normal samples. In general, the father's lack of involvement was more related to children's behavior problems than was the mother's (Bandura and Walters 1959; Dentler and Monroe 1961; Cortes and Gatti 1972). We were unable to find studies reporting on child-parent involvement as a predictor of delinquency.

B. Lack of Supervision

Nine concurrent studies are listed in table 3, which contains eleven analyses. Lack of supervision was significantly related to delinquency in ten of these analyses. Comparison group studies yielded only two values of RIOC (66.3 percent and 66.4 percent) and two values of d (.72 and .94). All four values were high, however, especially compared with the median RIOC for studies with normal samples, which was 14.6 percent, with a range from 0 to 21.5 percent. The evidence suggests a stronger relation between lack of supervision and official delinquency than between lack of supervision and self-reported delinquency. However, the number of analyses was not large. In a study in which both self-reported delinquency and police contacts were related to levels of supervision (Patterson and Stouthamer-Loeber 1984), the correlations were similar for both (r = .54 and .55, respectively).

If lack of supervision is related to delinquency, does this also imply that different levels of delinquency are related to different levels of supervision? This was tested by Patterson and Stouthamer-Loeber (1984), who found that 21 percent of the nondelinquents were poorly monitored by parents, compared with 50 percent and 73 percent for the one- to two-time offenders and multiple offenders, respectively. When self-reported delinquency was used as a criterion, the respective percentages of poorly monitored children were 10 percent, 30 percent, and 76 percent. If, instead of frequency, variety of delinquent acts is taken into account, one finds a similar relation. Loeber and Schmaling (1985b) found that children who both stole and fought were significantly less supervised than children who either stole or fought. Thus the amount of supervision was associated in these studies with both the frequency and the variety of delinquency in children.

Turning to the prediction studies, table 4 shows that poor parental supervision led to a median value of RIOC of 36.4 percent in predicting delinquency or antisocial behavior during adolescence or adulthood. The values ranged from about 21 percent in predicting frequent self-reported delinquency or aggressiveness (Farrington 1979) to 80.8 per-

TABLE 1

Concurrent Relation between Lack of Parent Involvement with the Child and the Child's Delinquency or Aggression

Study	Subjects	Age	Race	Parent Behavior	Respondent	Measurement Mode[a]	Conduct Problem	Strength of Relation[b]
Andry (1960)	80 del., 80 nondel. B	12–15	White	F-B: No outings	Child	Questionnaire (1)	Recidivist theft	RIOC = 61.5
Gold (1963)	93 del., 93 nondel. B	12–16	White	F-B: No activities together / M-B:	Child	Interview (1)	Recidivism	RIOC = 35.9 / RIOC = 32.4
Glueck and Glueck (1950)	500 del., 500 nondel. B	$\bar{X} = 14.5$	White	F-B: Poor concern for welfare / M-B: / F-B: Indifferent / M-B:	Child / Parents	Interview	Official delinquency	RIOC = 71.9 / RIOC = 87.1 / RIOC = 45.9 / RIOC = 72.1
Medinnus (1965)	30 del., 30 nondel. B	12–17	White	F-B: More neglecting / M-B:	Child	Questionnaire (15)	Official delinquency	d = 1.70 / d = .42****
Reid and Hendriks (1973)	14 stealers, 11 aggr., 27 nondel. BG	5–14	White	M-C: Less positive/friendly behaviors / F-C:	Observer	Observations in home	Parent-reported stealing	d = .00*****
Cortes and Gatti (1972)	100 del., 100 nondel. B	16.5–18.5	?	F-B: Less help / M-B: / F-B: Less praise / M-B: / F-B: Less understanding / M-B:	Child	Questionnaire (3) / Questionnaire (3) / Questionnaire (3)	Official delinquency	d = .64 / d = .04**** / d = .65 / d = .55 / d = .82 / d = .35

44

Study	Sample	Age	Race	Finding	Respondent	Method	Outcome	Effect size
Robinson (1978)	15 problem, 15 normal B	14–17	White	P-B: Less positive involvement	Child/mother, father	Questionnaire (16)	Beyond control	$d = .42$
Bandura and Walters (1959)	26 aggr., 26 nonaggr. B	14–17	White	F-B: Less time together M-B: F-B: Less praise M-B:	Parents	Interview	Aggression	$d = .64$ $d = .35$**** $d = .23$**** $d = .06$****
Hautzinger (1985)	54 aggr., 42 normal BG 28 aggr., 27 normal BG	$\bar{X} = 8$ $\bar{X} = 8$	White	M-C: Ignore F-C:	Observer	Observations in home	Aggression	$d = .63$ $d = .84$
Alexander (1973)	20 del., 22 normal BG	$\bar{X} = 15.3$	White	F-C: More defensive communication M-C: P-C: Supportive communication	Observer	Observations in lab	Runaway/ungovernable	ANOVA* ANOVA** ANOVA****
Slocum and Stone (1963)	1,674 B, 1,568 G	12–18	Mixed	Family with G: Less cooperative Family with B:	Child	Questionnaire	Self-reported "delinquent-type" behavior	$\bar{C} = .27$** $\bar{C} = .27$**

NOTE.—B = boy; G = girl; F = father; M = mother; P = parent; C = child; del. = delinquent; nondel. = nondelinquent; aggr. = aggressive; nonaggr. = nonaggressive.
[a] The number of items, if known, is shown in parentheses.
[b] RIOC = relative improvement over chance; d = effect size; ANOVA = analysis of variance; $\bar{C}$ = contingency coefficient.
* $p < .05$.
** $p < .01$.
**** Not significant.

45

TABLE 2
Concurrent Relation between Lack of Child's Involvement with Parent and the Child's Delinquency or Aggression

Study	Subjects	Age	Race	Child Behavior	Respondent	Measurement Mode[a]	Conduct Problem	Strength of Relation[b]
Hirschi (1969)	1,256 B	12–18	Mixed	B-F: Little intimate communication	Child	Questionnaire (2)	Self-reported delinquency	RIOC = 18.6
Belson (1975)	3,113 B	13–16	White	B: Dislikes being at home B: Desire to spend less than half time at home	Child	Interview (1) Interview (1)	Self-reported stealing	RIOC = 24.8 RIOC = 17.5
Dentler and Monroe (1961)	912 BG	12–14	?	C-M: Not confiding C-F: C: Less than four evenings per week home	Child	Questionnaire (1) Questionnaire (1)	High self-reported theft	RIOC = 17.9 RIOC = 26.4 RIOC = 15.0
Andry (1960)	80 del., 80 nondel. B	12–15	White	B-M: Seldom shares activities B-P: Does not seek help	Child	Questionnaire (1)	Recidivist theft	RIOC = 49.3 RIOC = 74.7
Gold (1963)	93 del., 93 nondel. B	12–16	White	B-P: No consulting	Child	Interview (1)	Recidivism	RIOC = 28.4
Dentler and Monroe (1961)	912 BG	12–14	?	C-M: Less talking about plans C-F:	Child	Questionnaire (1)	High self-reported theft	d = .40 d = .60
Cortes and Gatti (1972)	100 del., 100 nondel. B	16.5–18.5	?	B-F: Consults less B-M: B-F: Go less places together B-M: Go places together	Child	Questionnaire (1) Questionnaire (4)	Official delinquency	d = .52 d = .33 d = .66 d = .21****
Bandura and Walters (1959)	26 aggr., 26 nonaggr. B	14–17	White	B-F: Seeks less help B-M:	Father Mother	Interview	Aggression	d = 1.33 d = .39****

Study	Sample	Age	Race	Behavior	Source	Method	Outcome	Statistic
				B-F:	Child			$d = 1.44$
				B-M:				$d = .77$
				B-F: Resist help	Father			$d = 1.43$
				B-M:	Mother			$d = 1.44$
				B-F: Resist suggestions	Child			$d = .91$
				B-M:				$d = 1.05$
				B-F: Less time together	Father			$d = .64$
				B-M:	Mother			$d = .35$****
				B-F: Seeks less company	Child			$d = .67$
				B-M:				$d = .54$
				B-F: Resist company	Father			$d = .62$
				B-M:	Mother			$d = .55$
				B-F:	Child			$d = .48$
				B-M:				$d = .33$****
Solnick et al. (1981)	57 del. B in group homes	12–16	?	C-P: Less talk	Observer	Observations	Self-reported delinquency	$r = .38$**
				C-P: Less proximity				$r = .23$*
Canter (1982a)	1,725 BG	11–17	Mixed	C-P: Less family involvement	Child	Questionnaire (3)	Self-reported delinquency	$r = .28$***
Alexander (1973)	20 del., 22 normal BG	$\bar{X} = 15.3$	White	C-F: More defensive communication	Observer	Observations	Runaway/ ungovernable	ANOVA**
				C-M:				ANOVA**
				C-F: Less supportive communication				ANOVA**
				C-M:				ANOVA**
Slocum and Stone (1963)	1,674 B, 1,568 G	12–18	Mixed	B: More evenings out	Child	Questionnaire	Self-reported "delinquent-type" behavior	$\bar{C} = .20$*
				G:				$\bar{C} = .17$*

NOTE.—B = boy; G = girl; F = father; M = mother; P = parent; C = child; del. = delinquent; nondel. = nondelinquent; aggr. = aggressive; nonaggr. = nonaggressive.

a The number of items, if known, is shown in parentheses.

b RIOC = relative improvement over chance; d = effect size; r = product-moment correlation; ANOVA = analysis of variance; $\bar{C}$ = contingency coefficient.

* p < .05.   ** p < .01.   *** p < .001.   **** Not significant.

TABLE 3

Concurrent Relation between Lack of Parental Supervision and the Child's Delinquency or Aggression

Study	Subjects	Age	Race	Parent Behavior	Respondent	Measurement Mode[a]	Conduct Problem	Strength of Relation[b]
Hirschi (1969)	1,256 B	12–18	Mixed	M-B: Supervision score less than 3	Child	Questionnaire (2)	Self-reported delinquency	RIOC = 21.5
Belson (1975)	3,113 B	13–16	White	P-B: Supervision	Child	Interview (3)	Self-reported stealing (top 25 percent)	RIOC = .0****
Wilson (1980)	56 poor inner-city B	10–11	White	P-B: Intermediate/lax supervision	Mother	Interview	Self-reported delinquency (intermediate/serious)	RIOC = 13.6
Glueck and Glueck (1950)	500 del., 500 nondel. B	$\bar{X} = 14.5$	White	M-B: Unsuitable supervision	Parents	Interview	Official delinquency	RIOC = 66.3
Blakely, Stephenson, and Nichol (1974)	50 del., 37 nondel. BG	12–18	White	M-C: Unsuitable supervision	Parents	Interview	Official delinquency	RIOC = 66.4
McCord, McCord, and Howard (1961)	25 aggr., 149 assertive and nonaggr. B	9–15	Mixed	P-B: Supervision absent	Staff	Direct observations	Aggression	RIOC = 15.5
Cortes and Gatti (1972)	100 del., 100 nondel. B	16.5–18.5	?	F-B: Less supervision M-B:	Child	Questionnaire (9)	Official delinquency	$d = .94$ $d = .72$
Patterson and Stouthamer-Loeber (1984)	133 B	13, 16	White	P-B: Less supervision P-B:	Observers	Questionnaire (3)	Self-reported delinquency Police contacts	$r = .54***$ $r = .55***$
Jensen (1972)	1,588 B	12–18	White	F-B: Less supervision	Child	Questionnaire (2)	Self-reported delinquency	gamma = .28**

NOTE.—B = boy; G = girl; F = father; M = mother; P = parent; C = child; del. = delinquent; nondel. = nondelinquent; aggr. = aggressive; nonaggr. = nonaggressive.
[a] The number of items, if known, is shown in parentheses.
[b] RIOC = relative improvement over chance; d = effect size; r = product-moment correlation.
** $p < .01$.   *** $p < .001$.   **** Not significant.

48

TABLE 4
Lack of Parental Supervision as a Predictor of the Child's Delinquency or Aggression

Study	Subjects	Race	Interval	Parent Behavior	Respondent	Measurement Mode	Conduct Problem	Strength of Relation[a]
Farrington (1979)	409 B	White	8–(14–16)	Less supervision	Social worker	Rating of their reports	More than twenty self-reported acts	RIOC = 21.2
Farrington (1978)	401 B	White	8–(16–18)	Less supervision	Social worker	Rating of their reports	Aggressiveness (self-report)	RIOC = 21.9
McCord (1984)	232 B	Mixed	(5–19)–(38–52)	Less supervision	Staff	Rating of their reports	Serious criminality	RIOC = 29.2
McCord, McCord, and Howard (1963)	103 B	Mixed	(10–15)–(20–31)	Little supervision	Staff	Ratings of their reports	Aggressive or antisocial	RIOC = 42.8
Robins (1966, 1984)	262 BG, clinic	White	(−18)–(−48)	Poor supervision	Staff	Ratings of case records	Sociopathic personality	RIOC = 57.7
Wilson and Herbert (1978)	29 B, poor, inner city	White	(10–11)–(13–14)	No chaperonage	Parents	Interview (6)	Delinquency	RIOC = 80.8

NOTE.—B = boy; G = girl.

[a] RIOC = relative improvement over chance.

49

TABLE 5
Summary Table for the Neglect Paradigm

	All Studies			Comparison Samples			Normal Samples			Comparison Samples			Normal Samples		
Variable	Studies (N)	Analyses (N)	% Significant	Median RIOC	Analyses (N)	Range	Median RIOC	Analyses (N)	Range	Median d	Analyses (N)	Range	Median d	Analyses (N)	Range
Concurrent studies:															
Parent-child involvement	11	29	76	61.5	7	32.4–87.1	…	…	…	.55	17	.00–1.70	…	…	…
Child-parent involvement	11	40	90	49.3	3	28.4–74.7	18.3	6	15.0–26.4	.58	20	.21–1.44	.50	2	.40–.60
Supervision	9	11	91	66.3	2	66.3–66.4	14.6	4	.0–21.5	.83	2	.72–.94	…	…	…
All concurrent studies	31	80	85	63.9	12	28.4–87.1	17.7	10	.0–26.4	.64	39	.00–1.70	.50	2	.40–.60
Predictive studies:															
Parent-child involvement	1	1	100	…	…	…	31.0	1	…	…	…	…	…	…	…
Supervision	4	6	100	…	…	…	36.4	6	21.2–80.0	…	…	…	…	…	…

cent in predicting official delinquency in a sample of poor inner-city children (Wilson and Herbert 1978). The very high value for RIOC in the last study suggests that in some environments it may be necessary to apply strict supervision since the opportunities for deviance may be more abundant. Wilson (1974) found that, for children living in very disadvantaged neighborhoods, extremely strict supervision was more important in preventing delinquency than a warm and stable home.

C. The Neglect Paradigm: A Summary

Eighty-five percent of the concurrent analyses show a significant relation between parental neglect and children's behavior problems (see table 5). The data suggest a strong association between lack of parental involvement and children's official delinquency and aggression (median RIOC = 63.9 percent; median d = .64). This association was less strong, but in the same direction for self-reported delinquency (median RIOC = 17.7 percent; median d = .50). The median RIOC for predictive studies was 31 percent for poor parent-child involvement and 36.4 percent for poor supervision. These values were not as strong as those found for concurrent official delinquency studies, but they were still substantial and about twice as large as the values found in the self-reported delinquency studies.

III. The Conflict Paradigm

In this paradigm the emphasis is on strife and dissatisfaction between parents and children, as measured by discipline practices and parent-child and child-parent rejection. No studies were found for which the results could be converted into effect sizes.

A. Discipline

The term "discipline" has been used for a wide variety of parental child-rearing practices, such as physical punishment, withdrawal of affection by parents, and scolding. It has also been used to denote the consistency with which parents apply consequences. We try to disentangle the different definitions by discussing first the various kinds of discipline and then the evidence on strictness, consistency, and fairness.

1. *Physical Punishment and Deprivation.* Physical punishment has often been associated with child conduct problems, and child abuse has sometimes been seen as one of the precursors of delinquency (Brown 1984; Knutson, Mehn, and Berger 1984). Steinmetz (1979) summarized

the evidence on physical punishment and aggression of children up to the age of twelve (with most of the analyses referring to children up to age six) and found a positive relation between physical punishment and aggressiveness in children. However, as can be seen in table 6, the evidence is not strong. Six studies measured physical punishment as a separate variable, and they show a very weak and often nonsignificant relation. Of the sixteen analyses, seven were nonsignificant. The RIOC, in two analyses of comparison groups, was 2 percent and 13.4 percent. The median value for the effect size was .38 with a range of .03–1.23. No studies were found that used normal samples.

On the basis of Steinmetz's (1979) review, we expected to find some relation between physical punishment and children's aggression. However, in three studies the relation was not found consistently (Bandura and Walters 1959; Eron et al. 1971; Hautzinger 1985). Since physical punishment was probably administered less frequently to older children, it becomes a less important variable for that age group. This may explain why Brown (1984), in a retrospective study of high school freshmen, found no appreciable positive correlations between an index of physical abuse and various indices of self-reported delinquency. There are few predictive studies on physical punishment, and these are discussed later with other predictive studies on discipline.

2. *Nagging and Scolding.* Five studies, shown in table 7, have measured various forms of parental nagging and scolding, with fourteen of the eighteen analyses reaching significance. Comparison group studies yielded only one RIOC (70.4 percent), whereas the median for d was .77 (range .19–1.31) because of the fairly substantial effect sizes found in one observational study (Hautzinger 1985). For studies using normal samples, the median RIOC was 26.4 percent with a range between 7.9 and 36.2 percent.

3. *Lack of Reasoning.* Evidence for the relation between lack of reasoning and delinquency and aggression was scarce (see table 8). Only two studies measure this variable. In the Nye (1958) study on self-reported delinquency, four out of the six analyses were nonsignificant (median RIOC = 3.3 percent). In the Bandura and Walters (1959) study on aggression, the relation was significant for both the mother and the father (median d = .90).

4. *Love Withdrawal.* Love withdrawal as a discipline technique does not have a very strong relation with aggression and delinquency in the three studies reviewed (see table 9). Fifty percent of the analyses were

nonsignificant. In some situations encompassed within the neglect model, parent-child relations are devoid of positive interactions, so that love withdrawal becomes irrelevant. Instead, love withdrawal seems to be better suited to control children who have a strong attachment to their parents. For many delinquents, love withdrawal may be more a state than a technique to be used contingent on undesirable behavior. In the present review, the comparison group studies yielded a median d of only .33, whereas one self-reported delinquency study produced two values of RIOC that were both low (15.5 percent and 14.4 percent).

5. *Strictness of Discipline and Inconsistency.* Because most studies do not allow a clear distinction between strictness and inconsistency of discipline, studies on each have been combined in table 10. Compared with the different forms of discipline discussed above, more information was available about parents' general discipline style. Of the twenty-eight analyses in the eleven studies, seventeen showed a significant association between strictness, consistency, or both and conduct problems. However, the relations were not always in the same direction. Both strict and punitive, and lax and erratic, disciplining styles have been found to be related to delinquency and aggression. Comparison group studies produced a median RIOC of 82.1 percent, with a range between 42.7 and 87.9 percent. The median d was .28 with a range from 0 to 1.02. For the studies using normal samples, the median RIOC was 12.4 percent with a range between 0 and 34.7 percent. Thus the studies with the largest RIOCs compare official delinquents with nondelinquents (Glueck and Glueck 1950; Madoff 1959; Andry 1960).

6. *Unfairness of Punishment.* Four studies, shown in table 11, have measured children's perceptions of how fair their parents' punishment is. Of the eight analyses, five showed a significant relation between perceived unfairness of punishment and delinquency. The strongest relation was found in one study on recidivist stealing (Andry 1962), in which the RIOC was 76.5 percent. The self-reported delinquency studies showed a zero median RIOC, with a range between −5.4 and 21.7 percent.

Parental discipline as a predictor of child conduct problems and delinquency was measured in five studies (see table 12). Of the twelve analyses, seven showed a significant relation between discipline and later delinquency and aggression. The RIOC ranged from 12.2 to 46.1 percent, with a median of 17.6 percent.

B. Rejection

Two kinds of rejection can be distinguished: rejection by the parents of their children and rejection by children of their parents. Rejection can be mutual but does not have to be, although this was not considered in the following studies.

1. *Parental Rejection of Their Children.* Many terms are used in the different studies to measure rejection (rejection, not warm, lack of love, lack of affection, less affectionate, etc.). The unifying concept is that these terms reflect on the expression of the parents' appreciation of their children.

Parental rejection of their children was consistently related to delinquency and aggression. The twelve studies listed in table 13 show thirty-one analyses, of which all but one were significant. The comparison group studies on official delinquency showed a median RIOC of 62.6 percent, with a range between 38.7 and 84.6 percent. The median *d* was .79, with a range of .34–1.57. The median RIOC for studies with normal samples was 24 percent, substantially smaller than that for official delinquency but still showing a strong relation between parental rejection and self-reported delinquency. No consistent pattern was discerned as to whether rejection by a father or by a mother was more strongly related to delinquency and aggression.

Concurrent relations cannot resolve questions of cause and effect. Parental rejection is illustrative. Parental rejection may drive children to rebel. However, it is also difficult to love children who make one's life miserable. Thus parental rejection can be both cause and consequence of children's behavior.

Table 14 shows five studies on parental rejection as a predictor of aggressiveness and delinquency. Of the twenty analyses, thirteen were significant. The nonsignificant results were concentrated in two studies (Simcha-Fagan et al. 1975; Lefkowitz et al. 1977). In the Lefkowitz et al. (1977) study, neither parental rejection nor nurturance, measured when the boys and girls were eight, predicted aggressiveness at age eighteen. In the Simcha-Fagan et al. (1975) study, parents' coldness and rejection by the mother predicted the mother's later report of violence and delinquency, but not official delinquency. In the remaining studies, the median value of RIOC equals 35.8 percent, with a range between 26.8 and 43.8 percent. Judging from the McCord (1984) study, the results showed a slightly higher risk for fathers' compared with mothers' lack of affection as a predictor of serious criminality.

2. *Children's Rejection of Their Parents.* Many of the measures re-

ported in table 15 center around whether the children identify with their parents and accept them as role models. This emphasis derives from control theory in which identification and attachment are key concepts (Hirschi 1969).

Seven studies measured children's affective relations with their parents (see table 15). Twelve of fifteen analyses reported a significant relation between rejection and delinquency and aggression. Two studies dealing with official delinquency yielded a median RIOC of 56.3 percent, with a range between 20 and 79 percent. Comparison group studies in which the results were expressed in effect size showed a median d of .47, the values ranging from .41 to 1.03. The median RIOC for studies with normal samples was 22.9 percent (range 17.2–25.5 percent). The studies dealing with official and self-reported delinquency showed a consistent relation (except for the observation study by Reid and Hendriks [1973]); the study on aggression (Bandura and Walters 1959) showed it only for rejection of the father.

One longitudinal study used children's identification with the parents as a predictor for later aggression (Lefkowitz et al. 1977). Boys' and girls' identification with the father at age eight was significantly related to aggression at age eighteen ($r = -.16$ and $-.22$, respectively). Identification with the mother yielded similar correlations ($r = -.17$ and $-.19$, respectively).

C. The Conflict Paradigm: A Summary

Table 16 summarizes the data for the conflict paradigm. As the results for discipline and rejection are distinctly different, each is reported separately. Only 62 percent of the analyses relating to discipline were significant. The median RIOC was high for the comparison group studies (73.5 percent), but for the studies using normal samples the median RIOC was only 11.6 percent. Measures of effect size were found only in comparison group studies. Unfortunately, comparisons among the different discipline techniques are difficult to make because of the small number of studies. It seems safe to say, however, that nagging and scolding were relatively strongly related to conduct problems. These parental behaviors are probably good indicators of long-standing, unresolved conflicts.

Parent-child relationships tended to be strongly associated with delinquency and aggression. Ninety-one percent of the analyses were significant; the median RIOC for comparison group studies was 57.8 percent, while the median d was .65. This compares with an RIOC of

TABLE 6
Concurrent Relation between Physical Punishment and Deprivation and the Child's Delinquency or Aggression

Study	Subjects	Age	Race	Parent Behavior	Respondent	Measurement Mode[a]	Conduct Problem	Strength of Relation[b]
Gold (1963)	93 del., 93 nondel. B	12–16	White	F-B: Physical punishment or deprivation	Parents	Interview (1)	Recidivism	RIOC = 13.4
				M-B:				RIOC = 2.0
Cortes and Gatti (1972)	100 del., 100 nondel. B	16.5–18.5	?	P-B: More punitive control	Child	Questionnaire (2)	Official delinquency	d = .38
Medinnus (1965)	30 del., 30 nondel. B	12–17	White	F-B: Direct-object punishment	Child	Questionnaire (10)	Official delinquency	d = .51****
				M-B:				d = .20****
Bandura and Walters (1959)	26 aggr., 26 nonaggr. B	14–17	White	F-B: More physical punishment	Father	Interview	Aggression	d = .66
				F-B: More deprivation				d = 1.23
				M-B: More physical punishment	Mother			d = .37****
				M-B: More deprivation				d = 1.04
				F-B: More physical punishment	Child			d = .57
				F-B: More deprivation				d = .33****
				M-B:				d = .03****
				M-B: More physical punishment				d = .10****
Hautzinger (1985)	54 aggr., 42 normal BG	$\bar{X}$ = 8	White	M-C: Physical negative	Observer	Observations in home	Aggression	d = .68
	28 aggr., 27 normal BG	$\bar{X}$ = 8		F-C:				d = .36****
Eron, Walder, and Lefkowitz (1971)	875 BG	8–9	Mixed	P-C: More physical punishment	Parents	Interview	Aggression	ANOVA**

NOTE.—B = boy; G = girl; F = father; M = mother; P = parent; C = child; del. = delinquent; nondel. = nondelinquent; aggr. = aggressive; nonaggr. = nonaggressive.
[a] The number of items, if known, is shown in parentheses.
[b] RIOC = relative improvement over chance; d = effect size; ANOVA = analysis of variance. ** p < .01. **** Not significant.

TABLE 7

Concurrent Relation between Parental Nagging and Scolding and the Child's Delinquency or Aggression

Study	Subjects	Age	Race	Parent Behavior	Respondent	Measurement Mode[a]	Conduct Problem	Strength of Relation[b]
Andry (1962)	80 del., 80 nondel. B	12–15	White	P-B: Nagging	Child	Questionnaire (1)	Recidivist stealing	RIOC = 70.4
Nye (1958)	780 BG	14–18	White	M-C: Ever nagging	Child	Questionnaire (1)	Self-reported delinquency (most)	RIOC = 26.4
				F-C:		Questionnaire (1)		RIOC = 26.4
				M-C: Usually/always scold				RIOC = 7.9****
				F-C:				RIOC = 20.9
McCord, McCord, and Howard (1961)	25 aggr., 149 assertive and nonaggr. B	9–15	Mixed	P-B: Frequent threats	Staff	Direct observations	Aggression	RIOC = 36.2
Bandura and Walters (1959)	26 aggr., 26 nonaggr. B	14–17	White	F-B: Nag and scold	Parents	Interview	Aggression	$d = .71$
				M-B:				$d = .19$****
				F-B:	Child	Interview		$d = .38$****
				M-B:				$d = .31$****
Hautzinger (1985)	54 aggr., 42 normal BG	$\bar{X} = 8$	White	M-C: Command	Observer	Observations in home	Aggression	$d = 1.10$
				M-C: Command negative				$d = .83$
				M-C: Disapprove				$d = 1.31$
				M-C: Yell				$d = .48$
	28 aggr., 27 normal BG	$\bar{X} = 8$		F-C: Command				$d = .88$
				F-C: Command negative				$d = .97$
				F-C: Disapprove				$d = 1.17$
				F-C: Yell				$d = .65$

NOTE.—B = boy; G = girl; F = father; M = mother; P = parent; C = child; del. = delinquent; nondel. = nondelinquent; aggr. = aggressive; nonaggr. = nonaggressive.
[a] The number of items, if known, is shown in parentheses.   **** Not significant.
[b] RIOC = relative improvement over chance; d = effect size.

57

TABLE 8

Concurrent Relation between Lack of Reasoning by Parents and the Child's Delinquency or Aggression

Study	Subjects	Age	Race	Parent Behavior	Respondent	Measurement Mode[a]	Conduct Problem	Strength of Relation[b]
Nye (1958)	780 BG	14–18	White	F-C: Sometimes/seldom explanation	Child	Questionnaire (1)	Self-reported delinquency (most)	RIOC = 6.6
				M-C:				RIOC = 7.0****
				G-F: Sometimes/seldom allowed explanation		Questionnaire (1)		RIOC = 11.6
				G-M:				RIOC = .0****
				B-F:				RIOC = .0****
				B-M:				RIOC = .0****
Bandura and Walters (1959)	26 aggr., 26 nonaggr. B	14–17	White	F-B: Less reasoning	Parents	Interview	Aggression	d = .67
				M-B:				d = 1.13

NOTE.—B = boy; G = girl; C = child; M = mother; P = parent; F = father; C = child; aggr. = aggressive; nonaggr. = nonaggressive.
[a] The number of items, if known, is shown in parentheses.
[b] RIOC = relative improvement over chance; d = effect size.
**** Not significant.

58

TABLE 9
Concurrent Relation between Love Withdrawal by Parents and the Child's Delinquency or Aggression

Study	Subjects	Age	Race	Parent Behavior	Respondent	Measurement Mode[a]	Conduct Problem	Strength of Relation[b]
Nye (1958)	780 BG	14–18	White	M-C: Withdrawal F-C:	Child	Questionnaire (1)	Self-reported delinquency (most)	RIOC = 15.5 RIOC = 14.4
Medinnus (1965)	30 del., 30 nondel. B	12–17	White	F-B: More symbolic–love punishment M-B:	Child	Questionnaire (10)	Official delinquency	$d = 1.17$ $d = .78$
Bandura and Walters (1959)	26 aggr., 26 nonaggr. B	14–17	White	F-B: Withdrawal M-B: F-B: Withdrawal M-B:	Parents Child	Interview Interview	Aggression	$d = .25$**** $d = .19$**** $d = .28$**** $d = .38$****

NOTE.—B = boy; G = girl; F = father; M = mother; P = parent; C = child; del. = delinquent; nondel. = nondelinquent; aggr. = aggressive; nonaggr. = nonaggressive.
[a] The number of items, if known, is shown in parentheses.
[b] RIOC = relative improvement over chance; d = effect size.
**** Not significant.

TABLE 10

Concurrent Relation between Strictness of Discipline and Inconsistency by Parents and the Child's Delinquency or Aggression

Study	Subjects	Age	Race	Parent Behavior	Respondent	Measurement Mode[a]	Conduct Problem	Strength of Relation[b]
Nye (1958)	780 BG	14–18	White	F-B or -G: Easy	Child	Questionnaire (1)	Self-reported delinquency (most)	RIOC = .0****
				M-B: M-G: Fairly/very easy				RIOC = 5.6****
				F-B or -G: Erratic		Questionnaire (1)		RIOC = 13.8
				M-B: M-G: Very often/frequently erratic				RIOC = .0****
								RIOC = 12.4****
								RIOC = 10.1
Belson (1975)	3,113 B	13–16	White	P-B: Inconsistent	Child	Interview (1)	Self-reported stealing (top 50 percent)	RIOC = .0****
Andry (1960)	80 del., 80 nondel. B	12–15	White	P-B: Too strict/lenient	Child	Questionnaire (1)	Recidivist theft	RIOC = 82.8
Madoff (1959)	50 del., 57 nondel. B	11–18	Mixed	M-B: More suppression of aggression	Mother	Questionnaire (scale)	Institutionalized delinquency	RIOC = 42.7
Glueck and Glueck (1950)	500 del., 500 nondel. B	$\bar{X} = 14.5$	White	M-B: Lax, overstrict or erratic F-B:	Parents	Interview	Official delinquency	RIOC = 87.9
								RIOC = 81.5

Study	Sample	Age	Race	Parenting	Method	Informant	Outcome	Statistic
McCord, McCord, and Howard (1961)	25 aggr., 149 assertive and nonaggr. B	9–15	Mixed	M-B: Erratic F-B: M-B: Punitive F-B:	Direct observations	Staff	Aggression	RIOC = 34.7 RIOC = 14.9**** RIOC = 18.1 RIOC = 19.2****
Bandura and Walters (1959)	26 aggr., 26 nonaggr. B	14–17	White	F-B: Demands less obedience M-B: F-B: Consistency of demand M-B: Less consistent	Interview	Parents	Aggression	d = .19**** d = .83 d = .00**** d = 1.02
Robinson (1978)	15 problem, 15 normal B	14–17	White	P-B: Inconsistent	Questionnaire (8)	Child	Beyond control	d = .28****
Slocum and Stone (1963)	1,674 B, 1,568 G	12–18	Mixed	P-B: Less democratic P-G:	Questionnaire	Child	Self-reported "delinquent-type" behavior	$\bar{C}$ = .11* $\bar{C}$ = .20*
Patterson and Stouthamer-Loeber (1984)	133 B	13, 16	White	P-B: Less consistent P-B:	Questionnaire (3)	Observers	Self-reported delinquency Police contacts	r = .35* r = .30****
Imperio and Chabot (1980)	90 del. B	$\bar{X}$ = 15.7 ?		M-B: Psychological control factor F-B: M-B: Lax control factor F-B:	Questionnaire (scale)	Child	Institutionalized delinquency	20 percent common variance 25 percent common variance 14 percent common variance 12 percent common variance

NOTE.—B = boy; G = girl; F = father; M = mother; P = parent; del. = delinquent; nondel. = nondelinquent; aggr. = aggressive; nonaggr. = nonaggressive.

[a] The number of items, if known, is shown in parentheses.

[b] RIOC = relative improvement over chance; d = effect size; $\bar{C}$ = contingency coefficient; r = product-moment correlation.

* $p < .05$.

**** Not significant.

61

TABLE 11

Concurrent Relation between Unfairness of Punishment by Parents and the Child's Delinquency

Study	Subjects	Age	Race	Parent Behavior	Respondent	Measurement Mode[a]	Conduct Problem	Strength of Relation[b]
Nye (1958)	780 BG	14–18	White	F-B: Sometimes/seldom fair F-G: M-B: Unfair M-G:	Child	Questionnaire (1)	Self-reported delinquency (most)	RIOC = 21.7 RIOC = 15.3 RIOC = .0**** RIOC = .0****
Belson (1975)	3,113 B	13–16	White	P-B: Unfair	Child	Interview (1)	Self-reported stealing (top 25 percent)	RIOC = −5.4****
Andry (1962)	80 del., 80 nondel. B	12–15	White	P-B: Picked on	Child	Questionnaire (1)	Recidivist stealing	RIOC = 76.5
Slocum and Stone (1963)	1,674 B, 1,568 G	12–18	Mixed	P-B: More unfair P-G: More unfair	Child	Questionnaire	Self-reported "delinquent-type" behavior	$\bar{C}$ = .20* $\bar{C}$ = .25*

NOTE.—B = boy; G = girl; F = father; M = mother; P = parent; del. = delinquent; nondel. = nondelinquent.
[a] The number of items, if known, is shown in parentheses.
[b] RIOC = relative improvement over chance; $\bar{C}$ = contingency coefficient.
* $p < .05$.
**** Not significant.

62

TABLE 12

Parental Discipline as a Predictor of the Child's Delinquency or Aggressiveness

Study	Subjects	Race	Interval	Parent Behavior	Respondent	Measurement Mode[a]	Conduct Problem	Strength of Relation[b]
McCord (1981)	224 B	Mixed	(5–8)–(41–50)	More punitive	Staff	Ratings of their reports	Serious criminality	RIOC = 17.6
McCord, McCord, and Howard (1963)	86 B	Mixed	(10–15)–(20–31)	Extreme threats	Staff	Ratings of their reports	Aggressive or antisocial	RIOC = 46.1
West and Farrington (1973)	391 B	White	(9–10)–17	Authoritarian mother	Mother	Questionnaire	Conviction	RIOC = 22.6
Farrington (1978)	391 B	White	8–(8–10)	More harsh attitude and discipline			Aggressiveness	RIOC = 16.7
			8–(16–18)	More harsh attitude and discipline			Aggressiveness	RIOC = 12.2
Simcha-Fagan et al. (1975)	1,034 BG	Mixed	(6–18)–(11–23)	Punitive parents	Mother	Ratings of her reports	Mother report of child's delinquency	$r = .09**$
							Delinquent criminal record	$r = .04****$
							Mother report of child's violence	$r = .23***$
Sears (1961)	76 B, 84 G	?	5–12	Physical punishment	Child	Questionnaire (9)	Antisocial aggression	$r = -.08****$
								$r = -.06****$
Pulkkinen (1983)	77 B, 77 G	White	14–20	Physical punishment	Mother	Interview	Criminal offense	ANOVA***
								ANOVA****

NOTE.—B = boy; G = girl.
[a] The number of items, if known, is shown in parentheses.
[b] RIOC = relative improvement over chance; r = product-moment correlation; ANOVA = analysis of variance.

** $p < .01$.
*** $p < .001$.
**** Not significant.

63

TABLE 13

Concurrent Relation between Parental Rejection of the Child and the Child's Delinquency or Aggression

Study	Subjects	Age	Race	Parent Behavior	Respondent	Measurement Mode[a]	Conduct Problem	Strength of Relation[b]
Nye (1958)	780 BG	14–18	White	F-B: Most rejecting F-G: M-B: M-G:	Child	Questionnaire (10)	Self-reported delinquency (most)	RIOC = 18.7 RIOC = 22.2 RIOC = 17.1 RIOC = 21.1
Lewis (1954)	109 BG referred	B under 12, G under 15	White	M-C: Lacks affection F-C: P-C: Rejection	Case records	Various	Unsocialized aggression, socialized delinquency	RIOC = 30.3 RIOC = 25.7 RIOC = 42.0
Andry (1960)	80 del., 80 nondel. B	12–15	White	M or F: Too little love	Child	Questionnaire (1)	Recidivist theft	RIOC = 84.6
Andry (1962)	80 del., 80 nondel. B	12–15	White	M and F: Inadequate love	Child	Questionnaire (1)	Recidivist theft	RIOC = 73.9
Glueck and Glueck (1950)	500 del., 500 nondel. B	$\bar{X} = 14.5$	White	M-B: Hostile/rejecting F-B:	Parents	Interview	Official delinquency	RIOC = 73.6 RIOC = 67.3
Blakely, Stephenson, and Nichol (1974)	50 del., 37 nondel. BG	12–18	White	F-C: Not warm M-C: F-C: Not accepting M-C:	Parents	Interview	Official delinquency	RIOC = 38.7 RIOC = 54.8 RIOC = 57.8 RIOC = 57.8
McCord, McCord, and Howard (1961)	25 aggr., 149 assertive and nonaggr. B	9–15	Mixed	One parent affectionate, one parent rejecting	Staff	Direct observations	Aggression	RIOC = 76.5

Study	Sample	Age	Race	Variable	Respondent	Measure	Outcome	Effect size
Medinnus (1965)	30 del., 30 nondel. B	12–17	White	F-B: More rejecting M-B: F-B: Less loving M-B:	Child	Questionnaire (15) Questionnaire (15)	Official delinquency	$d = 1.57$ $d = .80$ $d = 1.28$ $d = .34$****
Bandura and Walters (1959)	26 aggr., 26 nonaggr. B	14–17	White	F-B: Less warm M-B: M-B: More rejection F-B:	Parents Child	Interview Interview	Aggression	$d = .85$ $d = .54$ $d = .64$ $d = .79$
Jensen (1972)	1,588 B	12–18	White	F-B: Less support	Child	Questionnaire (3)	Self-reported delinquency	gamma $= .30$**
Slocum and Stone (1963)	1,674 B, 1,568 G	12–18	Mixed	Family with G: Less affectionate Family with B:	Child	Questionnaire	Self-reported "delinquent-type" behavior	$\bar{C} = .21$** $\bar{C} = .29$**
Imperio and Chabot (1980)	90 del. B	$\bar{X} = 15.7$	?	M-B: Rejection versus aceptance factor F-B:	Child	Questionnaire	Institutionalized delinquency	26 percent of common variance 30 percent of common variance
Eron, Walder, and Lefkowitz (1971)	875 BG	8–9	Mixed	M-C: More rejection F-C:	Parents	Interview	Aggression	$r = .25$*** $r = .24$***

NOTE.—B = boy; G = girl; F = father; M = mother; P = parent; C = child; del. = delinquent; nondel. = nondelinquent; aggr. = aggressive; nonaggr. = nonaggressive.
[a] The number of items, if known, is shown in parentheses.
[b] RIOC = relative improvement over chance; d = effect size; $\bar{C}$ = contingency coefficient; r = product-moment correlation.
** $p < .01$.
*** $p < .001$.
**** Not significant.

65

TABLE 14

Parental Rejection as Predictor of Aggressiveness and Delinquency

Study	Subjects	Race	Interval	Parent Behavior	Respondent	Measurement Mode	Conduct Problem	Strength of Relation[a]
Robins (1966, 1984)	285 BG, clinic	?	(−18)–(−48)	More disinterested or lenient	Staff	Rating of case records	Sociopathic personality	RIOC = 26.8
McCord, McCord, and Howard (1963)	103 B	Mixed	(10–15)–(20–31)	More rejected	Staff	Rating of their reports	Aggressive or antisocial	RIOC = 37.9
McCord (1984)	232 B	Mixed	(5–19)–(38–52)	Father not affective Mother not affective	Staff	Rating of their reports	Serious criminality	RIOC = 43.8 RIOC = 33.7
Simcha-Fagan et al. (1975)	1,034 BG	Mixed	(6–18)–(11–23)	Parents cold Mother excitable, rejecting	Mother	Ratings of her reports	Mother report of child's delinquency Delinquent criminal record Mother report of child's violence Mother report of child's delinquency	$r = .35^{***}$ $r = .07^{****}$ $r = .23^{***}$ $r = .23^{***}$

Study	Race	N	Age	Predictor variable	Reporter	Method	Outcome measure	Statistic
							Delinquent criminal record	$r = .04$****
							Mother report of child's violence	$r = .32$****
Lefkowitz et al. (1977)	Mixed	211 B, 216 G	8–18	Parent's rejection	Parents	Interview	Aggressiveness (peer nomination)	$r = .10$****
				Parent's nurturance				$r = .04$****
								$r = -.15$****
								$r = -.09$****
				Child's identification with father				$r = -.16$*
								$r = -.22$*
				Child's identification with mother				$r = -.17$*
								$r = -.19$*
Pulkkinen (1983)	White	77 B, 77 G	14–20	Conflicting relationship with father	Mother	Interview	Criminal offense	ANOVA**
								ANOVA****

NOTE.—B = boy; G = girl.
[a] RIOC = relative improvement over chance; r = product-moment correlation; ANOVA = analysis of variance.
* $p < .05$.
** $p < .01$.
*** $p < .001$.
**** Not significant.

TABLE 15

Concurrent Relation between Child Rejection of Parent and the Child's Delinquency or Aggression

Study	Subjects	Age	Race	Child Behavior	Respondent	Measurement Mode[a]	Conduct Problem	Strength of Relation[b]
Nye (1958)	780 BG	14–18	White	B-M: Most rejecting	Child	Questionnaire (11)	Self-reported delinquency (most)	RIOC = 17.2
				G-M:				RIOC = 25.5
				B-F:				RIOC = 23.2
				G-F:				RIOC = 22.6
Hirschi (1969)	1,256 B	12–18	Mixed	B-F: No identification	Child	Questionnaire (1)	Self-reported delinquency	RIOC = 24.1
Hindelang (1973)	441 rural B, 445 rural G	11–18	White	B-F: No identification	Child	Questionnaire	High self-reported delinquency	RIOC = 18.6
Gold (1963)	93 del., 93 nondel. B	12–16	White	C-P: No identification (think/sure)	Child	Interview (1)	Recidivism	RIOC = 20.0

Glueck and Glueck (1950)	500 del., 500 nondel. B	$\bar{X}$ = 14.5	White	B-F: Indifferent/hostile B-M: B-F: Unacceptable model	Child	Interview	Official delinquency	RIOC = 54.1 RIOC = 79.0 RIOC = 61.6
Reid and Hendriks (1973)	27 del., 27 nondel. BG	5–14	White	C-P: Less positive/friendly behaviors	Observer	Observations	Parent-reported stealing	d = .65****
Bandura and Walters (1959)	26 aggr., 26 nonaggr. B	14–17	White	B-F: Less warm B-M: B-F: Less identification B-M:	Child, mother	Interview	Aggression	d = 1.03 d = .41**** d = .47 d = .44****

NOTE.—B = boy; G = girl; F = father; M = mother; P = parent; C = child; del. = delinquent; nondel. = nondelinquent; aggr. = aggressive; nonaggr. = nonaggressive.
a The number of items, if known, is shown in parentheses.
b RIOC = relative improvement over chance; d = effect size.
**** Not significant.

69

TABLE 16
Summary Table for the Conflict Paradigm

Variable	Comparison Samples						Normal Samples			Comparison Samples			Normal Samples		
	Studies (N)	Analyses (N)	% Significant	Median RIOC	Analyses (N)	Range	Median RIOC	Analyses (N)	Range	Median d	Analyses (N)	Range	Median d	Analyses (N)	Range
Concurrent studies:															
Physical punishment and deprivation	6	16	56	7.7	2	2.0–13.4	...	...	...	.38	12	.03–1.23	...	...	...
Nagging and scolding	5	18	78	70.4	1	...	26.4	5	7.9–36.2	.77	12	.19–1.31	...	...	...
Reasoning	2	8	50	...	...	...	3.3	6	0.0–11.6	.90	2	.67–1.13	...	...	...
Love withdrawal	3	8	50	...	...	...	14.9	2	14.4–15.5	.33	6	.19–1.17	...	...	...
Strictness and consistency	11	28	61	82.1	4	42.7–87.9	12.4	11	0.0–34.7	.28	5	.00–1.02	...	...	...
Fairness of punishment	4	8	63	76.5	1	...	0.0	5	−5.4–21.7	...	...	...	...	...	...
Total discipline	31	86	62	73.5	8	2.0–87.9	11.6	29	−5.4–36.2	.50	37	.00–1.31	...	...	...
Parental rejection	12	31	97	62.6	8	38.7–84.6	24.0	8	17.1–76.5	.79	8	.34–1.57	...	...	...
Child rejection of parent	7	15	80	56.3	4	20.0–79.0	22.9	6	17.2–25.5	.47	5	.41–1.03	...	...	...
Total rejection	19	46	91	57.8	12	20.0–84.6	22.6	14	17.1–76.5	.65	13	.34–1.57	...	...	...
All concurrent studies	50	132	72	64.5	20	2.0–87.9	18.1	43	−5.4–76.5	.54	50	.00–1.57	...	...	...
Predictive studies:															
Discipline	5	12	58	...	...	...	17.6	5	12.2–46.1	...	...	...	...	...	...
Parental rejection	5	20	65	...	...	...	35.8	4	26.8–43.8	...	...	...	...	...	...
Child rejection of parent	1	4	100	...	...	...	...	...	...	...	...	...	...	...	...

22.6 percent for the studies using normal samples. The longitudinal data showed a moderate RIOC for discipline (17.6 percent) and a higher value for parental rejection (RIOC = 35.8 percent). As with the data in the neglect paradigm, the predictive values fell in between the values of comparison group studies dealing mainly with official delinquency and the values for studies based on normal samples and dealing with self-reported delinquency.

IV. The Deviant Behaviors and Values Paradigm

In this paradigm, children are not necessarily in conflict with the parents or alienated from them. The children's deviant behavior may not be in conflict with the parents' attitudes toward deviant behavior.

A. Parental Criminality and Aggression

Parental involvement with the law and the emergence of delinquency in offspring can reflect genetic influences; alternatively, parental behaviors and attitudes about lawbreaking that accompany criminality can be witnessed by children and imitated by them.

Table 17 summarizes concurrent studies that measure parental criminality. The three studies measuring paternal criminality had a median RIOC of 34.8 percent (range 34.2–35.8 percent). Because criminality of the mother is infrequent, it was measured in only one study. The RIOC was 52.3 percent. Glueck and Glueck (1950) measured criminality in the parents' families as well and found a significant, but moderate, association with official delinquency (RIOC = 20.8 percent and 10.8 percent).

The concurrent results are consistent with those from five longitudinal studies on parental criminality or aggressiveness as a predictor of later delinquency or conduct problems in children (see table 18). Nine of the fourteen analyses were significant. The median RIOC was 21 percent, with a range between 10.8 and 37.6 percent. None of the studies used self-reported delinquency as a predictor or as a criterion.

Turning to the prediction of children's aggressiveness, the studies in table 18 support the notion that aggressiveness may become a family pattern. This was shown most markedly in a follow-up of subjects over twenty-two years (Huesmann et al. 1984): those who had been characterized as aggressive (which included theft) at the age of eight were later found to have significantly more aggressive children ($r = .31$). The results were in accord with the retrospective findings reported by Straus, Gelles, and Steinmetz (1980) that children who grew up in homes in which parents were violent to each other had a greater tendency to be violent in their own marriages.

B. Parental Deviant Attitudes

Parents may tolerate deviant behavior. This can take several forms, such as dishonesty and normlessness in parents, parents' tolerance of children's delinquency, and their encouragement of children's aggression. Four concurrent studies measured these qualities (see table 17). Eight of the nine analyses supported the relation between parental deviant values and children's delinquency or aggression. The median RIOC in a normal sample was 23.5 percent, ranging from 18.5 percent to 26.1 percent, and the size of effect in two comparison group studies had a median value for d of .61 with a range of .29 − .78. In addition, there is some evidence that parents of problem children are less perceptive of their children's positive behavior and often perceive neutral child behaviors as negative (Holleran et al. 1982).

C. The Deviant Behaviors and Values Paradigm: A Summary

Table 19 summarizes the studies referring to the deviant behaviors and attitudes paradigm. Overall, the median magnitude was the highest for studies on concurrent comparison groups. Because very different categories of parental behaviors are summarized, the results should be interpreted with caution.

V. The Disruption Paradigm

Many circumstances can disrupt family functioning and affect children's behavior. This section reviews studies relating to marital problems, parental absence, ill health, and mental problems.

The current divorce rate for first marriages is between 40 and 50 percent (*The State of Families* 1984). The number of children witnessing marital discord is substantial. Most marriage breakups are preceded by a period of strife, and 30 percent of children in intact families have parents whose marriage is unstable (Zill 1978).

Considerable research on the effect of broken homes and discord on children has been summarized in review articles (Herzog and Sudia 1970; Bane 1976; Rutter 1977a, 1977b; Goetting 1981; Blechman 1982; Emery 1982). The reviews usually minimize the importance of the relation between broken homes and children's behavior problems and stress marital discord as a stronger factor.

TABLE 1/

Relation between Parental Criminality and Other Deviant Behaviors with the Child's Delinquency or Aggression

Study	Subjects	Age	Race	Parent Behavior	Respondent	Measurement Mode[a]	Conduct Problem	Strength of Relation[b]
Glueck and Glueck (1950)	500 del., 500 nondel. B	$\bar{X}$ = 14.5	White	M: Criminal in family F: M: Criminality F:	Parents	Interview	Official delinquency	RIOC = 20.8 RIOC = 10.8 RIOC = 52.3 RIOC = 34.8
Offord, Allen, and Abrams (1978)	73 del., 73 nondel. B	$\bar{X}$ = 13.8	White	F: Law involvement	Parents	Interview	Official delinquency	RIOC = 34.2
Offord et al. (1979)	59 del., 59 nondel. G	$\bar{X}$ = 13.7	White	F: Law involvement	Parents	Interview	Official delinquency	RIOC = 35.8
Nye (1958)	780 BG	14–18	White	M: Truthfulness F: M: Honesty F:	Child	Questionnaire (1)	Self-reported delinquency (most)	RIOC = 26.1 RIOC = 23.1 RIOC = 18.5**** RIOC = 24.1
Gold (1963)	93 del., 93 nondel. B	12–16	White	M: Considers delinquent behavior less serious F:	Parent	Interview (1)	Recidivism	d = .29 d = .51
Bandura and Walters (1959)	26 aggr., 26 nonaggr. B	14–17	White	F: Encourage aggression M:	Parents	Interview	Aggression	d = .78 d = .70
Canter (1982a)	1,725 BG	11–17	Mixed	Family normlessness	Child	Questionnaire (4)	Self-reported delinquency	r = .37***

NOTE.—B = boy; G = girl; F = father; M = mother; del. = delinquent; nondel. = nondelinquent; aggr. = aggressive; nonaggr. = nonaggressive.
[a] The number of items, if known, is shown in parentheses. * $p < .001$.
[b] RIOC = relative improvement over chance; d = effect size; r = product-moment correlation. *,** Not significant.

TABLE 18

Parental Criminality and Aggressiveness as a Predictor of the Child's Delinquency or Aggressiveness

Study	Subjects	Race	Interval	Parent Behavior	Respondent	Measurement Mode	Conduct Problem	Strength of Relation[a]
McCord (1984)	232 B	Mixed	(5–19)–(38–52)	More aggressive	Staff	Rating of their reports	Serious criminality	RIOC = 34.4
Farrington (1978)	411 B	White	10–(16–18)	Criminal parent		Criminal record	Aggressiveness	RIOC = 17.9
Farrington (1979)	409 B	White	−10–(14–16)	Criminal parent		Criminal record	More than twenty self-reported delinquent acts	RIOC = 24.4
Osborn and West (1978)	185 B	White	8–(24–25)	Recidivist father		Criminal record	Recidivism	RIOC = 26.4
Robins, West, and Herjanic (1975)	86 B, select	Black	(10–11)–18+	Both parents arrested		Criminal record	Court or police contact before age 17	RIOC = 37.6
McCord (1984)	232 B	Mixed	(5–19)–(38–52)	Paternal alcoholism or crime	Staff	Rating of their reports	Serious criminality	RIOC = 22.5

Study	Sample		Age	Predictor	Source	Measure	Outcome	Result
Hutchings and Mednick (1975)	1,120 male nonadopted adults	White	?–(30–44)	Criminal biological father		Criminal record	Serious criminal record	RIOC = 10.8
	1,119 male adults adopted as children			Criminal adoptive father				RIOC = 13.0
	971 male adults adopted as children			Criminal biological fathers of adoptees				RIOC = 19.5
Lefkowitz et al. (1977)	211 B, 216 G	Mixed	8–18	Father's aggressiveness	Parents	Interview	Aggressiveness (peer nomination)	r = .11**** r = .06****
				Mother's aggressiveness				r = .03**** r = .06****
Huesmann et al. (1984)	82 BG	Mixed	8–22 years later	Parent's aggressiveness	Peers	Nomination	Aggressiveness (self-rating)	r = .31**

NOTE.—B = boy; G = girl.

[a] RIOC = relative improvement over chance; r = product-moment correlation.

** $p < .01$.

**** Not significant.

TABLE 19

Summary Table for the Deviant Behavior and Attitude Paradigm

Variable	All Studies			Comparison Samples			Normal Samples			Comparison Samples			Normal Samples		
	Studies (N)	Analyses (N)	% Significant	Median RIOC	Analyses (N)	Range	Median RIOC	Analyses (N)	Range	Median d	Analyses (N)	Range	Median RIOC	Analyses (N)	Range
Concurrent studies:															
Parent criminality and other deviant values	7	15	93	34.5	6	10.8–52.3	23.6	4	18.5–26.1	.60	4	.29–.78	...	...	...
Predictive studies:															
Parent criminality and aggressiveness	6	14	64	...	...	...	22.5	9	10.8–37.6	...	...	...	...	...	...

A. Marital Relations

Table 20 summarizes eleven studies that have measured marital relations. The measures include ratings of happiness, amount of conflict, lack of warmth, and hostility. Parents were generally the respondents. Of the twenty-two analyses listed, seventeen showed a significant relation between marital discord and children's delinquency and aggression. The RIOC was 29 percent and 29.4 percent for the two comparison group analyses, while other comparison group studies yielded a median d of .68 (range .60–.86). This compares with a median RIOC of 23.3 percent (range 6.8–28.3 percent) and a median d of .47 (range .15–.52) for normal samples.

Of the eight longitudinal analyses summarized in table 21, six were statistically significant. Three studies addressed marital conflict as a predictor of children's antisocial or delinquent behavior and produced RIOCs from 10.5 to 60.5 percent (with a median value of 28 percent). In McCord's (1984) study, the fathers' lack of respect for their wives produced an RIOC of 42.6 percent, compared with an RIOC of 26.2 percent for marital conflict in the same study. One study (Farrington 1978) found that, when marital disharmony emerged in families with a nonaggressive boy, the risk increased that the boy would become aggressive (RIOC = 29.8 percent).

B. Parental Absence

We found fifteen concurrent studies that have measured the effect of broken homes or parental absence (see table 22). Of the forty analyses, thirty-three were statistically significant. The median RIOC for comparison group studies was 27.7 percent (range 5.9–100 percent). No d's were reported for this group of studies. The median RIOC for the studies with normal samples was a low 12.2 percent, based on thirty analyses with a range of 0–42.8 percent. Only three analyses could be converted to the measure of effect size. The range for d was .16–.48 with a median value of .31.

In the predictive studies, parental absence showed a median RIOC of about the same magnitude (11.5 percent) as found in concurrent studies with normal samples (see table 23). Separation may have worse effects when children are young. Wadsworth's (1979) English longitudinal survey showed that 29 percent of the boys experiencing family disruption before the age of five became delinquent, compared with 16 percent for older boys (the figures for girls were 8 percent and 1.5–2.6 percent, respectively). Similar results were reported by Behar and

Stewart (1982), who compared hospitalized conduct problem children with children with other diagnoses. Perhaps a crucial factor, not measured in the studies reviewed, was the length of time since separation (Hetherington, Cox, and Cox 1978)—the effect of parental strife and family disruption may wear off over time.

Taking all the evidence together, marital discord has a stronger relation with delinquency and aggression than parental absence, concurrently as well as predictively. This finding strengthens Rutter's (1971) contention that children's behavior is disrupted by parental discord and quarreling rather than parental separation. This is consistent with studies that show that the death of a parent does not have the same effect on child behavior as divorce or separation (Glueck and Glueck 1950; Zill 1978).

Several studies have directly compared boys from broken homes with those with unhappily married parents. McCord (1982) compared the percentage of serious delinquents in intact homes in general (32 percent), in broken homes (41 percent), and in intact homes in which there was marital conflict (52 percent) and found the difference to be nonsignificant. Nye (1958) found that boys in broken homes were less delinquent than boys in homes with marital discord, while Power et al. (1974) showed that more delinquents from unhappy homes became recidivists than did delinquents from broken homes. Stouthamer-Loeber, Schmaling, and Loeber (1984), however, did not find a difference in self-reported or official delinquency between boys from unhappy marriages and boys from broken homes.

Witnessing parental discord may not be the only factor affecting children's behavior. Stouthamer-Loeber et al. (1984) in a study of ten-to sixteen-year-old boys found that both single mothers and unhappily married mothers supervised their children significantly less assiduously than did happily married mothers. They also had a more negative attitude toward their children. Both factors may make it easier for children to engage in nonsanctioned behaviors. Related findings were reported by Goldstein (1984), who found that, in low-supervision households, youths from families in which the father was absent had a higher probability of police contact than youths from intact families. This difference was absent in high-supervision households. In other words, high levels of supervision of youngsters in families in which the father is absent can reduce the likelihood of police contacts.

C. Parental Health

Studies of parental physical and mental health are summarized in table 24. Parental physical illness was measured in two concurrent studies; in one of these studies there was a moderate significant relation with official delinquency. The mother's physical illness was a predictor of later delinquency, but the relation for the father's illness was nonsignificant (see table 25).

Mental problems were measured more often. Five concurrent studies yielded eleven analyses, nine of which were significant. For comparison group studies, RIOC had a range of 0–65 percent, with a median value of 28.1 percent. The values in a study of a normal sample were 21.2 percent and 25.1 percent.

As shown in table 25, the mother's depression was a strong predictor of later antisocial child disorder in one study (Richman et al. 1982), with the RIOC ranging from 36.7 to 50.6 percent. In West and Farrington's (1973) study, parental nervousness was not predictive of delinquency, in contrast to parental instability (RIOC ranges from 18 to 22.9 percent).

D. The Disruption Paradigm: A Summary

Summarizing the evidence for the disruption paradigm, 80 percent of the analyses in concurrent studies were significant (see table 26). The median RIOC for comparison group studies was 28 percent with a median d of .68. For the studies with normal samples the values were 12.2 percent and .39, respectively, for concurrent studies. The median RIOC for longitudinal studies was somewhat higher because of higher values for marital relations and parental health. Disruption in marital relations was the strongest variable in this paradigm.

We return in the conclusion to other aspects of the meta-analyses such as the comparison of findings from concurrent and longitudinal studies and effects separately considered for mothers and fathers and for sons and daughters.

VI. Cumulative Effects

We now turn to the cumulative effects of familial handicaps that are associated with children's behavior problems. One major question concerns the extent to which multiple deficits in parenting coincide in certain families. Does the concurrence of such multiple deficits predict subsequent juvenile delinquency better than single-parenting deficits?

TABLE 20

Concurrent Relation between Marital Relations and the Child's Delinquency or Aggression

Study	Subjects	Age	Race	Parent Situation	Respondent	Measurement Mode[a]	Conduct Problem	Strength of Relation[b]
Nye (1958)	780 BG	14–18	White	F and M: Unhappy	Child	Questionnaire (1)	Self-reported delinquency (most)	RIOC = 28.3
				M: Somewhat/very unhappy F:				RIOC = 23.3 RIOC = 28.1
Belson (1975)	3,113 B	13–16	White	Family row (every day/most days)	Child	Interview (1)	Self-reported stealing (top 25 percent)	RIOC = 6.8
Andry (1960)	80 del., 80 nondel. B	12–15	White	P: Quarrel more than average	Child	Questionnaire (1)	Recidivist theft	RIOC = 29.4****
Glueck and Glueck (1950)	500 del., 500 nondel. B	$\bar{X}$ = 14.5	White	Conjugal relations (fair/poor)	Parents	Interview	Official delinquency	RIOC = 29.0
McCord, McCord, and Howard (1961)	21 aggr., 126 assertive and nonaggr. B	9–15	Mixed	Intense conflict	Staff	Observations	Aggression	RIOC = 12.4
Bandura and Walters (1959)	26 aggr., 26 nonaggr. B	14–17	White	M: Less warmth for father F: Less warmth for mother M: Hostility to father F: Hostility to mother	Parents	Interview	Aggression	d = .86 d = .74 d = .60 d = .63

Study	Sample	Age	Race	Variable	Parent	Method	Aggression	Effect size
Zill (1978)	2,279 BG	7–11	Mixed	Less than "very happy"	Parent	Interview (8)	Aggression	d = .15
Stouthamer-Loeber, Schmaling, and Loeber (1984)	190 B	10–16	White	P: Unhappy	Parents	Interview	Self-reported delinquency	d = .47
							Official delinquency	d = .52
Johnson and Lobitz (1974)	27 B, referred	2.4–12.5	White	P: Marital maladjustment	Parents	Questionnaire	Observed deviance	r = .45*
Emery and O'Leary (1982)	50 BG, referred	8–17	White	Marital discord	Mother of son	Questionnaire (9)	Delinquency (mother report)	r = .28****
					Mother of daughter			r = −.02*****
				Perceived marital discord	Son	Questionnaire (12)		r = .35*
					Daughter			r = −.08****
Alexander (1973)	20 del., 22 normal BG	X̄ = 15.3	White	F-M: More defensive communication	Observer	Observations	Runaway/ungovernable	ANOVA*
				M-F:				ANOVA*
				F-M, M-F: Supportive communications				ANOVA****

NOTE.—B = boy; G = girl; F = father; M = mother; P = parent; del. = delinquent; nondel. = nondelinquent; aggr. = aggressive; nonaggr. = nonaggressive.
[a] The number of items, if known, is shown in parentheses.
[b] RIOC = relative improvement over chance; d = effect size; r = product-moment correlation; ANOVA = analysis of variance.
* p < .05.
**** Not significant.

81

TABLE 21

Marital Relations as a Predictor of the Child's Delinquency or Aggressiveness

Study	Subjects	Race	Interval	Parent Behavior	Respondent	Measurement Mode	Conduct Problem	Strength of Relation[a]
Farrington and West (1971)	357 B	White	(8–9)–(14–15)	Parental disharmony	Social worker	Report	Aggressiveness	RIOC = 10.5
Farrington (1978)	156 B	White	14–(16–18)	New marital disharmony	Social worker	Report	Not aggressive before 14 but aggressive 14–16	RIOC = 29.8
McCord, McCord, and Howard (1963)	85 B	Mixed	(10–15)–(20–31)	Marital conflict	Staff	Ratings of their reports	Aggressive or antisocial	RIOC = 60.5
McCord (1984)	232 B	Mixed	(5–19)–(38–52)	Marital conflict Father does not respect mother	Staff	Ratings of their reports	Serious criminality	RIOC = 26.2 RIOC = 42.6
Robins (1966, 1984)	228 BG, clinic	White	(−18)–(−48)	Discordant home	Staff	Ratings of case records	Sociopathic personality	RIOC = 14.0
Lefkowitz et al. (1977)	211 B, 216 G	Mixed	8–18	Parents' disharmony	Parents	Interview	Aggressiveness (peer nomination)	r = .07**** r = .12****

NOTE.—B = boy; G = girl.
[a] RIOC = relative improvement over chance; r = product-moment correlation.
**** Not significant.

82

TABLE 22

Concurrent Relation between Parental Absence and the Child's Delinquency or Aggression

Study	Subjects	Age	Race	Parent Situation	Conduct Problem	Strength of Relation[a]
Wilkinson (1980)	2,909 BG	14–18	Mixed	Father-absent homes	Self-reported vandalism	RIOC = 13.5
	B					RIOC = 3.8****
	G					RIOC = 2.9****
	B				Self-reported assault	RIOC = 9.4
	G					RIOC = 3.1****
	B				Self-reported shoplifting	RIOC = 10.8
	G					RIOC = 4.7****
	B				Self-reported auto theft	RIOC = 8.1****
	G					RIOC = 12.2
	B				Self-reported marijuana	RIOC = 13.2
	G					RIOC = 21.7
	B				Self-reported drinking	RIOC = 23.6
	G					RIOC = 22.4
	B				Self-reported truancy	RIOC = 30.3
	G					RIOC = 13.1
	B				Self-reported runaway	RIOC = 12.8
	G					
Goldstein (1984)	3,288 B	12–17	Mixed	Father absent	Police contact	RIOC = 14.3
	2,999 G					RIOC = 1.1****
Nye (1958)	780 BG	14–18	White	Broken home	Self-reported delinquency	RIOC = 10.0
	B				(most)	
	G					RIOC = 10.7
	124 BG, broken home			Unhappy broken		RIOC = 25.2

TABLE 22 (*Continued*)

Study	Subjects	Age	Race	Parent Situation	Conduct Problem	Strength of Relation[a]
Belson (1975)	3,113 B	13–16	White	Broken at age 13	Self-reported stealing (top 25 percent)	RIOC = 3.2
Elliott, Knowles, and Canter (1981)	1,725 BG	11–17	Mixed	Broken home	Self-reported general delinquency	RIOC = 33.4
Dentler and Monroe (1961)	912 BG	12–14	?	Broken family	High self-reported theft	RIOC = .0****
Glueck and Glueck (1950)	500 del., 500 nondel. B	$\bar{X}$ = 14.5	White	Broken home	Official delinquency	RIOC = 27.7
Offord, Allen, and Abrams (1978)	73 del., 73 nondel. B	$\bar{X}$ = 13.8	White	Nonintact home	Official delinquency	RIOC = 27.3
Offord et al. (1979)	59 del., 59 nondel. G	$\bar{X}$ = 13.7	White	Nonintact	Official delinquency	RIOC = 50.9
Johnstone (1980)	2,933 B	14–18	Mixed	Nonintact	Police contact Brought before court	RIOC = 7.5 RIOC = 42.8

Study	Sample	Age	Race	Family	Outcome	Effect
Monahan (1957)	15,344 del. B	Under 18	White	Not with two parents	Recidivism	RIOC = 14.7
	14,414 del. B 2,488 del. G 3,668 del. G		Black White Black			RIOC = 11.1 RIOC = 30.2 RIOC = 21.9
Blakely, Stephenson, and Nichol (1974)	50 del., 37 nondel. BG	12–18	White	Father absent Mother absent	Official delinquency	RIOC = 100.0 RIOC = 5.9
Stouthamer-Loeber, Schmaling, and Loeber (1984)	190 B	10–16	White	Father absent	Self-reported delinquency Official delinquency	$d = .31$ $d = .48$
McCarthy, Gersten, and Langner (1982)	1,034 lower middle class, 605 welfare BG	6–18	Mixed	Surrogate father	Mother-reported delinquency	$d = .16$
Slocum and Stone (1963)	1,674 B 1568 G	12–18	Mixed	Broken home	Self-reported "delinquent-type" behavior	$\bar{C} = .13*$ $\bar{C} = .14**$

NOTE.—B = boy; G = girl; del. = delinquent; nondel. = nondelinquent.
[a] RIOC = relative improvement over chance; d = effect size; $\bar{C}$ = contingency coefficient.
* $p < .05$.
** $p < .01$.
**** Not significant.

85

TABLE 23

Parental Absence as a Predictor of the Child's Delinquency or Aggressiveness

Study	Subjects	Race	Interval	Parent Behavior	Conduct Problem	Strength of Relation[a]
Farrington and West (1971)	405 B	White	10–(14–15)	Temporary or permanent separations	Self-reported aggressiveness	RIOC = 6.3
Robins (1966, 1984)	504 BG, clinic	White	(−18)–(−48)	Broken home	Sociopathic personality	RIOC = 12.9
Wadsworth (1980)	2,191 BG	White	8–21	Death or separation before 3 years, 4 months	All reported offenses	RIOC = 7.4
Robins and Hill (1966)	296 B	Black	6–(15–17)	Father absent before age 15	Police or court record	RIOC = 30.2
Gregory (1965)	5,600 B		16–19	Separation through death or divorce	Police and court records; at least one minor offense	RIOC = 11.5
Simcha-Fagan et al. (1975)	732 BG	Mixed	5-year period?	Absence of one or both natural parents	Delinquent criminal record	RIOC = 25.1
McCord (1982)	201 B	Mixed	(5–18)–(35–48)	Broken home	Serious crime	RIOC = 8.5
Ensminger, Kellam, and Rubin (1983)	327 BG	Black	6–(16–17)	Mother alone Mother absent Mother/other families	High self-reported delinquency	RIOC = 18.6
Pulkkinen (1983)	77 B 77 G	White	14–20	Broken family	Criminal offense	ANOVA**** ANOVA**

NOTE.—B = boy; G = girl. ** $p < .01$.

[a] RIOC = relative improvement over chance; ANOVA = analysis of variance. **** Not significant.

TABLE 24

Concurrent Relation between Parental Health and the Child's Delinquency

Study	Subjects	Age	Race	Parent Situation	Respondent	Measurement Mode[a]	Conduct Problem	Strength of Relation[b]
Glueck and Glueck (1950)	500 del., 500 nondel. B	$\bar{X}$ = 14.5	White	M: Serious physical illness F:	Parents	Interview	Official delinquency	RIOC = 19.1 RIOC = 16.1
Lewis (1954)	119 normals, 109 unsocially aggr. and socially delinquent BG	G under 13 B under 16	White	M: Physical handicap	Case records	Various	Unsocially aggressive and socially delinquent	RIOC = .0****
Nye (1958)	780 BG	14–18	White	M: Nervousness F:	Child	Questionnaire (1)	Self-reported delinquency (most)	RIOC = 21.2 RIOC = 25.1
Glueck and Glueck (1950)	500 del., 500 nondel. B	$\bar{X}$ = 14.5	White	M: Emotional disturbance in family F: M: Emotional disturbance F:	Parents	Interview	Official delinquency	RIOC = 28.1 RIOC = 22.0 RIOC = 33.0 RIOC = 41.9
Lewis (1954)	119 normals, 109 unsocially aggr. and socially delinquent BG	B under 13 G under 16	White	M: Mental disability	Case records	Various	Unsocially aggressive and socially delinquent	RIOC = .0****
Offord, Allen, and Abrams (1978)	73 del., 73 nondel. B	$\bar{X}$ = 13.8	White	M: Mental illness	Parents	Interview	Official delinquency	RIOC = 42.3 RIOC = 28.0
Offord et al. (1979)	59 del., 59 nondel. G	$\bar{X}$ = 13.7	White	M: Mental illness F:	Parents	Interview	Official delinquency	RIOC = 65.0 RIOC = 8.6****

NOTE.—B = boy; G = girl; F = father; M = mother; del. = delinquent; nondel. = nondelinquent; aggr. = aggressive.
[a] The number of items, if known, is shown in parentheses.   **** Not significant.
[b] RIOC = relative improvement over chance.

TABLE 25
Parental Health as a Predictor of the Child's Antisocial or Delinquent Behavior

Study	Subjects	Race	Interval	Parent Behavior	Respondent	Measurement Mode	Conduct Problem	Strength of Relation[a]
Richman, Stevenson, and Graham (1982)	41 B, problem	White	3–8	M: Depressed	Mother	Interview/ questionnaire	Antisocial disorder	RIOC = 36.7
	86 BG, representative sample	White	4–8	M: Depressed			Antisocial disorder	RIOC = 50.6
West and Farrington (1973)	411 B	White	(8–9)–18	M: Physical illness F:	Parents	Interview	Conviction	RIOC = 15.0 RIOC = 10.4****
				M: Nervousness F:				RIOC = 13.3**** RIOC = 5.7****
				M: Instability F:				RIOC = 22.9 RIOC = 18.0

NOTE.—B = boy; G = girl; F = father; M = mother.

[a] RIOC = relative improvement over chance.

**** Not significant.

88

TABLE 26
Summary Table for the Disruption Paradigm

Variable	All Studies			Comparison Samples			Normal Samples			Comparison Samples			Normal Samples		
	Studies (N)	Analyses (N)	% Significant	Median RIOC	Analyses (N)	Range	Median RIOC	Analyses (N)	Range	Median d	Analyses (N)	Range	Median d	Analyses (N)	Range
Concurrent studies:															
Marital relations	11	22	77	29.2	2	29.0–29.4	23.3	5	6.8–28.3	.68	4	.60–.86	.47	3	.15–.52
Parental absence	15	40	82	27.7	5	5.9–100.0	12.5	30	.0–42.8	...	...	...	.31	3	.16–.31
Parental health	5	14	79	28.0	10	8.6–65.0	10.6	4	.0–25.1	...	...	...	...	...	...
All concurrent studies	31	76	80	28.0	17	5.9–100.0	12.2	39	.0–42.8	.68	4	.60–.86	.39	6	.15–.52
Predictive studies:															
Marital relations	4	8	75	...	...	...	28.0	6	10.5–60.5	...	...	...	...	...	...
Parental absence	9	10	90	...	...	...	12.2	8	7.4–30.2	...	...	...	...	...	...
Parental health	4	8	62	...	...	...	16.5	8	5.7–50.6	...	...	...	...	...	...

Further, which specific groups of parenting defects appear to increase the risk of children's delinquency?

A related question is whether particular patterns of handicaps within families generate particular categories of juvenile conduct problems and delinquency. For example, do children who are aggressive come from families with different handicaps than children who steal? And finally, which families appear most at risk?

A. *The Cumulative Effect of Multiple Familial Handicaps*

In some families the chance is high that poor parenting is common to both parents. For example, Hirschi (1969) found correlations averaging .75 between the youth's perception of paternal and of maternal behaviors, indicating high degrees of overlap between parent behaviors within the same family (although this could also reflect youngsters' response biases). Deficits in child rearing are also often associated with other kinds of handicaps. For example, in the Cambridge/Somerville study, the average intercorrelation between poor parental supervision, conflict, aggression, and the mother's affection was .20 (McCord 1979). In a study of seventh- and tenth-grade boys, the average intercorrelation between good parental discipline, supervision, and reinforcement was .57 (Patterson and Stouthamer-Loeber 1984). Similar low- to medium-level intercorrelations between various family handicaps have been noted by Kagan and Moss (1962), West (1969), West and Farrington (1973), and Pulkkinen (1982). McCord (1982) reported that 67 percent of the parents in intact homes supervised their children, compared with 44 percent in broken homes. Even within united homes, 81 percent of the boys with loving mothers were supervised, compared with 56 percent of those with mothers who were not loving. In comparison, in broken homes, 65 percent of the loving mothers and only 21 percent of the rejecting mothers supervised their sons.

Are multiple handicaps associated with a higher probability of juvenile delinquency compared with single handicaps? It can be expected that the overlap in handicaps is largest in those families with the most serious forms of juvenile delinquency. Data presented in table 27 suggest that multiple familial handicaps increase the risk of *later* delinquency. For example, two studies reported that parents with a delinquent record supervised their children less, which increased the probability of the children's delinquency compared with poor supervision by a nondelinquent parent (Farrington, Gundry and West 1975; Wilson 1980). McCord et al. (1969) found that children who were rejected by both parents were much more likely to become delinquent than were children who were rejected by one parent or whose parents were loving toward them (RIOC = 37.5 percent). Rutter (1978) reported that, even in homes with marked marital discord, if one of the parents had a warm, positive relationship with their children, the probability of child conduct disorders was reduced by about a third compared with the children of parents not having a good relationship with their children. The other examples shown in table 27 are organized by handicap. For example, it shows that broken homes in conjunction with parental conflict or parental criminality can further increase the likelihood of juvenile delinquency (McCord 1982).

Which overlap between familial handicaps is most predictive of later juvenile or adult delinquency? Several relevant longitudinal studies covering at least a decade are summarized in table 28. A number of studies used the Glueck Prediction Table, in either a three- or a five-factor format. The latter consisted of ratings of discipline by the father, supervision by the mother, affection by each, and family cohesiveness. The three-factor format was aimed at single-parent families and tapped maternal discipline and supervision and the family's cohesiveness. Compared with the RIOCs reviewed so far, the RIOCs are high in the studies using the Glueck Prediction Table (median 58.5, range 48.3–86.7).[3] The Glueck Prediction Table has, however, been criticized (Prigmore 1963; Weis 1974). The initial claims for its effectiveness were based on retrospective reports (Glueck and Glueck 1950, 1959) and for that reason have not been included here. Even the predictive studies included in table 28 are not always sufficiently clear in their definition of familial variables, and they often lack reliability checks, which may be why other studies have failed to replicate the findings (Whelan 1954, cited in Lundman and Scarpitti 1978; Dootjes 1972).

Nevertheless, other studies, not based on the Glueck formula, also show that a combination of familial handicaps can predict later delinquency more accurately than would any single handicap. The risk score in each of these studies included parenting variables in conjunction with other family factors (such as parental deviance and absence and low income). The risk scores achieved high RIOCs—45.7 percent in the McCord study (1979), 63 percent in the West and Farrington study (1973), and 49.5 percent in the Wadsworth (1979) study. That

[3] The Trevvett (1972) study has not been included in this computation as it concerns a reanalysis of the data used by Tait and Hodges (1972).

some familial risk scores also are predictive of the persistence of offending (in terms of juvenile and adult convictions) is evident from the report by Osborn and West (1978). Their risk score, based on the child's troublesomeness at ages eight to ten, parental criminality, and maternal or sibling criminality, produced an RIOC of 46.9 percent. This study found that early background adversities were more relevant for first convictions up to age eighteen, but not for first convictions from age nineteen and older (see also McCord et al. 1969).

These findings strongly suggest that familial handicaps "interlock" and increase the chances that children in these families will become delinquent. This is consistent with work by Rutter (1978), who demonstrated that the risk of child problem behavior increases rapidly as the number of handicaps in families increases. Several questions remain unanswered. First, the above findings need to be replicated in studies that use self-reports of delinquency as criteria. Second, it is not known what proportion of career criminals comes from families with multiple family handicaps. Third, cumulative deficits in parents' socialization practices may be more ominous for juvenile delinquency than is the cumulative effect of other familial handicaps. Finally, it is unclear to what extent the parental deficits in child-rearing practices early in the child's life were a concomitant rather than a cause of existing conduct problems.

B. Specific and Nonspecific Effects of Parental Factors

The effect of familial influences on child behavior can be conceptualized in several ways. Familial influences may be nonspecific and produce a wide range of undesirable juvenile behaviors. Repeated theft, for example, could be associated with the neglect paradigm but also with the conflict paradigm—this perspective is called the *nonspecific impact paradigm*. By contrast, specific risk factors may be responsible for specific juvenile problem behaviors. This is the *specific impact paradigm*.

The two perspectives have very different implications for theory, child rearing, and treatment programs. Most sociological theories that incorporate family variables have not claimed that specific influences are associated with specific forms of lawbreaking, even though subcategories of juvenile delinquency often have been chosen as outcome variables (e.g., Norland et al. 1979; Richards, Berk, and Forster 1979; Canter 1982a). Social learning theories, by contrast, rest on the assumption that conduct problems consist of certain skills that have emerged as a result of specific familial interactions; at least a proportion of children from a conflict-ridden home environment are hypothesized to adopt aggressive behavior patterns, while a neglectful household with little supervision is hypothesized to produce youngsters with covert conduct problem behaviors such as theft (Patterson 1982*b*).

Whether the nonspecific and the specific impact paradigms are useful constructs has repercussions for interventions. If specific social environments generate theft, then interventions prompted by concern for theft should be aimed at those environments. If other environments are associated with juvenile aggression and acts of violence, then interventions specifically aimed at aggression should address the inducing variables.

The specific impact paradigm implies that at least some youngsters confine themselves to certain problem behaviors and not others. The available evidence is equivocal. A number of researchers have concluded that most juvenile delinquent involvement is nonspecialized (e.g., Klein 1984); others have emphasized forms of specialization (Loeber 1985*a*).

There is substantial evidence (summarized by Loeber and Schmaling 1985*b*) that child conduct problems as perceived by parents and clinicians fall into two broad patterns: overt or confrontational (e.g., arguing, fighting, attacking, etc.) and covert (e.g., stealing, vandalism, truancy, drug use). It may be that some children develop specific propensities to overt forms of conduct problems and delinquency and others to covert counterparts and that a third group develops both overt and covert skills (Loeber 1985*a*). Evidence for the existence of the last group, who appear at high risk to be arrested for criminal acts, has been presented in a number of studies (Eisenberg et al. 1976; Langner et al. 1983; Loeber and Schmaling 1985*a*).

If distinct behavior patterns exist for juvenile conduct problems and delinquency, they may result from distinctly different influences. Hewitt and Jenkins (1946) distinguished between unsocialized aggressive youngsters and socialized nonaggressive delinquents. The latter came from households characterized by parental rejection, as measured by such factors as illegitimate or unwanted pregnancy, postdelivery rejection, unwilling mother, sexually unconventional mother, mother hostile to the child, or no contact with the natural parents. In contrast, the unsocialized aggressive youngsters came from households characterized by negligence and exposure. These households were unkempt; had irregular home routines, lack of supervision, lax discipline, harsh discipline, sibling delinquency, and a mother who was mentally inadequate or shielding; and often lived in a deteriorating neighborhood. Unfortunately, the study did not use well-developed measures of the variables and to our knowledge has not been replicated.

The Cambridge/Somerville study has also shed light on the specific impact paradigm. McCord (1979) reported that boys without supervision early in life had a high chance of being convicted later for serious property and personal crimes, whereas boys who had been rejected by their mothers were more likely later to be convicted for property crimes. Multiple regression analyses supported that distinction and revealed that family conflict, supervision, and lack of maternal affection were among the best predictors of later crimes against persons; the best predictors of crimes against property were lack of parental supervision and lack of maternal affection (see also McCord et al. 1969; McCord 1978).

Similarly, Pulkkinen (1983), in a Finnish longitudinal study, found that juvenile property offenses were related to broken homes, a "laissez-faire" atmosphere, the use of physical punishment, and the parents' negative comments on the son's character (which can be considered a form of rejection). Juvenile violent offenses were also associated with these familial factors, with the exception of physical punishment. In addition, violent offenders came from homes with a conflicting atmosphere, conflict with the father, poor parental supervision, poor communication between parents and the child, and no praise of the child by parents. The findings are remarkably congruent with observational data gleaned from family interactions within the home. Simard (1981) compared aggressive youngsters who did not steal (according to the mother), youngsters who stole but were not aggressive, and those who did both. The lowest rate of coercive behaviors by parents was observed in the stealer group, while the rate was significantly higher in the aggressor group but highest in the combined group. These findings have been replicated by Wahler and Dumas (1986b). That no firm conclusions can yet be drawn, however, appears from more recent cross-sectional work on nine- to sixteen-year-old boys, which found few differences between familial variables associated with children's self-reports and parents' reports of overt and covert forms of conduct problems (Loeber and Schmaling 1985a).

There is some support for the notion that covert conduct problems and delinquency in children are associated with a home environment that is characterized by parental neglect and an absence of open conflict. Chronic unresolved conflicts may lead to patterns of avoidance among family members rather than to patterns of overt aggression. For some children, the occasional physical punishment by parents leads them to avoid confrontations and encourages them to become more concealing. However, it is also likely that covert conduct problems emerge in families in which parents model covert behaviors to their children and thus indirectly encourage them to adopt these behaviors.

Violent offenses seem more a product of families in which open conflict is chronic and in which parents are actively discouraged by their youngsters from supervising them or executing other child-rearing practices. Future studies would greatly benefit from the use of self-reported delinquency as a criterion instead of relying solely on official records. Moreover, distinctions between different home environments are bound to be blurred when samples contain many subjects who engage in high rates of both overt and covert forms of delinquency. Whether current measurement instruments are sufficient for tapping offense-specific processes within the home remains to be seen.

C. Families at Risk

We first examine the few existing empirical studies that have looked at differences among families that relate to their probability of producing delinquent offspring. A study of welfare recipients in New York City found that three-quarters of the children did not have a father figure living in the home (Eisenberg 1979). The welfare families showed significantly higher rates of juvenile delinquency, in a cross-sectional sample of families, both at the beginning of the study and five years later. The effect was more pronounced for long-term than for short-term welfare families. It appears not so much that such high rates are a result of the welfare status itself as that they are associated with the emotional illness, poor child-rearing practices, and other handicaps in these families.

Investigators in the Manhattan study used a factor-analytic approach to classify families and then related family types to various child outcomes (Eisenberg, Langner, and Gersten 1975; Eisenberg et al. 1976; Langner 1979; Langner et al. 1983). The findings showed that 30.8 percent of the children from lower-middle-class, ethnic, mixed discordant homes were delinquent, compared with 19.4 percent in Spanish, welfare, and isolated families and 3 percent in white affluent cohesive families.

The risk of delinquency in certain families fluctuates with the emergence and termination of risk factors (see, e.g., Farrington 1978). This formulation of changing risk (Bell and Pearl 1982) also suggests that in some families the presence of unfavorable factors tends to increase over time with a concomitant increase in juvenile delinquency. The study of these emerging risk factors has been neglected. These factors may help to account for differences among families in changes in the risk that children will become delinquent. For example, Glidewell (1968) found that 2 percent of formerly adjusted, lower-class youth, aged eight and nine, *developed* conduct problems over a one-year period, compared with 0 percent for middle-class youths. Ghodsian et al. (1980) reported that a higher proportion of children from large families *became* deviant over time than children from small families.

Some families, however, are able to redress unfavorable factors, such as conflict with their children, and experience a concomitant decrease in juvenile delinquency. This is what perhaps happened in the white affluent families studied by Langner et al. (1983), who over a period of five years showed "a reduction of the rate of poor school outcomes and arrests from approximately 14 percent to 7 percent" (p. 62). The decrease was associated with improvements in home atmosphere, marriage, and other environmental variables. For disadvantaged families, the recovery from juvenile delinquency was less common (see also Cohen and Brook 1984). Similarly, Shepherd, Oppenheim, and Mitchell (1971) found that 41 percent of boys from a working-class background improved in behavior compared with 73 percent of boys from a skilled manual occupational background. This concurs with findings reported by Fréchette and LeBlanc (1979) showing that juvenile delinquency over time decreased less in lower than in higher socioeconomic strata.

In summary, the research findings support the notion that certain categories of families are more at risk of producing delinquent youngsters than others. The studies have rarely attempted to explain the reasons for this. Wilson and Herrnstein (1985) viewed risk in families as the result of interactions between genetic and social handicaps. They stressed the importance of individual differences between children and the fact that some youngsters—such as impulsive, hyperactive children—are much more difficult to handle than others. "Constitutional factors are implicated in the [child's] behavior, but they interact with family factors" (p. 511), in that negative family factors (and school and community factors) can *activate* child conduct problems, while other conditions can *deactivate* such problems.

On the basis of this formulation, the following group of families appears most at risk of producing delinquent youngsters: those that have to cope with a temperamentally difficult child, especially those who are overactive, impulsive, or with a short attention span, and those in which parents have limited resources to cope with such a child. These limited resources include parents' poor child-rearing skills, disruptions that interfere with these skills such as marital discord, loss of a partner, social isolation, or lack of social support from outside of the nuclear family, and poor parental physical or mental health. The latter can be aggravated by such handicaps as economic hardship and large family size.

TABLE 27

Selected Examples of Cumulative Effects of Family Handicaps

	RIOC of Child's Delinquency
Supervision:	
Lax supervision by delinquent versus nondelinquent parent (Wilson 1980)	24.5
Less supervision when parent had been convicted versus unconvicted parent (Farrington, Gundry, and West 1975)	[a]
Less supervision in broken home versus either less supervision or broken home (McCord 1982)	15.5
Low supervision in father-absent homes versus low supervision in father-present homes (Goldstein 1984)*	[a]
Parental rejection:	
Mother rejecting and father rejecting versus either one rejecting (McCord, McCord, and Zola 1969)	37.5
Mother nonloving and mother's deviant role model versus either nonloving or nondeviant role model (McCord, McCord, and Zola 1969)	25.7
Mother not affectionate and broken home versus either mother not affectionate or broken home (McCord 1982)	36.4
Parental conflict:	
Parental conflict and broken home versus broken home (McCord 1982)	29.6
Parental deviance:	
Father alcoholic or criminal and broken home versus father alcoholic or criminal or broken home (McCord 1982)	10.5

NOTE.—RIOC = relative improvement over chance.
[a] Data presented in this report are not suitable for computation of RIOC.
* Significant for boys but not for girls.

TABLE 28

Composite Family Handicaps as Predictors of the Child's Delinquency

Study	Subjects	Race	Interval	Parent Behavior	Respondent	Measurement Mode	Conduct Problem	Strength of Relation[a]
Tait and Hodges (1972)	116 B, select	Mixed	(5–14)–18	Gluecks' prediction table: (1) disciple by father; (2) supervision by mother; (3) affection by father; (4) affection by mother; (5) cohesiveness of family	Staff	Case records (?)	Known to juvenile court	RIOC = 56.4
	151 BG							RIOC = 58.5
Thompson (1952)	100 B	White	(5–11)–17	Gluecks' prediction table (5 factors)	Consultant	Case records (blind as regards to outcome)	Felony or misdemeanor	RIOC = 86.7
Trevvett (1972)	162 BG[b]	Mixed	5–14	Gluecks' prediction table (3 factors): (1) discipline by mother; (2) supervision by mother; (3) family cohesiveness	Staff	Case records (?)	Known to juvenile court	RIOC = 76.9
Craig and Glick (1968)	301 B	Mixed	6–16	Gluecks' prediction table (3 factors)	Parents	Interview (rated by staff)	Serious and persistent delinquency	RIOC = 81.9
Voss (1963)	223 B	Mixed	6–12	Modified Gluecks' prediction table (1 parent = 2 factors; 2 parents = 3 factors)			Police contact (?)	RIOC = 48.3

98

Study	N	Race	Age	Predictor			Outcome	RIOC
McCord (1979)	200 B	Mixed	(5–13)–21+	Home atmosphere, i.e.: (1) mother's affection; (2) supervision; (3) parents' aggression; (4) parents' conflict; (5) mother's self-confidence; (6) father's deviance; (7) parents' absence	Staff	Case records (rated by staff)	One or more convictions	RIOC = 45.7
West and Farrington (1973)	411 B	White	(8–10)–17	Combination of (1) parent criminality; (2) low family income; (3) poor parental behavior	Various		Conviction	RIOC = 63.0
Wadsworth (1979)	1,812 BG	White	0–21	Combination of (1) birth order; (2) family size; (3) family growth; (4) parental divorce, separation, death; (5) lengthy hospital stay; (6) social group	Various		Court appearance or cautioned by the police	RIOC = 49.5
Osborn and West (1978)	397 males	White	(8–10)–24	Two out of three: (1) troublesomeness; (2) father's criminality; (3) mother's or sibs criminality	Various		More than one finding of guilt as juvenile, and one conviction between 19 and 24	RIOC = 46.9

NOTE.—B = boy; G = girl.
[a] RIOC = relative improvement over chance.
[b] Same sample as Tait and Hodges (1972).

99

VII. The Influence of Siblings

The influence of siblings on children's conduct problems has received little attention in the sociological literature. This is surprising because of several consistent findings: (a) delinquents often come from families with large numbers of children; (b) cohort studies that focused on all siblings have shown that delinquency is concentrated in some families; (c) aggressive behaviors often accompany sibling conflict; and (d) some children learn and practice covert conduct problems with their siblings.

A. Large Families

Table 29 summarizes relevant concurrent studies. A variety of criteria have been used for family size, and both self-reported and official delinquency have been used as outcomes. In the studies with boys or mixed samples, the median value of RIOC was 9.5 percent, with a range of 7.4–15.8 percent. Predictive studies, summarized in table 30, produced much higher values. Here the median was 32.9 percent, with a range of 16.7–57.3 percent.

That even a family size criterion of more than two siblings produced a high RIOC shows that the effect does not require extremely large families (although this may result from a proportion of these small families growing over time). Only one study examined the effect of family size on delinquency in girls, and it reported no relation. Rutter et al. (1970), in an Isle of Wight study, also found that conduct problems in large families were significantly more prevalent in boys than in girls. Second, the sibling composition is usually not reported in the studies. It can be expected that, when there are more female than male siblings in a family, the effect of family size would be less than when more male siblings are present. However, this needs to be verified. Third, the findings may also differ depending on the ethnic background of the family. For example, Robins, West, and Herjanic (1975) found that the size of black families was related to police or court records for the subjects' siblings. If a sibling was delinquent, this increased the chances that the subject would also be delinquent. The effect held in *both* small and large families. This supports the notion that influences from siblings rather than family size itself are the major factors contributing to children's delinquency.

We are aware of no studies that concentrated on large families and examined the influences that helped to shape children's behavior problems. A variety of processes can be hypothesized. First, parents with large families have more difficulty disciplining and supervising their children than do parents with small families. The latter offer more opportunity for interactions between parents and the children and more intense emotional involvement (Nye 1958). Second, some parents with large families delegate child rearing to older siblings, who are not necessarily well skilled to execute this task (Bronfenbrenner 1970; Wilson 1974), especially with conduct problem children. Third, large families often are more exposed to illegitimacy, poverty, and overcrowding (Simcha-Fagan et al. 1975; Fischer 1984). Parents in these families may experience difficulties in rearing a large number of children. Finally, larger families may foster delinquency "through increasing the risk of exposure to a delinquent sibling" (Robins et al. 1975, p. 137). That sibling delinquency is a predictor of child delinquency is evident from findings by Farrington (1979) that produced an RIOC of 21.6 percent. Even if such a predictive link is replicated, it is unknown what processes influence the spread of delinquent activities from one sibling to another.

B. Concentrations of Delinquent Siblings

What proportion of families produces the majority of delinquent children? Wilson's (1975) study of disadvantaged inner-city families in England showed that 16 percent of the families produced 62 percent of the delinquent children. Farrington et al. (1975) reported that 4.3 percent of the families in a study cohort from a working-class neighborhood in London produced 46.9 percent of the convicted children. The New York City Youth Board found that 75 percent of the city's delinquents came from about 1 percent of the families (cited in Tait and Hodges 1962). These figures indicate that half to three-quarters of delinquent children derive from a small number of families. Whether many of these children are infrequent or frequent offenders needs to be determined.[4]

Do delinquent siblings from one family tend to engage in the same categories of delinquent acts? This finding, if true, would support the notion that factors that caused delinquency in one sibling also held for the other. If aggression among siblings is conducive to later violence, one would expect siblings to be overrepresented in populations of con-

---

[4] Another way of expressing the relation is the percentage of known juvenile delinquents who have delinquent siblings. Glueck and Glueck (1950) reported that 65.2 percent of delinquent youths had siblings who were also delinquent, compared with 25.8 percent of the siblings of youngsters in a nondelinquent sample (RIOC = 43.3 percent). For further supporting findings, see Jones, Offord, and Abrams (1980).

victs arrested for violent crime. Hamparian et al. (1978) found 12.7 percent of 1,138 violent offenders were siblings. Although the study does not indicate what percentage of such a group could be expected to be siblings merely by chance, it lends some support to the hypothesis that at least a proportion of siblings are arrested for similar crimes.

C. Sibling Conflict

Conflicts among siblings may often be more intense and more difficult to control for parents in large than in small families. The potential for quarrels over possessions, territory, and favoritism probably is exponentially related to the number of children in a family. In that sense, siblings, like the parents, are among the first victims of a child with conduct problems. These conflicts may be much more serious than the average sibling rivalry (see, e.g., Steinmetz and Straus 1974; Conway and Bucher 1976; Spungen 1984). It seems quite likely that early and persistent sibling conflict provides an intense training ground for aggression.

Sibling conflict often does not consist simply of a perpetrator and a victim. Observational studies on children referred for treatment for conduct problems indicate that, in these families, siblings show significantly higher rates of coercive behaviors than siblings in normal families (Patterson and Cobb 1971; Patterson, Cobb, and Ray 1973; Arnold, Levine, and Patterson 1975; Reid 1978). In one study, the correlation between the rate of coercive behavior of the referred child and that of his or her brothers and sisters was .61 and .63, respectively (Patterson 1982b). Siblings are also involved in the majority of coercive interchanges of referred children with family members (i.e., 59 percent in Patterson [1982b]; see also Loeber and Tengs [1986]).

On the basis of a small sample of families, Loeber and Weismann (1982) found that mothers intervened significantly less in conflict between children referred for treatment and their siblings than did mothers in normal families. This suggests that parental neglect may be one reason why sibling conflicts continue for long periods. There is evidence, however, that sibling conflicts become even more protracted once mothers intervene and reflect the often inadequate handling of conflicts by these mothers (Patterson 1982b; see also Eisenberg et al. 1975). There is a clear need to document further the role of parents in sibling conflict.

The sibling group can function as a training ground for child conduct problems in a number of ways. Frequent sibling conflict is associated with more serious coercive behaviors, such as threats and physical violence. Threats are of little use unless they are occasionally backed up by stronger measures such as beatings or other forms of violence.

Although physical abuse of children by parents has received increased attention in recent years, physical abuse by siblings probably is more prevalent (Steinmetz 1978). Cross-cultural comparisons of sibling conflict from study samples in Finland, Canada, Puerto Rico, Israel, and the United States have shown that the prevalence of physical violence was the highest in the United States (Steinmetz 1981). A second less documented training ground among siblings is the taking or vandalizing of siblings' possessions. In that sense, theft, vandalism, and robbery in the street can be mimicked in the family home.

A third aspect of sibling conflict, which has received very little attention, is that it has considerable continuity over time. This is borne out by a study of three-year-old children who were followed up till they were eight. Richman et al. (1982) found that sibling conflict was very stable, producing an RIOC of 80.5 percent (Loeber and Stouthamer-Loeber 1986). The Manhattan longitudinal study of six- to eighteen-year-olds also reported that sibling conflict was relatively stable over a period of five years, with test-retest correlations that averaged .48 (Gersten et al. 1976).

Aggression is stable over time in a proportion of children (Owens and Straus 1975; Olweus 1979; Magnusson, Stottin, and Duner 1983; Huesmann et al. 1984; Loeber 1985a), and it seems likely that violent adolescents or adults practiced frequent aggression with their siblings when they were children.

Sibling conflict is important for a fourth reason. Violent men victimize women through rape or wife abuse. Could it be that children who have acted aggressively for long periods of time toward female siblings or their mothers are more prone later to commit crimes against women compared with those children who early in life have not been aggressive toward females? Loeber, Weismann, and Reid (1983), in a small study of assaultive adolescents, found that 64 percent of their mothers reported that these adolescents engaged in frequent sibling fighting, compared with 20 percent in a group with children who stole. In addition, assaultive adolescents had about one and a half times more female than male siblings. Other research on much younger children is providing evidence that very aggressive boys who act aggressively toward preschool girls tend to come from households that include female siblings and are less likely to come from all-male sibling households (Fagot and Loeber 1986).[5]

Finally, researchers are increasingly more interested in finding out how behavior patterns established with siblings recur in interactions with peers (see, e.g., Pepler, Corter, and Abramovitch 1982). For example, in a retrospective study, Dengerink and Covey (1981) found that subjects who reported a history of violence with their siblings also reported significantly more violence toward individuals outside the family. It seems likely that early aggressive patterns practiced in the family home are later tried out on peers in other environments. Whether the same is true for deceptive practices remains to be investigated.

D. Covert Conduct Problems in Siblings

The last form of sibling influence considered here concerns the effect on children of having siblings who serve as role models for covert conduct problems, such as theft, lying, and substance use. At least two studies have found strong relations between substance use by older siblings and the child's substance use (Brook et al. 1983; Rittenhaus and Miller 1984). Stott (1966) and Nielsen and Gerber (1979) reported that half to three-quarters of habitually truant children had siblings who were also often truant.

The question is whether other behaviors such as theft tend to occur in the context if not the company of siblings. Wilkinson, Stitt, and Erickson (1982) studied adolescents who had either brothers or sisters in two- or three-child families. Among the boys, those second born with two sisters had the highest self-reported delinquency followed by boys with one to three male siblings. When boys having only male siblings were considered, more acts of vandalism and substance use were reported, behaviors that often take place within the peer context. Although the authors state that the data lent support for the imitation hypothesis, this is highly speculative without more detailed studies on the actual involvement of siblings in the same delinquent behavior over time, while controlling for peer influences.

To summarize, while there is evidence that siblings engage in similar

---

[5] It is not surprising that when the criterion is delinquency the proportion of female and male siblings is close to 50 percent for incarcerated delinquent adolescent boys (Clarke and Softley 1975).

delinquent activities, it is unclear how stable such patterns are over time. Anecdotal reports indicate that some children come to disapprove of a sibling's delinquent activity, presumably when that behavior has become more serious or when children are increasingly victimized or embarrassed by the sibling (Wilkinson et al. 1982; Spungen 1984). Subsequently, these children attempt to conform and reject the sibling's delinquent activities. How such reactive desistance actually takes place needs more study.

Siblings provide an opportunity for study of the causes of delinquency by means of comparing children who become delinquent with their siblings who do not. Reitsma-Street et al. (1984) undertook such a study and, on the basis of retrospective reports, found that delinquent and nondelinquent children acted very differently by the age of twelve. Temperament ratings later in life appeared to distinguish best the two groups. It is very likely that temperament characteristics *before the age of twelve* are also very different, but this needs empirical verification. In such a study, it would be opportune also to examine whether parents' different responses to each child further contribute to the widening gap between the delinquent and the conforming behaviors of the children, which often takes place as they become older.

In sum, there is evidence that sibling interactions have greater influence on children's aggression than on covert conduct problems. The findings from the sibling studies thus best fit our conflict paradigm. However, parental neglect and parents' deviant values may facilitate conduct problems in all children in a family to the same degree.

VIII. Shifts in Child Conduct Problems and Parental Behaviors over Time

The preceding summaries may suggest that parents' child-rearing practices and children's behavior are relatively static. This view can be supported by empirical findings. However, shifts do occur over time. First, although conduct problems are among the most stable of all forms of child psychopathology (Robins 1966; Loeber 1982; Kohlberg, Ricks, and Snarey 1984), considerable shifts take place in the *kinds* of conduct problems that youths display during childhood and adolescence. Second, even though there is evidence that particular child-rearing practices have some stability over time (Kagan and Moss 1962; Roberts, Block, and Block 1984), most parents change their practices as their children grow older. This is a normal process, but conduct problem children may interact with their parents in ways that debilitate the

TABLE 29

The Concurrent Relation between Family Size and the Child's Delinquency

Study	Subjects	Race	Family Size	Conduct Problem	Strength of Relation[a]
Nye (1958)	1,148 B, 1,152 G	White	More than two siblings	Self-reported delinquency	RIOC = 15.8
Glueck and Glueck (1950)	998 B, del. and nondel.	Mixed	More than five siblings	Court appearance	RIOC = 7.4
Hirschi (1969)	4,077 BG	Mixed	More than five siblings	More than two self-reported acts of delinquency	RIOC = 9.5

NOTE.—B = boy; G = girl; del. = delinquent; nondel. = nondelinquent.
[a] RIOC = relative improvement over chance.

TABLE 30
Family Size as a Predictor of Delinquency

Study	Subjects	Race	Interval	Family Size	Conduct Problem	Strength of Relation[a]
Farrington and West (1971)	411 B	White	(0–10)–14	More than two siblings	Conviction	RIOC = 57.3
Robins, West, and Herjanic (1975)	106 B	Black	0–(30–36)	More than two siblings	Police/court record for sibling	RIOC = 32.9
Simcha-Fagan et al. (1975)	732 BG	Mixed	5-year interval (?)	More than five siblings	Delinquent/ criminal record	RIOC = 16.7
Osborn and West (1978)	397 B	White	8–24	More than five siblings	More than one finding of guilt	RIOC = 33.6
Wadsworth (1980)	2,196 BG	White	2–21	Less than 2 years being only child	Reported offenses	RIOC = 50.0

NOTE.—B = boy; G = girl.
[a] RIOC = relative improvement over chance.

107

parents' child-rearing practices. When this happens repeatedly, the conduct problems can continue without impediment. We briefly discuss findings below on three forms of shifting behavior patterns.

A. Changes in Children's Conduct Problems

Three types of change in childrens' behavior can be contrasted.

1. *Normative Improvements in Early Conduct Problems.* A large proportion of youngsters show conduct problems in their early years. Most children outgrow behaviors typical of the toddler and preschool years, such as whining, temper tantrums, and seeking too much attention. Over time, many children learn to desist from verbal and physical aggression and irritating behaviors. They learn to deal with everyday frustrations other than by acting out, they learn alternative ways to get others to comply with their wishes, or they simply desist from offensive behaviors when told to do so. According to Patterson (1982b), children who do not outgrow these behaviors are arrested in their social development. They continue to perform immaturely during elementary school or later at frequency levels that characterize preschoolers.

2. *Progressions to More Varied and Serious Conduct Problems and Delinquent Acts.* Some youngsters fail to outgrow earlier problem behaviors, over time expand their repertoire of conduct problems, and eventually become enmeshed in illegal acts. Research findings increasingly point to the existence of developmental progressions that lead to more frequent, more varied, and more serious outcomes (Edelbrock and Loeber 1986; Loeber 1985b, 1986). This process starts early in a small proportion of youngsters. For example, two studies of nine- and ten-year-old children have shown that, judging from their self-reports, about 10–15 percent of the youngsters engage in theft and that 2 percent engage in major forms of shoplifting (Richards et al. 1979; Loeber 1985a). Aided by increased physical strength, some of these youngsters learn to bully others, using threats that victims find difficult to ignore and ganging up on age mates (Olweus 1978). Other research, reviewed by Loeber and Stouthamer-Loeber (1986), points to consistent findings that the majority of adult chronic offenders have displayed frequent conduct problems when young. Thus there is considerable evidence of progressions toward serious forms of delinquency, although the precise developmental sequences need further documentation.

3. *Desistance in Later Conduct Problems.* Not all youngsters who develop novel problematic behaviors during late childhood or adoles-

cence, such as theft, truancy, or fire setting, necessarily will persist in these behaviors; a proportion desists, especially during late adolescence.

B. Changes in Parents' Child-rearing Practices

Parents tend to change their child-rearing practices when their children grow older (Clifford 1959). For example, a large cross-sectional survey of parents, undertaken by Straus (1983), showed an almost linear decline with age in the percentage of parents who use physical punishment. At ages five and six, about 80–95 percent of children are sometimes physically punished, compared with only 10–20 percent by age seventeen. Similarly, Goldstein (1984) and Patterson and Stouthamer-Loeber (1984) have shown that parents monitor the activities of older children less often than they do those of younger children. The findings correspond to data reported by Ballenski and Cook (1982), who, after interviewing 278 mothers, found that mothers' discomfort in child rearing increased with the age of children. Disciplining and setting limits, especially, had become much more perplexing for many parents of adolescents. Adolescence also is a period in which conflict between parents and their children tends to increase (Gersten et al. 1977; Montemayor 1983; Olson et al. 1983). Often the conflict is directed more at the mother than at the father (Patterson 1976, 1980; Montemayor 1982).

Some of the conflicts emanate from increased demands by youngsters for independence and personal freedom. Parental supervision is seen by youngsters as an intrusion on their privacy and an undermining of their independence. Often parents have their own time schedule for acknowledging children's independence, which may lag far behind that of their children. Parents also differ in the speed with which they adopt novel, age-appropriate child-rearing practices. Research in these areas is wanting.

C. Unfavorable Shifts in Parent-Child Interactions

One devastating consequence of children's conduct problems occurs when parents are immobilized in their child-rearing practices. This usually results from long-standing, serious conflict. Although longitudinal research is lacking on this process, case and observational studies offer some basis for speculation about the course of events (see, e.g., Spungen 1984). First, some children from a very young age on are temperamentally more difficult to handle than others (Thomas, Chess, and Birch 1968; Thomas and Chess 1977). These children often are more active than others and are chronically disobedient. Observational research by Patterson (1980, 1982*b*) and his coworkers has shown how these children and their parents (especially the mother) can be embroiled in very frequent and long aversive interchanges. These interchanges are characterized by high rates of commands by the mother, high rates of oppositional behavior by the child, and lack of follow-up by mothers when they utter warnings, resulting in high rates of "nattering," that is, a "haphazard aversive reaction . . . [by which the parent] in no way clarifies or alleviates" the conflict with the child and that instead "serves to extend these low-intensity interchanges" (Patterson 1982*b*, p. 69).

Observational work shows the reciprocal nature of parent-child conflicts that are characteristic of children who are especially aggressive and coercive (Patterson 1982*b*). Some children ultimately "win" when they perform in such a way as to stop virtually all parental behaviors aimed at changing the misbehavior. Usually, children achieve this by escalating their level of aversive behavior by shouting, by threats, or by violent or subversive acts. This teaches parents two things. First, if they continue to resist, the youngster will usually follow through on threats, for example, put a fist through a window or hurt a sibling. Second, the outcome of the threats can be prevented by not persisting in whatever one was pursuing.

At this stage, as Samenow (1984) has graphically described, "the parents' interminable struggle to cope with this wayward youngster saps their energy" (p. 26). The parents give up parenting responsibility in order to achieve superficial peace and quiet and leave the children to act as they please. When this stage has been reached, children's conduct problems probably are qualitatively worse than those of children who are periodically disobedient.

One might consider the parents as the children's first really serious victims, although siblings are often victimized as well. This victimization of relatives frequently takes place before children victimize others outside the family, with the difference that parents rarely request assistance from the police. Those studies that focused on adolescents arrested for an assaultive crime found that these adolescents outranked their parents in terms of coercive behavior or in terms of who was seen as in charge of the family; the youngsters ruled the family (Loeber et al. 1983; Madden and Harbin 1983). As expressed in the *Report on the Causes of Crime* (1968), "The ordinary relationship between child and parent is reversed with the child developing a sense of superiority to the parent and an unwillingness to take any guidance from people" (cited in Silberman 1980, p. 42).

At this point, the parent's behavior has dramatically changed. Parents may not only cease disciplining and supervising the youngster but also come to dislike the problem child and wish that the child would leave the family home permanently (Robins 1966). This mirrors findings concerning hyperactive children who, because of their behavior problems, had been referred to a clinic (Mendelson, Johnson, and Stewart 1971). Interviews with the parents revealed that 34 percent of the children had threatened to kill the parents, 40 percent of the parents had seriously considered sending the child to a military school or to Boystown, and 46 percent were unable to think of a career for which their child was suited. In our experience, it is not uncommon for family members to feel enormous relief when the child finally is taken to a training school or a prison. These families often reconstitute the remaining family members in a more harmonious unit.

Not all families with conduct problem children go through all the stages described here. The major reason that we elaborate on the worsening stages in parent-child interactions and the changes in child conduct problems is to illustrate the need for more than one theoretical model. In the absence of empirical work to trace shifts in interactions between members of a family with a conduct problem child, our examples are mere descriptions of how our four paradigms probably interlock over time as a result of increasing conflict.

The temporally interlocking handicaps within families have implications for the interpretation of research findings and for the design of future studies. Conduct problem children and their relatives occupy different positions on dimensions of conflict, and it can be expected that scientific studies will capture this diversity. This requires an ability to disaggregate families into functionally different groups. This may then allow distinctions to be drawn between families whose youngsters are about to start conduct problems, those who are at an early stage of trivial conduct problems, and those who have advanced to serious conduct problems. Such a separation would shed better light on the factors that facilitate the onset of conduct problems, the factors that maintain or aggravate them, and the factors that result from prolonged confrontations with conduct problem children. As an illustration, some children may develop conduct problems following the emergence of a familial handicap. Most well known is the effect of divorce on young boys' aggression, as documented by Hetherington et al. (1978). Farrington (1978) showed that new marital discord by age fourteen was followed by the emergence of aggressiveness in boys who had not previously been aggressive (RIOC = 29.8 percent). This accords with findings from the Isle of Wight study that poor marital relations were associated with the development of new disorders in children after the age of ten (Rutter et al. 1976). Similar findings for younger children have been reported by Richman et al. (1982). The results support the notion that certain familial handicaps precede, and possibly cause, the emergence of problem behavior in children who did not show such behavior prior to the handicap occurring.

D. Favorable Shifts in Parent-Child Interactions

Data from studies on multiple risk factors are only suggestive that the familial factors rather than unmeasured variables contribute to undesirable outcomes. A more convincing demonstration of risk factors occurs when reductions in these factors are *systematically followed* by a reduction in children's problem behaviors. For example, Rutter (1981) described a sample of children who had been separated from a parent because of family discord or parental deviant behavior. Some families later became reasonably harmonious, while others remained discordant. If discordance is a critical variable, children's misbehavior would be expected to be reduced in the newly harmonious home but not in the discordant home. The results showed that the prevalence of antisocial children was twice as high in the discordant as in the harmonious homes (RIOC = 32.2 percent). Similarly, Langner (1979) noted in the Manhattan longitudinal study that, "if parents became warmer or less rejecting over the five-year period, their children demonstrated reductions in Conflict with Parents . . . , Fighting . . . , and Delinquency. Furthermore, changes in Parental Coldness and Excitability were tied to changes in children's aggressive behavior in all settings" (p. 136). Whether changes in the parents' behavior preceded or followed changes in children's behavior could not be determined, but both patterns were possible (Langner, Gersten, and Eisenberg 1977). Changes in parental behavior did not necessarily affect children's behavior outside the home; changes in parental punitiveness "were related only to changes in children's intrafamilial aggression, but not in aggression toward peers or society in general" (pp. 136–37). Parental child-rearing practices may improve when a parent divorces an antisocial or alcoholic partner and subsequently marries someone who is not involved in these behaviors (Stewart 1984).

The examples suggest that changes in child problem behaviors accompany changes in family handicaps. There is a need to replicate and extend these findings, particularly since they are so relevant for therapeutic interventions. The existing findings lend some support for causal interpretations of parent-child effects.

A series of experiments by Barkley and Cunningham (Cunningham and Barkley 1978; Barkley 1981) has greatly elucidated the direction of causal influences between parents and children. Hyperactive children were given stimulant drugs or placebos without the mother knowing which. Barkley (1981) postulated that "the mother's response to her hyperactive child may *not* be the cause of, but a reaction to, the child's difficult behaviors" (p. 305). The administration of Ritalin to the child resulted in significant improvements in compliance to maternal commands and off-task behaviors; at the same time, the mothers significantly reduced their frequency of commands and increased positive attention to the compliance of the child. Thus these studies demonstrate the effect that children's behavior can have on parental responses. The reverse causal sequence also exists. At least two studies, in which parental behavior was systematically varied, showed consequent changes in the child's problem behaviors (Johnson and Lobitz 1974; Green, Forehand, and McMahon 1979).

IX. Parental Training and Child Conduct
Problems and Delinquency

The most convincing test for understanding the causal status of familial variables associated with conduct problems is whether *systematic changes* in these variables bring about positive changes in children's behavior (Farrington 1982; Patterson 1982*b*). Without experimental manipulation, research results can remain ambiguous due to various sources of invalidity such as spurious influences, unmeasured variables, and failure to allow for maturational effects over time.

Some family variables can be varied systematically more easily than others. Parents can be taught better child-rearing practices, such as supervision, discipline, and positive interaction with their children. The effects of these improved practices can be tested in experimental studies in which families are randomly assigned to experimental and control groups. Findings of research on the following hypotheses are examined below. (*a*) Parent training programs will produce decreases in rates of juvenile conduct problems and delinquency—an implicit assumption is that parents' child-rearing practices will have changed by the end of the training program in the anticipated direction. (*b*) Parent training programs will decrease the rates of the conduct problems not only of referred children but also of their siblings. (*c*) Parent training programs will be more effective with younger than with older children as the former will not have progressed to serious forms of conduct problems. (*d*) Short-term treatment gains in the conduct problems of children will be associated with reduced risk of later delinquency.

A. Parent Training Programs

A number of systematic studies have been undertaken to train parents in better child-rearing practices. Most concerned parents of children with conduct problems. Preventive studies of families prior to the onset of the problem behaviors remain to be done. A number of recent reviews of parent training programs have evaluated their effect on children's behavior (Patterson 1979; Griest and Wells 1983; Kazdin 1984; Loeber 1984). In most studies, the intervention consisted of teaching parents to pinpoint the problem behavior better; to use nonphysical modes of disciplining, including the time-out, more systematically; and to reward for nonantisocial behaviors (see, e.g., Reid 1978; Forehand and McMahon 1981; Fleischman, Horne, and Arthur 1983). A number of the nonrandomized studies showed significant decreases in observed and in parent-reported problem behaviors of the referred children (Patterson and Reid 1973; Peed, Roberts, and Forehand 1977; Weinrott, Bauske, and Patterson 1979; Fleischman 1981). Treatment effects often were maintained over a period of up to at least a year, but, with one exception (Strain et al. 1982), their long-term effect is unknown because of the absence of extensive follow-up studies (Moreland et al. 1982). Moreover, replication has not been universally successful (Eyberg and Johnson 1974; Ferber, Keeley, and Schemberg 1974). Whether these treatments can reduce childrens' coercive behavior to levels normal for their ages remains to be seen. Hautzinger (1985), in her analysis of the Oregon Social Learning Center data, found that the coercive behavior of 42 percent of the treated children fell after treatment into the normal range, while that of the others was one-half to two standard deviations higher.

Four out of the five known randomized experimental studies showed significant reductions in the problem behavior of mostly preadolescent youngsters (Walters and Gilmore 1973; Karoly and Rosenthal 1977;

Martin 1977; Patterson, Chamberlain, and Reid 1982; but cf. Bernal, Klinnert, and Schultz 1980). These studies usually involved small numbers of subjects, which may have undermined equivalence in experimental and control groups. However, the significant changes usually were large. The nonsignificant findings in randomized and nonrandomized studies have been criticized on a number of grounds, for example, that relatively inexperienced therapists were used, that interference of treatment by marital conflicts and other crises was not sufficiently dealt with, and that time-limited therapy was used (Patterson et al. 1982). Loeber (1984) summarized the experimental studies on parental training and compared them with experimental studies in other areas such as cognitive/social skills training of youngsters, classroom interventions, et cetera. He concluded that "only in the case of parental training with mostly antisocial preadolescent youths is it possible to be guardedly optimistic, but long-term evaluations are badly needed to assess the maintenance of treatment effects" (p. 17).

This caution is all the more warranted given that the hypothesized change in parental behavior, thought to be necessary for changing the child problem behavior, did not always take place. One of the basic tenets of the social learning approach, and of "coercion theory" in particular, postulates that parents of conduct problem children are enmeshed in coercive interchanges that help to maintain the child's coercive behaviors. It is assumed that children's coercive behavior will decrease in frequency (Patterson 1982b) when parents learn to display fewer aversive behaviors (such as the use of ineffective commands) and more positive behaviors (contingent on children's prosocial behavior). Hautzinger (1985) concluded from observational data from the Oregon Social Learning Center that there was no evidence that either the fathers or the mothers of referred children decreased the frequency of their coercive behavior or commands as a result of treatment.[6] In contrast, a few studies have reported that parents after treatment showed reduced rates of commands or aversive behavior in general (Forehand and King 1977; Peed et al. 1977; Reid 1983). The equivocal findings are perplexing and show the current lack of measurement sophistication for tapping behavioral change in parents as a result of a training program. The changing of parental habits requires effort and persistence, which are barriers for some parents. Some parents leave parent training before

[6] Earlier analyses of part of these data had shown that maternal aversive consequences contingent on deviant child behavior significantly decreased after treatment for fathers but not for mothers (Taplin and Reid 1977).

it is well under way (Forehand et al. 1983). Other parents are seen by therapists as "resistant" because they do not deal with the issues that really matter. A third group may dislike treatment because they feel that they are being blamed for children's problem behavior (Spungen 1984; York, York, and Wachtel 1984). The simplistic message of some of the programs would be, If only the parent were able to change, then the child would follow suit. We agree with York et al. (1984) that " 'parenting' . . . carries a kind of product orientation that sees the family as an assembly line, with parents manipulating different factors to produce a certain kind of kid. If parents could only perfect their technique, then they could turn out consistently wonderful children. When the kid is not wonderful, people assume that the parents goofed" (p. 43). This view puts all the emphasis on parents' shortcomings and is a pitfall that familial treatment should avoid.

The implementation of parent training programs is not always easy, especially when the parents face problems other than those presented by their children. Parents often need positive support in the community for pursuing a more firm and loving approach with their children. The lack of such support, with or without other familial disadvantages, has been seen as one of the major reasons why a group of mothers reverted to pretreatment levels of coercive interactions with their children, accompanied by a relapse in children's problem behavior (Wahler, Leslie, and Rogers 1979; Wahler, Hughey, and Gordon 1981; Dumas and Wahler 1983). One of the redeeming features of the Toughlove movement is the support generated among parents to be firm with their youngsters (York et al. 1984). The Toughlove agenda emphasizes that other adults sometimes are needed to help youngsters face the consequences of real life and that the youngsters themselves are ultimately responsible for the consequences of their misbehavior. Scientific investigators who design treatment programs for conduct problem children may be able to learn from this movement.

Although parent training programs can be improved, it is clear that treatment programs involving random assignment of families to experimental and control groups have contributed substantially to our knowledge of the causal role that these programs can play in decreasing juvenile conduct problems.

B. The Effects on Siblings

When parents change their child-rearing practices as a result of a training program, both referred children and their siblings should benefit. Many of the social learning–oriented training programs have reported that the rate of the siblings' overt conduct problems had significantly decreased at the end of parent training programs (Arnold et al. 1975; Humphreys et al. 1978; Horne and Van Dyke 1983; Haut-zinger 1985). A similar finding was noted by Klein, Alexander, and Parsons (1977) in their familial treatment of known delinquents. Siblings in 20 percent of families in treatment had a court contact, compared with 40 percent of the siblings in the no-treatment control group and 59–63 percent for an alternative treatment.

These results are encouraging, but a number of important issues remain to be clarified. Did changes in parental behavior as a result of the training generalize to the siblings? Or could it be that the training program decreased the overall level of family conflict, including that between referred children and the siblings? And if the rate of siblings' overt conduct problems is reduced, what processes are responsible? Moreover, can one exclude as causes maturational changes in the sibling behavior rather than changes brought about from within the family?

C. The Child's Age at Intervention

Younger children usually present less serious and less numerous conduct problems. Moreover, it is easier to discipline younger children and supervise them since the majority of their problem behaviors occur in or around the house; for older children these behaviors often occur outside the parents' view. When unfavorable conditions fostering child conduct problems have existed for a long time, it probably is more difficult to reduce both the inappropriate parenting and the children's behaviors (Loeber 1982). One might conclude that parent training programs are likely to be more effective with younger than with older children.

The treatment studies partly support this conclusion. Peed et al. (1977) found that student therapists could help parents of conduct problem children of an average age of five. In a three- to nine-year follow-up of treated preschoolers, Strain et al. (1982) found that the age at which treatment began correlated $-.49$ with the children's compliance at follow-up; in other words, the later treatment began, the lower the levels of compliance. Evaluating a parent training program for multiple offenders (of an average age of thirteen), Reid (1983) found that the level of coercive child behavior was not significantly reduced.

These findings give some indirect support for the early intervention hypothesis, but there is need for more systematic research.

For those children who already show high rates of serious problem behaviors, early age does not necessarily mean easier intervention. There is increasing evidence that, the earlier the age of onset of serious conduct problems, the more persistent these behaviors are (Loeber 1982). Robins (1970) reported that boys whose misbehavior began between the ages of eight and ten had a much worse diagnosis compared with those who began later. Data from the Cambridge Study on Delinquent Development indicates that the average number of convictions per year was higher for those who were first convicted for delinquency between ages ten and twelve, compared with those first convicted at a later age (Farrington 1986). This probably means that early starters are more difficult for parents to handle than those who start misbehavior later. This may have to do with a tendency of early starters to develop different problem behaviors and different forms of delinquency at a higher rate than do those who start later. As a consequence, the early starters tend to display a greater *variety* of antisocial acts and have a lower probability of remission than those who commit fewer antisocial acts (Loeber 1986). In sum, the scant evidence we have suggests that early intervention is probably more effective and less arduous than late intervention. However, there is a need for therapeutic studies to address this question more systematically than has so far occurred.

D. *The Effects of Parent Training Programs on Later Delinquency*

The majority of the experimental studies reviewed by Loeber (1984) had at most a one-year follow-up period. Consequently, the long-term outcome in delinquency reduction remains unknown. Traditional forms of parent training programs may not reduce the risk of later theft or other covert forms of delinquency as they are aimed mostly at reductions in coercive child behaviors. This is suggested by a two- to nine-year follow-up of children initially seen in a parent training program (Moore, Chamberlain, and Mukai 1979).

Eighty-four percent of the children with early stealing problems incurred nonstatus offense records, compared with 24 percent of aggressive children and 21 percent of a normative sample. Even when offense records before the end of treatment were taken into account, the stealer group still appeared to be at the highest risk for delinquency.

A few experimental studies have attempted to instill better parenting behaviors and communications within families of known juvenile delinquents. Alexander and Parsons (1973), through their training program, were able significantly to reduce recidivism and improve familial communication. A replication of this important study is badly needed. Byles and Maurice (1979) compared crisis family therapy with traditional contacts and failed to find significant results in terms of later police contacts of recidivist offenders. Finally, Reid and his colleagues (Reid 1983) evaluated a parent training program over three years, on the basis of their earlier social learning paradigm for parents who had court-referred juveniles but who also were instructed how to deal with youngsters' thefts (Reid and Hendriks 1973; Reid 1975). Comparisons between parent training and behavior contracts with court programs for these youths and controls did not reveal significant differences in observed aggression in the home and in the number of offenses.[7]

The above studies show the strengths and weaknesses of treatments. Particularly wanting are studies that concentrate on familial conditions that foster early covert conduct problems and that experimentally change these conditions and then evaluate the long-term outcome both for official delinquency records and for self-reported delinquency.

X. Conclusions and Next Steps

Overviews of large areas of research present major trends in relations between family and child variables. Almost unavoidably, however, such overviews have limitations. They often do little justice to the interplay between the variables and how they change during the course of children's growing up. Moreover, the varying degrees of sophistication in measurement of variables probably has set an upper limit to the explanatory power of familial and other variables. Typically, familial variables have been measured through verbal reports by the parents or, more frequently, by the children. As mentioned, we know from several studies that parents' and children's reports on family functioning often diverge. Observational studies on family processes have been in the minority. Although this survey contained a number of longitudinal studies, most of them had infrequent assessments of family processes, which makes it hard to reconstruct changes in parent-child and sibling-child interactions over time.

---

[7] Reid (1983) mentioned that the number of high-rate offenders was smaller for the experimental group, but whether this reached statistical significance is not clear.

A. *The Results of the Meta-Analyses*

Despite these reservations, the meta-analyses produced some striking results. In both concurrent and predictive studies, at least 70 percent of the analyses for each paradigm showed a significant effect in the expected direction. Thus family variables and child conduct problems or delinquency were consistently related to each other. Certain aspects of family functioning were more strongly related to children's behavior than others, and family variables can be ranked according to the strength of their relation with children's behavior. We use RIOC and *d* values, not the number of significant analyses, as a basis for the ranking because the significance levels depend on the number of subjects, which varied from thirty to several thousand. The median values of the RIOCs and *d*'s have been summarized in table 31. It should be kept in mind that the ranges of RIOC and *d* varied from variable to variable and therefore may affect the following conclusions.

1. *The Paradigms.* The set of familial paradigms proposed in this study—neglect, conflict, deviant behaviors and attitudes, and disruption—are heuristic tools to organize the data, not causal models that could be completely verified. Therefore the following conclusions should be regarded with caution. The concurrent meta-analyses revealed that the RIOC tended to be highest for the neglect paradigm, intermediate for the deviant behaviors and attitudes and the conflict paradigms, and lowest for the disruption paradigm. The results indicate that conduct problems and delinquency are all positively associated with each familial paradigm but that socialization variables are more strongly related than familial background variables. Many aspects of these paradigms are not unique to the American, English, and Scandinavian studies in our review but have also been documented in cross-cultural studies in other countries or cultures (see, e.g., Whiting and Whiting 1975; Werner and Smith 1977, 1982; Montegu 1978). The evidence for the four paradigms probably means that distinctly different processes contribute to the same outcomes. The characteristics of each paradigm need clarification, as do the ways they coincide within certain families and evolve over time.

2. *The Rank Ordering of Familial Variables in Concurrent Studies.* Concurrent studies produced different results depending on whether they concerned comparison samples or normal samples. Among the highest median RIOC values in concurrent comparison samples were parent-child involvement (61.5 percent), supervision (66.3 percent), discipline (73.5 percent), and parental rejection (62.6 percent). Slightly lower, but

TABLE 31

Summary of Familial Variables Associated with the Child's Conduct Problems and Delinquency

| | Conduct Problems and Delinquency | | | | |
| Variable | Concurrent Studies, Median RIOC | | Predictive Studies, Median RIOC, Normal Sample | Concurrent Studies, Median d | |
	Comparison Sample	Normal Sample		Comparison Sample	Normal Sample
Parent-child involvement	61.5	...	31.0	.55	...
Child-parent involvement	49.3	18.3	...	.58	.50
Supervision	66.3	14.6	36.4	.83	...
Discipline	73.5	11.6	17.6	.50	...
Parental rejection	62.6	24.0	35.8	.79	...
Child rejection of parent	56.3	22.9	...	.47	...
Parental criminality, deviant values, or aggressiveness	34.5	23.6	22.5	.60	...
Marital relations	29.1	23.3	28.0	.68	.47
Parental absence	27.7	12.5	12.2	...	.31
Parental health	28.0	10.6	16.5	...	...
Family size	7.4	33.6	32.9	...	...
Composite family factors	...	...	57.5	...	...

NOTE.—For details, see preceding tables.

still high, were children's rejection of parents (56.3 percent) and child-parent involvement (49.3 percent). Still lower were variables that did not directly reflect parent-child interactions, such as parental criminality (34.5 percent), marital discord (29.1 percent), parental absence (27.7 percent), and parental health (28 percent). Unexpectedly, the least powerful correlate was family size (7.4 percent). In these studies, the ranking based on the measure of d was very similar for the most powerful socialization variables, parental supervision and rejection. However, parental criminality and discord had higher ranking in this instance.

In all, the studies on comparison groups showed that familial relations, in families with a delinquent or a conduct problem child, were very disturbed, parents' child-rearing practices were impaired, and negative perceptions between children and parents were common.

The RIOC values in the concurrent normal samples are lower than in the comparison group studies. However, one would expect lower RIOC values because normal samples have more complete distributions of subject characteristics than do the comparison samples. The ranking of the median RIOCs was somewhat different from that for comparison groups. Among the highest values were variables such as parents' rejection of children (24 percent), children's rejection of parents (22.9 percent), parental criminality (23.6 percent), and marital discord (23.3 percent).

Note that a majority of the studies with normal samples focused on the youth's self-reported delinquency. Sociological control theory (Hirschi 1969) based on these studies has often emphasized the attachment between parents and children as one of the more critical variables; this is consistent with the present findings. In comparison, parents' child-rearing variables, usually not highlighted in control theory studies, produced relatively low RIOCs, such as for supervision (14.6 percent) and discipline (11.6 percent). The results could not be replicated with the measure of d because too few of these could be computed to make realistic comparisons possible.

3. *The Rank Ordering in Longitudinal Studies.*   Virtually all the longitudinal studies in our survey involved relatively normal samples. Only RIOC could be computed. The ranking of the median values of RIOC partly matched the ranking for the concurrent comparison group studies. The highest RIOC values were for the parents' involvement with their children (31 percent), parental rejection of their children (35.8 percent), and supervision (36.4 percent). Thus the highest values in the

longitudinal studies refer to parent-child socialization variables, with the exception of discipline (17.6 percent). The familial background variables all have lower values—parental criminality (22.5 percent), marital discord (28 percent), parental absence (12.2 percent), and parental health (16.5 percent). Overall, the ranking of most familial variables replicated the order formerly reported by Loeber and Dishion (1983) for the prediction of delinquency, except that the present meta-analysis was based on a much larger survey of studies with a higher variety of conduct problems.

4. *Possible Sleeper Effects.* The results show a tendency for socialization variables to have stronger relations to child conduct problems over time in normal samples than concurrently. This applies especially to parental supervision and parental rejection. In the concurrent studies, based on normal samples, the median RIOC for supervision and rejection was 14.6 percent and 24 percent, respectively, compared with 36.4 percent and 35.8 percent in the longitudinal studies.

These are startling results. Normally, longitudinal studies show decrements over time in the magnitude of relations between independent and dependent variables (see, e.g., Olweus 1979), but here exactly the opposite was evident. This may be an artifact of use of different independent and dependent measures in the different studies. However, studies measuring familial variables over time point to a similar effect. For example, data reported by Simcha-Fagan et al. (1975) showed that three parent characteristics—coldness, punitiveness, and the mother's excitability or rejection—correlated an average of .15 with mother's report of juvenile violence and delinquency and with criminal record. Five years later, the average correlation amounted to .23. These data suggest that certain parenting behaviors have stronger long-term than short-term effects.[8]

These findings are similar to the "sleeper effect" noted by Kagan and Moss (1962) in their longitudinal study from birth to adulthood. They noted that "certain classes of maternal practices have a latent or sleeper effect and require several years before their influence is evidenced in the child's behavior" (p. 3). We expect that the effect of lack of supervision and parental rejection becomes more apparent when they endure over extended periods. The development of children's conduct problems and delinquency may lag behind the poor disciplining, supervi-

[8] Two exceptions should be noted. Kagan and Moss (1962) and Eron, Walder, and Huesmann (1978) did not find sleeper effects for parental variables related to children's aggressiveness.

sion, and parental feelings of dislike for their children. A supplementary explanation is that over time conduct problem children may develop coercive behaviors that disable the parents' child-rearing practices. In either case, the sleeper effect assumes that parent behaviors have a considerable stability over time. This assumption is supported by several studies (Kagan and Moss 1962; Schaefer and Bayley 1963; Roberts et al. 1984). These estimates of sleeper effects probably are underestimates because attrition in most studies has usually been high, especially for the most deviant youngsters (Lefkowitz et al. 1977; Polk and Ruby 1978; Robins 1978).[9] The sleeper effects for parental supervision and rejection are more striking because potential sleeper effects were not noted in our analyses for a set of variables that do not directly measure parent-child contacts, for example, broken home, marital conflict, and parental criminality.

The existence of sleeper effects agrees with the thesis, developed by Cohen and Brook (1984), that the *duration* of familial handicaps is associated with the future onset or exacerbation of juvenile problem behaviors. The authors, in their eight-year follow-up study of juveniles, found evidence that worsening forms of child rearing were significantly and independently related to increases in the prevalence of conduct disorders. This supports the notion that extended exposure to such risk factors facilitates the deterioration of children's problem behavior.

5. *The Findings in the Context of Sociological and Social Learning Theories.* Sociological and social learning theories have often been seen as antithetical in their approach to familial influences. Our meta-analysis provides support for each. Parent-child and child-parent involvement and rejection, reflecting the attachment characteristic for control theory, were prominent in concurrent, self-reported delinquency studies but carried less weight in prospective ones. The converse was true for child-rearing factors, integral to social learning approaches, which were not powerful in self-report studies but ranked higher in longitudinal studies.

6. *Conduct Problems, Self-reported Delinquency, and Official Delinquency.* We assume that familial variables are related to the full range of child conduct problems. This was borne out by the meta-analyses. The familial factors were positively associated with children's conduct

---

[9] An alternative explanation is that the systematic increase in the relation between parental and child behavior over time is a result of changing base rates of the two variables. However, we think that this is less likely than the sleeper effect, but, admittedly, more evidence is needed for either interpretation.

problems, self-reported delinquency, and arrest or court records. In discussing the results concerning supervision, we reported data showing that the amount of supervision was inversely related to the amount or the seriousness of delinquency. Moreover, the association of supervision and delinquency was stronger for official delinquency than for self-reported delinquency. Judging from the tables presented above, this finding was not limited to supervision only. The median RIOC for all parenting variables using official delinquency as the dependent variable was 41.9 percent. This compares with 14 percent for self-reported delinquency. If we compare only family variables for which there were at least four values of RIOC for official delinquency and for self-reported delinquency, the median RIOCs are 31.7 percent and 17.1 percent, respectively. This is a solid finding since there were no family variables for which the pattern was reversed.

It is more difficult to establish whether aggression is associated with the family variables to the same degree as official delinquency. Most of the analyses in the aggression studies have been expressed in effect size rather than RIOC. Where comparisons could be made, the median d values were quite similar for official delinquency and aggression (.60 and .63, respectively). The little evidence available suggests the same strength of association of familial variables with juvenile delinquency and with aggression. However, in one study the aggression group consisted to a large extent of official delinquents (Bandura and Walters 1959).

Although this review does not include studies on conduct problems such as juvenile substance use or abuse, many of our findings on familial factors also hold for juvenile alcohol use and drug taking (see, e.g., reviews by Zucker 1976; Kandel 1978; Glynn 1981; concurrent studies by Smart, Gray, and Bennett 1978; Lassey and Carlson 1980; Brook et al. 1983; Jensen and Brownfield 1983; Newcomb, Huba, and Bentler 1983; Dishion and Loeber 1985; and longitudinal studies by Brook, Lukoff, and Whiteman 1980; McCord 1981).

7. *Fathers and Mothers.* Fathers' roles have not been studied well (Lamb 1976, 1979), perhaps because researchers make assumptions about fathers' roles or because mothers are often more available to participate in interviews. Fathers' roles in the family have been conceptualized in several ways. Fathers have been described as lodgers in their own homes, who bring in money but leave the child rearing to the mother, except for occasional shows of authority (Patterson 1980). Fathers have also been seen as important role models, especially for

boys. From a third perspective, each parent has similar influence on the child's development, but in most families mothers spend more time with their children.

In order to evaluate the association of fathers' and mothers' behaviors with child conduct problems, we compared the findings in studies in which the behavior of both fathers and mothers was measured on the same variables. Of seventy-five analyses, the values for the father data were larger than for the mother data in forty-eight analyses. This tendency of paternal behavior to have a somewhat stronger association with delinquency and aggression was mainly reflected in the median d for those seventy-five analyses, .64 for fathers and .46 for mothers. This difference was not evenly spread throughout the data and is clearly evident mainly in parental lack of involvement. Overall, the results on differential influences by fathers and mothers only partly overlap those reported by McCord et al. (1969). Whether this is because most of the studies relied on children's or mothers' reports of fathers' behavior rather than on reports from fathers themselves is unclear.

8. *The Influence of Siblings.* Studies have shown that a relatively small proportion of families tend to produce a large number of delinquent youths. The evidence is strong that problem youths practice aggressive and coercive behaviors with their siblings, who often respond in kind. Few studies have examined the phenomenon of youngsters who acquire covert antisocial behaviors through interaction with their siblings.

9. *The Effect of Family Factors on Boys and Girls.* Girls are involved in different behavior problems than boys, and parents often deal differently with boys than with girls (McCord et al. 1969). Only twenty-two analyses were found in which boys' and girls' delinquency and aggression were separately related to parental behaviors. In general, parental behavior was related to child conduct problems to the same degree for each sex. This conclusion is drawn with caution since the data on which it is based are not extensive.

B. The Causal Status of Family Factors

Not all the results discussed here directly address the question of whether delinquency is caused primarily by social or by hereditary factors. The meta-analyses showed that a number of family handicaps were more likely to occur in families with conduct problem or delinquent children than in families with less difficult children. Moreover, the studies show that the higher the degree of impairment in the parents' child-rearing practices, the more serious the delinquent involvement of the offspring. Survey studies have found that a small group of families produces a large proportion of all delinquents, and this is reinforced by still other studies that have demonstrated a relation between sibling conflict and engagement in covert delinquent activities. The meta-analyses showed that familial variables predict later delinquency and conduct problems. The risk of delinquency in offspring tends to increase with the number of handicaps a family experiences. Studies that measured both handicaps and child behavior over time showed that changes in the handicaps varied directly with changes in child behavior. Systematic training of parents to improve child-rearing practices has strengthened the notion that aggressive and coercive child behavior can be reduced, although this is less clear for delinquent acts. In aggregate, the findings from our analyses consistently point to social influences that determine whether or not children become delinquent. In contrast, our review of predictors shows that the often quoted biological factor of criminality in the family is a modest predictor of delinquency in comparison with other familial factors. In addition, other biological studies, not reviewed here, although demonstrating positive relations between biological factors and delinquency, concern effect sizes that are not very large (see e.g., Hutchings and Mednick 1975; Dalgard and Kringlen 1976; Cadoret 1980; Mednick and Volavka 1980; Cloninger et al. 1982; Cadoret, Cain, and Crowe 1983).

A word of caution, however; the social influences impinging on children can also easily be overestimated. There are large individual differences among children in terms of their risk-taking behavior, activity level, and intelligence, to mention but a few factors that influence how their parents and siblings react to them. Given that these child characteristics partly or largely are biologically determined, it is necessary to view causal effects in delinquency as an interaction between both hereditary components and social influences (Wilson and Herrnstein 1985).

The causal interpretations also should explain why the effects take place for some but not all children in a family. The effect of familial changes on child conduct problems may be moderated by children's temperaments (e.g., McCord et al. 1969; Rutter 1978). The latter noted that when "parents are depressed"—or, we would add, when they are involved in marital strife or exposed to other serious stresses—"they do not 'take it out' on all their children to the same extent. Children with 'difficult' personality features tend to be the butt or scapegoat (Redl and

Wineman 1951). Conversely, easy, adaptable children tend to be protected even in a stressful home environment simply because much of the hostility and discord is focused on other members of the family" (p. 109). We still need to learn much about how children's temperaments interact with parental responses to stress.

In summary, we agree with Rutter and Giller's (1983) conclusion that "the evidence suggests a relatively weak hereditary influence for juvenile delinquency as a whole (although a rather stronger one for recidivist delinquency which persists into adult life . . .)" (p. 182). However, there is a scarcity of studies that have attempted to isolate the effects of heredity and social influences in order to establish the effect of each independently from the other.

For practical purposes, the major question is not what the relative contributions of hereditary and social factors are but which factors are *modifiable* in order to influence juvenile delinquency careers and which of such modifiable influences potentially have the greatest effect on specific constitutional characteristics of children and the subsequent course of delinquency. Answers to this question are particularly important because of the current lack of insight into breaking the cycle of delinquency transmission from one generation to the next.

Family factors never operate in a vacuum but take place against a backdrop of other influences such as those exercised by children's peers, their school, and society in general. Lack of space here prohibits a review of studies that in multivariate analyses have attempted to control for the main effects and interactions of these variables.

C. Intervention

Juvenile conduct problems and delinquency pose formidable challenges to parents, teachers, and therapists. Most of the data presented here have been available for years. Despite that, amazingly little has penetrated into policy planning on federal, state, or regional levels. Some people think that *any* type of intervention in families undermines people's right to privacy. Others believe that people should not have the right to rear career offenders, who will eventually leave in their wake a multitude of victims. About eight years ago the Office for Juvenile Justice and Delinquency Prevention (1977) observed that "there are many aspects of family life which we generally regarded as private matters, such as patterns of authority or styles of parenting, but the psychological theories presented lead one to believe that educational and therapeutic services for families should be available, and that many youngsters and parents might benefit from these services" (p. 99).

We agree, and when we discuss interventions in the following pages, we always refer to voluntary, noncompulsory forms of educational and therapeutic services. We anticipate that interventions probably will become more common since naturally occurring parent education has become less likely for large groups of parents. The need for alternative parental education is becoming more acute because of the increasing breakdown of traditional buffers for parents—live-in partners, support from relatives or others in the community, and religious values.

1. *The Need for Primary Prevention.* It makes more sense to strengthen available informal ties to kin and community than it does to introduce additional layers of bureaucracy to help problem children.

a) There is a need to evaluate and further perfect preventive community programs through the media, especially television. Certain special interest groups already promote television spots for parents and for children that are aimed at reducing misbehavior. Rodman and Grams (1967) called for "parent-education television" almost twenty years ago; to our knowledge this still has not taken place in a systematic fashion.

b) Early training in parenting skills has been advocated for high school students (Farrington and West 1981). Wilson (1983) made the excellent suggestion to replace lectures on parenting by the scoring of videotapes of adaptive and nonadaptive family interactions and ways that child behavior can be changed.

c) In the line of the Toughlove movement (York et al. 1984), there is a great need for parents experiencing crises with their conduct problem children to gain information and support through community self-help programs.

d) Community-wide media programs can convince parents that they can help to clean up their neighborhood from drug pushers and others, who eventually can entice children to engage in delinquent acts.

e) Community or professionally sponsored group sessions for parents probably are best when geared for specific age-related problems in children. One kind of group, similar to the birth-to-three parenting groups, could deal with preschool conduct problems. A second type of group could focus more on late childhood and early adolescence (Montemayor 1983) and prepare the parent for emerging substance use, truancy, theft, and other covert conduct problems.

f) Another form of community program could promote temporary placement of those conduct problem children who have exhausted the patience of their parents in the home of experienced relatives or friends.

g) Rutter and Giller (1983) recommended early adoption for potential problem children, especially in the case of parents who have persistent difficulties accepting their children.

2. *Professional Services.* Community-wide media programs may help parents with children whose problems have not advanced to a serious level, but there undoubtedly will remain a need to retain and improve existing professional services.

a) Further evaluations are needed of temporary specialized foster care placements in homes in which professional foster parents have been trained in managing difficult children (see, e.g., Hawkins and Meadowcroft 1984).

b) Improvements in residential services are needed to ensure the generalizability of child behavior change from the residential to the family home.

c) Parents and children will be particularly well served when professional assessments go beyond the list of past misdeeds and current risk variables and produce instead assessments to show children's strengths and ways to optimize behavioral improvements.

3. *High Priority Areas for Future Research.* The following list is our personal ranking of research priorities in the area of family studies.

a) There is a great need to establish the long-term effect of parent training programs to decrease coercive and aggressive behavior of youngsters. Ideally such a follow-up should establish whether these programs reduce the risk for physical aggression and violent crime.

b) The present review shows that of all the possible conduct problems only aggression served as a criterion measure in many studies. However, considering that theft and other covert illegal behaviors (fraud, breaking and entering, scams, etc.) constitute the majority of all delinquent acts, it is remarkable how little research has been done to relate covert conduct problems to familial factors.

c) Considering these two points, there is an urgent need to optimize the evaluation of treatment and prevention programs in order to separate spurious from causal factors. Intervention studies should randomly assign subjects or families to experimental and control groups.

d) A proportion of delinquent youngsters tends to desist over time. For some, the desistance occurs prior to the peaking of delinquency around the ages of sixteen and seventeen; for many others the desistance takes place later. Very little is known about the factors that contribute to such desistance and about the speed with which it takes place. Systematic research on naturally occurring familial interventions that lead to desistance is likely to produce knowledge that can be applied to future interventions for parents.

e) Because most career offenders appear to have started misbehaving early in life, there is a need to study family conditions that facilitate these children's early development of serious conduct problems.

f) Our review unequivocally shows the scarcity of studies of family processes in black or other minority-group families. This is surprising given the relatively high rates of juvenile delinquency in these groups. The study of both risk factors and risk-reducing factors in these families has high priority.

g) Future research should be aimed at further elucidating the mechanisms underlying the cumulative and compensatory effects of risk variables within families and should seek to clarify which handicaps are susceptible to easiest intervention and greatest payoff in terms of behavioral change in children.

h) While it is easy to blame high-risk families for the crime problem in our society, a more advantageous approach is to examine how, for example, a proportion of single parents or parents in a high crime neighborhood are able to bring up children in a nondelinquent fashion.

i) Research is badly needed to document how some children debilitate their parents' child-rearing practices and what parents can best do to regain control.

It is clear that much research needs to be done. However, policymakers need not wait until all that has been accomplished. One of the major aims of this essay is to show the high degree of agreement among a large body of research findings. The findings show that in a number of areas of family life there are changes that can be made so that children can be brought up with fewer conduct problems and less risk for delinquency.

APPENDIX A

Bibliographical Note

The following are some major sources on the influence of the family on juvenile conduct problems and delinquency. Nye (1958) and McCord et al. (1969) accomplished the most extensive investigations of family functioning as relating to the youths' delinquency. A milestone is the Patterson (1982*b*) volume, which summarizes more than a decade of observational work on families with aggressive children and, to a lesser extent, on families with children who steal. Equally thorough is the summary of the work done on families of antisocial children by Wahler and Dumas (1986a). Good reviews of conduct disorders and their treatment can be found in Herbert (1982) and Kazdin (1984).

Among the best review papers that discuss empirical findings relating overt antisocial behavior to family functioning are Peterson and Becker (1965), Hetherington and Martin (1979), Steinmetz (1979), and Maccoby and Martin (1983). Slightly broader reviews that also include delinquency have been produced by Hirschi (1969), Wilson (1983), and Wilson and Herrnstein (1985). General reviews of family aspects relating to delinquency can be found in Rodman and Grams (1967), Bahr (1979), and Rutter and Giller (1983), while Belsky (1984) has given us one of the better conceptualizations of family functioning.

A number of biographical works can be recommended that, while written by family members, shed much light on the nature and the development of trivial and serious conduct problems within the family (Wolff 1979; Spungen 1984). Special mention should be made of Redl and Wineman's (1951) book on their experiences with conduct problem children in the context of a treatment home.

APPENDIX B

The Characteristics of RIOC and d

As mentioned in the text, RIOC corrects for chance and maximum levels within a 2×2 table. This is illustrated in figure A1, which gives an example of data. In this case, there are 100 subjects, of whom thirty have characteristic B and sixty have characteristic A. Figure A1 gives the observed values, the expected values (in parentheses), and the maximum values (in square brackets). For example, in cell a (the valid positives), the observed value is twenty-five, but the expected value by chance is eighteen. The latter is calculated by $(a + d) \times (a + b/t)$. Cell a has a maximum value in that it can never contain more than thirty subjects because of the difference between the base rate, $(a + d)/t$, and the selection ratio, $(a + b)/t$. As a consequence, the maximum table in this case contains zero subjects in cell d and forty subjects in cell c. This means that, under this condition, the maximum valid positives (a) and the valid negatives (c) is seventy. In other words, thirty of the subjects can *never* be correctly identified in this table. The larger the difference between the selection ratio and the base rate, the higher the proportion of subjects that fall in this unidentifiable category.

The formula for RIOC is

$$\text{RIOC} = \frac{\text{Total correct} - \text{Chance correct}}{\text{Maximum correct} - \text{Chance correct}} \times 100.$$

Using the parameters shown in figure A1, this is computed in the following way:

$$\text{RIOC} = \frac{(a + c) - \dfrac{(a + d) \times (a + b)}{t} + \dfrac{(b + c) \times (d + c)}{t}}{\max (a + c) - \dfrac{(a + d) \times (a + b)}{t} + \dfrac{(b + c) \times (d + c)}{t}} \times 100.$$

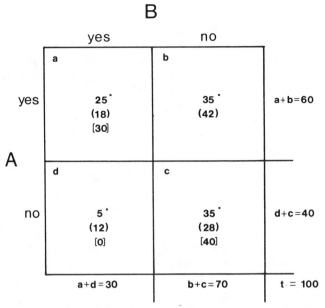

FIG. A1.—An illustration of observed, expected, and maximum values in a 2 × 2 table: ■ = observed value; numbers in parentheses are expected value; and numbers in square brackets are maximum value.

Confidence intervals have been computed for RIOC.

Turning to the standard effect size estimate, Cohen's d (Cohen 1977; Miller and Berman 1983), its formula is

$$d = t \sqrt{\frac{1}{n_1} + \frac{1}{n_2}}$$

or

$$d = \sqrt{F\frac{1}{n_1} + \frac{1}{n_2}},$$

where n_1 and n_2 are the sample sizes of the two groups. For F-ratios with more than one degree of freedom in the numerator, the standard deviation was estimated by

$$s = \sqrt{\frac{n_i(\overline{X}_i - \overline{G})^2/(k - 1)}{F}},$$

where $\overline{X}$ is the individual group mean, $\overline{G}$ is the grand mean of all groups, and k is the number of groups.

REFERENCES

Alexander, J. R. 1973. "Defensive and Supportive Communications in Normal and Deviant Families." *Journal of Consulting and Clinical Psychology* 40:223–31.

Alexander, J. R., and B. J. Parsons. 1973. "Short-Term Behavioral Intervention with Delinquent Families: Impact on Family Processes and Recidivism." *Journal of Abnormal Psychology* 81:219–25.

Andry, R. G. 1960. *Delinquency and Parental Pathology.* London: Methuen.

————. 1962. "Parental Affection and Delinquency." In *The Sociology of Crime and Delinquency,* edited by M. E. Wolfgang, L. Savitz, and H. Johnston. New York: Wiley.

Arnold, J. E., A. G. Levine, and G. R. Patterson. 1975. "Changes in Sibling Behavior Following Family Intervention." *Journal of Consulting and Clinical Psychology* 43:683–88.

Bahr, S. J. 1979. "Family Determinants and Effects of Deviance." In *Contemporary Theories about the Family,* edited by W. R. Burr, R. Hill, F. I. Nye, and I. L. Reiss. New York: Macmillan.

Ballenski, C. B., and A. S. Cook. 1982. "Mothers' Perceptions of Their Competence in Managing Selected Parenting Tasks." *Family Relations* 31:489–94.

Bandura, A., and R. H. Walters. 1959. *Adolescent Aggression.* New York: Ronald Press.

Bane, M. J. 1976. "Marital Disruption and the Lives of Children." *Journal of Social Issues* 32:103–17.

Barkley, R. A. 1981. "The Use of Psychopharmacology to Study Reciprocal Influences in Parent-Child Interaction." *Journal of Abnormal Child Psychology* 9:303–10.

Behar, D., and M. A. Stewart. 1982. "Aggressive Conduct Disorder of Children: The Clinical History and Direct Observations." *Acta Psychiatrica Scandinavia* 65:210–20.

Bell, R. Q., and D. Pearl. 1982. "Psychosocial Change in Risk Groups: Implications for Early Identification." *Journal of Prevention in Human Services* 1:46–59.

Belsky, J. 1984. "The Determinants of Parenting: A Process Model." *Child Development* 55:83–95.

Belson, W. A. 1975. *Juvenile Theft: The Causal Factors.* London: Harper & Row.

Bernal, M. E., M. D. Klinnert, and L. A. Schultz. 1980. "Outcome Evaluation of Behavioral Parent Training and Client-centered Parent Counseling for Children with Conduct Problems." *Journal of Applied Behavior Analysis* 13:671–76.

Blakely, B., P. S. Stephenson, and H. Nichol. 1974. "Social Factors Compared in a Random Sample of Juvenile Delinquents and Controls." *International Journal of Social Psychiatry* 20:203–17.

Blechman, E. 1982. "Are Children with One Parent at Psychological Risk? A Methodological Review." *Journal of Marriage and the Family* 44:179–95.

Bronfenbrenner, U. 1970. *Two Worlds of Childhood: U.S. and USSR.* New York: Russell Sage.

————. 1974. "The Roots of Alienation." In *Raising Children in Modern America,* edited by N. B. Talbot. Boston: Little Brown.

Bronson, W. C. 1966. "Control Orientations: A Study of Behavior Organizations from Childhood to Adolescence." *Child Development* 37:125–55.

Brook, J. S., I. F. Lukoff, and M. Whiteman. 1980. "Initiation into Adolescent Marijuana Use." *Journal of Genetic Psychology* 137:133–42.

Brook, J. S., M. Whiteman, A. S. Gordon, and C. Brenden. 1983. "Older Brother's Influence on Younger Sibling's Drug Use." *Journal of Psychology* 114:83–90.

Brown, S. E. 1984. "Social Class, Child Maltreatment, and Delinquent Behavior." *Criminology* 22:259–78.

Burt, C. 1930. *The Young Delinquent.* New York: Appleton.

Byles, J. A., and A. Maurice. 1979. "The Juvenile Services Project: An Experiment in Delinquency Control." *Canadian Journal of Criminology* 21:155–65.

Cadoret, R. J. 1980. "Sex Differences in Predictors of Antisocial Behavior in Adoptees." *Archives of General Psychiatry* 37:1171–75.

Cadoret, R. J., C. A. Cain, and R. R. Crowe. 1983. "Evidence for Gene-Environment Interaction in the Development of Adolescent Antisocial Behavior." *Behavior Genetics* 13:301–10.

Canter, R. J. 1982a. "Family Correlates of Male and Female Delinquency." *Criminology* 20:149–67.

———. 1982b. "Sex Differences in Self-Report Delinquency." *Criminology* 20:373–93.

Clarke, R. V. G., and P. Softley. 1975. "The Male:Female Ratio among the Siblings of Delinquents." *British Journal of Psychiatry* 126:249–51.

Clifford, E. 1959. "Discipline in the Home: A Controlled Observational Study of Parental Practices." *Journal of Genetic Psychology* 95:45–82.

Cloninger, C. R., S. Sigvardsson, M. Bohman, and A. L. VonKnorring. 1982. "Predisposition to Petty Criminality in Swedish Adoptees: Cross-fostering Analysis of Gene-Environment Interaction." *Archives of General Psychiatry* 39:1242–47.

Cohen, J. 1977. *Statistical Power Analysis for the Behavioral Sciences.* Rev. ed. New York: Academic Press.

Cohen, P., and J. Brook. 1984. "Family Factors Related to the Persistence of Psychopathology in Childhood and Adolescence." Paper presented to the Society for Life History Research in Psychopathology, Baltimore.

Conway, J. B., and B. D. Bucher. 1976. "Transfers and Maintenance on Behavior Change in Children: A Review and Suggestions." In *Behavior Modification and Families*, edited by E. J. Walsh, L. A. Hamerlynck, and L. C. Handy. New York: Brunner/Mazel.

Cortes, J. B., and F. M. Gatti. 1972. *Delinquency and Crime: A Biopsychological Approach.* New York: Seminar Press.

Craig, M. M., and S. J. Glick. 1968. "School Behavior Related to Later Delinquency and Nondelinquency." *Criminologica* 5:17–27.

Cunningham, C. E., and R. A. Barkley. 1978. "The Effects of Ritalin on the Mother-Child Interactions of Hyperkinetic Twin Boys." *Developmental Medicine and Child Development* 20:634–42.

Dalgard, O. S., and E. A. Kringlen. 1976. "Norwegian Twin Study of Criminality." *British Journal of Criminology* 16:213–32.

Dengerink, H. A., and M. K. Covey. 1981. "Implications for an Escape-Avoidance Theory of Aggressive Responses to Attack." In *Aggression: Theoretical and Empirical Review*, edited by R. Green and E. Donnerstein. New York: Academic Press.

Dentler, R. A., and L. J. Monroe. 1961. "Social Correlates of Early Adolescent Theft." *American Sociological Review* 26:733–43.

Dishion, T. J., and R. Loeber. 1985. "Adolescent Marijuana and Alcohol Use: The Role of Parents and Peers Revisited." *American Journal of Drug and Alcohol Abuse* 11:11–26.

Dootjes, I. 1972. "Predicting Juvenile Delinquency." *Australian and New Zealand Journal of Criminology* 5:157–71.

Dumas, J. E., and R. G. Wahler. 1983. "Predictors of Treatment Outcome in Parent Training: Mother Insularity and Socioeconomic Disadvantage." *Behavioral Assessment* 5:301–13.

Edelbrock, C., and R. Loeber. 1986. "The Development of Antisocial Behavior in Childhood and Adolescence." Unpublished manuscript. Worcester: University of Massachusetts Law School.

Eisenberg, J. G. 1979. "The Welfare Children: An Overview of Longitudinal Findings." In *Research in Community and Mental Health: An Annual Compilation of Research*, edited by R. G. Simmons. Greenwich, Conn.: JAI.

Eisenberg, J. G., J. C. Gersten, T. S. Langner, E. D. McCarthy, and O. Simcha-Fagan. 1976. "A Behavioral Classification of Welfare Children from Survey Data." *American Journal of Orthopsychiatry* 46:447–63.

Eisenberg, J. G., T. S. Langner, and J. G. Gersten. 1975. "Differences in the Behavior of Welfare and Non-welfare Children in Relation to Parental Characteristics." *Journal of Community Psychology* 3:311–40.

Elliott, D. S., S. S. Ageton, and R. J. Canter. 1979. "An Integrated Theoretical Perspective on Delinquent Behavior." *Journal of Research in Crime and Delinquency* 16:3–27.

Elliott, D. S., B. A. Knowles, and R. J. Canter. 1981. "The Epidemiology of Delinquent Behavior and Drug Use among American Adolescents, 1976–1978." Unpublished progress report to the National Institute of Mental Health. Boulder, Colo.: Behavioral Research Institute.

Emery, R. E. 1982. "Interparental Conflict and the Children of Discord and Divorce." *Psychological Bulletin* 92:310–30.

Emery, R. E., and K. D. O'Leary. 1982. "Children's Perceptions of Marital Discord and Behavior Problems of Boys and Girls." *Journal of Abnormal Child Psychology* 10:11–24.

Ensminger, M. E., S. G. Kellam, and B. R. Rubin. 1983. "School and Family Origins of Delinquency: Comparisons by Sex." In *Antecedents of Aggression and Antisocial Behavior*, edited by K. T. Van Dusen and S. A. Mednick. Boston: Kluwer-Nijhoff.

Eron, L. D. 1983. "The Consistency of Aggressive Behavior across Time and Situations." Paper presented at the meeting of the American Psychological Association, Anaheim, California.

Eron, L. D., L. O. Walder, and L. R. Huesmann. 1978. "The Convergence of Laboratory and Field Studies of the Development of Aggression." In *Origins of Aggression*, edited by W. W. Hartup and J. DeWit. The Hague: Mouton.

Eron, L. D., L. O. Walder, and M. M. Lefkowitz. 1971. *Learning of Aggression in Children*. Boston: Little Brown.

Eyberg, S., and S. M. Johnson. 1974. "Multiple Assessment of Behavior Modification with Families: The Effects of Contingency Contracting and Order of Treated Problems." *Journal of Consulting and Clinical Psychology* 42:594–606.

Fagot, B. I. 1978. "The Influence of Sex of Child on Parental Reactions to Toddler Children." *Child Development* 49:459–65.

Fagot, B. I., and R. Loeber. 1986. "Developmental Determinants of Male to Female Aggression." In *Violence in Intimate Adult Relationships*, edited by G. W. Russell. New York: Spectrum.

Farrington, D. P. 1978. "The Family Background of Aggressive Youths." In *Aggression and Antisocial Behavior in Childhood and Adolescence*, edited by L. A. Hersov, M. Berger, and D. Schaffer. Oxford: Pergamon.

———. 1979. "Environmental Stress, Delinquent Behavior, and Convictions." In *Stress and Anxiety*, vol. 6, edited by I. G. Sarason and C. D. Spielberger. Washington, D.C.: Hemisphere.

———. 1982. "Randomized Experiments on Crime and Justice." In *Crime and Justice: An Annual Review of Research*, vol. 4, edited by Michael Tonry and Norval Morris. Chicago: University of Chicago Press.

———. 1986. "Stepping Stones to Adult Criminal Careers." In *Development of Antisocial and Prosocial Behavior*, edited by D. Olwens, J. Block, and M. R. Yarrow. New York: Academic.

Farrington, D. P., G. Gundry, and D. J. West. 1975. "The Familial Transmission of Criminality." *Medicine, Science and the Law* 15:177–86.

Farrington, D. P., and D. J. West. 1971. "A Comparison between Early Delinquents and Young Aggressives." *British Journal of Criminology* 11:341–58.

———. 1981. "The Cambridge Study in Delinquent Development." In *Prospective Longitudinal Research: An Empirical Basis for Primary Prevention*, edited by S. A. Mednick and A. E. Baert. Oxford: Oxford University Press.

Federal Bureau of Investigation (U.S. Department of Justice). 1984. *Uniform Crime Reports for the United States, 1983*. Washington, D.C.: U.S. Government Printing Office.

Ferber, H., S. M. Keeley, and K. M. Schemberg. 1974. "Training Parents in Behavior Modification: Outcomes of and Problems Encountered in a Program after Patterson's Work." *Behavior Therapy* 5:415–19.

Fischer, D. G. 1984. "Family Size and Delinquency." *Perceptual and Motor Skills* 58:527–34.

Fischer, M., J. E. Rolf, J. E. Hasazi, and L. Summings. 1984. "Follow-up of a Preschool Epidemiological Sample: Cross-Age Continuities and Predictions of Later Adjustment with Internalizing and Externalizing Dimensions of Behavior." *Child Development* 55:137–50.

Fleischman, M. J. 1981. "A Replication of Patterson's Intervention for Boys with Conduct Problems." *Journal of Consulting and Clinical Psychology* 49:342–51.

Fleischman, M. J., A. M. Horne, and J. L. Arthur. 1983. *Troubled Families: A Treatment Program.* Champaign, Ill.: Research Press.

Forehand, R., and H. E. King. 1977. "Noncompliant Children: Effects of Parent Training on Behavior and Attitude Change." *Behavior Modification* 1:93–108.

Forehand, R., and R. J. McMahon. 1981. *Helping the Noncompliant Child: A Clinician's Guide to Parent Training.* New York: Guilford.

Forehand, R., J. Middlebrook, T. Rogers, and M. Steffe. 1983. "Dropping out of Parent Training." *Behavior Research and Therapy* 21:663–68.

Fréchette, M., and M. LeBlanc. 1979. "Délinquance cachée à l'adolescence." Unpublished manuscript. Groupe de Recherche sur l'Adaptation Juvènile. Montreal: University of Montreal.

Gersten, J. C., T. S. Langner, J. G. Eisenberg, and O. Simcha-Fagan. 1977. "An Evaluation of the Etiological Role of Stressful Life-Change Events in Psychological Disorders." *Journal of Health and Social Behavior* 18:228–44.

Gersten, J. C., T. S. Langner, J. G. Eisenberg, O. Simcha-Fagan, and E. D. McCarthy. 1976. "Stability and Change in Types of Behavioral Disturbances of Children and Adolescents." *Journal of Abnormal Child Psychology* 4:111–27.

Ghodsian, M., K. Fogelman, L. Lambert, and A. Tibbenham. 1980. "Changes in Behaviour Ratings of a National Sample of Children." *British Journal of Social and Clinical Psychology* 19:247–56.

Glidewell, J. C. 1968. "Studies of Mothers' Reports of Behavior Symptoms in Their Children." In *The Definition and Measurement of Mental Health*, edited by S. B. Sells. U.S. Public Health Service, National Center for Health Statistics. Washington, D.C.: U.S. Government Printing Office.

Glueck, S., and E. T. Glueck. 1934. *One Thousand Juvenile Delinquents.* Cambridge, Mass.: Harvard University Press.

———. 1940. *Juvenile Delinquents Grown Up.* New York: Commonwealth Fund.

———. 1950. *Unraveling Juvenile Delinquency.* Cambridge, Mass.: Harvard University Press.

———. 1959. *Predicting Delinquency and Crime.* Cambridge, Mass.: Harvard University Press.

Glynn, T. J. 1981. "From Family to Peer: A Review of Transitions of Influence among Drug-using Youth." *Journal of Youth and Adolescence* 10:363–83.

Goetting, A. 1981. "Divorce Outcome Research." *Journal of Family Issues* 2:350–78.

Gold, M. 1963. *Status Forces in Delinquent Boys.* Ann Arbor: University of Michigan, Institute for Social Research.

Goldstein, H. S. 1984. "Parental Composition, Supervision, and Conduct Problems in Youths 12 to 17 Years Old." *Journal of the American Academy of Child Psychiatry* 23:679–84.

Green, K. D., R. Forehand, and R. J. McMahon. 1979. "Parental Manipulation of Compliance and Noncompliance in Normal and Deviant Children." *Behavior Modification* 3:245–66.

Gregory, I. 1965. "Anterospective Data Following Childhood Loss of a Parent:

Delinquency and High School Dropout." *Archives of General Psychiatry* 13:99–109.

Griest, D. L., and K. C. Wells. 1983. "Behavioral Family Therapy with Conduct Disorders in Children." *Behavior Therapy* 14:37–53.

Hamparian, D. M., R. Schuster, S. Dinitz, and J. P. Conrad. 1978. *Violent Few—a Study of Dangerous Juvenile Offenders.* Lexington, Mass.: D. C. Heath.

Hautzinger, C. 1985. *The Case of Incomplete Therapy: Treatment Outcome Study of Aggressive Behavior.* Ph.D. dissertation, Free University, Berlin, Psychological Institute.

Hawkins, R. P., and P. Meadowcroft. 1984. "Practical Program Evaluation in a Family-based Treatment Program for Disturbing and Disturbed Youngsters." Unpublished manuscript. Morganstown: West Virginia University, Department of Psychology.

Healy, W. 1915. *Honesty.* Indianapolis: Bobbs-Merrill.

Herbert, M. 1982. "Conduct Disorders." In *Advances in Clinical Child Psychology,* vol. 5, edited by B. B. Lahey and A. E. Kazdin. New York: Plenum.

Herzog, E., and C. E. Sudia. 1970. *Boys in Fatherless Families.* Washington, D.C.: Office of Child Development.

Hetherington, E., M. Cox, and R. Cox. 1978. "The Aftermath of Divorce." In *Mother/Child, Father/Child Relationships,* edited by J. H. Stevens and M. Matthews. Washington, D.C.: National Association for the Education of Young Children.

Hetherington, E. M., and B. Martin. 1979. "Family Interaction." In *Psychopathological Disorders of Childhood,* edited by H. C. Quay and J. S. Werry. 2d ed. New York: Wiley.

Hewitt, L. E., and R. L. Jenkins. 1946. *Fundamental Patterns of Maladjustment.* Springfield, Illinois: Michigan Child Guidance Institute.

Hindelang, M. J. 1973. "Causes of Delinquency: A Partial Replication and Extension." *Social Problems* 20:471–87.

Hirschi, T. 1969. *Causes of Delinquency.* Berkeley: University of California Press.

———. 1983. "Crime and the Family." In *Crime and Public Policy,* edited by James Q. Wilson. San Francisco: Institute for Contemporary Studies Press.

Holleran, P. A., D. C. Littman, R. D. Freund, and K. B. Schmaling. 1982. "A Signal Detection Approach to Social Perception: Identification of Negative and Positive Behaviors by Parents of Normal and Problem Children." *Journal of Abnormal Child Psychology* 4:547–58.

Horne, A. M., and B. Van Dyke. 1983. "Treatment and Maintenance of Social Learning Family Therapy." *Behavior Therapy* 14:606–13.

Huesmann, L. R., L. D. Eron, M. M. Lefkowitz, and L. O. Walder. 1984. "The Stability of Aggression over Time and Generations." *Developmental Psychology* 20:1120–34.

Humphreys, L., R. Forehand, R. McMahon, and M. Roberts. 1978. "Parental Behavior Training to Modify Child Noncompliance: Effects on Untreated Siblings." *Journal of Behavior Therapy and Experimental Psychiatry* 9:235–38.

Hutchings, B., and S. A. Mednick. 1975. "Registered Criminality in the Adoptive and Biological Parents of Registered Male Criminal Adoptives." In

Genetic Research in Psychiatry, edited by R. R. Fieve, D. Rosenthal, and H. Brill. Baltimore: Johns Hopkins University Press.

Imperio, A. M., and D. R. Chabot. 1980. "Male Delinquents' Perceptions of Their Parents—a Factor Analysis." *Perceptual and Motor Skills* 51:829–30.

Jensen, G. F. 1972. "Parents, Peers and Delinquent Action: A Test of the Differential Association Perspective." *American Journal of Sociology* 78:562–75.

Jensen, G. F., and D. Brownfield. 1983. "Parents and Drugs: Specifying the Consequences of Attachment." *Criminology* 21:543–54.

Johnson, S. M., and G. R. Lobitz. 1974. "The Personal and Marital Status of Parents as Related to Observed Child Deviance and Parenting Behaviors." *Journal of Abnormal Child Psychology* 3:193–208.

Johnstone, J. W. C. 1980. "The Family and Delinquency: A Reappraisal." Unpublished manuscript. Chicago: University of Illinois at Chicago Circle.

Jones, M. B., D. R. Offord, and N. Abrams. 1980. "Brothers, Sisters, and Antisocial Behavior." *British Journal of Psychiatry* 136:139–45.

Kagan, J., and H. A. Moss. 1962. *Birth to Maturity*. New York: Wiley.

Kandel, D. B. 1978. "Convergence in Prospective Longitudinal Surveys of Drug Use in Normal Populations." In *Longitudinal Research on Drug Use*, edited by D. B. Kandel. New York: Wiley.

Karoly, P., and M. Rosenthal. 1977. "Training Parents in Behavior Modification: Effects on Perceptions of Family Interaction and Deviant Child Behavior." *Behavior Therapy* 8:406–10.

Kazdin, A. E. 1984. "Treatment of Conduct Disorders." In *Psychotherapy Research: Where Are We Going?* edited by J. W. Williams and R. L. Spitzer. New York: Guilford.

Klein, M. W. 1984. "Offense Specialization and Versatility among Juveniles." *British Journal of Criminology* 24:185–94.

Klein, N. C., J. F. Alexander, and B. V. Parsons. 1977. "Impact of Family Systems Intervention on Recidivism and Sibling Delinquency: A Model of Primary Prevention and Program Evaluation." *Journal of Consulting and Clinical Psychology* 45:469–74.

Knutson, J. F., J. G. Mehn, and A. M. Berger. 1984. "Is Violence in the Family Passed from Generation to Generation?" Unpublished manuscript. Iowa City: University of Iowa, Department of Psychology.

Kohlberg, L., D. Ricks, and J. Snarey. 1984. "Childhood Development as a Predictor of Adaptation in Adulthood." *Genetic Psychology Monographs* 110:91–172.

Kraus, P. E. 1973. *Yesterday's Children: A Longitudinal Study of Children from Kindergarten into Adult Years*. New York: Wiley.

Lamb, M. E. 1976. *The Role of the Father in Child Development*. New York: Wiley.

———. 1979. "Paternal Influences and the Father's Role: A Personal Perspective." *American Psychologist* 34:938–43.

Langner, T. S. 1979. "Predictors of Child Behavior and Their Implications for Social Policy." In *Research in Community and Mental Health: An Annual Compilation of Research*, edited by R. G. Simmons. Greenwich, Conn.: JAI.

Langner, T. S., J. C. Gersten, and J. G. Eisenberg. 1977. "The Epidemiology of Marital Disorder in Children." In *New Trends in Psychiatry in the Community*, edited by G. Serban. Cambridge, Mass.: Ballinger.

Langner, T. S., J. C. Gersten, T. A. Wills, and O. Simcha-Fagan. 1983. "The Relative Roles of Early Environment and Early Behavior as Predictors of Later Child Behavior." In *Origins of Psychopathology*, edited by D. F. Ricks and B. S. Dohrenwand. New York: Cambridge University Press.

Lassey, M. L., and J. E. Carlson. 1980. "Drinking among Rural Youth: The Dynamics of Parental and Peer Influences." *International Journal of the Addictions* 15:61–75.

Lefkowitz, M. M., L. D. Eron, L. O. Walder, and L. R. Huesmann. 1977. *Growing Up to Be Violent: A Longitudinal Study of the Development of Aggression.* New York: Pergamon.

Lewis, H. S. 1954. *Deprived Children.* Oxford: Oxford University Press.

Loeber, R. 1982. "The Stability of Antisocial and Delinquent Child Behavior: A Review." *Child Development* 53:1431–46.

———. 1984. "Experimental Studies to Reduce Antisocial and Delinquent Child Behavior: Implications for Future Programs and Optimal Times for Intervention." Paper presented at the Alcohol, Drug Abuse, and Mental Health Administration/Office of Juvenile Justice and Delinquency Prevention Conference on Juvenile Offenders with Serious Drug, Alcohol, and Mental Health Problems, Bethesda, Maryland.

———. 1985a. "Patterns and Development of Antisocial Child Behavior." In *Annals of Child Development*, vol. 2, edited by G. J. Whitehurst. Greenwich, Conn.: JAI.

———. 1985b. "The Prevalence, Correlates, and Continuity of Serious Conduct Problems in Elementary School Children." Unpublished manuscript. Pittsburgh: University of Pittsburgh, Western Psychiatric Institute and Clinic.

———. 1986. "The Natural Histories of Juvenile Conduct Problems, Substance Use, and Delinquency: Evidence for Developmental Progressions." Unpublished manuscript. Pittsburgh: University of Pittsburgh, Western Psychiatric Institute and Clinic.

Loeber, R., and T. J. Dishion. 1983. "Early Predictors of Male Delinquency: A Review." *Psychological Bulletin* 94:68–99.

Loeber, R., and K. B. Schmaling. 1985a. "Empirical Evidence for Overt and Covert Patterns of Antisocial Conduct Problems: A Meta Analysis." *Journal of Abnormal Child Psychology*. 13:337–52.

———. 1985b. "The Utility of Differentiating between Mixed and Pure Forms of Antisocial Child Behavior." *Journal of Abnormal Child Psychology*. 13:315–36.

Loeber, R., and M. Stouthamer-Loeber. 1986. "The Prediction of Delinquency." In *Handbook of Juvenile Delinquency*, edited by H. C. Quay. New York: Wiley.

Loeber, R., and T. Tengs. 1986. "Coercive Chains between Children, Mothers and Siblings." *Journal of Family Violence* (in press).

Loeber, R., and W. Weismann. 1982. "Mother Intervention in Sibling Fighting." Unpublished manuscript. Eugene: Oregon Social Learning Center.

Loeber, R., W. Weismann, and J. B. Reid. 1983. "Family Interaction of Assaultive Adolescents, Stealers, and Nondelinquents." *Journal of Abnormal Child Psychology* 11:1–14.

Lundman, R. J., and F. R. Scarpitti. 1978. "Delinquency Prevention: Recommendations for Future Projects." *Crime and Delinquency* 24:207–20.

McCarthy, E. D., J. C. Gersten, and T. S. Langner. 1982. "The Behavioral Effects of Father Absence on Children and Their Mothers." *Social Behavior and Personality* 10:11–23.

Maccoby, E. E., and C. M. Jacklin. 1974. *The Psychology of Sex Differences*. Stanford: Stanford University Press.

Maccoby, E. E., and J. A. Martin. 1983. "Socialization in the Context of the Family: Parent-Child Interactions." In *Handbook of Child Psychology*, vol. 4, *Socialization, Personality, and Social Development*, edited by E. M. Hetherington. New York: Wiley.

McCord, J. 1978. "A Thirty Year Follow-up of Treatment Effect." *American Psychologist* 32:284–89.

———. 1979. "Some Child-rearing Antecedents of Criminal Behavior in Adult Men." *Journal of Personality and Social Psychology* 9:1477–86.

———. 1981. "Alcohol and Criminality." *Journal of Studies on Alcohol* 42:739–48.

———. 1982. "A Longitudinal Study of the Link between Broken Homes and Criminality." In *Abnormal Offenders, Delinquency and the Criminal Justice System*, edited by J. Gunn and D. P. Farrington. London: Wiley.

———. 1984. "Family Sources of Crime." Paper presented at the meeting of the International Society for Research on Aggression, Turku, Finland, July.

McCord, W., J. McCord, and A. Howard. 1961. "Familial Correlates of Aggression in Non-delinquent Male Children." *Journal of Abnormal Social Psychology* 62:79–93.

———. 1963. "Family Interaction as Antecedent to the Direction of Male Aggressiveness." *Journal of Abnormal and Social Psychology* 66:239–42.

McCord, W., J. McCord, and I. K. Zola. 1969. *Origins of Crime*. Montclair, N.J.: Patterson Smith. (Originally published 1959. New York: Columbia University Press.)

MacFarlane, J. W., L. Allen, and M. P. Honzik. 1962. *A Developmental Study of the Behavior Problems of Normal Children between Twenty-one Months and Fourteen Years*. Berkeley: University of California Press.

Madden, D. J., and H. T. Harbin. 1983. "Family Structures of Assaultive Adolescents." *Journal of Marital and Family Therapy* 9:311–16.

Madoff, J. 1959. "The Attitudes of Mothers of Juvenile Delinquents toward Child Rearing." *Journal of Consulting Psychology* 23:518–20.

Magnusson, D., H. Stottin, and A. Duner. 1983. "Aggression and Criminality in a Longitudinal Perspective." In *Antecedents of Aggression and Antisocial Behavior*, edited by K. T. VanDusen and S. A. Mednick. Boston: Kluwer-Nijhoff.

Martin, B. 1977. "Brief Family Intervention: Effectiveness and the Importance of Including Father." *Journal of Clinical and Consulting Psychology* 45:1002–10.

Medinnus, G. R. 1965. "Delinquents' Perceptions of Their Parents." *Journal of Consulting Psychology* 29:592–93.

Mednick, S. A., and J. Volavka. 1980. "Biology and Crime." In *Crime and*

Justice: An Annual Review of Research, vol. 2, edited by Norval Morris and Michael Tonry. Chicago: University of Chicago Press.

Mendelson, M., N. Johnson, and M. A. Stewart. 1971. "Hyperactive Children as Teenagers: A Follow-up Study." *Journal of Nervous and Mental Disease* 153:273–79.

Miller, R. C., and J. S. Berman. 1983. "The Efficacy of Cognitive Behavior Therapies: A Quantitative Review of the Research Evidence." *Psychological Bulletin* 94:39–53.

Monahan, T. P. 1957. "Family Status and the Delinquent Child: A Reappraisal and Some New Findings." *Social Forces* 35:251–58.

Montegu, A. 1978. *Learning Non-aggression: The Experience of Non-literate Societies.* Oxford: Oxford University Press.

Montemayor, R. 1982. "The Relationship between Parent-Adolescent Conflict and the Amount of Time Adolescents Spend Alone and with Parents and Peers." *Child Development* 53:1512–19.

———. 1983. "Parents and Adolescents in Conflict: All Families Some of the Time and Some Families Most of the Time." *Journal of Early Adolescence* 3:83–103.

Moore, D. R., P. Chamberlain, and L. Mukai. 1979. "Children at Risk for Delinquency: A Follow-up Comparison of Stealing and Aggression." *Journal of Abnormal Child Psychology* 7:345–55.

Moreland, J. R., A. I. Schwebel, S. Beck, and R. Wells. 1982. "Parents as Therapists: A Review of the Behavior Therapy Parent Training Literature—1975 to 1981." *Behavior Modification* 6:250–76.

Newcomb, M. D., G. J. Huba, and P. M. Bentler. 1983. "Mothers' Influence on the Drug Use of Their Children: Confirmatory Tests of Direct Modeling and Mediational Theories." *Developmental Psychology* 19:714–26.

Nielsen, A., and D. Gerber. 1979. "Psychosocial Aspects of Truancy in Early Adolescence." *Adolescence* 14:313–26.

Norland, J. S., M. Shover, W. E. Thornton, and J. James. 1979. "Intra Family Conflict and Delinquency." *Pacific Sociological Review* 22:223–40.

Nye, F. I. 1958. *Family Relations and Delinquent Behavior.* New York: Wiley.

Office for Juvenile Justice and Delinquency Prevention. 1977. *Preventing Delinquency.* Washington, D.C.: U.S. Government Printing Office.

Offord, D. R., N. Abrams, N. Allen, and M. Poushinsky. 1979. "Broken Homes, Parental Psychiatric Illness, and Female Delinquency." *American Journal of Orthopsychiatry* 49:252–64.

Offord, D. R., N. Allen, and N. Abrams. 1978. "Parental Psychiatric Illness, Broken Homes and Delinquency." *Journal of the American Academy of Child Psychiatry* 17:224–38.

Olson, D. H., H. I. McCubbin, M. Barnes, A. Larsen, M. Muxen, and M. Wilson. 1983. *Families: What Makes Them Work.* Beverly Hills, Calif.: Sage.

Olweus, D. 1978. *Aggression in the Schools.* New York: Wiley.

———. 1979. "Stability of Aggressive Reaction Patterns in Males: A Review." *Psychological Bulletin* 86:852–57.

Osborn, S. G., and D. J. West. 1978. "The Effectiveness of Various Predictors of Criminal Careers." *Journal of Adolescence* 1:101–17.

Owens, D. J., and M. A. Straus. 1975. "The Social Structure of Violence in

Childhood and Approval of Violence as an Adult." *Aggressive Behavior* 1:193–211.

Patterson, G. R. 1976. "The Aggressive Child: Victim and Architect of a Coercive System." In *Behavior Modification and Families*, edited by E. J. Mash, L. A. Hamerlynck, and L. C. Handy. New York: Brunner/Mazel.

———. 1979. "Treatment for Children with Conduct Problems: A Review of Outcome Studies." In *Aggression and Behavior Change*, edited by S. Feshbach and A. Fraczek. New York: Praeger.

———. 1980. *Mothers: The Unacknowledged Victims*. Monographs of the Society for Research in Child Development, vol. 45, no. 5, serial no. 186. Chicago: University of Chicago Press.

———. 1982a. "A Macrosocial Analysis of the Contribution of Siblings to Antisocial Process in the Family." Paper presented at the Conference of the Development of Antisocial and Prosocial Behavior, Voss, Norway.

———. 1982b. *A Social Learning Approach: Coercive Family Process*. Vol. 3. Eugene, Oreg.: Castalia.

———. 1983. "Stress: A Change Agent for Family Process." In *Stress, Coping, and Development in Children*, edited by N. Garmezy and M. Rutter. New York: McGraw-Hill.

Patterson, G. P., P. Chamberlain, and J. B. Reid. 1982. "A Comparative Evaluation of Parent Training Programs." *Behavior Therapy* 13:638–50.

Patterson, G. R., and J. A. Cobb. 1971. "A Dyadic Analysis of 'Aggressive' Behaviors." In *Minnesota Symposia on Child Psychology*, vol. 5, edited by J. P. Hill. Minneapolis: University of Minnesota Press.

Patterson, G. R., J. A. Cobb, and R. S. Ray. 1973. "A Social Engineering Technology for Retraining the Families of Aggressive Boys." In *Issues and Trends in Behavior Therapy*, edited by H. E. Adams and I. P. Unkel. Springfield, Ill.: Thomas.

Patterson, G. R., and J. B. Reid. 1973. "Intervention for Families of Aggressive Boys: A Replication Study." *Behaviour Research and Therapy* 11:383–94.

Patterson, G. R., and M. Stouthamer-Loeber. 1984. "The Correlation of Family Management Practices and Delinquency." *Child Development* 55:1299–1307.

Peed, S., M. Roberts, and R. Forehand. 1977. "Evaluation of the Effectiveness of a Standardized Parent Training Program in Altering the Interaction of Mothers and Their Non-compliant Children." *Behavior Modification* 1:323–50.

Pepler, D., C. Corter, and R. Abramovitch. 1982. "Social Relations among Children: Comparison of Sibling and Peer Interaction." In *Peer Relationships and Social Skills in Childhood*, edited by K. H. Rubin and H. S. Ross. New York: Springer-Verlag.

Peterson, D. R., and W. C. Becker. 1965. "Family Interaction and Delinquency." In *Juvenile Delinquency*, edited by H. C. Quay. Princeton, N.J.: VanNostrand.

Polk, K., and C. H. Ruby. 1978. *Respondent Loss in the Longitudinal Study of Deviant Behavior*. San Francisco: National Council on Crime and Delinquency.

Power, M. J., P. M. Ash, E. Schoenberg, and E. C. Sirey. 1974. "Delinquency and the Family." *British Journal of Social Work* 4:13–38.

Powers, E., and H. Witmer. 1951. *An Experiment in the Prevention of Delinquency: The Cambridge-Somerville Youth Study*. New York: Columbia University Press.

Prigmore, C. S. 1963. "An Analysis of Rater Reliability on the Glueck Scale for the Prediction of Juvenile Delinquency." *Journal of Criminal Law, Criminology and Police Science* 54:30–41.

Pulkkinen, L. 1982. "Self-control and Continuity from Childhood to Late Adolescence." In *Life-Span Development and Behavior*, vol. 4, edited by P. B. Baltes and O. G. Brim. New York: Academic.

———. 1983. "Search for Alternatives to Aggression in Finland." In *Aggression in Global Perspective*, edited by A. P. Goldstein and M. Segall. New York: Pergamon.

Redl, F., and D. Wineman. 1951. *Children Who Hate: A Sensitive Analysis of the Antisocial Behavior of Children in Their Response to the Adult World*. New York: Free Press.

Reid, J. B. 1975. "The Child Who Steals." In *A Social Learning Approach to Family Intervention: The Socially Aggressive Child*, edited by G. R. Patterson, J. B. Reid, R. R. Jones, and R. E. Conger. Eugene, Oreg.: Castalia.

———. 1978. *A Social Learning Approach to Family Intervention: Observations in Home Settings*. Vol. 2. Eugene, Oreg.: Castalia.

———. 1983. "Home-based Treatment for Multiple Offending Delinquents." Final report to the National Institute of Mental Health. Eugene: Oregon Social Learning Center.

Reid, J. B., and A. F. C. J. Hendriks. 1973. "A Preliminary Analysis of the Effectiveness of Direct Home Intervention for Treatment of Pre-delinquent Boys Who Steal." In *Behavior Therapy: Methodology, Concepts and Practice*, edited by L. A. Hamerlynck, L. C. Handy, and E. J. Mash. Champaign, Ill.: Research Press.

Reitsma-Street, M., D. R. Offord, T. Finch, and G. Dummitt. 1984. "Antisocial Adolescents and Their Non-antisocial Siblings." Final Report. Hamilton, Ont.: McMaster University, Department of Psychiatry.

Richards, P., R. A. Berk, and B. Forster. 1979. *Crime as Play—Delinquency in a Middle Class Suburb*. Cambridge, Mass.: Ballinger.

Richman, N., J. Stevenson, and P. J. Graham. 1982. *Pre-school to School: A Behavioural Study*. London: Academic Press.

Rittenhaus, J. D., and J. D. Miller. 1984. "Social Learning and Teenage Drug Use—an Analysis of Family Dyads." *Health Psychology* 3:329–46.

Roberts, G. C., J. H. Block, and J. Block. 1984. "Continuity and Change in Parents' Child-rearing Practices." *Child Development* 55:586–97.

Robins, L. N. 1966. *Deviant Children Grow Up: A Sociological and Psychiatric Study of Sociopathic Personality*. Baltimore: Williams & Wilkins.

———. 1970. "The Adult Development of the Antisocial Child." *Seminars in Psychiatry* 2:420–34.

———. 1978. "Study Childhood Predictors of Adult Antisocial Behavior: Replication from Longitudinal Studies." *Psychological Medicine* 8:611–22.

————. 1984. "The Epidemiology of Antisocial Personality." In *Psychiatry*, edited by J. O. Cavenar. Philadelphia: Lippincott.

Robins, L. N., and S. Y. Hill. 1966. "Assessing the Contribution of Family Structure, Class and Peer Groups to Juvenile Delinquency." *Journal of Criminal Law, Criminology and Police Science* 57:325–34.

Robins, L. N., P. A. West, and B. L. Herjanic. 1975. "Arrests and Delinquency in Two Generations: A Study of Black Urban Families and Their Children." *Journal of Child Psychology and Psychiatry* 16:125–40.

Robinson, P. A. 1978. "Parents of Beyond Control Adolescents." *Adolescence* 13:109–19.

Rodman, H., and P. Grams. 1967. "Juvenile Delinquency and the Family: A Review and Discussion." In *Juvenile Delinquency and Youth Crime*, compiled by the Presidents' Commission on Law Enforcement and Administration of Justice. Task Force Report. Washington, D.C.: U.S. Government Printing Office.

Rutter, M. 1971. "Parent-Child Separation: Psychological Effects on the Children." *Journal of Child Psychology and Psychiatry* 12:233–60.

————. 1977a. "The Family Influences." In *Child Psychiatry: Modern Approaches*, edited by M. Rutter and L. Hersov. Oxford: Blackwell.

————. 1977b. "Separation, Loss, and Family Relations." In *Child Psychiatry: Modern Approaches*, edited by M. Rutter and L. Hersov. Oxford: Blackwell.

————. 1978. "Family, Area and School Influences in the Genesis of Conduct Disorders." In *Aggression and Antisocial Behavior in Childhood and Adolescence*, edited by L. A. Hersov, M. Berger, and D. Shaffer. Oxford: Pergamon.

————. 1981. "Epidemiological-Longitudinal Strategies and Causal Research in Child Psychiatry." *Journal of the American Academy of Child Psychiatry* 20:513–44.

Rutter, M., and H. Giller. 1983. *Juvenile Delinquency: Trends and Perspectives*. Harmondsworth: Penguin.

Rutter, M., P. Graham, O. Chadwick, and W. Yule. 1976. "Adolescent Turmoil: Fact or Fiction?" *Journal of Child Psychology and Psychiatry* 17:35–56.

Rutter, M., J. Tizard, and K. Whitmore. 1970. *Education, Health and Behavior*. New York: Wiley.

Samenow, S. E. 1984. *Inside the Criminal Mind*. New York: Time Books.

Schaefer, E. S., and N. Bayley. 1963. *Maternal Behavior, Child Behavior and Their Intercorrelations from Infancy through Adolescence*. Monographs of the Society for Research in Child Development, vol. 28, no. 3, serial no. 87. Chicago: University of Chicago Press.

Sears, R. R. 1961. "The Relation of Early Socialization Experiences to Aggression in Middle Childhood." *Journal of Abnormal and Social Psychology* 63:466–92.

Shepherd, M., B. Oppenheim, and S. Mitchell. 1971. *Childhood Behavior and Mental Health*. London: University of London Press.

Silberman, C. E. 1980. *Criminal Violence, Criminal Justice*. New York: Vintage.

Simard, K. A. F. 1981. "From Here to Delinquency: An Investigation of Achievement and Home Quality Characteristics in Delinquent and Socially Aggressive Preadolescent Males." M.A. thesis, University of Oregon, Department of Psychiatry.

Simcha-Fagan, O., T. S. Langner, J. C. Gersten, and J. G. Eisenberg. 1975. "Violent and Antisocial Behavior: A Longitudinal Study of Urban Youth." Report no. OCD-CB-480. Washington, D.C.: Office of Child Development.

Slocum, W. L., and C. L. Stone. 1963. "Family Culture Patterns and Delinquent-Type Behavior." *Marriage and Family Living* 25:202–08.

Smart, R. G., G. Gray, and C. Bennett. 1978. "Predictors of Drinking and Signs of Heavy Drinking among High School Students." *International Journal of Addictions* 13:1079–94.

Solnick, J. V., C. J. Braukmann, M. M. Bedlington, K. A. Kirigin, and M. M. Wolf. 1981. "The Relationship between Parent-Youth Interaction and Delinquency in Group Homes." *Journal of Abnormal Child Psychology* 9:107–19.

Spungen, D. 1984. *And I Don't Want to Live This Life*. New York: Fawcett Crest.

The State of Families, 1984. 1984. New York: Family Service America.

Steinmetz, S. K. 1978. "Sibling Violence." In *Family Violence*, edited by J. M. Eckelaar and S. N. Katz. Toronto: Butterworths.

———. 1979. "Disciplinary Techniques and Their Relationship to Aggressiveness, Dependency, and Conscience." In *Contemporary Theories about the Family*, vol. 1, edited by W. R. Burr, R. Hill, F. I. Nye, and I. L. Reiss. New York: Free Press.

———. 1981. "A Cross-cultural Comparison of Sibling Violence." *International Journal of Family Psychiatry* 2:337–51.

Steinmetz, S. K., and M. H. Straus. 1974. *Violence in the Family*. New York: Dodd, Mead.

Stewart, M. A. 1984. "Aggressive Conduct Disorder." Paper presented at the meeting of the International Society for Research on Aggression, Turku, Finland, July.

Stott, D. H. 1966. *Studies of Troublesome Children*. London: Tavistock.

Stouthamer-Loeber, M., K. B. Schmaling, and R. Loeber. 1984. "The Relationship of Single Parent Family Status and Marital Discord to Antisocial Child Behavior." Unpublished manuscript. Pittsburgh: University of Pittsburgh, Department of Psychiatry.

Strain, P. S., P. Steele, T. Ellis, and M. A. Timm. 1982. "Long-Term Effects of Oppositional Child Treatment with Mothers as Therapists and Therapist Trainees." *Journal of Applied Behavior Analysis* 15:163–69.

Straus, M. A. 1983. "Ordinary Violence, Child Abuse, and Wife Beating: What Do They Have in Common?" In *The Dark Side of Families*, edited by D. Finkelhor, R. J. Gelles, G. T. Hotaling, and M. A. Straus. Beverly Hills, Calif.: Sage.

Straus, M. A., R. J. Gelles, and S. K. Steinmetz. 1980. *Behind Closed Doors: Violence in the American Family*. Garden City, N.Y.: Anchor.

Sutherland, E. H., and D. R. Cressey. 1960. *Principles of Criminology*. 6th ed. Philadelphia: Lippincott.

———. 1966. *Principles of Criminology*. 7th ed. Philadelphia: Lippincott.

Tait, C. D., and E. F. Hodges. 1962. *Delinquents, Their Families and Their Communities*. Springfield, Ill.: Thomas.

———. 1972. "Follow-up Study of Glueck Table Applied to a School Population of Problem Boys and Girls between the Ages of Five and Fourteen." In

Identification of Predelinquents, edited by S. Glueck and E. Glueck. New York: Intercontinental Medical Book Co.

Taplin, P. S., and J. B. Reid. 1977. "Changes in Parent Consequation as Function of Family Intervention." *Journal of Consulting and Clinical Psychology* 45:973–81.

Thomas, A., and S. Chess. 1977. *Temperament and Development*. New York: Brunner/Mazel.

Thomas, A., S. Chess, and H. G. Birch. 1968. *Temperament and Behavior Disorders in Children*. New York: New York University Press.

Thompson, R. E. 1952. "A Validation of the Glueck Social Prediction Scale for Process to Delinquency." *Journal of Criminal Law, Criminology, and Police Science* 43:451–70.

Tims, A. R., and J. D. Masland. 1985. "Measurement of Family Communication Patterns." *Communication Research* 12:35–58.

Trevvett, N. B. 1972. "Identifying Delinquency-prone Children." In *Identification of Predelinquents*, edited by S. Glueck and E. Glueck. New York: Intercontinental Medical Book Co.

U.S. Bureau of the Census (U.S. Department of Commerce). 1984. *Statistical Abstract of the United States*. 104th ed. Washington, D.C.: U.S. Government Printing Office.

Voss, H. T. 1963. "The Predictive Efficiency of the Glueck Social Prediction Table." *Journal of Criminal Law and Criminology* 54:421–30.

Wadsworth, M. 1979. *Roots of Delinquency, Infancy, Adolescence and Crime*. Oxford: Robertson.

Wadsworth, M. E. J. 1980. "Early Life Events and Later Behavioral Outcomes in a British Longitudinal Study." In *Human Functioning in Longitudinal Perspective*, edited by S. B. Sells, R. Crandell, M. Roff, J. S. Strauss, and W. Pollin. Baltimore: Williams & Wilkins.

Wahler, R. G., and J. E. Dumas. 1986*a*. "Family Factors in Childhood Psychopathology: A Coercion-Neglect Model." In *Family Interaction and Psychopathology*, edited by T. Jacob. New York: Plenum.

———. 1986*b*. "Stimulus Class Determinants of Mother-Child Coercive Interchanges in Multidistressed Families: Assessment and Intervention." In *Prevention of Delinquent Behavior*, edited by J. D. Burchard and S. Burchard. Beverly Hills, Calif.: Sage.

Wahler, R. G., J. B. Hughey, and J. S. Gordon. 1981. "Chronic Patterns of Mother-Child Coercion: Some Differences between Insular and Noninsular Families." *Analysis and Intervention in Developmental Disabilities* 1:145–56.

Wahler, R. G., G. Leslie, and E. G. Rogers. 1979. "The Insular Family: A Deviance Support Mechanism for Oppositional Children." In *School and Family Environments*, vol. 1 of *Behavioral Systems for the Developmentally Disabled*, edited by L. A. Hamerlynck. New York: Brunner/Mazel.

Walters, H. I., and S. K. Gilmore. 1973. "Placebo versus Social Learning Effects in Parental Training Procedures Designed to Alter the Behavior of Aggressive Boys." *Behavior Therapy* 4:361–77.

Weinrott, M. R., B. W. Bauske, and G. R. Patterson. 1979. "Systematic Replication of a Social Learning Approach to Parent Training." In *Trends in*

Behavior Therapy, edited by P. O. Sjoden, S. Bates, and W. S. Docken. New York: Academic Press.

Weis, K. 1974. "The Glueck Social Prediction Table: An Unfulfilled Promise." *Journal of Criminal Law and Criminology* 65:397–404.

Werner, E. E., and R. S. Smith. 1977. *Kauai's Children Come of Age*. Honolulu: University of Hawaii Press.

———. 1982. *Vulnerable, but Invincible: A Longitudinal Study of Resilient Children and Youth*. New York: McGraw-Hill.

West, D. J. 1969. *Present Conduct and Future Delinquency*. London: Heinemann.

West, D. J., and D. P. Farrington. 1973. *Who Becomes Delinquent?* London: Heinemann.

———. 1977. *The Delinquent Way of Life*. London: Heinemann.

Whelan, R. 1954. "An Experiment in Predicting Delinquency." *Journal of Criminal Law, Criminology, and Police Science* 45:432–41.

Whiting, B. B., and J. W. M. Whiting. 1975. *Children of Six Cultures: A Psychocultural Analysis*. Cambridge, Mass.: Harvard University Press.

Wilkinson, K. 1980. "The Broken Home and Delinquent Behavior: An Alternative Interpretation of Contradictory Findings." In *Understanding Crime: Current Theory and Research*, edited by T. Hirschi and M. Gottfredson. Beverly Hills, Calif.: Sage.

Wilkinson, K., B. G. Stitt, and M. L. Erickson. 1982. "Siblings and Delinquent Behavior." *Criminology* 20:223–40.

Wilson, H. 1974. "Parenting in Poverty." *Journal of Social Work* 4:241–54.

———. 1975. "Juvenile Delinquency, Parent Criminality and Social Handicap." *British Journal of Criminology* 15:241–50.

———. 1980. "Parental Supervision: A Neglected Aspect of Delinquency." *British Journal of Criminology* 20:203–35.

Wilson, H., and G. W. Herbert. 1978. *Parents and Children in the Inner City*. London: Routledge & Kegan Paul.

Wilson, J. Q. 1983. "Raising Kids." *Atlantic* 252(4):45–51.

Wilson, J. Q., and R. Herrnstein. 1985. *Crime and Human Nature*. New York: Simon & Schuster.

Wolff, G. 1979. *The Duke of Deception: Memories of My Father*. New York: Random House.

York, P., D. York, and T. Wachtel. 1984. *Toughlove Solutions*. Garden City, N.Y.: Doubleday.

Zill, N. 1978. "Divorce, Marital Happiness and the Mental Health of Children: Findings for the FCD National Survey of Children." Paper presented to the National Institute of Mental Health Workshop on Divorce and Children, Bethesda, Maryland.

Zucker, R. A. 1976. "Parental Influences upon Drinking Patterns of Their Children." In *Alcoholism Problems in Women and Children*, edited by M. Greenblatt and M. A. Schuckit. New York: Grune & Stratton.

Zucker, R. A., and F. H. Barron. 1971. "Toward a Systematic Family Mythology: The Relationship of Parents' and Adolescent's Reports of Parent Behavior during Childhood." Paper presented at the meeting of the Eastern Psychological Association, New York.

Peter W. Greenwood

Differences in Criminal Behavior and Court Responses among Juvenile and Young Adult Defendants

ABSTRACT

The peak ages of criminality fall between the sixteenth and twentieth birthdays, with participation rates falling off rapidly for older age groups. Young men under the age of twenty-one account for half of all felony arrests. However, these arrest figures tend to overestimate the seriousness of the youthful offender crime problem somewhat because their crimes tend to be less serious and are committed in groups. There is a strong and direct connection between juvenile criminal activity and adult criminal careers. Chronic juvenile offenders have a high probability of continuing in crime as adults, while juveniles who were never arrested are unlikely to develop criminal careers as adults. Predictors of chronic juvenile offending include predelinquent deviant or troublesome behavior, physiological deficits associated with abnormal brain development, poor parenting, and evidence of criminal conduct or mental disorder among parents or siblings. In recent years juvenile and criminal courts have been criticized for failing to deal with young chronic offenders severely enough. The common belief was that the juvenile court was excessively lenient in all types of cases because of its concern for the welfare of the minor, while the criminal courts were probably forced to be lenient because they did not have unrestricted access to juvenile records. Analysis of case disposition patterns suggests that chronic juvenile and young adult offenders are sentenced to incarceration or state custody at least as frequently as is any other age group (for some types of crime) and that

Peter W. Greenwood is Senior Researcher at the Rand Corporation in Santa Monica, California.

the seriousness of their juvenile records affects the severity of their sentences.

Every major jurisdiction in the United States has two discrete legal systems for responding to criminal conduct: a juvenile or family court, given responsibility for most young offenders who fall under a specified age, and a criminal court, which is responsible for all the rest. These two systems are generally operated by different personnel, guided by different philosophies and goals, and governed by different laws. This division of authority has been referred to as the "dual" or "two-track" system for responding to youthful criminality.

The underlying assumptions, characteristics, and effects of this division of responsibility have only recently been subjected to close scrutiny. Of particular interest are the effects of this two-track system on two classes of offenders: (1) the offenders who, while legally juveniles and therefore the beneficiaries of the juvenile court's supposedly benevolent concern for their future welfare, have demonstrated such sustained commitment to serious criminal activity that the probability of their continued involvement is extremely high and (2) the slightly older group of equally persistent and risky offenders who are only one or two years past the age of transition from juvenile to criminal courts and for whom the two-track system may obscure their prior criminal activities.

Recent commentaries have asserted that these youthful but chronic offenders receive more lenient sentences than their records warrant, particularly when compared with the sentences received by older peers.

This concern is more than academic. Many jurisdictions are considering reforms relating to serious youthful offenders, including changing the bases for waiver of juvenile court jurisdiction; implementing parole guidelines that increase the minimum amount of time that serious juvenile offenders must remain in secure custody; forming special "juvenile career criminal prosecution" units; and making juvenile proceedings and records more accessible to public scrutiny and the criminal courts. In many jurisdictions there appears to be a political consensus that chronic youthful offenders are not being dealt with appropriately and that organizational or procedural changes are needed.

Many recent criminal justice reforms and innovations, such as career criminal prosecution units, targeted apprehension programs, and anti-truancy efforts, have been specifically designed to reduce the risks of particular types of serious criminal behavior such as robbery, burglary, or sexual assault. Most of these programs initially focused on adult offenders and criminal courts, where issues of public safety have historically been predominant. However, there is increasing pressure to include serious juvenile offenders within the focus of these crime control efforts.

There are several reasons why interest in chronic youthful offenders has increased. One is the perception that youthful offenders constitute a majority of the active offenders. Another is the finding that a small number of chronic offenders account for a disproportionate share of all crimes. A third is a general belief that youthful offenders are treated much more leniently than are their older colleagues because both juvenile and criminal court judges treat their youthfulness as a mitigating factor and emphasize rehabilitation in sentencing at the expense of community protection.

This essay reviews recent research that bears on the accuracy of these perceptions. The first section focuses on what we know about the age distribution of offenders. How much of the crime problem is due to juvenile offenders or young adult offenders who are just past the age boundaries of the juvenile court? The second section looks at the phenomenon of criminal careers. How much of the crime problem can be attributed to chronic juvenile or young adult offenders, and how well can such offenders be identified early in their careers? The third section looks at how these two categories of offenders are now being sentenced in juvenile and criminal courts. The last section discusses a number of policy issues that are raised by the youthful criminal career patterns that this essay describes.

I. The Amount of Crime That Is Attributable to
Youthful Offenders

A considerable body of evidence shows that many offenses, including robbery, burglary, and theft, are committed predominantly by young men between the ages of sixteen and twenty-five (Farrington 1979; Petersilia 1980). The age group with the highest arrest rate (arrests per 100,000 population) for robbery or burglary comprises young men between the ages of sixteen and eighteen (Twentieth Century Fund 1978). In 1984, half of those arrested for Index crimes[1] were between

---

[1] Index crime in the FBI's Uniform Crime Report includes murder, rape, robbery, aggravated assault, burglary, larceny, auto theft, and arson.

the ages of sixteen and twenty-five (U.S. Department of Justice 1985). By age twenty-three, the arrest rate for robbery is only half what it was at age eighteen; the rate at which twenty-three-year-olds are arrested for burglary is about one-quarter of what it is for sixteen-year-olds (Zimring 1978). Petersilia, Greenwood, and Lavin's (1977) criminal career study, based on interviews with forty-nine incarcerated robbers, suggested that, even among chronic adults, offense rates were highest in their young adult years. If one purpose of criminal sanctions is to protect the public from further crime, at least half of the offenders the public must be protected from are under twenty-five.

Juvenile and youthful offender crimes pose two general policy questions. (1) To what degree must crime control strategies reach juvenile or youthful offenders in order to be effective? (2) To what degree are juvenile courts being asked to deal with criminal behavior that represents a real threat to community safety as opposed to crime that is only bothersome and merely predictive of more serious criminal behavior to come?

A. *Arrests by Age*

The primary source of information on the age distribution of the offender population is aggregate data on reported arrests. To the extent that all age groups are subject to the same probability of arrest given the commission of a specific crime type, the recorded arrests will provide a reasonably accurate sample of all offenders.

Table 1 shows the percentages of property, violent, and total Part I arrests[2] attributable to specific age groups in 1980 along with the percentage each represents of the total population. (Data for 1980, rather than for more recent years, are used here because of the availability of accurate population data from the 1980 census. Age-specific estimates for later years must be based on projections from the 1980 census data.) In 1980, juvenile offenders under age eighteen accounted for 36 percent of all Part I arrests. Including those between the ages of eighteen and twenty brings the percentage of Part I crime attributable to offenders under age twenty-one to 54.5 percent.

A rough check on the accuracy of arrest distributions by age is provided by victimization surveys that ask victims about the characteristics of offenders. This information is obviously only available for

---

[2] Part I violent offenses include murder, rape, robbery, and aggravated assault; Part I property offenses include burglary, larceny-theft, motor vehicle theft, and arson.

TABLE 1

Distribution of Arrests by Age Groups, 1980

Age Group	Total U.S. Population	Total Part I Crimes	Violent Crimes	Property Crimes
1–12 (%)	19.4	4.5	1.1	5.3
13–14 (%)	3.2	8.3	3.6	9.6
15–17 (%)	5.5	23.2	14.6	25.3
18–20 (%)	5.7	18.5	17.7	18.7
21–24 (%)	7.5	15.3	19.6	14.1
25–29 (%)	8.6	11.6	16.4	10.4
30–39 (%)	14.0	10.8	16.4	9.3
40–49 (%)	10.1	4.2	6.3	3.6
50–59 (%)	10.3	2.3	2.9	2.1
60 + (%)	15.7	1.4	1.3	1.4
Total Arrests (N)		2,198,077	446,373	1,751,704

SOURCE.—U.S. Department of Justice 1983.

crimes against the person, and the estimates of age are crude and subject to considerable error. For instance, using National Crime Survey (NCS) data for 1979, Cook (1983) estimated the percentage of robbery offenders who were under twenty-one years of age to be 56 percent, which is very close to the Uniform Crime Report's figure of 54.5 percent, based on reported arrests.

Self-reports of offenders could conceivably provide another basis for checking the accuracy of arrest distributions by age, but, to date, they have not. Self-report surveys have traditionally focused on specific age groups or captive populations and thus do not reflect a complete or accurate picture of the entire offender population. Most researchers tend to focus exclusively on either juveniles or adults, thereby eliminating any possibility of comparing participation in crime or offense rates.

In recent years, the percentage of arrests attributable to juveniles under age eighteen has been on the decline. Between 1971 and 1984 the percentage of Part I arrests involving juveniles has declined from 45 to 31 percent (U.S. Department of Justice 1982, 1985). In those years, the percentage of violent arrests has declined from 22 to 17 percent, while the percentage of property crimes has declined from 51 to 35 percent. For the past few years, many states have been showing an absolute decline in the number of juveniles arrested for Part I crimes due, in part, to the aging of the members of the postwar baby boom.

The most important feature of the arrest distributions shown in table 1 is the difference in participation rates for juveniles between violent and property crimes. In 1980 juveniles under eighteen years of age accounted for 40 percent of all Part I property arrests but only 19 percent of all Part I arrests for violence. While juveniles are clearly overrepresented among persons arrested, their representation is also clearly biased toward the less serious property crimes as opposed to the more serious crimes of violence.

B. *A Closer Look at Age and Crime Seriousness*

Just as total aggregate arrest figures tend to overestimate the participation of youthful offenders in the most serious crime categories, so arrest figures for specific offense categories may also inflate the seriousness of crime by youth. The aggregate arrest figures cited above show that juveniles under age eighteen account for 36 percent of all Part I arrests but for only 19 percent of all Part I arrests for violence. A further breakdown by crime type shows that they account for only 9 percent of the arrests for murder and nonnegligent manslaughter.

Even within the offense types in which young men predominate— robbery and burglary—there is room for considerable variation in seriousness. Robberies can range from simple school-yard extortions to armed assault on a business or a residence. Burglaries can range from poking around in a neighbor's garage to surreptitious entry by an armed intruder into an occupied dwelling.

Within a single crime category such as robbery, we find that these same age-related patterns of seriousness hold up. Younger offenders are less likely to be armed with guns and are less likely to rob businesses and residences than pedestrians on the street. The amount of loss from their crimes is likely to be less, and they are more likely to commit their crimes in groups (Greenwood, Petersilia, and Zimring 1980).

Juveniles tend to commit crimes the way they lead the rest of their lives, in groups of two or more. Victim surveys indicate that two-thirds of all robberies by juveniles involve two or more perpetrators, compared with one-third of robberies by adults (Greenwood et al. 1980). A sample of 400 armed robbery arrests drawn from the records of the Los Angeles Police showed that only 23 percent of those involving a sixteen- to seventeen-year-old were committed alone, compared with 34 percent of those committed by offenders eighteen to nineteen years of age (Greenwood et al. 1983). Since juvenile arrests are more likely to involve multiple perpetrators for a single crime, this means that aggregate arrest statistics for specific age groups will tend to overestimate the true risk of victimization by juveniles. By combining NCS data on the frequency of group offending and weapon use, Zimring (1981) estimated that offenders under the age of twenty-one accounted for 60 percent of all robbery arrests but for only 31 percent of all armed robberies. Also, since accessories are invariably sentenced more leniently than are principals, the higher group-participation pattern of juveniles will also tend to underestimate the severity of sanctions received compared with offenders from different age groups.

Arrest figures leave little doubt that male juveniles between the ages of thirteen and seventeen and young men between the ages of eighteen and twenty-nine account for the bulk of criminal activity. The most high-risk groups are those between the ages of sixteen and twenty-one, whose arrest rates are three to five times the proportion represented by their age group. However, the amount of serious crime attributed to juveniles by these figures is somewhat inflated because of systematic differences in offense severity with age and the greater proportion of crimes committed by juveniles in groups. Any attempt to reduce property crime rates must deal with the crimes of the juvenile and young adult population. Efforts to reduce violent crime rates must begin at least during the young adult years. If these interventions are to be at all selective, then the targeted offenders must be selected on the basis of information about crimes committed even earlier.

II. Criminal Career Patterns among the Young

Studies of criminal careers have established that a disproportionate share of crime is attributable to a small subset of "chronic" or "high-rate" offenders. Inmate surveys have focused on a small subset who commit crimes at a high rate (Chaiken and Chaiken 1982; Greenwood and Abrahamse 1982). Longitudinal cohort studies have focused on the small subset who are arrested most frequently over the span of the study (Farrington 1979). Both types of studies conclude that crime control policies should focus on chronic or high-rate offenders—for whom incapacitation or successful rehabilitative treatment would have the highest payoff.

One key question is the age at which chronic offenders can first be identified. If they begin their criminal careers in their early teens, this raises the issue of whether incapacitative sentences are appropriate for this group or whether rehabilitative or preventive interventions are justified at even younger ages. These questions in turn raise important issues about the role of juvenile courts. Further, even if incapacitative sentences are inappropriate at fourteen or fifteen, if early onset is predictive of later criminality, this factor may be a useful discriminant indicator for adult sentencing years later.

From a theoretical perspective, the earlier the age at which chronic careers begin, the greater the emphasis that must be given to causal theories that emphasize early child-rearing and socialization practices, schooling, or even physiological predisposition as opposed to theories emphasizing employment opportunities and other influences that begin to have effects later in life.

The crudest evidence on juvenile criminal careers comes from retrospective studies of adult chronic offenders. The Rand Inmate Surveys found that conviction prior to age sixteen or commitment to a state juvenile facility were predictive of high-rate offending (Greenwood and Abrahamse 1982). Age at first arrest has traditionally been found to be a strong predictor of subsequent recidivism. This evidence is crude because it may be biased and unreliable. Juvenile records are often sealed or purged within several years after their subjects pass the maximum age jurisdiction of the juvenile court. These records are also usually kept on a limited geographic basis, such as for an individual police department or county probation department, rather than in state or national systems like adult records. Even when available, juvenile records are often difficult to link up with the records of adult subjects because of prohibitions on the recording of unique identifiers, such as fingerprints, for juveniles. Samples of incarcerated adults may be unrepresentative because they include a higher proportion of offenders with prior juvenile records than normal (if the courts use early arrests as a basis for harsher sentencing).

The best sources of data for examining patterns of onset in criminal careers are those longitudinal studies that have obtained accurate information on both juvenile and adult arrests (Farrington 1979). The best of these—in that it tracks a large number of subjects over an extended period of time, contains complete juvenile and adult criminal record information, and includes a significant number of serious chronic offenders—is Farrington and West's (1981) Cambridge study.

This study covers 411 boys who were aged eight to nine in 1961–62 and who attended six schools in a working-class area of London. The boys were contacted every two years up to age twenty-one, while their families were contacted every year up to age fifteen. The study includes all recorded convictions up through age twenty-five.

Other longitudinal studies containing data on the relation between juvenile and adult criminality include McCord's (1979) follow-up through 1975 of 325 boys who had participated in the Cambridge-Somerville project in the late 1930s, Robins's (1966) study of 524 children treated in a St. Louis child guidance clinic between 1924 and 1929 and followed up thirty years later, and Shannon's (1978) study of 1,352 youths born in 1942 and of 2,099 youths born in 1949 in Racine, Wisconsin. The records of both groups were followed up through 1973.

A. The Connection between Juvenile and Adult Careers

The Farrington and West data provide the most complete and compelling picture of the connection between juvenile and adult crime (Farrington 1983). In that study 70 percent of the sample who were *convicted as juveniles* (between the ages of ten and sixteen) were subsequently convicted as adults (over age sixteen) by the time they had reached age twenty-four. The prevalence of convictions for adults who had not received any juvenile convictions was only 16 percent, more than a *four-to-one difference*. Only thirteen out of 411 boys sustained more than *three juvenile convictions*. Of these thirteen, *77 percent* had *four or more convictions as an adult*. Only 2 percent of those adults without any juvenile convictions received four or more convictions. The small group of boys who were first convicted between ages ten and twelve averaged six convictions apiece by their twenty-first birthdays (Farrington 1979).

In the McCord (1979) study, 46 percent of those with juvenile (under age eighteen) arrests went on to sustain adult arrests, compared with only 18 percent of those without juvenile records, a three-to-one difference in adult arrest prevalence. In the latest report on the Racine cohorts published by Shannon (1981), 35 percent of those who committed a felony or major misdemeanor as a juvenile also committed one as an adult, compared with a 6 percent prevalence rate for those without a significant juvenile record, a six-to-one difference.

All these studies indicate a fair degree of continuity between juvenile offending and later criminal behavior. However, there is considerable disagreement among criminologists whether this degree of continuity is sufficient to justify selectively targeting special intervention efforts on chronic juvenile or young adult offenders over and above what any one particular offense might call for.

B. Assessing the Significance of Predictive Increments

Some criminologists argue that we cannot predict well enough to have any effect on crime rates (Hamparian et al. 1978; Shannon 1983). Others claim that they can identify a group of chronic offenders who are responsible for a disproportionate share of crime (Wolfgang, Figlio, and Sellin 1972; Greenwood and Abrahamse 1982; Farrington 1983). Are these authors looking at different data, or are they reaching different conclusions from the same data? The truth is a little of both.

The accuracy of any prediction device in discriminating between two groups of subjects (i.e., delinquents and nondelinquents, or chronics and nonchronics) can be displayed fully in a 2 × 2 matrix such as that shown in table 2. This table is taken from a paper by Shannon (1983), which disparages the value of several recent prediction efforts, including those of Wolfgang and Farrington. The data is taken from Farrington and West's (1977) longitudinal study of young men from a working-class area of London.

The rows represent the two prediction categories—not criminal (no) and criminal (yes)—based on juvenile convictions; the columns represent the actual categories of adult criminality—experiencing (yes) and not experiencing (no) an adult conviction. The decimal figures in each cell show the fraction of cases falling into each category. The numbers at the margins are the sums of their respective rows or columns. The

TABLE 2

Predicting Adult Conviction from Juvenile Conviction:
Cambridge Study

	Actual Adult Convictions		
	No	Yes	Total
Predicted future criminality based on prior juvenile convictions (ages 14–17):			
No	.69	.10	.79
	(269)	(38)	
Yes	.08	.13	.21
	(32)	(50)	
Total	.77	.23	1.00

NOTE.—Total number of subjects equals 389. The numbers in parentheses show the actual distribution of the 389 subjects.

numbers in parentheses show the actual distribution of the 389 subjects.

The data in table 2 show that 23 percent of the sample experienced at least one conviction between the ages of eighteen and twenty-one, while 21 percent were predicted to receive convictions. Of the 23 percent convicted, 13 percent were accurately predicted, while 10 percent were not. The juvenile conviction data divide the juvenile population into two groups, one with a 62 percent (thirteen in twenty-one) chance of being convicted as an adult, the other with a 13 percent (ten in seventy-nine) chance, a five-to-one difference. Is this a reasonable level of discrimination on which the system might act? Shannon argues it is not. Others might disagree. It obviously depends on the reasons for discrimination.

There is no one statistic that captures all the possible differences among prediction scales that can appear in such a 2 × 2 table. Different summary statistics emphasize different aspects of comparison. For instance, Shannon computes what he calls a *coefficient of predictability*, which measures the percentage reduction in error over that which could arise through chance. Shannon points out, on the basis of the data in table 2, that a prediction that no one would experience an adult conviction would be correct for 77 percent of the cases, the true percentage of those with no convictions. The twenty-three incorrect predictions would all be false negatives. Using juvenile convictions to predict adult convictions as shown in table 2 results in 82 percent correct predictions, the 69 percent correctly predicted to have no convictions and the 13 percent correctly predicted to be convicted. Shannon's coefficient of predictability, which he claims is low, is simply the difference between these two percentage error terms divided by the percentage error under chance:

$$\frac{23 - 18}{23} = .22.$$

Notice that Shannon's proposed "chance-method" of prediction does not do very well at identifying future offenders in that it predicts that none will have convictions. The use of this measure for comparison assumes that all errors in prediction, whether false positives or false negatives, have equal weight. This is not usually the case. For instance, in predicting which defendants are guilty for purposes of conviction, we tolerate many false negatives in order to keep the percentage of false positives extremely low. However, in screening airport travelers for guns or explosives, we accept a large percentage of false positives in order to keep the false negatives extremely low. The weight to be given to false positives and false negatives in screening offenders for risk of future criminality will usually fall somewhere between these two extremes and will depend on the consequences of each type of mistake to the subject and the community. Assigning high-risk juveniles to a program that was very effective in reducing later delinquency might be justified in some instances, while assignment to programs of more limited effectiveness would not. Other measures of predictive accuracy are available, and their use can lead to conclusions far different from Shannon's. An article by Loeber and Dishion (1983), for example, applied an analysis called "random improvement over chance" to the Farrington data in table 2 and concluded that it yielded a substantial improvement over chance.

Regardless of which statistical measures we use to describe the accuracy of a prediction scale, its true value can be known only by determining how it performs its intended purpose. No one has ever suggested doing anything special to juveniles, in order to reduce the level of adult crime, on the basis of only one arrest or conviction. A more realistic evaluation of predictive capability is provided by data developed by Farrington (1983) in attempting to predict the chronic offenders in his sample.

His sample of 411 subjects contains twenty-three (5.5 percent) who experienced six or more convictions prior to their twenty-fifth birthdays. These "chronics" accounted for half of all the convictions experienced by the sample and, presumably, for at least half of all the crimes. If chronics have lower probabilities of arrests than have other offenders, a conclusion suggested by Rand's Inmate Survey data,[3] then chronics would account for an even higher percentage of crimes than indicated by the percentage of arrests or convictions that they account for.

Farrington attempted to predict the chronics at age thirteen on the basis of data collected earlier, whether or not they had yet been convicted. The scale predicts accurately in 95 percent (92 + 3) of the cases.

[3] Analyses of inmate self-reported offense data show that age of onset and extent of delinquency, both predictors of subsequent offending, are also predictive of high rates of offending (Chaiken and Chaiken 1982; Greenwood and Abrahamse 1982). Analyses of individual probabilities of arrest, computed by dividing either self-reported or recorded arrests by self-reported offenses, show that high-rate offenders are on the average less likely to be arrested for any one offense, compared to low-rate offenders (Greenwood and Turner 1986).

It divides the sample into two groups, one (predicted no) containing 2.6 percent chronics and the other (predicted yes) containing 55 percent chronics. By focusing on 5.5 percent of the sample, or about 20 percent of those with juvenile records, Farrington has identified more than half (55 percent) of his chronics. The predicted yes group would then presumably be responsible for at least 25 percent of all future crimes attributable to that sample. If some of the false positives include offenders who continued to commit crimes but who were not chronic, then the percentage of crime attributable to this group is even higher than 25 percent.

No mathematical formula can be selected as the appropriate guide for criminal justice policy. The degree of predictive accuracy required to justify policy consequences must depend on a weighing of values as well as a weighing of probabilities. At the same time, the potentially harsh consequences of predictions should not lead to statistical hyperbole in describing basic patterns of statistical regularity. It is preferable to separate the empirical and value decisions in research than to merge them prematurely.

In summary, a fairly clear statistical picture of the connection between juvenile and adult crime emerges from these figures, and it holds up over vastly different populations and using different research methods. Most individuals who are arrested as juveniles (under age eighteen) will not be arrested as adults; and a large fraction of adults arrested may never have been arrested as juveniles. However, those individuals who are arrested as juveniles are three to four times more likely to be arrested as adults than are those who are not arrested as juveniles. Juvenile record is predictive of adult crime, but, of course, having a juvenile record does not predestine one to commit crimes as an adult.

Lowering the age that defines the transition from juvenile to adult status probably increases the strength of the apparent relation between juvenile and adult careers. This is because prevalence rates peak somewhat before the eighteenth birthday and because early arrests or convictions are more predictive of sustained criminality than are later ones. A higher proportion of those convicted before age sixteen will still be active as seventeen-year-olds than will be the proportion of those convicted prior to age eighteen who are still active at nineteen. The proportion of those arrested prior to age twenty-one who are still active at twenty-two would be lower still.

Restricting attention to those individuals with the more frequent or serious juvenile contacts (i.e., convictions rather than arrests, arrests for felonies rather than "any crime," or at least three arrests) also increases the strength of the apparent relation between juvenile and adult crime.

C. System Capacity to Identify Serious Career Prospects
When They Are Young

The issue addressed in this section is the degree to which these future chronic or high-rate offenders can be identified at a young age, before their criminal activity has reached its peak.

Much, if not all, recent longitudinal study and research concerning criminal careers has been justified in part on the notion that the early prediction of chronic offenders will allow the system to do "something" that it would not be able to do in the absence of this predictive capacity. That something, depending on the philosophy of the researcher and the nature of the predictor variable being used, ranges from early prevention (day care, parent training), to heavy investment in treatment programs that focus on specific correlates of crime (drug or alcohol abuse), to selective incapacitation. Many negative reactions to the use of predictions are actually negative reactions to specific forms of intervention that a predictive capability might justify or imply.

The same longitudinal studies that provide information on the links between juvenile and adult criminality also provide the best data for prediction modeling. These studies are summarized in recent articles by Farrington (1979) and Loeber and Dishion (1983). Other sources of data for exploring predictive relations are provided by studies assembling retrospective longitudinal information on samples of active offenders (Greenwood and Abrahamse 1982) or matched delinquent and nondelinquent groups (Glueck and Glueck 1950).

D. Types of Variables Predicting Chronic Delinquency

The different types of factors that have been shown to be associated with excessive criminal behavior can be grouped into five broad categories, reflecting different levels of causation and generally coming into ascendancy for prediction purposes at different stages in the criminal career.

1. *Prior Criminal Record.* A juvenile with four prior arrests is much more likely to commit further crimes than is any juvenile of the same age with fewer arrests no matter how they may differ in other characteristics. The best predictor of immediate future behavior is immediate past behavior (Monahan 1981). By the time juveniles have reached the age of fourteen or fifteen, their official records, including drug use and

type of crimes committed, have become the best predictor of their subsequent behavior.

In their study of males born in Philadelphia in 1945, Wolfgang et al. (1972) showed that the probability that any one boy would be arrested prior to his eighteenth birthday was .35; the probability of a subsequent arrest increased with each prior arrest up to about five prior arrests, where it leveled off at .72. Prior arrest types had very little power to predict subsequent arrest types. The earlier a juvenile's first arrest and the more serious the crime types with which he was charged, the greater the likelihood he will become a chronic offender.

Shannon's (1981) cohort studies in Racine, Wisconsin, also show a strong correlation between juvenile arrests and adult crime, but his samples do not contain a significant number of serious chronic offenders.

In Farrington's (1983) study of 411 males from working-class families in London, "number of juvenile convictions" and whether a juvenile was convicted prior to age thirteen were both strongly predictive of later adult convictions. Out of twenty-nine individuals with four or more adult convictions, ten had four or more juvenile convictions (77 percent of those with four or more juvenile convictions), and six had at least two juvenile convictions (29 percent of those with at least two juvenile convictions). Only 2 percent of those with no juvenile convictions experienced four or more convictions as an adult.

Knight and West (1975) found that youths who committed crimes alone were more likely to become chronic offenders. Greenwood and Abrahamse (1982) showed that prior convictions for robbery or burglary increased the likelihood that a defendant convicted of those crimes did them at a high rate.

Among juveniles and young men admitted to the California Youth Authority in 1975, the probability of parole failure increased with the number of prior commitments, from 29 percent for those with no prior commitments to 80 percent for those with three or more commitments (Greenwood et al. 1983).

Among prison and jail inmates in California, Michigan, and Texas, "conviction prior to age sixteen" and "commitment to a state juvenile facility" were both found to be predictive of high-rate adult offending (Greenwood and Abrahamse 1982).

The obvious problem with using only arrest records to predict chronic delinquency is that the chronicity is already well established by the time the youth is identified, making any treatment efforts that much harder and eliminating the possibility of preventing many of his crimes.

2. *Predelinquent Behavior.*   At a somewhat younger age, say, between the ages of eight and fourteen, lying, stealing, or excessively aggressive or passive behavior are among the best predictors of subsequent criminal activity. Other signs include poor academic achievement and poor verbal ability. At the youngest age level these children are simply labeled as troublesome or antisocial by their teachers or parents, and they usually do not get along with other children.

Delinquent children do not materialize out of thin air; neither do very good children suddenly become very bad. The onset of chronic delinquency, like the development of most other behavior patterns, appears to be a gradual process. A number of studies have shown that predelinquent problem behaviors in children between the ages of six and twelve are predictive of later delinquency.

Specific problem behaviors that tend to be correlated with later delinquency include being daring or disobedient, stealing, lying, truancy before age twelve, wandering, and excessive aggressiveness (Loeber and Dishion 1983). For older children predelinquent behavior can include heavy drinking and smoking, drug use, promiscuous sex, and fighting (Osborne and West 1978). Robins (1966) found that adult sociopaths were likely to have engaged in incorrigible behavior, running away, promiscuous sex, and theft. This problem behavior often started as early as age seven. Most studies also find that low academic achievement and poor verbal skills are associated with later delinquency.

3. *Family Functioning.*   A third category of predictor variables is associated with the child-rearing practices of the parents. Lack of affection, failure to monitor or discipline antisocial behavior, or physical abuse are all associated with later criminal behavior.

Inadequate or incompetent parenting has been known for some time to be associated with later delinquency. Fifty years ago Glueck and Glueck (1930) cited poor supervision and lack of affection or family cohesiveness as strong predictors of delinquency. McCord, McCord, and Howard (1963) found that aggressive, antisocial men were likely to have experienced family discord, neglect, and parental attacks when they were boys. In the Cambridge study, Farrington (1983) also found poor child-rearing practices to be associated with delinquency.

As with any other variable that is correlated with delinquency, it is difficult to know whether certain child-rearing practices simply happen to be found in families that also produce delinquents or whether the practices themselves cause delinquency. One promising contribution in this area has been the development of procedures for teaching parents improved child-rearing practices and the conduct of subsequent evaluations that show that adoption of these procedures does substantially reduce antisocial behavior (Patterson, Chamberlain, and Reid 1982).

4. *Family Characteristics.* The fourth category has to do with the characteristics of the individual's parents and other family members. Parents with criminal records, low social class, psychotic mothers, and alcoholic fathers are all more likely to have delinquent children. The number of siblings and the criminal record of siblings is also predictive of subsequent crimes.

Certain categories of families can be predicted to produce children with higher rates of delinquency even before anything about the child is known. Income and social class are clearly related, as is the size of the family (Farrington and West 1971; Wolfgang et al. 1972), the criminal record of the family members (particularly the father and siblings), and the mental health of the mother (Robins 1966; Knight and West 1975). In this country, race is clearly associated with risk of delinquency, with black males facing a risk of arrest for serious crime five to ten times higher than whites (Blumstein and Graddy 1982; Greenwood et al. 1983).

The most logical interpretation of the data concerning the relation between family characteristics and the delinquency of the children is that family characteristics affect family functioning. Poor parents and parents of large families are likely to have less time to devote to supervising any one child. They are also likely to be less well trained in how to do it. Antisocial fathers and psychotic mothers are also less likely to be warm, affectionate, patient, loving, effective parents.

5. *Physical Characteristics.* Physical characteristics are correlated with criminal behavior and may be linked in a causal way. They include slow autonomic nervous systems, higher than normal alpha in EEG readings, left-handedness, low IQ, psychomotor clumsiness, and minor birth defects. While these physical characteristics probably do not cause criminal behavior directly, they may lead to criminal behavior by acting as a handicap or by interfering with normal socialization or child-rearing processes; or they may be indicators of more serious neurological damage. For reviews of research on biology and crime, see Mednick and Volavka (1980), Freier (1985), and Wilson and Herrnstein (1985).

E. The Bottom Line

Merely knowing that variables are related to future criminality is not enough. We need to know how these different classes of variables would perform when combined. That information comes from analyses performed by Farrington (1983), using the Cambridge data, and Ratcliff and Robins (1979), using data on a cohort of 233 black males who grew up in St. Louis.

In the Farrington study, twenty-three out of 411 male subjects had been convicted six or more times by their twenty-fifth birthday. Farrington calls these his chronics. They accounted for half of all convictions for the entire sample, and all twenty-three were first convicted as juveniles. Farrington developed a "Burgess Scale,"[4] consisting of seven factors, all equally weighted, in order to see how accurately the chronics could be identified. The seven factors were rated troublesomeness by teachers at ages eight to ten, conduct disorder, acting out, social handicap, criminal parents, poor potential child-rearing practices, and low IQ. Applying this scale to all 411 boys at age thirteen, fifty-five boys scored four or higher. These fifty-five included fifteen of the twenty-three chronics, twenty-two others who were convicted at least once, and eighteen who were never convicted.

Limiting the prediction sample to only those boys who were convicted as youths and using the variables shown in table 3 in a logistic regression model, Farrington obtained the following results. Of the seventeen youths with the highest predicted probability of becoming chronic, fourteen were chronics. Lowering the threshold to predict twenty-three chronics (the same number as there actually were) still only identified fourteen true chronics. Of the thirty-four youths first convicted before age thirteen, fourteen became chronics; thirteen of these were among the fourteen predicted above. Therefore, Farrington points out that the addition of elementary school variables to indicators of early criminal behavior can greatly improve the accuracy with which chronics are predicted.

The Ratcliff and Robins (1979) study did not focus exclusively on criminal behavior as the dependent variable but used instead a number of measures of adult antisocial behavior (the number of behaviors was counted) as determined by two psychiatrists. They were marital trouble, financial dependency, poor work history, alcohol problems, drug problems, multiple arrests or felony conviction, impulsivity, vagrancy,

---

[4] Burgess scales, unlike regression or discriminate analysis, are less susceptible to shrinkage in cross-validation (Loeber and Dishion 1983).

TABLE 3

Prediction Variable	Age When Measured
Convicted	10–13
Low family income	8
Troublesome	8–10
Poor junior attainment	10
Psychomotor clumsiness	8–10
Low nonverbal IQ	8–10
Convicted sibling	10
Catholic family	. . .

physical aggression, and deviant life-style. Individuals with four or more of these characteristics as adults were rated highly antisocial.

Nine different behaviors were measured during each subject's childhood. These were arrests, incarceration, truancy, drinking, alcohol problems, sexual intercourse, marriage, drug use, and having delinquent friends. Children were defined as highly antisocial if they exhibited at least three of these factors or if they used drugs before age fifteen.

Analysis of the relationship between childhood and adult behavior was asserted to show the following. (1) Serious antisocial behavior in adults rarely occurs in the absence of high levels of childhood antisocial behavior—70 percent of highly antisocial adults were highly antisocial children. (2) Only about half of very antisocial children become antisocial adults. (3) The number of antisocial behaviors in childhood is the best indicator of severe antisocial behavior in adults. (4) Among mildly antisocial children, having an antisocial father is the best predictor of severe antisocial behavior in adulthood. (5) Social class or rearing is not an important predictor of severely antisocial behavior in adults. (6) Three family background characteristics make a substantial contribution to identifying which highly antisocial children will become highly antisocial adults: (a) being placed away from both parents; (b) severe poverty; and (c) having few childhood years with parents of both sexes in the home. Their predictive efficiency is shown in table 4. Eighty-nine percent of highly antisocial children with all three adverse family variables became highly antisocial adults. Only 15 percent of highly antisocial children with none of the adverse family variables become highly antisocial adults. (7) Illicit drug use after the late teens had very little predictive power.

The predictive accuracy achieved by Farrington for juvenile offenders at age thirteen is consistent with that found in other studies that

TABLE 4

Number of Family Variables as a Predictor of Highly Antisocial Adult Behavior among Highly Antisocial Children

No. of Family Variables That Apply	Those Who Become Highly Antisocial Adults		Percent of Highly Antisocial Adults (53) Identified	Percent of Whole Sample Selected (223)
	No.	Percent		
3	7	89	12	3
2 or more	39	66	50	18
1 or more	64	52	63	29
None	23	15	7	11
All antisocial children	88	42	70	39

SOURCE.—Ratcliff and Robins (1979).
NOTE.—Variables are being placed away from natural parents, severe poverty, and missing parent.

have attempted to predict high-rate or chronic offenders (Chaiken and Chaiken 1982; Monahan, Brodsky, and Shah 1982) and appears to be near the maximum we can expect.[5] Without these early childhood factors that Farrington used in his prediction scale, attempts to predict chronic offenders would be even less accurate or would have to wait until more of a criminal record had been accumulated.

Is the degree of accuracy achieved by Farrington a sufficient basis for treating some juveniles differently from others even though the number of times they have been convicted may be similar? This is where the concept of bringing just deserts into juvenile court runs headlong into the traditional approach of providing treatment according to needs. If the use of predictions allows the low-risk juvenile to avoid any punishment or treatment while the high-risk juvenile is removed from his home or is required to participate in an extensive treatment program, then this difference in dispositional severity may be difficult to sustain. If, however, both youths were required to participate in some type of programming, the predictive factors might be more easily justified in determining the type of program to which each should be assigned. The low-risk youth might be assigned to community service. The high-risk youth might be assigned to a more structured and highly supervised program that would address his behavioral problems or skill deficits through counseling, skill training, or other techniques.

[5] See Gottfredson and Gottfredson (1986) for a recent review of the criminal career prediction literature.

The window of opportunity for dealing with serious delinquent behavior is only about five years in length, extending from the thirteenth to the eighteenth birthday. We cannot afford, nor is it productive in most cases, to make much of a response in the first one or two instances that a juvenile may be arrested. However, waiting for chronic offenders to build up a record of many arrests and minor dispositions only compounds the problems that must be dealt with later.

In summary, chronic offenders can usually be identified solely on the basis of their juvenile records. However, this evidence normally does not accumulate until after the youth's sixteenth birthday. If additional factors describing the youth's school performance and home situation are included, the age at which chronics can be predicted can be moved up several years, possibly to the thirteenth birthday. This earlier identification might facilitate more productive programming, but it also runs the risk of treating some juveniles who would have desisted on their own. There is little evidence on the effects of different policies in this area. The balance we strike must depend on the nature of the interventions imposed and the effects they achieve.

III. A Comparison of Disposition Patterns in Criminal and Juvenile Courts

Why would youthful chronic offenders be treated too leniently in juvenile and criminal courts? At least seven reasons are frequently cited.

The first is the "least restrictive alternative" and "best interests of the minor" language embodied in juvenile court law and juvenile justice standards. This language sounds as if the court is bound to put the interests of the child ahead of the community interest in protection from crime.

A second reason is the availability of diversion as an informal disposition. In most jurisdictions the police take juveniles to the probation department, which conducts its own investigation of the matter, including the juvenile's social history. Probation then decides which cases to handle informally and refers the others to the prosecutor. This process must result in lesser sanctions for some chronic offenders than if cases were taken to the prosecutor in the first instance.

A third reason is the heavy emphasis that has been placed on deinstitutionalization and diversion in the past few years. Surely, these efforts have resulted in many chronic offenders being placed, perhaps inappropriately, in community or other nonrestrictive placements.

The fourth reason is provided by aggregate statistics on the disposition of juvenile arrests. More than 80 percent of juvenile arrests do not result in a sustained petition; most are settled without a court hearing; fewer than 5 percent result in confinement of any type (Greenwood et al. 1983).

The reasons for expecting undue leniency toward young offenders in criminal courts are somewhat different. First, there is the issue of records. We know that access to juvenile records is somewhat restricted under the premise that juvenile offenders should be allowed to put their past misdeeds behind them. These restrictions on juvenile records, when combined with the natural clutter and confusion of the criminal courts, must result in many former chronic juvenile offenders being misidentified as adult "first offenders."

Another reason for expecting leniency in criminal courts involves assumptions about career criminal prosecution (CCP) programs for older adult offenders. Career criminal prosecution is designed to ensure that career criminals, who are by definition older chronic offenders, experience high convictions rates and long periods of incarceration. It might be assumed that younger chronic offenders, who do not fall within the formal definition of career criminals used to select the targets for CCP, must therefore receive lighter sentences. Career criminal prosecution would not have been necessary if chronic offenders were receiving appropriate sentences without it. Therefore, the chronics who are excluded as targets of the program because their juvenile records cannot be considered must still be getting lenient sentences (Boland and Wilson 1978; Greenwood et al. 1980).

Finally, for many people who still believe in special deterrence and rehabilitation, the clearest evidence of undue leniency is found in the records of almost all chronic offenders. When they observe repeated instances of diversion, dismissals, or lenient sentences, they find it difficult not to conclude that the system "spared the rod and spoiled the child." Virtually every chronic offender's record is a Monday morning indictment of last Saturday's game plan. All the breaks granted in "the best interests of the minor" come back to haunt us if the minor does not straighten out. Of course, one of the reasons that the evidence provided by these false negatives is so persuasive is that the records of those who did straighten out are sealed from our view.

A. Juvenile Records in Criminal Courts

Prior to 1979 there had been no studies of how juvenile records were used in criminal courts or how youthful chronic offenders were sentenced relative to older offenders. Debates prior to that time were based on speculations or anecdotal information (Boland and Wilson 1978; Twentieth Century Fund 1978). Information on juvenile records was first provided by a national survey of prosecutors that was conducted by Greenwood et al. (1980). The survey was mailed to the two largest prosecutors' offices in all fifty states and to the three largest offices in the ten most populous states, and 66 percent responded.

The general pattern that was disclosed was one of individual initiative. Few jurisdictions routinely denied or provided for access to the juvenile records of adult criminal defendants. The retrieval and documentation of juvenile records was left to the discretion of individual investigators and prosecutors.

Although almost every state has some statutory requirements for maintaining the confidentiality of juvenile records, these statutes are generally aimed at preventing public disclosure, not the sharing of records among criminal justice agencies. Criminal justice agencies may be specifically exempted from the confidentiality requirement of the statute, or the statute may allow the sharing of information under circumstances to be governed by orders from the juvenile court.

Most states also have statutes providing for the destruction of juvenile records (usually on the motion of the former delinquent) after a specified number of years have elapsed without further convictions. However, such statutes appear to pose few constraints on the identification of chronic offenders, who would seldom qualify for such expungement because of their continuing involvement in crime. Attempts to trace the records of individuals three or four years beyond the maximum age jurisdiction of the juvenile court suggest that the wholesale purging of records, as a cost-saving measure, may be a more severe limitation on the identification of chronic offenders than are these formal expungement provisions (Greenwood et al. 1980). However, even here, the percentage of chronic offenders who would be affected is probably small because their juvenile records will be permanently recorded in subsequent adult presentence reports.

A prosecutor's first opportunity to learn about a criminal defendant's record occurs when the police bring in the case for filing. The difference between the treatment of juvenile and adult records is striking. Seventy-four percent of prosecutors responded that adult criminal records were always or usually provided at the time of filing, compared with 20 percent who reported that juvenile records were usually provided. Sixty percent of the prosecutors responded that juvenile records were provided rarely or never at the time of filing.

Even if the local police department provides its record of juvenile arrests, that record is not likely to be comprehensive. Eighty percent of prosecutors reported that the juvenile information provided by the police is local only and does not include contacts in other cities.

Fewer than 20 percent of the responding prosecutors indicated that their offices consistently attempted to obtain juvenile record information beyond that provided by the police. Those who sought out additional information were more likely to have been those who were provided with better juvenile record information initially. Seventy-five percent of the responding prosecutors always or usually sought additional adult criminal history information over and above that provided by the police. Any comparison between the quality or completeness of juvenile and adult record systems invariably favors the adult system.

Of course, the amount of information collected on any one individual can continue to grow throughout a case. Even if juvenile record information is provided only at the sentencing hearing, it can still have substantial effect. Only 23 percent of the prosecutors responded that the criminal court would be unaware of a convicted felon's juvenile record at the time of sentencing; another 45 percent indicated that they would expect to know such information by the time of any potential pretrial settlement.

The prosecutors were also fairly optimistic about the effect that juvenile records would have. More than 60 percent believed that they would affect the defendant's chances for diversion or dismissal. Sixty-three percent thought that access to records would affect the kind of plea bargain the defendant was offered.

B. Defining Relative Severity

How do we know when sentences are too lenient or too harsh? The only valid standard of comparison is with other types of offenders in the same jurisdiction. Concerns about undue leniency focus on two categories of offenders: (1) older chronic juvenile offenders who are still within the jurisdiction of the juvenile court and (2) young adults who were chronic offenders as juveniles. These two groups can be compared with two different sets of offenders who are charged with similar crimes to assess sentencing severity. The first comparison is with other offenders of the same age but with less serious prior records. The second comparison is with offenders with similar prior records who are between the ages of twenty-one and twenty-five. This latter group is well beyond the juvenile court, and chronic offenders have had at least three years to build up an adult record. None of the reasons advanced at the beginning of this section to explain leniency for young offenders should apply to this group.

C. The Effect of Juvenile Records on Criminal Court Dispositions

At the time of the prosecutors survey, there were no data sets available that would have permitted an examination of how young adults with chronic juvenile records were sentenced in comparison with less serious peers. The several cohort studies (Wolfgang et al. 1972; Farrington and West 1981; Shannon 1981) that contain accurate juvenile record data for adult offenders contain too few adult felony convictions to permit statistical comparisons.

In order to investigate the potential effect of juvenile records on criminal court dispositions, Greenwood, Abrahamse, and Zimring (1984) collected and analyzed case records from three jurisdictions selected to represent a range of information-sharing practices. The three jurisdictions were as follows.

Las Vegas represents a frequently occurring low-information-sharing situation[6] in which information about a young adult defendant's prior juvenile record is not disclosed to the prosecutor or the court until it is presented in the presentence investigative report following conviction.

Los Angeles represents a frequently occurring high-information-sharing situation in which there are no limitations on access to juvenile records by criminal court personnel. In Los Angeles, police investigators frequently include juvenile sheets as part of the arrest package that is turned over to the prosecutor at the time of filing. Juvenile records are routinely included in presentence investigative reports.

Seattle represents a less frequent complete-information-sharing situation in which the county prosecutor maintained a complete criminal history record on every defendant handled by his office, both juvenile and adult.

In all three sites the juvenile records available to the courts consisted of the charged offenses for arrests in that jurisdiction and their disposition. Presentence investigation reports frequently contained a brief de-

---

[6] All three of the jurisdictions are in states where the eighteenth birthday marks the upper boundary on the jurisdiction of the juvenile court. Most of the sites that reported the absence of any information sharing were in much less populated areas or states in which the jurisdiction of the juvenile court terminated at a younger age.

scription of the more serious offenses and the defendant's alleged role in them. Records available to prosecutors in Los Angeles and Seattle at early stages in the proceedings frequently did not contain disposition data. The case samples selected in each site consisted of young men between the ages of eighteen and twenty who were arrested for armed robbery or residential burglary. The information coded included characteristics of the offense (type of premises, weapons used, number of victims, etc.), the defendant's juvenile and adult criminal record as reflected in law enforcement records, and the disposition of the case. In Los Angeles and Las Vegas, the samples also included juveniles between the ages of sixteen and seventeen and older adults twenty-one to twenty-five.

In all three sites, lengthy juvenile records were associated with harsher sentences for some types of cases. Sentence severity was also affected by the presence of a gun or a prior adult arrest for a crime against the person. The number of prior adult arrests did not appear to make a difference.

In Los Angeles, a lengthy juvenile record, use of a gun, or a prior adult arrest for a crime of violence all had a substantial effect on the likelihood that armed robbers would be incarcerated or committed to state terms in either the Youth Authority or the Department of Corrections. These same factors had no apparent effect on the disposition of young adult burglars. In Las Vegas, only the presence of several of these aggravating factors, including juvenile records, was associated with higher conviction and incarceration rates for armed robbers, but the presence of any one factor increased the likelihood of incarceration or state commitments for burglars. In Seattle, the number of prior juvenile petitions did not appear to affect the probability of conviction or incarceration. The only effect of a record of prior petitions was to increase the likelihood that an incarcerative term would be served in state prison.

D. Sanctions for Young Adults Compared with Juveniles and Older Adults

When the sentencing of young adults (eighteen to twenty) in Los Angeles and Las Vegas was compared with that for juveniles (sixteen to seventeen) or older adults (twenty-one to twenty-five) it was found that young adults were generally sentenced as harshly as was any other age group. Figures 1–4 display the disposition patterns for each of the two offense types in these two sites. In both sites, juveniles with extensive records are incarcerated or sentenced to state facilities about as often as are the more serious young adults.

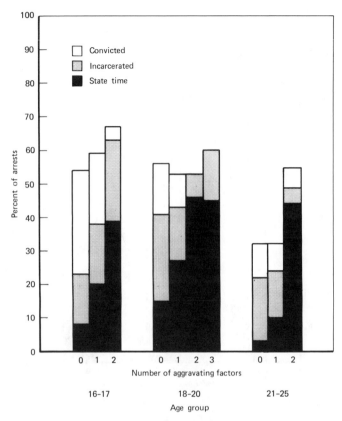

FIG. 1.—Disposition of Los Angeles robbers: All ages

This analysis leads to several conclusions about factors affecting the severity of dispositions for older juveniles and young adult defendants. First, in the two jurisdictions where data are available to make the appropriate comparisons, young adults were convicted and incarcerated as frequently as was any other age group for some categories of offenses, even without attempting to control on aggravating factors. When we control on offense severity and prior record, young adults are frequently sentenced more harshly than are other age groups.

Note, however, that this analysis deals only with convictions and commitments, not with time served. It may well be that those young adults who are incarcerated serve shorter average terms than do older inmates convicted of similar crimes. In California this is certainly the case for that substantial fraction of young men between the ages of eighteen and twenty who are sentenced to the Youth Authority instead of to state prison. But even here, the percentage of young adults who

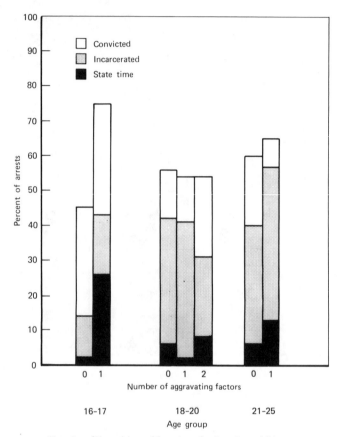

FIG. 2.—Disposition of Los Angeles burglars: All ages

receive Youth Authority commitments has declined considerably in the last few years.

The second point is that the availability of juvenile or adult records does not guarantee that they will have an effect. If there is a very strong predisposition for or against incarceration for a particular type of offense, then prior record will not exert much influence. It is principally in those types of cases in which the decision can go either way that prior records may have a pronounced effect.

These data also suggest that the effects of juvenile records are not all in one direction. A reliable juvenile record index can be used to rebut a presumption of chronic criminality as well as to identify chronic offenders. This is evident in the relative leniency with which Seattle treats its young adult burglars who do not have extensive prior records.

A final point concerns the question of what juvenile record informa-

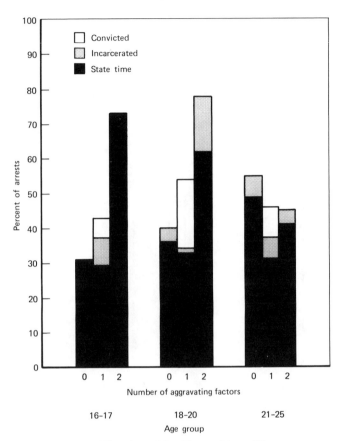

FIG. 3.—Dispositon of Las Vegas robbers: All ages

tion should be shared with criminal courts. In Los Angeles and many other counties, adult felony presentence reports routinely contain allegations associated with many arrests for which no petition was ever filed or sustained. In fact, a majority of juvenile arrests do not result in any "findings" in court. Nevertheless, these alleged charges are currently reviewed and summarized as descriptive of an individual's involvement in juvenile crime. When and how it is appropriate to use these unsubstantiated allegations are key issues confronting those concerned with the use of juvenile records in adult courts.

E. The Disposition of Delinquency Cases in Juvenile Court

The juvenile court process can be distinguished from the criminal court process by its speed and informality. The options available for

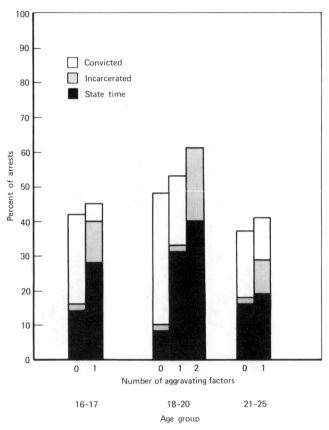

FIG. 4.—Disposition of Las Vegas burglars: All ages

handling any particular delinquency case are also wider, ranging from counseling and release by the arresting officer, through diversion to community programs by the police or probation, to placement in group homes or secure institutions under orders from the court. Under specified conditions, the more serious juvenile offenders can be remanded to the criminal court if found not to be amenable to treatment by juvenile court programs.

In theory, the disposition of juvenile adjudication should be based on a comprehensive assessment of the juvenile's needs and background. The disposition selected should be the least restrictive alternative consistent with the needs of the minor and the protection of the public. In practice, the pattern of dispositions appears to follow a "just deserts" model, with longer placements associated with more serious offenses or longer prior records.

An analysis of disposition patterns in California suggests that the juvenile system in that state is becoming increasingly punitive, particularly for the more serious offenders (Greenwood et al. 1983). Between 1978 and 1981, the number of juveniles placed in secure county facilities jumped by 23 percent, while California Youth Authority placements increased by more than 10 percent. At the same time, arrest rates for most crime categories were either leveling off or declining.

Because of their volume, minor nature, and the supporting theory that formal intervention is often counterproductive, most juvenile arrests do not result in a formal court hearing. In the California study more than 60 percent were handled by informal counseling or referral to other agencies. Juvenile arrests for more serious crimes such as burglary or robbery were filed and settled in court about as often as were adult arrests. At the upper limits of offense and prior record severity, juveniles were sentenced to secure institutions about as frequently as were young adults with comparable records, although they did not serve as long on any given commitment (Greenwood et al. 1983). The effects of either offense or prior record severity on sanction severity were large.

F. Juveniles in Adult Court

Every state has a least one method for removing specific types of juvenile offenders from juvenile courts and trying them as adults, although there are considerable differences in how waiver laws operate and how often they are used. In 1978, over 9,000 juveniles were waived to adult courts, 2,000 were prosecuted as adults because of concurrent jurisdiction, and over 250,000 sixteen- and seventeen-year-olds were prosecuted as adults in the twelve states in which the maximum age jurisdiction of the juvenile court is lower than the eighteenth birthday (Hamparian et al. 1982).

The primary motivation for transferring juveniles to criminal courts is to increase the severity of the sentences to which they can be subjected. However, this harsher treatment is not always imposed. An analysis of a nationally representative sample of cases that had been waived to adult court revealed that, while 91 percent of those waived were convicted, less than half of those convicted were sentenced to confinement. Among those confined, 40 percent had maximum sentences of less than one year. Therefore, in at least three-quarters of those cases in which waiver provisions were invoked, the juvenile was sentenced to a term that was no more severe than the juvenile court could have imposed (Hamparian et al. 1982).

IV. Concluding Thoughts

This essay has reviewed evidence concerning the connections between juvenile and adult criminal careers and how knowledge about these connections is reflected in court disposition policies. Arrest data show that the peak ages of criminality lie between the sixteenth and the twentieth birthdays, with crime rates falling off rapidly for older age groups. Because of this age distribution pattern, young men under the age of twenty-one account for approximately half of all serious felony arrests. While these arrest figures tend to inflate the relative contribution of younger offenders to overall crime rates because their crimes tend to be somewhat less serious and to be committed in groups, they demonstrate the importance of dealing with this age group in any policy initiative designed to increase public safety.

There is a clear connection between juvenile criminal activity and adult criminal careers. Chronic juvenile offenders have a high probability of continuing their involvement in crime as adults, whereas those juveniles who are never arrested are unlikely to develop criminal careers as adults. Our ability to identify potential chronic offenders at an early age, when they first begin to appear in the juvenile justice system, can be improved by using measures of school performance and family characteristics as additional predictor variables.

Analyses of court disposition patterns reveal that, in all the jurisdictions considered, prior juvenile record severity was associated with harsher dispositions for at least some categories of offenses, for both juveniles and young adults. One recurring problem in the way that juvenile records tend to be used is that judgments about the extensiveness of an offender's prior juvenile record frequently are based on a summary of all recorded arrests, without regard for their ultimate disposition, because the majority of juvenile arrests are settled without formal adjudication.

Increasing knowledge about the connections between juvenile and adult criminality can lead in a number of different policy directions. For those who believe that rehabilitation or primary prevention efforts are futile, this evidence can be used to support demands that chronic offenders be sentenced to longer periods of confinement in order to incapacitate them during their peak years of criminality. If individual crime rates cannot be reduced by rehabilitative programs, this argument will have merit on utilitarian grounds whether or not it can survive challenges on legal or other bases (Moore et al. 1983). However, knowledge about juvenile careers can also be used to justify more vigorous efforts to develop or to identify intervention methods that can reduce subsequent criminality without reliance on long and expensive periods of incarceration.

The major stumbling block that must be dealt with in any discussion of rehabilitative programs is the widespread perception that rehabilitative programs "do not work," an oversimplification and distortion of previous evaluation efforts.

The perception that rehabilitation programs are ineffective is based on certain critical assumptions, namely, that the principal difference that would distinguish successful from unsuccessful programs would be the theories and methods on which the program was based and not the quality of its management or staff, the skill with which it was implemented, or other characteristics of where it takes place (Lipton, Martinson, and Wilks 1975; Sechrest, White, and Brown 1979).

It is not true that no program has ever worked. Some, though not many, programs have been successful in producing lower recidivism rates among their graduates. The problem has been that no particular treatment method has worked consistently, producing lower recidivism rates wherever it is applied.

This finding should not be surprising since it is also true in business management, investment portfolio management, football coaching, teaching, and many other similar fields. What the treatment-evaluation literature suggests is not that nothing works but rather that, in order to find out what programs are working, it is necessary to measure results continuously instead of simply ensuring that the program is following a particular model. The absence of any such performance-measurement effort will probably ensure that rules and practices that promote custodial serenity will win out over more controversial treatment practices whenever these two objectives are in conflict (Greenwood et al. 1983).

When one looks beyond the juvenile court to identify other community agencies that might deal with troublesome but predelinquent youth, the public schools loom large. Only they have the appropriate level of resources, authority, and existing contacts with high-risk juveniles to make any systematic intervention efforts feasible (Greenwood and Zimring 1985). It remains to be seen whether those practices that have been identified in the "safe schools" (Kimbrough 1985) or "effective schools" (Rutter et al. 1979) literature as contributing to improved academic performance of children from poor families will also achieve significant declines in their rate of delinquency. At an even earlier point of intervention, recent results from Headstart evaluations suggest that such early education programs can be effective in reaching high-risk youth, improving their level of school attendance and academic performance, and reducing the frequency with which they are arrested (U.S. Department of Health, Education and Welfare 1978; Berrueta-Clement et al. 1984).

In the final analysis the reduction of chronic criminal behavior by youthful offenders can be approached in two radically different ways. The incapacitation approach accepts criminal behavior as a given and attempts to identify and isolate the most active offenders (Greenwood and Abrahamse 1982). The treatment approach assumes that future behavior can be altered. Both approaches suggest that resources be targeted on youthful chronic offenders because of their disproportionate contribution to the crime problem. The incapacitation approach would spend those resources on secure custody, spreading them out over all the years that the offender could be expected to be active. The treatment approach would concentrate resources on remedial programs at an earlier point in the career in an attempt to avoid the necessity of later incarceration.

A rough analysis of how these two approaches compare as crime reduction strategies suggests that treatment programs must achieve something like a 30 percent reduction in average individual offense rates in order to be as cost-effective as selective incapacitation in reducing the future crimes of chronic youthful offenders (Greenwood and Zimring 1985; Rydell 1985). Given the underlying factors that appear causally related to chronic offending, it would seem that vigorous efforts to identify and support effective early intervention and treatment programs can be justified on both moral and utilitarian grounds. Problematic as they may be, early intervention programs offer one of the primary means of easing our continued reliance on long-term imprisonment—and the growing prison population it generates—as our primary crime control strategy.

REFERENCES

Berrueta-Clement, John R., Lawrence J. Schweinhart, W. Steven Barnett, Ann S. Epstein, and David P. Weikhard. 1984. *Changed Lives: The Effects of the Perry Preschool Program on Youths through Age 19*. Ypsilanti, Mich.: High/ Scope.

Blumstein, Alfred, and Elizabeth Graddy. 1982. "Prevalence and Recidivism in Index Arrests: A Feedback Model Approach." *Law and Society Review* 16(2):265–90.

Boland, Barbara, and James Q. Wilson. 1978. "Age, Crime, and Punishment." *Public Interest* 51:22–34.

Chaiken, Jan M., and Marcia Chaiken. 1982. *Varieties of Criminal Behavior.* Santa Monica, Calif.: Rand.

Cook, Philip J. 1983. *Robbery in the United States: An Analysis of Recent Trends and Patterns.* Working paper. Durham, N.C.: Duke University, Institute of Policy Sciences and Public Affairs.

Farrington, David P. 1979. "Longitudinal Research on Crime and Delinquency." In *Crime and Justice: An Annual Review of Research*, vol. 1, edited by Norval Morris and Michael Tonry. Chicago: University of Chicago Press.

———. 1983. *Further Analyses of a Longitudinal Survey of Crime and Delinquency.* Cambridge: Cambridge University, Institute of Criminology.

Farrington, D. P., and D. J. West. 1971. "A Comparison between Early Delinquents and Young Aggressives." *British Journal of Criminology* 11:341–58.

———. 1977. *The Cambridge Study in Delinquency Development.* Cambridge: Cambridge University, Institute of Criminology.

———. 1981. "The Cambridge Study in Delinquent Development (United Kingdom)." In *Prospective Longitudinal Research: An Empirical Basis for Primary Prevention of Psychosocial Disorders*, edited by S. A. Mednick and A. E. Baert. New York: Oxford University Press.

Freier, Michelle. 1985. "The Biological Bases of Criminal Behavior." In *The Juvenile Rehabilitation Reader*, edited by Peter W. Greenwood. Santa Monica, Calif.: Rand.

Glueck, Sheldon, and Eleanor T. Glueck. 1930. *500 Criminal Careers.* New York: Knopf.

———. 1950. *Unraveling Juvenile Delinquency.* New York: Commonwealth Fund.

Gottfredson, Stephen D., and D. M. Gottfredson. 1986. "Accuracy of Prediction Models." In *Criminal Careers and Career Criminals*, edited by Alfred Blumstein, Jacqueline Cohen, J. Roth, and C. Visher. Washington, D.C.: National Academy of Sciences.

Greenwood, Peter W., with Allan Abrahamse. 1982. *Selective Incapacitation.* Santa Monica, Calif.: Rand.

Greenwood, Peter W., Allan Abrahamse, Albert Lipson, and Franklin Zimring. 1983. *Youth Crime and Juvenile Justice in California: A Report to the Legislature.* Santa Monica, Calif.: Rand.

Greenwood, Peter W., Allan Abrahamse, and Franklin Zimring. 1984. *The Role of Juvenile Delinquency Records in Criminal Court Proceedings.* Santa Monica, Calif.: Rand.

Greenwood, Peter W., Joan Petersilia, and Franklin Zimring. 1980. *Age, Crime, and Sanctions: The Transition from Juvenile to Adult Court.* Santa Monica, Calif.: Rand.

Greenwood, Peter W., and Susan Turner. 1986. *The Identification of High-Rate Offenders from Their Criminal Histories.* Santa Monica, Calif.: Rand.

Greenwood, Peter W., and Franklin E. Zimring. 1985. *One More Chance: The Pursuit of Promising Intervention Strategies for Chronic Juvenile Offenders.* Santa Monica, Calif.: Rand.

Hamparian, Donna M., L. Estep, S. Muntean, R. Pristino, R. Swisher, P. Wallace, and J. White. 1982. *Major Issues in Juvenile Justice Information and Training: Youth in Adult Courts: Between Two Worlds.* Washington, D.C.: U.S. Department of Justice, Office of Juvenile Justice and Delinquency.

Hamparian, Donna Martin, Richard Schuster, Simon Dinitz, and John P. Conrad. 1978. *The Violent Few: A Study of Dangerous Juvenile Offenders.* Lexington, Mass.: Lexington Books.

Kimbrough, Jackie. 1985. "School-based Strategies for Delinquency Prevention." In *The Juvenile Rehabilitation Reader,* edited by Peter W. Greenwood. Santa Monica, Calif.: Rand.

Knight, B. J., and D. J. West. 1975. "Temporary and Continuing Delinquency." *British Journal of Criminology* 15:43–50.

Lipton, Douglas, Robert Martinson, and Judith Wilks. 1975. *The Effectiveness of Correctional Treatment: A Survey of Treatment Evaluation Studies.* New York: Praeger.

Loeber, R., and T. Dishion. 1983. "Early Predictors of Male Delinquency: A Review." *Psychological Bulletin* 94(1):68–99.

McCord, J. 1979. "Some Child-rearing Antecedents of Criminal Behavior in Adult Men." *Journal of Personality and Social Psychology* 37:1477–86.

McCord, J., W. McCord, and A. Howard. 1963. "Family Interaction as Antecedent to the Direction of Male Aggressiveness." *Journal of Abnormal and Social Psychology* 66:239–42.

Mednick, Sarnoff A., and Jan Volavka. 1980. "Biology and Crime." In *Crime and Justice: An Annual Review of Research,* vol. 2, edited by Norval Morris and Michael Tonry. Chicago: University of Chicago Press.

Monahan, John. 1981. *The Clinical Prediction of Violent Behavior.* Rockville, Md.: Institute of Mental Health.

Monahan, John, Stanley L. Brodsky, and Saleem A. Shah. 1982. *Predicting Violent Behavior: An Assessment of Clinical Techniques.* Beverly Hills, Calif.: Sage.

Moore, Mark H., Susan Estrich, and Daniel McGillis, with William Spelman. 1983. *Dealing with Dangerous Offenders, Final Report.* Vol. 1. Cambridge, Mass.: Harvard University, John F. Kennedy School of Government.

Osborn, S. G., and D. J. West. 1978. "The Effectiveness of Various Predictors of Criminal Careers." *Journal of Adolescence* 1:101–17.

Patterson, Gerald R., Patricia Chamberlain, and John B. Reid. 1982. "A Comparative Evaluation of a Parent-training Program." *Behavior Therapy* 13:638–50.

Petersilia, Joan. 1980. "Criminal Career Research: A Review of Recent Evidence." In *Crime and Justice: An Annual Review of Research,* vol. 2, edited by Norval Morris and Michael Tonry. Chicago: University of Chicago Press.

Petersilia, Joan, Peter W. Greenwood, and Marvin Lavin. 1977. *Criminal Careers of Habitual Felons.* Santa Monica, Calif.: Rand.

Ratcliff, Katherine S., and Lee N. Robins. 1979. "Risk Factors in the Continuation of Childhood Antisocial Behaviors into Adulthood." *International Journal of Mental Health* 7:96–116.

Robins, L. N. 1966. *Deviant Children Grown Up*. Baltimore: Williams & Williams.

Rutter, Michael, Barbara Maughan, Peter Mortimore, and Janet Ouston, with Alan Smith. 1979. *Fifteen Thousand Hours*. Cambridge, Mass.: Harvard University Press.

Rydell, Peter. 1985. "The Economics of Early Intervention vs. Later Incarceration." In *The Juvenile Rehabilitation Reader*, edited by Peter W. Greenwood. Santa Monica, Calif.: Rand.

Sechrest, Lee, Susan O. White, and Elizabeth D. Brown, eds. 1979. *The Rehabilitation of Criminal Offenders: Problems and Prospects*. Washington, D.C.: National Academy of Sciences.

Shannon, Lyle. 1978. "A Longitudinal Study of Delinquency and Crime." In *Quantitative Studies in Criminology*, edited by Charles Wellford. Beverly Hills, Calif.: Sage.

————. 1981. *Assessing the Relationship between Juvenile and Adult Criminal Careers*. Iowa City: University of Iowa.

————. 1983. *The Prediction Problem as It Applies to Delinquency and Crime Control*. Department of Justice, Office of Juvenile Justice and Delinquency Prevention. Washington, D.C.: U.S. Government Printing Office.

Twentieth Century Fund. 1978. *Confronting Youth Crime*. Task Force on Sentencing Policy. New York: Holmes & Meier.

U.S. Department of Health, Education, and Welfare. 1978. *Lasting Effects after Preschool*. Washington, D.C.: U.S. Government Printing Office.

U.S. Department of Justice. 1983. *Sourcebook of Criminal Justice Statistics, 1982*. Washington, D.C.: U.S. Government Printing Office.

U.S. Department of Justice. Federal Bureau of Investigation. 1982. *Uniform Crime Reports, 1981*. Washington, D.C.: U.S. Government Printing Office.

————. 1985. *Uniform Crime Reports, 1984*. Washington, D.C.: U.S. Government Printing Office.

Wilson, James Q., and Richard J. Herrnstein. 1985. *Crime and Human Nature*. New York: Simon & Schuster.

Wolfgang, M., R. M. Figlio, and T. Sellin. 1972. *Delinquency in a Birth Cohort*. Chicago: University of Chicago Press.

Zimring, Franklin E. 1978. *Confronting Youth Crime: Report of the Twentieth Century Fund Task Force on Sentencing Policy toward Young Offenders*. New York: Holmes & Meier.

Zimring, Franklin E. 1981. "Kids, Groups, and Crime: Some Implications of a Well-kept Secret." *Journal of Criminal Law and Criminology* 72(3):867–85.

David P. Farrington

Age and Crime

ABSTRACT

The age-crime curve, increasing to a peak in the teenage years and then decreasing, is well-known. Less well-known is that it seems to reflect variations in prevalence (the proportion of persons who are offenders) rather than incidence (the rate of offending by offenders). Age-crime curves for individuals do not resemble the aggregate curve since incidence does not change consistently between the onset and the termination of criminal careers. This has major implications for criminal justice policy since the greatest residual length of criminal careers, and hence the greatest potential incapacitative effect, may be between ages thirty and forty, not at the peak age. Different types of offenses peak at different ages; this probably reflects crime switching rather than the replacement of one group of offenders by another. There is little specialization in offending, but specialization does increase with age. Age effects need to be separated from period and cohort effects. The age-crime curve probably reflects decreasing parental controls, a peaking of peer influence in the teenage years, and then increasing family and community controls with age.

The relation between age and crime, as seen in official criminal statistics for any given year, is well-known. Typically, the crime rate increases from the minimum age of criminal responsibility to reach a peak in the teenage years; it then declines, at first quickly, but gradually more slowly. While the form of the curve is widely appreciated, its

David P. Farrington is University Lecturer in Criminology, Cambridge University. He is grateful to Pat Altham, Al Blumstein, Daniel Glaser, Patrick Langan, Rolf Loeber, Joan McCord, Sheldon Messinger, Michael Tonry, and Nigel Walker for comments on an earlier version of this essay. National American data relating age to Index crimes over time have recently been published in *Age-specific Arrest Rates, 1965–1983* (Washington, D.C.: Federal Bureau of Investigation, 1984), which was not available in time to be considered in this essay. These data permit an age-period-cohort analysis of the type shown in fig. 6 below for England, although the percentage of the U.S. population covered is not constant (increasing from 65 percent in 1965 to 86 percent in 1983).

meaning is not. For example, does the peak in the teenage years reflect a peak in the number of different offenders, in the number of different types of offenses committed by each offender, or in the number of offenses of each type committed by each offender (or in some combination of these)? Why does the crime rate reach a peak in the teenage years, and why does it decline afterward?

Just as the answers to substantive questions about the age-crime curve are not widely known, methodological questions are also perplexing. For example, the age-crime curve in any one year is essentially a cross-sectional phenomenon, with persons of each age compared with different persons of other ages. Would the same relation between age and crime be obtained in a longitudinal survey in which the same persons were followed up at different ages? Also, how far does the age-crime curve seen in official criminal statistics reflect variations with age in official reactions to crime, as opposed to variations in crimes committed? Would the same curve be obtained if crime rates were measured by self-reports rather than by official records?

Interest in the relation between age and crime has recently been rekindled by a provocative article by Hirschi and Gottfredson (1983). They have argued that the age-crime curve is invariant over different times, places, crime types, sexes, and so on. Furthermore, they have claimed that the relation between age and crime cannot be explained by changes in other factors with age and hence that age has a direct causal influence on crime. These arguments are controversial, but they have important implications for criminology if they are correct. No other factor has yet been shown to have an invariant and directly causal effect on crime.

This essay aims to summarize the current state of knowledge about the relation between age and crime. Section I describes in some detail the age-crime curve seen in cross-sectional official criminal statistics and investigates variations in this curve over time, place, sex, and type of crime. Section II reviews age-crime curves obtained with longitudinal as opposed to cross-sectional methods and with self-reports as opposed to official statistics of crime. Section III attempts to disentangle the different elements of the age-crime curve such as prevalence and incidence and also reviews the ages of onset and termination of criminal careers. Section IV considers a number of explanations for why crime varies with age, and the final section draws conclusions, summarizes needed research, and reviews policy implications.

This essay is concerned with the ages of offenders. There have also been a number of studies of the ages of victims. For example, Langan and Innes (1985) showed age-victimization curves for the violent crimes of rape, robbery, and assault, based on the U.S. National Crime Survey. Victimization rates for these offenses peaked at ages sixteen to nineteen. Many of the questions about age and offending rates would probably apply also to age and victimization rates. However, partly because the study of age-victimization curves is relatively undeveloped, and partly because of limitations of space, this essay does not attempt to consider the ages of victims.

I. The Age-Crime Curve

Considerable evidence indicates that the relation between age and crime is not invariant. Aggregate age-crime curves are similar in some respects, but measures of distribution and central tendency show that they vary substantially over time, over types of offenses, between males and females, and between England and the United States. While the general age-crime pattern appears to hold independently of sex, the ratios of male to female offending vary substantially with age and with type of offense.

A. Annual Official Criminal Statistics

Figure 1a shows the relation between age and (recorded, detected) crime for English males in the years 1983, 1961, and 1938. Figure 1b shows the same curves for English females.[1] These curves are based on age-specific figures published annually in the *Criminal Statistics, England and Wales* (e.g., Home Office 1984, table 5.19). At the time of writing, 1983 was the latest year for which data were available; 1938 was the last year before World War II (in Europe); and 1961 was a convenient middle point (and also a census year). The Criminal Statistics currently show age-specific rates for each age from ten to twenty and then for twenty-one to twenty-four, twenty-five to twenty-nine, thirty to thirty-nine, forty to forty-nine, fifty to fifty-nine, and sixty or over. The minimum age of criminal responsibility was raised from eight to ten in 1964.

The "crime rate" is the rate of convictions and police cautions for indictable offenses per 100 population. Convictions and cautions for indictable offenses in England are roughly comparable to arrests for Index offenses in the United States.[2] Convictions and cautions are slightly less inclusive than arrests, although most arrests in England

---

[1] All references to England should be taken to include Wales.
[2] Index offenses consist of murder, forcible rape, robbery, aggravated assault, arson, burglary, theft, and motor vehicle theft.

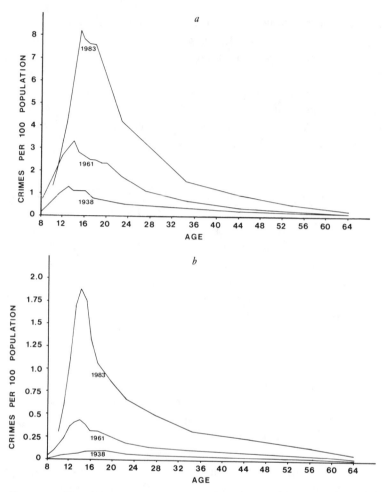

FIG. 1.—*a*, The relation between age and crime for English males. *b*, The relation between age and crime for English females. The graphs in both *a* and *b* show the rate of findings of guilt and cautions per 100 population for indictable offenses in the years 1938, 1961, and 1983. Source: Home Office (1940, 1962, 1984).

lead to convictions or cautions. Unlike all persons arrested, all persons convicted or cautioned have been found guilty of offending. Indictable offenses in England are slightly more inclusive than Index offenses in the United States are since indictable offenses include fraud, receiving, vandalism, and sex offenses other than forcible rape as well as Index offenses.

Figure 1*a* shows that the crime rate for English males peaked in 1983 at age fifteen at 8.2 offenses per 100 population, in comparison with the

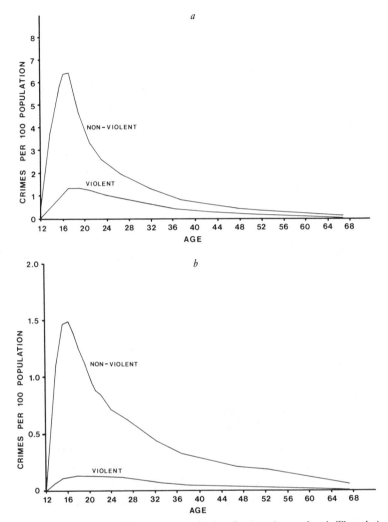

FIG. 2.—a, The relation between age and crime for American males. b, The relation between age and crime for American females. The graphs in both a and b show the rate of arrests per 100 population for Index offenses in the year 1982. Source: Federal Bureau of Investigation (1983).

1961 peak at age fourteen of 3.3 and the 1938 peak at age thirteen of only 1.3. Therefore, over time, the peak age has increased slightly, and the rate of offending at the peak has increased considerably. Figure 1b shows that the crime rate for females peaked in 1983 at age fourteen at 1.9 offenses per 100 population, in comparison with the 1961 peak at age fourteen of 0.46 and the 1938 peak at age nineteen of only 0.11.

For comparison, figure 2*a* shows the age-crime curves for American males in the year 1982, for violent and nonviolent offenses separately, and figure 2*b* shows the same curves for American females. These figures show the rate of arrests per 100 population for Index offenses. The total crime curve is not shown; it is similar in shape to the nonviolent crime curve and slightly above it. These curves are based on age-specific data published in the *Uniform Crime Reports* for 1982 (Federal Bureau of Investigation 1983, app. 4). It is difficult to obtain comparable age-crime curves for the United States over a long time period, partly because age-specific data are not published every year, and partly because of changes in the geographic coverage of the statistics. The *Uniform Crime Reports* for 1982 show age-specific arrest rates for different offenses at age twelve and under, age thirteen to fourteen, each age from fifteen to twenty-four, at five-year intervals from ages twenty-five to twenty-nine to ages sixty to sixty-four, and then for age sixty-five or over. The English *Criminal Statistics* do not show detailed age-specific crime rates for different categories of offenses.

Figure 2*a* shows that the nonviolent crime rate for American males peaked in 1982 at age seventeen at 6.4 offenses per 100 population, in comparison with the peak for violence at age eighteen of 1.3. Figure 2*b* shows that the nonviolent crime rate for females peaked at age sixteen at 1.5 offenses per 100 population, in comparison with the peak for violence at age twenty of 0.13. It seems, therefore, that the peak age for violent crime is slightly later than the peak age for nonviolent crime. For all Index crimes, the 1982 peak for American males was at age seventeen at 7.7 offenses per 100 population, in comparison with the 1983 peak at age fifteen at 8.2 for English males. For American females, the peak for all Index crimes was at age sixteen at 1.6 offenses per 100 population, in comparison with the peak at age fourteen at 1.9 for English females.

These curves have been reproduced here as a starting point. It was not too implausible for Hirschi and Gottfredson (1983) to conclude that the relation between age and crime was invariant. Superficially, the curves for different places, times, sexes, and crime types are similar, reaching a peak (usually) in the teenage years and then declining.

The curves raise many problems of interpretation that will be discussed later, in regard to offending versus official reactions, prevalence versus incidence, and explaining the relation between age and crime. However, one problem that is not so obvious is in measuring the population at risk or the denominator in the rate calculation. Between censuses (e.g., in England between 1971 and 1981), the population at each age is estimated, and the following census often indicates that the population estimates were inaccurate (Home Office 1984, p. 102). Also, the population figures typically include persons who are in institutions or temporarily abroad (e.g., in the military), who are not really at risk of offending in the country of origin. This leads to an underestimate of crime rates at each age.

Other problems arise in measuring crime. For example, temporary visitors are typically included in the crime figures but not in the population at risk, leading to an overestimate of crime rates at each age. The use of conviction measures in England is especially problematic because delays between arrests and convictions for adults can distort the age curve. When an offender is remanded to a higher court, the delay between arrest and conviction can exceed one year. Also, one conviction may represent several different offenses, so the distribution of convictions may be different from the distribution of offenses. (National arrest figures are not available in England.) These problems suggest ways in which the national statistics should be modified to produce more accurate age-crime curves.

B. Summarizing the Curve

In general, age-crime curves are unimodal (i.e., have only one peak) and peak in the teenage years. However, from these facts alone it cannot be concluded that the relation between age and crime is invariant. Any researcher who wished to test this hypothesis convincingly would have to compare age-crime curves on a variety of measures such as those outlined below.

There are many measures that can be used in summarizing distributions, and curves that are similar according to one criterion may be different according to others. Table 1 shows some summary measures derived from the English curves shown in figure 1a, b. The peak age is shown first, and then the crime rate at the peak. The next two measures show the age at which half the peak crime rate is reached on the increasing (left-hand) side of the curve and the age at which half the peak crime rate is reached on the decreasing side of the curve. These ages were estimated roughly from the figures and give some indication of how narrow or broad the peak is. For example, the peak for females in 1938 was very broad, ranging from a half-peak at eleven before to one at forty-four after. In contrast, the peak for females in 1983 was much sharper, ranging from a half-peak at twelve before to one at nineteen after.

There are other common methods of summarizing the central ten-

TABLE 1

Summarizing English Age-Crime Curves

	English Males			English Females		
	1938	1961	1983	1938	1961	1983
Peak age	13	14	15	19	14	14
Crime rate at peak*	1.32	3.35	8.25	.11	.46	1.89
Half of peak before	10	10	13	11	11	12
Half of peak after	21	23	22	44	21	19
Median age	21	20	21	29	24	21
Twenty-fifth percentile	15	15	16	19	16	15
Seventy-fifth percentile	33	29	29	42	40	34
Mean age	25.3	23.5	24.9	31.5	28.8	26.3
Standard deviation	13.5	11.8	11.8	14.3	15.3	14.1
Skewness	1.18	1.71	1.68	.22	.51	1.10
Kurtosis	3.44	4.35	4.20	2.25	2.38	3.15

SOURCE.—Home Office (1940, 1962, 1984).

* Findings of guilt and cautions per 100 population.

dency of a distribution, using the mean and median, and its dispersion, using the standard deviation and interquartile range (i.e., the distance between the twenty-fifth and the seventy-fifth percentiles). All these are shown in table 1. In calculating these, it has been assumed that each age group contains the same number of people, in order to eliminate effects of different cohort sizes. Also, crime rates of those aged eight and nine have been eliminated from the 1938 and 1961 statistics, to make them consistent with 1983. Table 1 shows that the median age of female offenders has decreased dramatically, from twenty-nine in 1938 to twenty-one in 1983. Also, since the peak age roughly coincides with the twenty-fifth percentile, only a quarter of all offenders have ages below or at the peak. Perhaps more surprisingly, despite the sharp peak of 1983 females at age fourteen (see figure 1b), as many as a quarter of female offenders were over thirty-four.

The mean ages of offenders in table 1 are remarkably high. For example, while the peak age for male offenders increased from thirteen to fifteen between 1938 and 1983, the mean age hovered around twenty-four to twenty-five. While the peak age for female offenders decreased from nineteen to fourteen, the mean age decreased from thirty-one to twenty-six. The standard deviations were consistently lower for males than for females, showing that female offenders tended to be more widely distributed over all ages. The interquartile range demonstrates the same phenomenon.

The two remaining measures in table 1 are of skewness and kurtosis. Skewness, as the name suggests, shows the extent to which a distribution is skewed or symmetrical. A skewness of zero reflects a symmetrical distribution, while a positive value (as here) indicates a distribution that is skewed to the right.[3] Table 1 shows that the curve for English females was nearly symmetrical in 1938 (skewness = 0.22) but had become skewed to the right in 1983 (skewness = 1.10). Kurtosis measures the degree to which a distribution is flattened or peaked around its center. The normal distribution has a kurtosis value of three. Values greater than three indicate that the curve is more peaked (or narrower) than the normal distribution, while values less than three show that the curve is flatter. Table 1 shows that the curve for English males in 1983 was more peaked than the normal distribution, while the curve for English females in 1938 was flatter.

For comparison, table 2 shows the same measures for the American curves shown in figure 2a, b. Generally, nonviolent offenders tended to be younger than violent ones, as shown by a lower peak age, a lower median, and a lower mean. Violent offenders tended to be more variable in age according to the distance between the two half peaks but not according to the interquartile range or the standard deviation. The male

TABLE 2

Summarizing American Age-Crime Curves

	American Males		American Females	
	Violent	Nonviolent	Violent	Nonviolent
Peak age	18	17	20	16
Crime rate at peak*	1.33	6.45	.13	1.51
Half of peak before	15	13	13	13
Half of peak after	32	21	32	23
Median age	25	20	26	23
Twenty-fifth percentile	19	16	19	17
Seventy-fifth percentile	34	29	35	34
Mean age	28.4	24.7	28.5	27.4
Standard deviation	11.6	11.5	11.5	13.2
Skewness	1.08	2.15	.85	1.19
Kurtosis	3.56	4.75	3.32	3.37

SOURCE.—Federal Bureau of Investigation (1983).
* Arrests per 100 population.

[3] If a curve is skewed to the right, the mean is greater than the median, the peak is to the left of the mean, and the long tail is to the right of the mean.

nonviolent offenders tended to have the most skewed and sharply peaked age distribution.

Comparing the ten curves summarized in tables 1 and 2, the peak age varied from thirteen to twenty, but the age at which the half peak afterward was attained varied from nineteen to forty-four. The median age varied from twenty to twenty-nine and the mean from twenty-three to thirty-one; but the interquartile range varied from thirteen years (sixteen to twenty-nine) to twenty-four years (sixteen to forty). Furthermore, the skewness varied from a near symmetrical 0.22 to a highly skewed 2.15, and the kurtosis varied from being flatter than the normal distribution at 2.25 to being sharper at 4.75. On the basis of these figures, it would be difficult to conclude that the relation between age and crime was invariant.

Figure 3 shows curves that can usefully be derived from the age-crime curve and that illustrate the concepts of the maximum ages of acceleration and deceleration. This figure shows the rate of change in the crime rate per year. Assuming that the crime rate is in some sense analogous to a speed of offending, these curves show the acceleration in

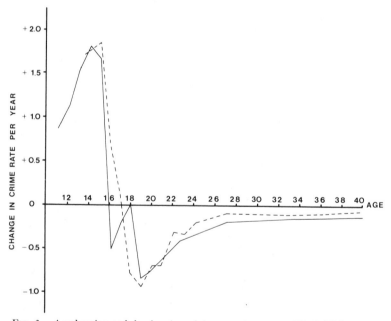

FIG. 3.—Acceleration and deceleration of the age-crime curve. The solid line represents English males (findings of guilt and cautions per 100 population for indictable offenses in 1983) and the broken line American males (arrests per 100 population for nonviolent offenses in 1982). Source: Home Office (1984) and Federal Bureau of Investigation (1983).

that speed before the peak age and deceleration after. For English males in 1983, the peak age of acceleration was fourteen and the peak age of deceleration nineteen. For American males arrested for nonviolent offenses in 1982, the peak age of acceleration was fifteen and of deceleration was nineteen. These ages of maximum change may be more important theoretically than the peak age of offending. They draw attention to ages when important life changes may be occurring that influence the commission of crimes.

C. Different Types of Crimes

It might be expected that the relation between age and crime would vary with the type of crime, and this is indeed true. Using FBI figures for 1977, Cline (1980) calculated median ages of arrest for different offenses. The lowest median ages were for vandalism (seventeen) and for motor vehicle theft, arson, burglary, larceny-theft, and liquor law violations (all eighteen). Cline regarded these as the offenses of adolescence. The next lowest median ages were for handling stolen property (twenty), narcotic law violations (twenty-one), violence, disorderly conduct, and prostitution (all twenty-four), sex offenses other than forcible rape and prostitution (twenty-six), white-collar offenses such as forgery and fraud (twenty-six), and abuse and neglect of family and children (twenty-eight). These were the offenses of young adulthood. Finally, there were the crimes of middle-age, drunkenness and drunk driving (median age thirty-five in both cases) and gambling (thirty-seven). Wilson and Herrnstein (1985) also showed relative changes in the pattern of offenses with age, using FBI figures for 1980. Burglary declined from the third most frequent arrest under age eighteen to the thirteenth most frequent at age forty or over. Robbery declined from eleventh to twenty-first, motor vehicle theft from ninth to twenty-second, and vandalism from sixth to fifteenth. In contrast, drunkenness increased from the tenth most frequent arrest under age eighteen to the most frequent at age forty or over, as did drunk driving (fourteenth to second), fraud (nineteenth to seventh), and gambling (twenty-fifth to twelfth).

As might be expected from the skewness of the distributions, peak ages do not vary as widely as median ages. For example, for males arrested for Index offenses in 1982 (Federal Bureau of Investigation 1983), the lowest peak age was for arson (fifteen), followed by motor vehicle theft (sixteen), robbery, burglary, and larceny-theft (seventeen), and murder, forcible rape, and aggravated assault (twenty). The range for females was from fifteen for arson, motor vehicle theft, and burglary to twenty-one for aggravated assault and twenty-three for murder. These differences in the peak age again suggest that it is unlikely that the age-crime curve is invariant of type of offense.

D. Sex, Age, and Crime

National criminal statistics are notoriously uninformative. They enable aggregate crime rates to be compared with only a very small number of variables, notably, age, sex, and crime type. In order to explain why age is related to crime, it would be helpful to know, first, if the relation between age and crime held independently of other variables and, second, if the relation between other variables and crime held independently of age. Using national statistics, these questions can be investigated in regard to the "other variable" of sex.

Posing the first question brings out the difficulty of answering it using conventional multivariate methods. Does the relation between age and crime hold independently of sex? A perusal of figures 1a, b, and 2a, b, and of tables 1 and 2 suggests that the answer to this question is probably yes since the age-crime curves are generally similar for males and females. However, it would be desirable to quantify our intuition and investigate whether the curve for males was significantly different from the curve for females. This is not straightforward and is discussed in more technical terms in the Appendix.

Figure 4 suggests that the answer to the second question is also yes. This figure shows the male-female ratios at different ages. At all ages, males were more likely to commit offenses than were females. However, for English offenders (who were mainly nonviolent), and for American nonviolent offenders, there were indications of an interaction between age and sex. The male-female ratio reached a peak at age sixteen to twenty-two, at 4.6 for American nonviolent offenders and at 7.5–9.5 for English offenders. It then declined steadily to only about two at the oldest ages. This is another age-crime phenomenon that needs to be explained. For American violent offenders, the male-female ratio reached a peak of 10.4 at age eighteen, but then never fell below 7.7, and reached 10.4 again at age sixty to sixty-four. It would be possible to calculate an "average" strength of association between sex and crime over different age levels, but the interactions seen in figure 4 suggest that any average would be misleading.

II. Other Ways of Studying Age and Crime

Section I was entirely concerned with age-crime curves derived from national criminal statistics showing crime rates in one year for persons

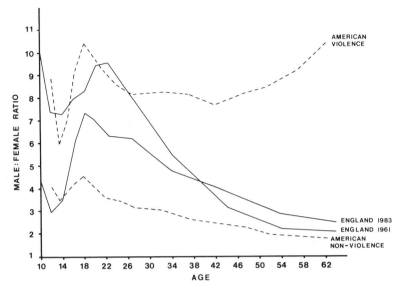

FIG. 4.—Male-female ratios at different ages. Source: derived from figs. 1a, b, and 2a, b.

of different ages. This is essentially a cross-sectional method of derivation. It is also possible to obtain age-crime curves longitudinally, by studying crime rates of the same persons at different ages. Furthermore, the longitudinal and cross-sectional methods can be used either with national statistics or in smaller-scale research projects, and the smaller scale studies can yield age-crime curves not only for official records of offending but also for self-reports. All these different methods of studying the age-crime curve are reviewed in this section.

A. Longitudinal Follow-up of Cohorts in Official Statistics

Longitudinal research based on national statistics follows up cohorts of persons born in one particular year. For example, the follow-up of persons born in 1960 would involve studying crime rates of ten-year-olds in 1970, eleven-year-olds in 1971, twelve-year-olds in 1972, and so on. The persons studied in one year are not exactly the same as those studied in any other year because of immigration, emigration, and deaths. However, this is a reasonable approximation to a true longitudinal study in which the same people are followed up.

Figure 5a shows age-crime curves obtained from the English criminal statistics in following up cohorts of males born in 1940, 1950, and 1960, and figure 5b shows the same curves for females. These curves are directly comparable with those shown in figure 1a, b, in showing con-

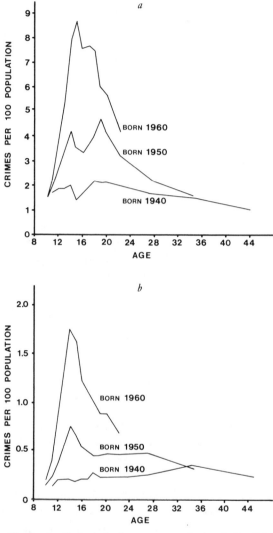

FIG. 5.—*a*, The longitudinal relation between age and crime for English males. *b*, The longitudinal relation between age and crime for English females. The graphs in both *a* and *b* show the rate of findings of guilt and cautions per 100 population for indictable offenses for cohorts born in 1940, 1950, and 1960. Source: Derived from annual *Criminal Statistics, England and Wales*.

victions and cautions per 100 population for indictable offenses. However, some of the curves shown in figure 5a, b, are very different from the familiar unimodal skewed curves seen in figure 1a, b. The curves for males and females born in 1960 certainly resemble the corresponding curves for males and females of different ages in 1983. However, the curve for males born in 1950 seems to have two peaks, at ages fourteen and nineteen, and the curve for females born in 1940 is skewed to the left and reaches a peak at age thirty to thirty-nine. How can we say that crime invariably reaches a peak in the teenage years when it clearly did not for females born in 1940?

The basic problem in interpreting these curves is the potential confusion between aging and period effects. Official crime rates in England increased considerably between the mid-1960s and mid-1970s, and this effect could be masking the true relationship between age and crime. There is always a problem of distinguishing between aging, period, and cohort effects. *Period effects* refer to influences specific to a particular time period; for example, a period of high unemployment or economic depression may influence the crime rates of all ages and all cohorts. *Cohort effects* follow from membership in one cohort (e.g., persons born in a particular year) rather than another; for example, persons born at the peak of a "baby bulge" might suffer more intense competition for resources at all ages and all periods. *Aging effects* refer to changes that occur with age; for example, aging eventually leads to physical deterioration for all cohorts at all periods.

In figure 5a, b, the identity of the birth cohort is held constant in each curve, but aging and period effects are then confounded. In the more usual cross-sectional curves for any given year, the period is held constant, but aging and cohort effects are confounded. Differences in crime rates between fifteen-year-olds and sixty-year-olds in 1983, for example, may reflect differences in cohort composition (e.g., a higher proportion of blacks among fifteen-year-olds than among sixty-year-olds), in cohort size (e.g., there may have been more persons born in 1968 than in 1923, leading possibly to more peer influence), or in other factors specific to a birth cohort.

In an attempt to disentangle aging, period, and cohort effects, it is desirable to study age-crime curves over time. For example, figure 1a, b, and table 1 show how the English age-crime curves have changed over time. Between 1938 and 1983, the peak crime rate increased dramatically, the curves became more skewed and more peaked, and (in the case of females) the average age of offenders decreased markedly.

These changes could reflect differences in periods or in cohorts or even interactions among aging, period, and cohort effects.

The basic analytic problem is that aging, period, and cohort effects are always confounded because age in general equals current year (period) minus birth year (cohort). Several researchers have tried to disentangle the three effects assuming that the crime rate is some additive function of aging, period, and cohort effects. Fienberg and Mason (1979) justified this kind of an analysis on the ground that, although the measured age, period, and cohort variables were confounded, the theoretical constructs underlying them were not necessarily. Rodgers (1982) also argued that age, period, and cohort variables were not of intrinsic interest in themselves but were used as indicators of biological or intellectual development, economic conditions, or the effects of childhood environments. He proposed that, in order to avoid the confounding, one of the three variables should be replaced by a more valid measure of the underlying theoretical construct; for example, period could be replaced by the unemployment rate if it was felt that unemployment was the important causal factor that varied over time. Unfortunately, it is difficult to establish what the important underlying theoretical constructs are.

There are simpler ways of investigating the three effects, as table 3 (based on Glenn 1977) shows. Aging effects are represented by the 1–4 progression, period effects by the A–D progression, and cohort effects by the I–VII progression. If crime rates were entered into the cells of an age-year table and then contour lines were drawn, predominantly horizontal contours would indicate an aging effect, predominantly vertical contours a period effect, and predominantly left-right diagonal contours a cohort effect. This was investigated for English males, using all ages from ten to twenty and all years from 1961 to 1983. The

TABLE 3

Aging, Period, and Cohort Effects

Age	Year			
	1950	1960	1970	1980
10	1-A-IV	1-B-III	1-C-II	1-D-I
20	2-A-V	2-B-IV	2-C-III	2-D-II
30	3-A-VI	3-B-V	3-C-IV	3-D-III
40	4-A-VII	4-B-VI	4-C-V	4-D-IV

SOURCE.—Based on Glenn (1977, tables 7–9).

contours were predominantly horizontal, beginning around the age fifteen crime rates and then spreading out vertically. There was no sign of cohort effects, as evidenced by diagonal contours. Therefore, the major influences in this English table seemed to be aging and period effects.

This is rather ironic because the major use of age-year tables in criminology has been to investigate cohort effects—the hypothesis of "delinquent generations." Wilkins (1960) examined the table showing convictions of English males aged eight to twenty in the years 1946–57 and compared the observed crime rates with those expected on the basis of row and column totals. He found clear diagonal effects since the cohort of males born in 1935–42 had higher crime rates than expected and concluded that children who had been four or five during World War II were especially crime prone. Somewhat similar results were obtained by Christiansen (1964) in Denmark and Jasinski (1966) in Poland. Interestingly, the peak age for crime in both countries was nineteen, in comparison with fourteen in Wilkins's English data. McKissack (1974) repeated the analysis in Scotland and concluded that children born in 1947 were a less delinquent cohort, perhaps because they were part of the postwar baby bulge.

Unfortunately for the delinquent generations hypothesis, Walters (1963) showed that Wilkins's results essentially reflected two trends over time: a decreasing conviction rate of eight- to eleven-year-olds (probably because the police became increasingly reluctant to take them to court) and an increasing conviction rate of seventeen- to twenty-one-year-olds. Rose (1968) then showed that these trends continued up to 1965 and always made the middle-born cohort appear more delinquent, no matter what time period was studied. The basic problem was that the period effects differed at different ages so that there was an interaction between aging and period effects. Carr-Hill, Hope, and Stern (1972) then used an additive cohort analysis model of the type described above and could not detect cohort effects in the English data. However, using essentially additive models, Slater, Darwin, and Richie (1966) in New Zealand and Maxim (1985) in Canada claimed that there were cohort effects, probably associated with cohort size. Interestingly, none of this research on crime rates in age-year tables has been carried out in the United States, presumably because of the difficulty of constructing comparable national age-year tables, although there has been a great deal of American interest in the use of cohort size in predicting crime rates (e.g., Wellford 1973; Blumstein, Cohen, and Miller 1980).

Finally, whether there are period or cohort effects is less important

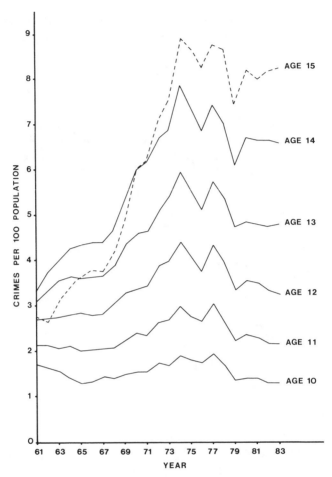

FIG. 6.—Changes in crime rates over time for English males aged ten to fifteen. The graph shows the rate of findings of guilt and cautions per 100 population for males of each age from ten to fifteen. Source: Based on annual *Criminal Statistics, England and Wales*.

for this essay than whether the relation between age and crime holds independently of period and cohort. Figure 6 suggests that it does. This shows the crime rate of English males aged ten to fifteen from 1961 to 1983. There were clear period effects, as already mentioned. For example, the crime rates of males of all these ages increased between 1967 and 1974, possibly because of the great expansion in police cautioning (Farrington and Bennett 1981), then decreased in 1974–76, increased in 1976–77, and decreased again in 1977–79. However, in every year, the crime rate increased from age ten to age fourteen. After 1970–71, it also increased up to fifteen.

Changes in crime rates with age for different birth cohorts can be studied in figure 6 by tracing the points diagonally. Thus fifteen-year-olds in 1983 were fourteen-year-olds in 1982, thirteen-year-olds in 1981, and so on. It can be seen that the increase in crime rate from age ten to age fourteen (or fifteen after the 1955–56 birth cohort) occurred for all cohorts. The curves for ages sixteen to twenty are not shown, but were they shown, they would indicate that the crime rate decreased from fifteen to twenty in almost every year and for almost every cohort. Therefore, the increase in crime rates from ten to fourteen or fifteen and the subsequent decrease to twenty held independently of period and cohort. This analysis suggests that it is desirable to investigate the age-crime curve by following up multiple cohorts in longitudinal research.

B. Smaller-Scale Cross-sectional Research

Studying the crime rates in one year of persons of different ages is essentially a large-scale cross-sectional research project. However, national criminal statistics provide information about only a very limited range of variables. More detailed data can be collected in smaller-scale projects, especially in those using interviews and self-reports.

Not all national statistics are as limited as those published in England and the United States. For example, Sveri (1965) was able to show how the number of persons involved in an offense varied with age, using national statistics for Norway. Generally, the proportion of offenses committed alone increased with age for all types of crimes. Offending in a group of three or more was especially common at the youngest ages (under fifteen). These results are very important since the age-crime curves discussed above show the total number of offenders at each age, not the total number of offenses. No researcher has yet published an age-crime curve for the total number of offenses, correcting for the number of offenders involved in each offense. However, such a curve might not show such a sharp peak in the teenage years, assuming that group offending is most common at this time.

One of the few projects providing information about self-reports of offending by representative samples of people of widely different ages was carried out by Rowe and Tittle (1977) (see also Tittle 1980). They interviewed random samples of persons aged fifteen or over (totaling 2,000) in three states—New Jersey, Iowa, and Oregon—and asked them about crimes they had committed in the previous five years. Rowe and Tittle found that thefts, marijuana smoking, and physical assaults decreased steadily with age, from ages fifteen to twenty-four to ages sixty-five or over. However, illegal gambling and cheating on income tax increased from ages fifteen to twenty-four to ages twenty-five to forty-four before decreasing. These results are consistent with Cline's (1980) conclusions, which are based on official records.

Gold and Reimer (1975) carried out national surveys of self-reported offending in two years, 1967 and 1972, but only with juveniles. In both years self-reported offending increased from thirteen to sixteen, for males and females. Williams and Gold (1972) were able to compare self-reported and official offending in the first of these surveys and concluded that the relation between age and crime was greater in official records than in self-reports.

One of the most interesting cross-sectional surveys providing information about age and crime was completed by Peterson, Braiker, and Polich (1981). They interviewed over 600 male inmates of five California state prisons and asked them about their commission of eleven types of crimes during the three-year period before their present incarceration. Unlike most other researchers, they divided the crime rate into prevalence, incidence, and the number of types of crimes. Their results are discussed in Section III. They were also careful to relate offending at different ages to "street time" or time not incarcerated.

Occasionally, cross-sectional victimization surveys provide information about the ages of offenders on the basis of victim reports. This is primarily obtained for crimes in which there was personal contact between the victim and the offender, such as rape, robbery, assault, and theft from persons. Unfortunately, victims' estimates of offenders' ages are likely to be inaccurate. Nevertheless, Hindelang (1981) linked up victim reports with demographic data and concluded that, for personal crimes in which victims saw their assailants, offenders aged eighteen to twenty had the highest crime rates.

There have been many cross-sectional surveys that yield data about the relation between age and behaviors related to crime. For example, Flanagan (1983) reviewed a number of previous American studies and concluded that the most adequately established correlate of misconduct in prison was the age of the inmates. Porporino and Zamble (1984) also found a significant negative correlation between age and disciplinary violations for Canadian prisoners. Of course, since prisoners are generally above the peak age of offending, it is not surprising that prison offenses should decrease steadily with age. Alcoholism, drug addiction, psychiatric distress, and sexual promiscuity also peak in the teenage or early adult years (Gove 1985).

Below the peak age, a number of studies have investigated the relation between age and behavior problems of children. Achenbach and Edelbrock (1981) published graphs showing how more than 100 behavior problems (reported by parents) varied in prevalence between age four and age sixteen. For example, alcohol and drug use increased with age, but stealing outside the home did not. If behavior problems of children vary in the same way crime does, this suggests that the age-crime curve may reflect changes in behavior rather than in police reactions.

C. Longitudinal Studies Using Official Records

Longitudinal studies can be prospective or retrospective (see, e.g., Farrington 1979*b*). The Gluecks were the pioneers of prospective longitudinal research providing information about officially recorded offending at different ages. In their fifteen-year follow-up of 1,000 juvenile delinquents, Glueck and Glueck (1940) reported that 80 percent were arrested within five years of the end of the treatment, 80 percent in the next five years, and 78 percent in the next five years—remarkably consistent figures, between ages fourteen and twenty-nine on average. The average number of arrests per arrested person increased slightly with age, from 3.4 in the first period to 3.8 in the last. The types of offenses changed since crimes against property (burglary, theft, receiving, and forgery) decreased steadily, while crimes of drunkenness increased steadily.

Similar results were obtained by Glueck and Glueck (1943) in their fifteen-year follow-up of 510 reformatory inmates between the average ages of twenty-five and forty. The percentage arrested in each five-year period decreased between these ages from 70 percent in the first period to 58 percent in the third, but the average number of arrests of those arrested increased from 3.3 to 3.6. As before, property crimes decreased dramatically with age and tended to be replaced by drunkenness offenses. In their third long-term study, Glueck and Glueck (1968) followed up the 500 delinquents from *Unraveling Juvenile Delinquency* (Glueck and Glueck 1950) from age fourteen to age thirty-one. Once again, burglary and theft decreased between these ages, while drug and drink offenses increased. It seems clear that the changes in offending patterns with age seen in national statistics (Cline 1980; Wilson and Herrnstein 1985) are at least partly due to crime switching by offenders.

Farrington (1983) also reported changes in officially recorded offending with age in a prospective longitudinal study of 400 London males. The peak age for the total number of convictions was seventeen, and by age twenty-four this total number had decreased to about a quarter of the peak value. The peak age for burglary and shoplifting was at fourteen to sixteen, while the peak age for assault, damage, and thefts of vehicles was at seventeen to twenty. All offenses increased from ages ten to thirteen to ages fourteen to sixteen and then decreased from ages seventeen to twenty to ages twenty-one to twenty-four, mirroring the familiar curvilinear pattern seen in the national statistics.

Miller, Dinitz, and Conrad (1982) carried out an interesting retrospective longitudinal study of the arrest histories of some 1,600 male violent offenders in Ohio. They published age-crime curves for homicide, rape, robbery, and assault that generally showed peaks at age twenty to twenty-four. Wolfgang, Figlio, and Sellin (1972) also reported age-crime curves in their retrospective Philadelphia cohort study of 10,000 males, but these only extended up to age seventeen. Interestingly, the black-white ratio decreased steadily from age ten or less to age seventeen. Van Dusen and Mednick (1983) replicated the Wolfgang et al. project with a Copenhagen cohort of nearly 29,000 males followed in records from birth to age twenty-six. The peak age of offending in this sample was seventeen to eighteen, although violence peaked later, at twenty to twenty-one. Finally, Shannon (1981) studied three birth cohorts in Racine, Wisconsin, born in 1942, 1949, and 1955. The total number of police contacts peaked at sixteen to seventeen for males and at seventeen to nineteen for females. The results of these projects are reviewed in more detail in Section III.

D. Longitudinal Studies Using Self-Reports

These studies also can be prospective or retrospective. The Farrington (1983) prospective longitudinal survey included self-reports of offending at different ages as well as official records. These self-reports showed that most offenses peaked during the period fifteen to eighteen, although shoplifting and burglary peaked earlier. Self-reports of offending at different ages were also included in the Bachman, O'Malley, and Johnston (1978) national survey of about 2,200 boys and in the Elliott et al. (1983) national study of about 1,700 youngsters. The self-reports in the Bachman et al. project are difficult to interpret because they covered different time periods. However, stealing cars seemed to decrease steadily from ages twelve to fifteen to ages twenty-two to twenty-three, while taking marijuana seemed to increase steadily from ages seventeen to eighteen to ages twenty-two to twenty-three (although this may be a period effect, from 1969 to 1974). The Elliott et al. study is discussed in more detail in Section III. Unlike any other criminological survey, it included repeated interviews with multiple cohorts (aged eleven to seventeen at the beginning).

An interesting retrospective self-report survey was carried out by Petersilia, Greenwood, and Lavin (1978) with forty-nine prisoners serving sentences for armed robbery. They were asked about offending during their juvenile, young adult, and adult career periods. Generally, the prevalence of burglary and auto theft seemed to decrease with age, while the prevalence of drug sales and robbery seemed to increase. However, it was difficult to make exact comparisons because of the differing lengths of the three periods. The Shannon (1981) and Wolfgang (1980) longitudinal surveys also included retrospective self-reports. Persons in the Philadelphia sample, during an interview at age twenty-six, were asked to report offending during their juvenile and adult years, and Collins (1981) found that robbery, burglary, and shoplifting all decreased with age.

Most of the results presented in this section concern aggregate crime rates at different ages. In Section III, attempts are made to disentangle prevalence and incidence rates and to determine what is really varying with age. Also, many of the quoted surveys have not tried to obtain exact information about ages of offending. It is impossible to draw conclusions about the relation between age and crime if people are merely asked about total offenses before or after age eighteen, for example. These surveys draw attention to the advantages and disadvantages of the different methods of studying age and crime.

E. Advantages and Disadvantages of Different Methods

The relation between age and crime can be investigated in cross-sectional or longitudinal research using official records or self-reports of offending, and the longitudinal research can be prospective or retrospective. These various possibilities all have advantages and disadvantages.

An advantage of cross-sectional research is that the results can be obtained more quickly and contemporaneously. In a longitudinal project, the conclusions are delayed by the necessity to wait while the subjects of the investigation get older. Taking the extreme case, the complete relationship between age and crime can only be determined in a longitudinal project when the subjects die, at which point the information will be out of date and inapplicable to persons currently living. Also, in a longitudinal survey including interviews, there are the considerable practical problems of attrition and maintaining contact with the sample, and one interview may affect later ones.

An advantage of longitudinal research is the decreased problem of selection effects. In a cross-sectional project comparing people of different ages, those of one age are likely to differ from those of another in many factors other than age, and it may be difficult to disentangle aging effects from the influences of other factors. In a longitudinal project, to a large extent each person acts as his or her own control, so there is less variation in extraneous factors that is confounded with variation in age. Period effects may be a problem in longitudinal research, but even in cross-sectional research, in which the period is held constant, the results may be distorted by unusual events that occur at one particular time.

Another advantage of longitudinal research is the possibility of studying continuity or discontinuity between different ages, the relation between earlier and later events, prediction, developmental sequences, specialization, versatility, and escalation in offending. In a cross-sectional study, for example, it is impossible to know whether the property offenders at one age switch to violent offending later or whether the property offenders desist and a new sample of violent offenders emerges. Also, longitudinal research is needed to establish cumulative phenomena such as the cumulative prevalence of offending or the proportion of crimes committed by "chronic" offenders. The cumulative prevalence of offending can be estimated in an ostensibly cross-sectional study, but only if essentially longitudinal information is available about the presence or absence of previous offenses.

Another advantage of a longitudinal study is its superiority over cross-sectional research in establishing cause and effect, by showing that changes in one factor are followed by changes in another. Another variant of this is the ability in longitudinal research to establish the effects of specific events on the course of development by quasi-experimental analysis (Cook and Campbell 1979). Ultimately, in studying the relation between age and crime, or any other criminological correlation, the goal must be to establish causal relations.

An advantage of using official records of offending, in comparison with self-reports, is the greater comprehensiveness of the data. The losses in surveys are often substantial. For example, in the Elliott et al. (1983) study, only 1,725 out of a target sample of 2,360 (73 percent) participated in the first interview, and this number had shrunk to 1,494 (63 percent) by the fifth. This will not matter so much if the people lost constitute a representative sample, but often they are the most delinquent and hence the most interesting to criminological researchers (West and Farrington 1973). Even those who die tend to be disproportionally delinquent (Sarnecki and Sollenhag 1985).

There are losses even in studies based on official records, but these tend to be less serious in prospective than in retrospective projects. In prospective surveys, the number of persons lost can be specified more exactly, and the information collected about them before the loss can be used to calculate the degree of error introduced into estimates. In Wadsworth's prospective national survey (1975), only 1.9 percent of males were lost by emigration and 0.8 percent by death between the eighth and twenty-first birthdays (the period of the official record follow-up). However, Gordon (1976) concluded that the requirement that subjects live in Philadelphia at least between age ten and age eighteen led to a loss of 30.5 percent of the original birth cohort in the retrospective Wolfgang et al. (1972) study.

Another advantage of official records is that they often contain more specific information about the dates of offenses than do self-reports. This is needed especially in investigating the relation between age and crime. There is no reason in principle why self-report researchers should not also seek detailed information about the dates of offenses, although the extent to which people can report these accurately needs to be established by a reverse record check, as in victim surveys.

Official records and self-reports of offending are both biased measures. Official records reflect police reactions to crime at different ages, while self-reports reflect people's willingness to admit offenses at different ages. A great advantage of self-reports is that the researcher is not limited by what is available in records but can choose which questions to ask. Therefore, in self-report surveys it is possible to obtain information about a much richer array of factors, enabling fuller testing of causal hypotheses and better statistical control of extraneous variables.

The main advantages of retrospective surveys are feasibility and speed of obtaining answers to questions. They have many disadvantages. For example, in retrospective self-report surveys, the memory problems are likely to be severe if middle-aged people are asked to remember what happened when they were juveniles. In retrospective surveys using official records, there are likely to be problems caused by the tendency of record-keeping systems to lose records or to destroy them after a certain length of time. Methodological problems are likely to ensue if a sample is defined by the occurrence of a certain event (e.g., conviction or imprisonment) that is then included in the analysis. Glueck and Glueck (1940) had the sense to exclude the current arrest when calculating the prior arrest history of their 1,000 juvenile delinquents, but some subsequent researchers have not.

In general, all methods of studying age and crime have advantages and disadvantages. The best solution is to combine methods, if possible, by following up multiple cohorts and by deriving information both from official records and from self-reports.

III. What Factors Vary with Age?

The age-crime curves seen in cross-sectional official criminal statistics are essentially aggregate curves. They show how many crimes were committed by persons of any given age, but they do not divide this into prevalence (defined here as the number of different persons committing crimes or the participation rate) and incidence (defined here as the rate at which offenders commit crimes or the individual crime rate). For example, does the peak age reflect a peak in prevalence, in incidence, or in both? This section reviews knowledge about more subtle questions of this kind.

A. Prevalence of Offending at Each Age

A distinction is usually made between the prevalence of offending at each age and the cumulative prevalence up to any given age. The first of these is sometimes called "point prevalence," but it should be realized that both these measures involve cumulation over time. They differ in the length of time over which the cumulation occurs. For example, the prevalence of offending at age seventeen is obtained by comparing the number of people who offend between the seventeenth and the eighteenth birthday with the population at risk. The more familiar cumulative prevalence of offending up to the eighteenth birthday is calculated by comparing the number of people who offend between the minimum age of criminal responsibility and the eighteenth birthday with the population at risk for the whole period.

If offending is viewed as a random process, the period of cumulation can affect the prevalence estimate. For example, in the theory outlined by Cohen (1983), a criminal career begins when a person's individual crime rate (r) is greater than zero. Crimes occur probabilistically according to a Poisson process, so the expected number of crimes committed during any time interval T is rT. With this conception of offending, there is a certain probability (e^{-rT}) that any "offender" (i.e., a person with a nonzero rate of offending) will not commit an offense during a given time interval T. Therefore, the measured prevalence (i.e., the number of persons who actually commit an offense during the time interval) will be the true prevalence of offenders multiplied by the factor $(1 - e^{-rT})$. For example, if the rate of offending is one crime per year, 36.8 percent of "offenders" will not commit a crime during a year, so the measured prevalence would be only 63.2 percent of the true prevalence. Obviously, this problem becomes less acute as the rate of offending increases; at a rate of two crimes per year, only 13.5 percent would not actually offend, and at a rate of three crimes per year, only 5.0 percent would not actually offend.

Existing prevalence measures are based on crimes actually committed. Generally, the prevalence curve closely mirrors the aggregate age-crime curve. In the Philadelphia cohort study, Collins (1981) reported that the peak age for the prevalence of arrests was sixteen, while in their Copenhagen replication Van Dusen and Mednick (1983) found that prevalence peaked at seventeen to eighteen. In England, Farrington (1983) showed that the age curve for the number of different persons convicted was similar to the curve for the total number of convictions. It seems that the peak age seen in official statistics reflects a peak in the prevalence of offending.

Farrington (1983) also showed that the prevalence of offending according to self-reports peaked at fifteen to eighteen for most offenses. The most extensive American data relating age to self-reports of offending has been produced by Elliott et al. (1983). Unfortunately, their figures seem to be subject to a great deal of sampling variability. Restricting the analysis to ages with at least three estimates from different cohorts, the peak age for the prevalence of Index offenses was fifteen to seventeen (with 18 percent of the sample committing at least one Index offense at each of these ages). Therefore, self-reports also show a peak in the prevalence of offending at about fifteen to eighteen.

B. Cumulative Prevalence

Like other features of the age-crime curve, the cumulative prevalence of offending up to a certain age can be estimated either cross-sectionally or longitudinally. The cross-sectional calculation requires a knowledge of the proportion of persons of each age who offend for the first time in a given year. If these proportions are added up over all ages, this yields an estimate of the cumulative prevalence of offending in a cohort, on the assumption that first offending rates do not change over time.

The first cross-sectional estimate of the prevalence of offending (defined as a court appearance on a delinquency charge) was made by Monahan (1960) in Philadelphia. Unfortunately, Monahan's calculations were incorrect. Gordon and Gleser (1974) explained the error and published the correct figures. These showed that 51 percent of black males, 18 percent of white males, 16 percent of black females, and 3 percent of white females had appeared in court by the eighteenth birthday. Ball, Ross, and Simpson (1964) used the correct method in Kentucky, calculating that 21 percent of males and 5 percent of females had appeared in the juvenile court by the eighteenth birthday. Christensen (1967) then extended the technique to calculate the lifetime probability of arrest for nontraffic offenses in the United States as 50 percent for males and 12 percent for females. More recent estimates have been made by Blumstein and Graddy (1982), showing that the probability of arrest of a male for an Index offense by age fifty-five in large American cities was 51 percent for nonwhites and 14 percent for whites. These cumulative prevalence figures are surprisingly high.

The cross-sectional method of estimating prevalence has also been used in other countries. In England, McClintock and Avison (1968) calculated the lifetime risk of conviction for a nontraffic offense to be 31 percent for males and 8 percent for females. Just over a decade later, these rates had increased to 44 percent for males and 15 percent for females (Farrington 1981). The lifetime prevalence of convictions may be lower in the Scandinavian countries. Christiansen and Jensen (1972) used 1968 figures to estimate that 12 percent of males and less than 2 percent of females in Denmark would be convicted and receive sanctions more severe than fines in their lifetimes.[4] (These severe sanctions constituted about 60 percent of all sanctions.)

Longitudinal methods of estimating cumulative prevalence have become common since the pioneering work of Wolfgang et al. (1972). They showed that the cumulative prevalence of nontraffic arrests in their cohort of Philadelphia males was 35 percent up to age eighteen, with a marked racial differential (50 percent of the blacks versus 29 percent of the whites). Later work by Wolfgang (1983) demonstrated that the overall prevalence increased to 47 percent by age thirty, and Wolfgang and Tracy (1982) reported a cumulative prevalence of 33 percent up to age eighteen for males in a second Philadelphia cohort. In Racine, Wisconsin, Shannon (1981) studied three birth cohorts, fol-

---

[4] The low prevalence in this study is partly due to the severe criterion for counting offenses. The longitudinal prevalence figures quoted below for Copenhagen are higher.

lowed up in records to ages thirty-three, twenty-six, and twenty-one, respectively. The proportions with police contacts up to these ages for relatively serious offenses (felonies and major misdemeanors) were 22–23 percent for males and 2–6 percent for females. In another small-town study, in Marion County, Oregon, Polk et al. (1981) found a cumulative prevalence of 25 percent up to the eighteenth birthday for police contacts of males for nontraffic offenses.

Similarly high cumulative prevalence figures have been reported in England. In a national sample, Wadsworth (1975) discovered that 15 percent of males were convicted or cautioned for nontraffic offenses by the twenty-first birthday, and Farrington (1983) found that about one-third of a cohort of London males were convicted of nontraffic offenses by the twenty-fifth birthday. A national follow-up of persons born in 1953 in the official criminal records (Home Office 1985) showed that 31 percent of the males and 6 percent of the females had been convicted of nontraffic offenses by the twenty-eighth birthday.

The cumulative prevalence of police contacts is also high in other countries. In Copenhagen, Wolf (1984) in the Danish *Project Metropolitan* reported that 35 percent of males had been registered by the police for an offense committed by age twenty-three. According to Wolf (personal communication), 21 percent were registered for nontraffic offenses. In the Swedish *Project Metropolitan*, Wikstrom (1985) found that 31 percent of males had a police record by age twenty-five to twenty-six.

These cumulative figures show that, at least for males, police records are not confined to a small deviant minority. Indeed, in some studies the noncriminals are in the minority. Little seems to be known about the cumulative prevalence of offending as measured by self-reports. It would be desirable to publish national cumulative prevalence figures versus age on a regular basis. The ages at which cumulative prevalence is increasing fastest (the ages of maximum acceleration) may be particularly significant in the explanation of crime, as these indicate the most usual ages at which nonoffenders become offenders.

C. Incidence

"Incidence" here refers to the rate of committing crimes by offenders. Comparatively little is known about how incidence varies with age. This is surprising in light of the pioneering work of Glueck and Glueck (1940, 1943), who published the average number of arrests per arrested person in successive five-year periods. It is clear from the Gluecks' figures that the prevalence of arrests varied far more than the incidence.

For example, Glueck and Glueck (1940) reported that, while the percentage of their released offenders arrested for property crimes such as burglary and theft decreased from 60 percent (between, on average, fourteen and nineteen) to 25 percent (between, on average, ages twenty-four and twenty-nine), the incidence of such arrests decreased only from 2.3 to 1.9. Similarly, while the prevalence of arrests for drunkenness increased from 11 percent to 27 percent, the incidence increased only from 2.4 to 4.1.

Knowledge about the incidence of offending advanced little during the forty years that separated the Gluecks' work and Blumstein and Cohen's (1979), who more recently have emphasized the importance of the individual crime rate. In a sample of adults arrested for serious crimes in Washington, D.C., Blumstein and Cohen found that the individual arrest rate decreased with age, from below age twenty to above age thirty. However, they explained this decrease away on two grounds. First, there were cohort effects confounded with age since arrest rates were higher among those born more recently. Second, the calculation did not take account of time incarcerated, which affected the older offenders more than the younger ones. When Blumstein and Cohen allowed for both these effects in more sensitive analyses, they found that the arrest rate did not tend to decrease with age. They have consistently argued that the individual crime rate or incidence of offending is constant during a criminal career and that changes in aggregate crime rates reflect changing prevalence.

In support of Blumstein and Cohen's (1979) arguments, Farrington (1983) in the London cohort found that the peak in the number of convictions was primarily affected by prevalence, not by incidence. The number of convictions per convicted person varied only between 1.0 and 1.5 at each age. However, the problem with convictions and arrests as measures of incidence is that there are limits on the number that can be incurred in any time period, partly because of the official reaction that follows. Also, the probability of an arrest or a conviction following an offense may vary systematically with age. It might be more satisfactory to measure incidence using self-reports, taking account of time at risk.

Peterson et al. (1981) obtained self-reports in their cross-sectional survey of California prisoners and published figures showing how prevalence and incidence varied with age. Unfortunately, while the prevalence figures generally decreased with age, the incidence figures showed no consistent pattern. For example, the incidence of burglary was high at twenty-one to twenty-five and twenty-six to thirty and low at under twenty-one and over thirty; in contrast, the incidence of auto theft was high at under twenty-one and over thirty and low at twenty-one to twenty-five and twenty-six to thirty. Peterson et al. also calculated the probability of an offense being followed by an arrest at different ages, but again there were no clear trends. Earlier, Petersilia et al. (1978) had found that this probability increased with age during the adult years.

Farrington (1983) obtained incidence rates from self-reports as well as from official records. As with the official records, the peak in self-reported crime at age fifteen to eighteen generally reflected a peak in prevalence, not in incidence. The decrease in prevalence after the peak could coincide with a decrease in incidence (for fighting and burglary), with an increase in incidence (for damaging property and stealing from vehicles), or with no consistent change in incidence (for shoplifting and stealing from automatic machines). It is also possible to calculate incidence rates for Index offenses in the Elliott et al. (1983) national self-report survey, and these also did not seem to vary systematically with age.

The reciprocal of the incidence rate is the average time between offenses. This was calculated by Glueck and Glueck (1940, 1943) for arrests but by few subsequent researchers. As might have been expected, the average time between arrests did not vary greatly in the Gluecks' research: from one arrest every fourteen months at age fourteen to nineteen to one arrest every 12.6 months at age twenty-four to twenty-nine, for example (Glueck and Glueck 1940). The Gluecks deducted time spent in institutions in making these calculations. Subsequent researchers who have studied time between arrests (e.g., Miller et al. 1982) have not related it to age and not deducted time spent in institutions.

The limited amount of present knowledge, then, suggests that the peak in the crime rate in the teenage years reflects a peak in prevalence and that incidence does not vary consistently with age. This has the clear implication that individual curves relating age and crime will be very different from aggregate curves.

D. Age of Onset

The age of onset of offending is of course related to the cumulative prevalence. If the age-crime curve reflects primarily prevalence, it follows that the peak age of onset should coincide with the peak age of acceleration of the age-crime curve, just as it must coincide with the peak age of acceleration of the cumulative prevalence curve. Both curves are accelerating because more nonoffenders are becoming offenders. Figure 3 suggests that the peak age of onset will be before the peak age of offending, at fourteen to fifteen for English and American males in the 1980s. It would be interesting to plot age of onset curves not only in relation to the whole population but also in relation to the number of nonoffenders at each age. The proportion of nonoffenders who become offenders at each age can be regarded as a "hazard rate" (Gordon and Gleser 1974).

Several of the studies of cumulative prevalence include detailed curves showing age of onset. This is true, for example, in the Blumstein and Graddy (1982) research on cumulative prevalence in large American cities. It is clear from their results that the age of onset curves for white and nonwhite males both peak at fifteen, although the nonwhite probabilities are much higher. Similarly, Fry (1985) has provided detailed age of onset information for the Swedish *Project Metropolitan* in Stockholm. The peak ages of first arrests for males and females were both at thirteen.

The peak ages of onset in English studies seem to be less sharp. In Wadsworth's (1975) national longitudinal survey, the peak for convictions and cautions was at fourteen to sixteen. In Farrington's (1983) London cohort, the peak age was at thirteen to seventeen, with two noticeable peaks at fourteen and seventeen. The boys in this survey were born mostly in 1953. Interestingly, in the Home Office (1985) follow-up in the criminal records of a national sample of persons born in 1953, there were also two peaks for first convictions of males, at fourteen and seventeen. In contrast, the peak age of onset for females was at seventeen. These peak ages may be related to English legal categories; at fourteen a "child" becomes a "young person," while at seventeen a "young person" becomes a "young adult."

In their longitudinal self-report survey, Elliott and Huizinga (1984) provided interesting information not only about the prevalence of different kinds of offending at each age but also about the percentage of persons initiating and terminating. Unfortunately, it is difficult to be sure that all initiations and terminations are genuine, in view of the limited period covered by this survey (five annual interviews). However, their combined data from three birth cohorts indicated that initiation peaked at thirteen to fifteen, prevalence at sixteen to seventeen, and termination at eighteen to nineteen.

It is important to know how age of onset is related to incidence as well as to prevalence. Hirschi and Gottfredson (1983) argued that groups with a higher aggregate peak offending rate (such as blacks) would inevitably have an earlier age of onset, a later age of termination, and hence a longer criminal career. This is essentially arguing that the whole age-crime curve tends to be magnified for blacks or that, once the peak of the curve is known, every other feature of it follows. Unfortunately, Hirschi and Gottfredson did not distinguish between prevalence and incidence in their article. However, one possible interpretation of their argument is that an early age of onset tends to be followed by a high incidence of offending.

A number of studies have related the age of onset to the number of offenses per year after onset. Hamparian et al. (1978), in a retrospective longitudinal survey of violent juveniles in Columbus, Ohio, showed that the number of arrests after the age of onset increased linearly with the time available up to the eighteenth birthday. In other words, after the age of onset, these juveniles offended at a constant (incidence) rate. Similar results were obtained by Miller et al. (1982) with violent adults in Ohio, by Van Dusen and Mednick (1983) in Copenhagen, and in the English follow-up of cohorts by the Home Office (1985). However, Farrington (1983) found that those first convicted at the earliest age (ten to twelve) offended consistently at a higher rate and for a longer time period than those first convicted at later ages, up to age twenty-five. Similarly, McCord (1980) reported that those first convicted under age sixteen were more likely to be convicted later, at different ages.

There are many other questions that could be asked about age of onset. How do those who offend at an early age differ from those who do not offend until later? In the London cohort, West (1982) reported that those first convicted after age eighteen were less likely to share the deprived backgrounds—low-income families, convicted parents, and poor parental child-rearing behavior—of those who offended at earlier ages. However, the latecomers to crime were just as likely to have had low intelligence at age eight to nine. Another important issue is the extent to which the early offenders who persist in crime differ from those who desist. Blumstein, Farrington, and Moitra (1985) showed that factors that predicted those who became chronic offenders out of all convicted youths were offending at an early age, having a convicted sibling, being troublesome, and performing badly at school at age eight to ten.

E. Age of Termination

Less is known about the age at which offending ceases than about the age at which it begins. This is partly because of the difficulty of distinguishing between a gap in a criminal career and true termination and of the very long term follow-ups that are required to establish the age at termination. Assuming that offending occurs probabilistically, there are bound to be crime-free periods in the middle of criminal careers. Barnett and Lofaso (1985) carried out an interesting analysis of the Philadelphia cohort, showing that the primary predictor of future arrest rate was past arrest rate. They could find no evidence of termination of offending up to the eighteenth birthday. Virtually all apparent termination was "false desistance" caused by the artificial truncation of the data at eighteen.

Glueck and Glueck (1943) were probably the first to publish information about the age of termination. They concluded that 140 of their 510 reformatory inmates had "reformed" since they had no recorded arrests during the third follow-up period (average ages thirty-five to forty). Eighteen were last arrested under age twenty-one, thirty-eight at age twenty-one to twenty-seven, forty-five at age twenty-seven to thirty-three, and the remaining thirty-nine over age thirty-three. The Gluecks were interested in predicting those who reformed. Unfortunately, a five-year or even a ten-year crime-free period is no guarantee that offending has terminated. For example, Gibbens (1984) followed up a sample of 200 English borstal boys in records for twenty-five years after conviction. After ten years, forty-three had not been reconvicted, but as many as one-third of these were reconvicted subsequently.

It might be thought that recidivism is the other side of the coin from termination. A great deal is known about the relation between age and recidivism. For example, Hoffman and Beck (1984, p. 617) stated that "one of the most firmly established pieces of statistical knowledge is that the older a man is when released from prison the less likely he is to return to crime." They carried out a study that showed that, for federal prisoners, the recidivism rate (defined as the commission of an offense leading to imprisonment for sixty days or more, within two years of release) varied from 36 percent for those under twenty-five to 23 percent for those over forty. Kitchener, Schmidt, and Glaser (1977), in an eighteen-year follow-up of federal prisoners, showed a more dramatic relationship between recidivism and age at first arrest. Unfortunately, it is difficult to draw conclusions about termination from information about recidivism because those who do not recidivate within two years include true desisters, undetected offenders, and those who will persist later.

Assuming that the age-crime curve primarily reflects prevalence, the peak age of termination should coincide with the peak age of deceleration of this curve. As already mentioned, Elliott and Huizinga (1984) provided information about the proportion of persons initiating and terminating at each age in their five-year follow-up study. Also, Polk et al. (1981) produced a distribution of the year of the last arrest for their sample, for men with no arrests in the last three years of their project (ages twenty-seven to thirty). This peaked at age seventeen. However, the table published by Hamparian et al. (1978, p. 71) is potentially more interesting, as it shows the age of the first arrest versus the age of the last arrest. This makes it possible to calculate the length of criminal careers and to relate length to the ages of onset and termination. Unfortunately, the Hamparian et al. analysis is limited to juvenile arrests, but it might serve as a useful model for other researchers.

Just as little is known about ages of termination, the same is inevitably true of the lengths of criminal careers. Blumstein, Cohen, and Hsieh (1982) drew attention to the importance of the concept of residual career length at each age. Using cross-sectional data and assuming that offending was a probabilistic process, they used a life-table method to calculate both career length (which averaged 5.6 years for Index arrests) and residual career length (which peaked between age thirty and age forty). It is important to know both residual career length and the incidence rate in order to estimate the number of crimes prevented by incapacitation. It may be that incapacitation has its greatest crime-reducing potential for offenders aged between thirty and forty despite the peak age of offending in the teenage years. This is an example of how more subtle relationships between age and crime than the well-publicized gross curve are often needed.

There is a great deal yet to be established about how criminal careers vary with age, including the interrelations among prevalence, incidence, age of onset, age of termination, and career length (residual or total). It is also important to know how these factors are related to other variables such as sex, race, family background, intelligence, and so on. Predictive analyses are especially desirable to establish how far the future course of a criminal career (in terms of residual length and incidence rate) can be predicted at any age on the basis of the past course (in terms of the length of time elapsed in the career, the incidence rate, and perhaps even the rate of acceleration or deceleration of the incidence rate; see Barnett and Lofaso [1985]).

F. Crime Types and Transitions

Changes in the commission of different types of crimes with age have already been discussed. Violent crimes generally peak at a later age than property crimes, for example. However, there is a need for careful data on the prevalence and incidence of different types of crimes at different ages, and the overall age-crime curves do not help in answering questions about changes between ages for particular individuals. Does the seriousness of offending tend to increase with age, or is it just that less serious offenders drop out and more serious ones appear for the first time? How far are offenders specialized or versatile in their offending patterns at different ages? How far do the types of offenses committed at one age predict the types committed at another, and how far can offending at one age be predicted from offending at another? These are the questions of interest here.

Unfortunately, studies of changes in the seriousness of offending with age have produced inconsistent results. In the Philadelphia cohort, using the Sellin-Wolfgang (1964) index of seriousness, Wolfgang (1980) found that the average seriousness of offenses was reasonably constant during the juvenile years but then increased during the young adult years. Collins (1981) reported that the seriousness of Index offenses peaked at age twenty to twenty-one. However, in the older two of Shannon's (1981) Racine cohorts, the average seriousness of offenses decreased steadily with age. This may be because Shannon's data, unlike Wolfgang's, included traffic violations. In Van Dusen and Mednick's (1983) replication of the Philadelphia study in Copenhagen, the average seriousness of Index offenses decreased with age to reach a minimum level at age seventeen to eighteen and then increased again. None of these results show changes in offense seriousness for individuals. It may be that changes in the pattern of offending with age can only be understood by investigating the actual types of crimes committed rather than by using summary measures of seriousness.

Petersilia et al. (1978) and Peterson et al. (1981), in their retrospective self-report studies of prisoners, both found that the number of different types of crimes committed decreased with age, in agreement with the hypothesis of increasing specialization. Petersilia et al. concluded that the average seriousness of offenses decreased from the juvenile to the adult years, but this seemed to be largely because of the low seriousness score of drug sales, which increased markedly with age.

Wolfgang et al. (1972) popularized the study of offense to offense transitions with increasing age. Generally, their transition matrices show no specialization from one age to the next, just as they showed no specialization from one arrest to the next. However, the probability of an Index offense being followed by no offense declined steadily with age (from ten to sixteen), just as the probability of no offense being followed by any offense increased steadily with age (from ten to sixteen). The probability of transition from a non-Index to an Index offense remained fairly constant over age, as did the probability of transition from one Index offense to another.

Rojek and Erickson (1982) essentially replicated the Wolfgang et al. transition matrices analysis for arrests. However, they also showed that the lack of specialization held independently of the age at the first arrest. Rankin and Wells (1985) derived transition matrices for self-reported offending in their reanalysis of the Bachman et al. (1978) longitudinal survey. They were interested in the concept of escalation, but they found that there was almost as much de-escalation from delinquency to status offenses (between age twelve to fifteen and age sixteen to eighteen) as escalation from status to delinquency offenses.

These analyses of transition matrices are bedeviled by methodological problems. First, there is the difficulty of disentangling the effects of age from those of other variables confounded with age, such as the number of previous offenses. Second, the more frequent offenders contribute more transition matrices to the total than do the less frequent offenders, so that a lack of specialization may be true of the more frequent offenders but possibly not of the less frequent ones. Third, some offenders may switch only between a small number of types of crimes, so it may be misleading to refer to them as generalists. Fourth, it is important to determine how the results are affected by the number of categories of crime used. As the number of categories decreases, the likelihood of concluding that offenders specialize should increase, but so too will the likelihood of this conclusion being misleading.

Most important, there is a need for a standard summary measure of specialization versus generalization. One possibility will be illustrated by reference to table 4, which is derived from Phillpotts and Lancucki's (1979) six-year follow-up in records of a nationally representative sample of 5,000 English nontraffic offenders. Table 4A shows the type of offense committed on conviction and on the first reconviction for 1,194 males who were under twenty-one on conviction and who were reconvicted, while table 4B shows the same figures for 1,130 males who were twenty-one or over on conviction. Offenses were divided up into three types, personal (violence and sex), property (burglary, robbery, theft, handling), and others (principally fraud, forgery, and damage to property).

The figures in parentheses show the expected cell entries on the assumption that there is no relation between conviction and reconvic-

TABLE 4

Specialization in Offending

A. Under Twenty-one on Conviction

Conviction Offense	Reconviction Offense			Total	Coefficient	z
	Personal	Property	Other			
Personal	42 (25.8)	67 (84.7)	21 (19.5)	130	.15	3.77
Property	182 (185.6)	630 (609.2)	123 (140.2)	935	.06	3.06
Other	13 (25.6)	81 (84.1)	35 (19.3)	129	.14	4.09
Total	237	778	179	1194		

B. Twenty-one or Over on Conviction

Conviction Offense	Reconviction Offense			Total	Coefficient	z
	Personal	Property	Other			
Personal	52 (20.0)	55 (87.4)	38 (37.6)	145	.26	8.25
Property	76 (102.4)	515 (447.2)	151 (192.4)	742	.23	8.68
Other	28 (33.5)	111 (146.4)	104 (63.0)	243	.23	6.77
Total	156	681	293	1130		

SOURCE.—Phillpotts and Lancucki (1979, table 4.3).
NOTE.—Figures in parentheses are expected figures based on row and column totals. See text for definition of coefficient. z = the adjusted standardized residual.

tion offenses (i.e., complete generalization). It can be seen that the observed figures are greater than the expected figures in all diagonal cells (personal conviction–personal reconviction, etc.), suggesting some degree of specialization. The observed and expected figures in both tables are significantly different according to the χ^2 test, again showing some specialization (under twenty-one: $\chi^2 = 36.0$; twenty-one or over: $\chi^2 = 115.1$; both significant at $p < .001$). Furthermore, the larger value of χ^2 in table 4B indicates that specialization increases with age.

The following coefficient of specialization is proposed for each diagonal cell:

$$\text{Coefficient} = \frac{\text{observed} - \text{expected}}{\text{row total} - \text{expected}}.$$

This coefficient seems useful because it is zero when there is complete generalization (and hence the observed figure equals the expected one) and one when there is perfect specialization (and hence every conviction offense becomes the same type of reconviction offense). The coefficients are shown in the right-hand column of table 4. They are not very high, indicating perhaps that these tables show a low degree of specialization superimposed on a high degree of generalization. The coefficients in table 4B are higher, again indicating more specialization at older ages. The statistical significance of each coefficient could be tested using the adjusted standardized residual (Bursik 1980). All the coefficients were significantly different from zero, at least partly because of the large numbers involved in the tables.

One interesting question is the extent to which offenders at one age tend also to be offenders at other ages. Farrington (1986) showed that the best predictor of offending at all ages between ten and twenty-five was offending at the immediately prior age and that these results held for both self-reported and official measures of offending. Generally, there is considerable continuity in offending between the juvenile and the adult years (Langan and Farrington 1983).

Shannon (1985) has argued that juvenile offending is not a useful predictor of adult offending. He concentrates on errors in prediction. For example, in his 1949 cohort, fifteen out of forty-five males (33 percent) with three or more juvenile offenses also had three or more adult offenses, in comparison with sixteen out of 560 males (3 percent) with two or fewer juvenile offenses. Therefore, having three or more juvenile offenses would only identify about half of those with three or more adult offenses. However, the contrast between a "hit rate" of 33 percent and one of 3 percent does nothing to shake my belief in the continuity of offending from the juvenile to the adult years.

IV. Why Are Age and Crime Related?

Hirschi and Gottfredson (1983) argued that the relation between age and crime was invariant or, in other words, that it held independently of, and could not be explained by reference to, other variables. Consequently, age had a direct causal effect on crime. They also argued that the causes of crime were the same at every age, so longitudinal research was unnecessary in studying crime causation. In discussing possible causal relationships involving age and crime, the key questions are those raised earlier in connection with sex. First, does the relation between age and crime hold independently of other variables? Second, does the relation between other variables and crime hold independently of age?

Before discussing these questions, it is desirable to clarify the concept of a causal relationship. Ideally, what is meant is a functional relationship of the following kind: $y = f(x)$. For example, in physics, Boyle's law specifies that decreasing the volume of a gas will cause a predictable increase in its pressure. In other words, the pressure (y) is a reciprocal function of the volume (x). This relationship, like many others, only holds within certain boundary conditions of pressure and volume. In criminology, the dependent variable of interest might be conceptualized as the underlying rate of offending, or incidence rate, which may be probabilistically related to actual offending as in the Cohen (1983) model.[5] In other words, the number of offenses a person actually commits in any given time period depends on his or her incidence rate and on situational factors that can be viewed as random or unpredictable. The key causal question in criminology is, How does the incidence of offending change as a function of changes in other variables?

Answering this question is complicated by the different kinds of other variables that are possible. Some factors (e.g., the number of delinquent peers) can vary within individuals and, at least in principle, can be manipulated in an experiment. Age is a factor that varies within individuals but that cannot be manipulated. Other factors vary only between individuals and cannot be manipulated (e.g., sex and race). Again, some factors can vary continuously, while others (e.g., the death of a parent) occur at one particular time. The simplest way of interpreting the statement that "x is a cause of crime" is that "changes in x will cause changes in the incidence rate." Clearly, it is easiest to demonstrate that a factor causes crime if it varies within individuals and if it can be manipulated in an experiment. For example, Feldman,

---

[5] Hirschi and Gottfredson (1985*b*) have proposed a distinction between criminality (the propensity to commit crimes) and crimes. In some respects, this seems similar to Cohen's (1983) distinction between underlying and observed incidence rates.

Caplinger, and Wodarski (1983) demonstrated experimentally that anti-social youths placed in groups of prosocial peers showed less antisocial behavior than those placed in groups of antisocial peers.

Saying that age causes crime is equivalent to saying that changes in age in some way cause changes in incidence rates. It seems more likely that age measures an underlying theoretical construct that causes crime than that age is itself a causal factor. Since age cannot be manipulated in an experiment, it is essential to show that changes in incidence rates that are correlated with changes in age are not caused by changes in other factors. This requires information about how incidence rates (and other variables) vary with age within individuals. In turn, this means that longitudinal research involving frequent data collection is required. Unfortunately, almost all existing age-crime curves are essentially aggregate curves that probably bear little relation to individual ones. Much more detailed information is needed about how age and crime vary within individuals before it is possible to determine whether any relationships hold independently of other variables.

It may be easier to determine whether relationships between other variables and crime hold independently of age. Some factors only apply at certain ages. For example, the relation between marriage and crime cannot be studied among ten-year-olds, any more than the relation between truancy and crime can be studied among sixty-year-olds. Other factors may have different meanings at different ages. For example, since the socioeconomic status of youngsters is determined according to the jobs of their parents, while the socioeconomic status of older people depends on their own jobs, different relations at different ages between socioeconomic status and crime (Thornberry and Farnworth 1982) are not too surprising. Again, increased unemployment of adults may lead to increased crime by adults but to decreased crime by juveniles (Glaser and Rice 1959), perhaps because the unemployed adults are able to exercise closer supervision over their children. It seems implausible to argue that all variables are related to crime in the same way at all ages.

The present state of knowledge does not permit an answer to either of the questions posed above. However, if it is accepted that the best way of determining the causes of crime is to study changes within individuals, this indicates that the best method of investigation is longitudinal (preferably including experimental elements; see Farrington, Ohlin, and Wilson [1986]).

A. Possible Explanations

Many explanations have been proposed for the aggregate age-crime curve, on the basis of individual or environmental factors that change with age. If the age-crime curve primarily reflects prevalence, researchers should concentrate on explaining onset and termination rather than changes in incidence.

There may be biological factors that influence some crimes at different ages. For example, it has often been argued (Gibbens and Prince 1962) that shoplifting by females increases at the time of menopause. Crimes have been linked to testosterone levels in males, which increase during adolescence and early adulthood and thereafter decline. However, the age-testosterone curve does not have the same sharp peak in the teenage years that the age-crime curve does (Gove 1985; Hirschi and Gottfredson 1985a). Physical factors may be important in some crimes. For example, the ability to climb buildings and hence to commit burglaries may peak in the teenage years. Some offenses, such as car theft, depend on skills and knowledge acquired during the period from childhood to adulthood. As skills and knowledge increase, so too will offending.

Kohlberg (1976) suggested that offending was linked to changes in moral reasoning with age. Each person was supposed to pass through three stages of moral development: preconventional, conventional, and postconventional. The preconventional person was one who had not yet come to understand and obey the law and whose conformity to the law depended on the likelihood of legal punishment. According to Kohlberg, this was the level of most children under nine, some adolescents, and many criminal offenders. The conventional person was one who obeyed the law purely because it was the law, because of conscience, or to avoid the breakdown of society. The postconventional individual obeyed the law to the extent that it conformed with higher moral principles such as rights and duties. The conventional level was said to characterize most adolescents and adults, while the postconventional level was reached by a minority, usually only after age twenty. This theory has been criticized (Kurtines and Grief 1974), but there is some empirical support for it (Scharf and Hickey 1976). By itself, it cannot explain why crime reaches a peak in the teenage years, but it may account for the termination of offending. It is similar in some respects to Glueck and Glueck's (1940) proposal that desistance from offending is linked to maturation.

Explanations that link the age-crime curve to changes in the social environment are more popular and probably more important than those stressing changes only in individual factors. From birth, children are under the influence of their parents, who generally discourage offending. It is interesting that the best predictor of the onset of offending is poor parental control (Loeber and Dishion 1983). However, during their teenage years, children gradually break away from the control of their parents and become influenced by their peers, who may encourage offending in many cases. Elliott, Huizinga, and Ageton (1985) found that the most important correlate of offending in their longitudinal survey was having delinquent friends, and this factor also proved to be an important predictor in the Farrington (1986) survey. Group offending is most common in the teenage years.

After age twenty, offending declines as peer influence gives way to family influence, except this time the family influence originates in spouses rather than in parents. Spontaneous comments by the youths in the London longitudinal survey indicated that withdrawal from the delinquent peer group was seen as an important factor in ceasing to offend (West and Farrington 1977). Also, West (1982) reported that marriage led to a decline in offending, providing that a young man married a nondelinquent woman. If he married a delinquent woman, his offending seemed to get worse.

Trasler (1979) outlined a variant of this theory in which the emphasis was on reinforcement contingencies in the environment. Parents tended to reward conformity and punish offending, and these external controls in many cases led to internal controls (a strong conscience) in the child. However, during the teenage years, offending tended to be reinforced by peer approval and excitement, and so it became more likely. As adults, people tended to desist from offending as adult reinforcers (employment, income, spouses, and children) became available. A similar explanation was proposed by Wilson and Herrnstein (1985), who also emphasized people's increasing ability with age to delay gratification and to take account of the possible future consequences of their actions. A major implication of this approach is that offending can be reduced by changing the pattern of reinforcements in the community (Farrington 1979a).

It is interesting to study the reasons given for crime at different ages. Petersilia et al. (1978) reported that the main reasons given by their armed robbers for crimes in the juvenile years were thrills and peer influence. In the adult years, the main reason given for crime was to obtain money, most commonly for drugs, alcohol, or self-support, but sometimes for women or for family support. West and Farrington (1977) also found that a significant proportion of reasons given in the juvenile years mentioned excitement or enjoyment (especially in stealing cars, vandalism, and shoplifting), while more rational or economic reasons stressing material gain became more common as their cohort got older.

Greenberg (1979a, 1983) has emphasized the role of economic factors in explaining the age-crime curve. He argued that juveniles desire to participate in social activities but that, because they are excluded from the labor market or limited to part-time, poorly paid jobs by child labor laws, they have insufficient funds from legitimate sources to finance these. Therefore, they commit crimes in order to meet their perceived needs. Furthermore, the absence from home of parents working means that juveniles are often not subject to informal social control. When they become adults, employment, leaving school, military enlistment, and marriage eliminate major sources of criminogenic frustration and at the same time supply informal social control. Greenberg also drew attention to the changing opportunities for crime (e.g., employee theft) with age. However, Hirschi and Gottfredson (1985b) argued against this theory, claiming that the adult institutions of employment and marriage were not related to offending as predicted.

McKissack (1967, 1973) noted that, in England, the peak age of offending coincided with the last year of compulsory schooling. It may be that this is the age of maximum boredom for many low-achieving children and hence the age at which the need for excitement outside school becomes most intense. If the school has a role in producing offending, crime should decrease after people leave school. In agreement with this, Elliott (1966) and Elliott and Voss (1974) found that dropping out of school seemed to produce a decline in offending.

Many of the ideas put forward in this section can be found in classic theories of delinquency. For example, Cohen (1955) emphasized the role of school failure in producing delinquent subcultures and argued that working-class boys were likely to fail in school because their parents were less likely to have taught them reasoning, middle-class manners, the avoidance of aggression, and the postponement of immediate gratification in favor of long-term goals. Cloward and Ohlin (1960) stressed the rational element in delinquency as a way of achieving culturally induced goals (such as material success) by illegitimate means. Hirschi (1969) proposed that offending depended on the strength of a person's bond to society, which in turn depended on attachment to parents and internalization of their wishes, and also emphasized the rational weighing of costs against benefits in deciding whether to offend. The differential association theory of Sutherland and Cressey (1974) would also predict that offending would vary with changes in social influence, from parents to peers, for example. Hence, as Greenberg (1985) argued, a substantial part of the relation between age and crime could be explained by familiar social concepts. Nevertheless, while it may not be necessary at present to propose that age causes crime, it cannot yet be concluded that the relation between age and crime has been explained convincingly by reference to other factors.

B. Criminal Justice System Influences

The most obvious way in which the criminal justice system influences the age-crime curve is through cutoff points defined by law. In England, the age of criminal responsibility is ten, so no person under ten can commit a crime in the strictly legal sense. However, in behavioral terms, it seems likely that many children under ten engage in stealing, vandalism, aggression, and so on. Committing an offense at an early age is a bad sign since the earliest offenders tend to be the most serious and persistent in later life. It may be that more attention should be given to "offending" before the age of criminal responsibility, to establish whether this is followed by an especially serious and persistent adult criminal career. Another important question is whether interventions designed to prevent crime are more effective if applied at earlier ages, possibly under age ten. The preschool "Head Start" program described by Berrueta-Clement et al. (1984) was surprisingly effective in preventing later arrests.

Setting a minimum age of criminal responsibility was originally justified by reference to the intellectual capacities of children. Keasey and Sales (1977a) reviewed some of the many definitions of criminal responsibility, including knowledge of the nature and illegality of the offense, awareness that the act is wrong, capability of entertaining a criminal intent, comprehension of the consequences of the offense, power to discriminate right from wrong, demonstration of intelligent design and malice in executing the act, and a mischievous inclination or disposition. They argued that the key element underlying a court's enquiry into mens rea was whether the child intended to commit the act and hence that research on the development of the concept of intention was especially important.

Many years ago, Piaget (1932) found that children under seven judged naughtiness not in terms of intentions but in terms of the consequences of the act (e.g., the resulting damage). This research was used to justify the age of criminal responsibility of seven that had prevailed in England from the seventeenth century up to the 1933 Children and Young Persons Act (Kean 1937). If children under seven could not understand the concept of intent, then they could not intentionally commit criminal acts. However, Keasey and Sales (1977b) asked children aged five, six, and seven to judge stories about arson, assault, theft, and homicide. They found that the judgments of naughtiness were based on intent rather than consequences for 67 percent of the five-year-olds, 83 percent of the six-year-olds, and 89 percent of the seven-year-olds. Therefore, it is hard to justify an age of criminal responsibility of even seven on the grounds of children's lack of understanding of the concept of intent.

There are a number of key questions about the minimum age of criminal responsibility that are as yet unanswered. At what age is it better to deal with offending through the criminal justice system as opposed to the social welfare system? What is the effect on children's offending of the possibility of criminal justice system intervention? For example, do English nine-year-olds feel that they can commit offenses with impunity? And how much offending is there by children under ten? It would be desirable to breach the legal barrier to complete the age-crime curve and obtain more accurate information about the age of onset of offending.

Rather similar questions arise in connection with an arguably more important legal cutoff point, namely, between juvenile and adult offending. In England, it is notable that the peak age for convictions of seventeen coincides with the minimum age of adult court processing. In general, the police hold off prosecuting offenders as long as they are legally juveniles (preferring instead to caution them), but these inhibitions disappear once an offender becomes legally adult. Again, it is important to establish the effect of juvenile as opposed to adult court processing. In the United States, Ruhland, Gold, and Hekman (1982) compared the official and self-reported offending of seventeen-year-olds in states where they were legally juveniles and in states where they were legally adults. They found that seventeen-year-olds who would be processed as juveniles committed more offenses, suggesting that the adult criminal justice system had more of a deterrent effect.

The increasing severity of legal penalties is often cited as a major reason for the decline in offending with age (Greenberg 1979a). Shover

(1983) interviewed fifty previously incarcerated men at an average age of fifty-one and asked them why they had given up crime. Generally, what had changed was their calculation of costs and benefits. The perceived costs of crime increased greatly as they got older, not only in terms of the increased likelihood of lengthy prison sentences, but also in terms of the consequent risk of losing their families and their jobs. Many felt that the criminal justice system had gradually worn them down over the years.

While it is widely believed that the probability and length of prison sentences increase with age (at least from eighteen to thirty), there is surprisingly little evidence about this. Petersilia et al. (1978) showed that both the probability of conviction after an arrest and the probability of incarceration after a conviction increased for their robbers from the juvenile through the young adult to the adult years. However, Greenwood, Abrahamse, and Zimring (1984) and Greenwood, Petersilia, and Zimring (1980) did not find a consistent increase with age in incarceration probabilities in various sites across the United States, and neither did Langan and Farrington (1983) in England. In investigating the relation between age and sentence severity, what is needed is research that controls for other relevant factors such as type of offense and number of previous convictions. Greenwood et al. (1984) reported that young adults with extensive juvenile records were sentenced more severely than those without such records.

V. Conclusions

The age-crime curve is not invariant. Many curves appear to be superficially similar in peaking in the teenage years, but more subtle aspects of the distribution (such as the extent to which it is skewed or sharply peaked) vary considerably with such basic variables as sex and crime type. The more detailed summary measures of the curves show that offending is not predominantly a teenage phenomenon. The average age of offenders is twenty-five to thirty, and only about a quarter are aged up to and including the peak in the teenage years.

The familiar age-crime curve is an aggregate curve and reflects variations in the prevalence of offending rather than in incidence. Age-crime curves for individuals are likely to be very different from the aggregate curve since current evidence suggests that incidence does not increase or decrease systematically between onset and termination. The aggregate age-crime curve peaks at about sixteen to seventeen, with the peak age of acceleration at about fourteen to fifteen and of deceleration at about eighteen to nineteen. These peaks in acceleration and deceleration, which probably coincide with peak ages of onset and termination, are likely to identify ages at which important developmental changes are occurring. The cumulative prevalence of arrests over age is surprisingly high, and in some cases (e.g., black males) nonarrested persons are in the minority.

Different types of offenses peak at different ages, and this probably reflects crime switching by offenders rather than one group of persons ending their criminal careers and another group starting. Characteristics of crimes change with age, with group offending and the motive of excitement peaking in the teenage years. There is generally little specialization in offending, but this does seem to increase with age, and the number of types of crimes committed decreases. There is continuity in offending from one age to the next since the worst offenders at one age tend also to be the worst at others. However, there is no consistent evidence of escalation in the seriousness of offending with increasing age. An early age of onset seems to be followed by a long criminal career, but whether it is followed by a higher incidence rate is not clear. The residual length of criminal careers may peak at age thirty to forty.

It is unnecessary to postulate that age has a direct effect on crime. It is difficult to study whether age is related to crime independently of other variables because of the nonlinear relationship between age and crime. Also, it is desirable to take account of the different kinds of variables and especially of whether they vary within or only between individuals, whether they are manipulable, and whether they change at one time or vary continuously. Age effects need to be separated from period and cohort effects in particular as well as from the influences of other variables. The most plausible theory is that the age-crime curve reflects decreasing parental controls, a peaking of peer influence in the teenage years, and then increasing family and community controls with age.

It is very unlikely that other variables are related to crime in the same way at different ages. For example, the ratio of male to female offenders generally decreases with age. Therefore, it cannot be deduced that longitudinal research is unnecessary. The advantages of longitudinal studies have been discussed earlier in this essay.

A. Implications for Policy

That the age-crime curve primarily reflects changing prevalence has major implications for policy. A court faced with an offender aged twenty-five, for example, cannot necessarily assume that that person's criminal behavior will decline in the next few years as the aggregate curve does. The probability of termination may be lower at twenty-five than at eighteen, the expected residual career length may be higher, the incidence of offending may be just as great, and the seriousness of offenses may be higher. In other words, characteristics of the aggregate age-crime curve cannot necessarily be imputed to the individual offender at any given age. It is important to develop predictors of quantities such as the residual career length, termination, and the future incidence rate at different ages, in evaluating penal policy options such as incapacitation.

Since the age-crime curve reflects prevalence, a major aim of public policy should be to prevent onset and encourage termination. It is especially desirable to prevent the onset of offending at an early age since that is often a precursor of a long criminal career. In the past, some commentators have deduced from the age-crime curve that the best policy is to "leave them alone and they will grow out of it." This policy is most plausible if applied to offenders of relatively late onset (say at fourteen or fifteen), who may offend in groups primarily for excitement and who may have short criminal careers. It would be ineffectual with those first offending at an early age. It may be that the criminal justice system should not deal so leniently with offenders under age thirteen since effective treatment at this age would have disproportionate benefits. It is certainly essential to target these offenders for special efforts, whether within or outside the criminal justice system.

It is important to establish the relative effects of different kinds of interventions at different ages. At present, penalties are thought to be lenient in the juvenile years and then increasingly severe for adults. It is interesting that the increasing legal penalties are quoted as a reason for giving up crime, just as is the influence of a spouse or a job. If the penalties for juveniles were increased, or if the separate juvenile court were abolished, would offenders terminate earlier? An alternative strategy would be to increase agency efforts to help ex-offenders settle down with spouses and jobs as early as possible.

The remarkably high cumulative prevalence of arrests and convictions is a matter for concern. Is it in the best interests of society to criminalize such a high proportion of the population, especially when there is some evidence that one effect of a conviction is to make the convicted person more hostile to the police (Farrington 1977)? It might be better to concentrate resources on the more serious crimes and ignore some of the more trivial ones, at least in the absence of evidence of escalation. What is needed is more information about the future criminal careers of different types of offenders at different ages, to know in which cases trivial crimes are stepping stones in a developmental sequence leading to more serious offenses.

B. Future Research

In order to advance knowledge about the relation between age and crime, multiple cohort longitudinal studies are needed. It is impracticable to follow a single cohort from the cradle to the grave. The most feasible design is to follow a number of cohorts for a number of years, combining the results to build up a complete picture of the relation between age and crime. It should be possible to take advantage of the cross-sectional and longitudinal elements to achieve some separation of aging, period, and cohort effects. Frequent data collection is essential, using a variety of methods, including interviews and searches of records. This would make it possible to relate changes in criminal behavior at different ages to changes in parental controls, peer influences, unemployment, and so on. In turn, this would help in establishing the extent to which the age-crime curve can be explained by changes in other variables with age.

The aim should be to collect detailed information for individuals at different ages about prevalence, incidence, and different types of crimes committed. Efforts should be made to identify ages of onset and termination for different types of crimes and hence lengths of criminal careers. It is important to establish relations between these different variables. For example, do those who offend at the earliest ages differ in the types of crimes committed or in subsequent incidence rates? Predictive analyses are desirable at different ages. There is scope for obtaining much more detailed information from self-reports about the exact ages of offending, transition matrices between different ages, group offending, reasons for offending, cumulative prevalence, and so on.

In my estimation, a multiple cohort longitudinal study focusing on age and crime as a unifying principle would greatly advance our knowledge about the causes of crime and would also help in evaluating public policies for dealing with crime.

APPENDIX

It is not easy to summarize the relation between age and crime. In general, measures of association in the social sciences assume linear (straight line) relations. The product-moment correlation, for example, essentially measures how closely the relation between two variables approximates a straight line. A low correlation is usually interpreted as indicating no relation between the variables, whereas in fact it may reflect a nonlinear relation. Where two variables have a nonlinear relation (as in the case of age and crime), there is no generally accepted method of measuring strength of association. The best way of summarizing such a relation is probably to propose a mathematical function that fits the data. Essentially, the same approach underlies the use of the product-moment correlation for the special case in which two variables have a straight line relation. If crime rates increased linearly with age, there would be no problem.

Just as there is no generally accepted measure of association for two variables that are not linearly related, there is no generally accepted measure of partial association after controlling for a third variable. Conventional partial correlation measures assume not only linear but also additive relations, of the following kind:

$$y = a + b_1x_1 + b_2x_2,$$

where y is a dependent variable and x_1 and x_2 are independent variables. In studying how age was related to crime independently of some third variable, it would be necessary to specify not only the functional relation between the third variable and crime but also how crime varied as a function of age and of the third variable. Again, different mathematical functions and methods of combining functions could be tested to see which ones fit the data best. By appropriate transformations and substitutions, it may be possible to derive an equation like the above, where y is a function of crime, x_1 is a function of age, x_2 is a function of the third variable, and there are interaction terms such as $b_3x_1x_2$. In this case, b_1 would measure the contribution of age independently of the third variable, b_2 would measure the contribution of the third variable independently of age, and b_3 would measure the interaction between age and the third variable.

This approach is undoubtedly complex. One unfortunate implication is that it is difficult to answer questions such as, Is age or sex more strongly related to offending? However, an advantage of studying the relation between age and crime is that it forces researchers to study distributions and to grapple with the problem of nonlinear relations. Researchers may be too ready to assume that a relation is linear, because of mathematical convenience, without testing whether it approximates a straight line in reality. There may be variables that have been neglected in the literature because of their low correlations with criminal behavior but that on closer inspection show marked nonlinear relations.

Because sex is a dichotomous (as opposed to a continuous) variable, it is more feasible to investigate whether age is related to crime independently of sex than independently of other variables. The hypothesis to be tested is that the age-crime curve is the same for males and females. Each age could be regarded as analogous to a score on a test. The distribution of "scores" of male offenders could then be compared with that of female offenders, to see whether they differed significantly. The usual test for differences between distributions of scores is Student's t-test, based on means and standard deviations. Even if the scores are not normally distributed, the t-test can be used with large samples because the sampling distribution of the difference between two sample means will be normally distributed (Blalock 1972, p. 220). Another possible approach is to use a nonparametric test of the difference between two distributions, such as the Kolmogorov-Smirnov test (Siegel 1956, p. 127). Another possibility is to analyze the relation between age, sex, and crime (the number of offenders and nonoffenders) as a large contingency table, using loglinear methods (Fienberg 1980).

All these methods are complex and/or not easily applicable to types of variables other than sex. It might be more satisfactory to base analyses on mathematical functions linking crime with age and other variables.

Mathematical Specification of the Age-Crime Curve

In specifying the mathematical function relating age and crime, the problem is as follows. If crime $= y$ and age $= x$, what is the function f in $y = f(x)$? It is clear that $f(x)$ must specify a unimodal, positively skewed probability distribution. It would no doubt be possible to fit a complex polynomial equation to the empirical curve, but it would be more satisfactory to discover a simpler function, especially one that made sense theoretically.

An immediate problem is where to set the origin for age. In England, where the minimum age of criminal responsibility is ten, all crime rates under age ten are by definition zero. Therefore, in fitting curves derived from official records, it would be plausible to set

$$x = (\text{age} - 9) \text{ years,}$$

where age is an integer. One of the simplest probability distributions that resembles the age curve, and that has only one parameter (or theoretical variable), is the Poisson distribution. This has been used widely in criminology (e.g., Cohen 1983). The equation is as follows:

$$y = \frac{e^{-\lambda}\lambda^x}{x!},$$

where λ is the parameter. However, despite the superficial resemblance, it is clear that the age-crime curve is not a Poisson distribution. In a Poisson distribution, the mean and variance are equal to each other and to λ. However, in the age-crime curve, the variance far exceeds the mean. For example, table 1 shows that, for English males in 1983, the mean age was 24.9 and the standard deviation was 11.8. The variance, which is the square of the standard deviation, was 140.2 or 8.8 times the mean value of x of 15.9 (age $- 9$).

Another simple probability distribution that resembles the age curve and that has only one parameter is the χ^2 distribution. The equation is as follows:

$$y = \frac{e^{-(x/2)}x^{(v/2)-1}}{2^{v/2}\left(\dfrac{v}{2} - 1\right)!},$$

where v is the parameter or the number of degrees of freedom of the distribution. However, since the mean of this distribution is v and the variance is only $2v$, it is clearly not a good model for the age-crime distribution.

Moving up to two parameters, another simple distribution that resembles the age-crime curve is the gamma distribution (e.g., Greenberg 1979b, pp. 271–72). The equation is as follows:

$$y = \frac{b^a e^{-bx} x^{a-1}}{G(a)},$$

where a and b are parameters and $G(a)$ is the gamma function:

$$G(a) = \int_{z=0}^{\infty} z^{a-1} e^{-z} dz.$$

With this distribution, the mean equals a/b and the variance equals a/b^2. Given a mean value of x of 15.9 for English males in 1983 and a variance of 140.2, $a = 1.8$ and $b = 0.11$. Figure A1a shows the gamma distribution in comparison with the age-crime curve for English males, and figure A1b shows the same curves for English females. The age-crime curves are expressed as probability distributions, again assuming the same number of people at each age. Thus the curve for English males peaks at age fifteen at .065 (or 6.5 percent of all crimes) rather than at 8.2 crimes per 100 population, but otherwise it is identical to the curve in figure 1a. Figure A1a, b, shows that the gamma distribution is not as sharply peaked as the age-crime curve. Also, the peak age, which occurs at $x = (a - 1)/b$, is slightly too high, being sixteen for males and fifteen for females.

A better fit can be achieved by moving up to three parameters and assuming the following functional relationship between x and y:

$$y = ax^b e^{-cx},$$

where a, b, and c are parameters. Essentially, what this equation indicates is that the age-crime curve is a combination of two functions, one (x^b) increasing with age and the other (e^{-cx}) decreasing. The χ^2 and gamma distributions are both of this general form. An increase in b will shift the peak to the right, while an increase in c will shift the peak to the left. The third parameter (a) essentially sets the overall height of the curve.

There are various ways of determining the parameters. Because of the importance attached to the peak age, I decided to require that the peak age of the fitted curve was correct. For any unimodal curve of the form $y = f(x)$, the peak occurs when $dy/dx = 0$. If

$$y = ax^b e^{-cx},$$

then

$$\frac{dy}{dx} = ax^{b-1} e^{-cx}(b - cx).$$

Therefore, at the peak, $b - cx = 0$, or $x = b/c$. For English males in 1983, the peak age was at fifteen. Since $x = $ age $- 9$, it followed that $b = 6c$. The

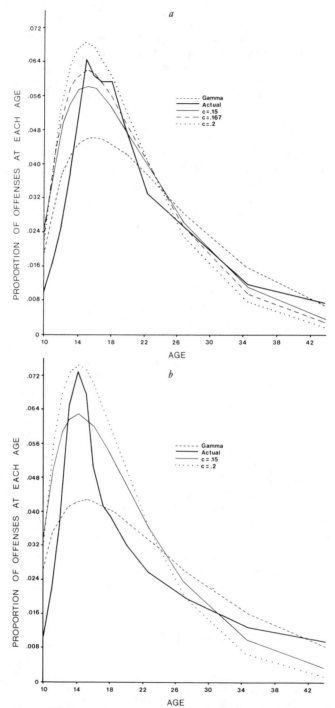

FIG. A1.—*a*, Fitting the age-crime curve for English males in 1983. *b*, Fitting the age-crime curve for English females in 1983. Source of actual curves: Home Office (1984).

parameter a was set to determine a probability distribution with the sum of all the crime rates at all ages as one. Figure A1a shows that values of c of .15 and .20 produced reasonable fits to the observed distribution, as did the special case of c = .167 (when b = 1). For English females in 1983, the peak age was at fourteen, leading to a requirement that b = 5c. Figure A1b shows that values of c of .15 and .20 (when b = 1) again produced reasonable fits to the observed distribution. In both cases, the fit might have been improved by assuming that x = age − 10, but it would have been incorrect and undesirable to assume that the crime rate was zero at age ten.

This section shows that it is possible to fit the age-crime curve approximately with a mathematical model containing only three parameters. One (b) determines the speed of increase of the curve up to the peak, one (c) determines the speed of decrease of the curve after the peak, and one (a) determines the height of the peak. The relative sizes of b and c determine the peak of the curve in the teenage years. For c = .15, a = .0287 for males and .04 for females. Age-crime curves can be compared more easily if they can be summarized by only three parameters.

No doubt a better fit to the data could be achieved with a more complex mathematical model containing more parameters. For example, in figure A1a, c = .167 is a reasonable fit to the left-hand peak, but c = .10 is a better fit to the right-hand tail of the distribution. Therefore, a more complex model might be

$$y = a_1 x^{b_1} e^{-c_1 x}$$

for ages up to forty and

$$y = a_2 x^{b_2} e^{-c_2 x}$$

for ages over forty, with c_1 = .167 and c_2 = .10. However, there is a trade-off between the complexity of a model and the fit to the data. The most useful model is often a simple one with a reasonable fit, and that is what has been proposed here.

REFERENCES

Achenbach, Thomas M., and Craig S. Edelbrock. 1981. *Behavior Problems and Competencies Reported by Parents of Normal and Disturbed Children Aged 4 through 16*. Monographs of the Society for Research in Child Development, vol. 46, no. 1, serial no. 188. Chicago: University of Chicago Press.

Bachman, Jerald G., Patrick M. O'Malley, and Jerome Johnston. 1978. *Youth in Transition*. Vol. 6. Ann Arbor: University of Michigan, Institute for Social Research.

Ball, John C., Alan Ross, and Alice Simpson. 1964. "Incidence and Estimated Prevalence of Recorded Delinquency in a Metropolitan Area." *American Sociological Review* 29:90–93.

244   David P. Farrington

Barnett, Arnold, and Anthony Lofaso. 1985. "Selective Incapacitation and the Philadelphia Cohort Data." *Journal of Quantitative Criminology* 1:3–36.

Berrueta-Clement, John R., Lawrence J. Schweinhart, W. Steven Barnett, Ann S. Epstein, and David P. Weikart. 1984. *Changed Lives.* Ypsilanti, Mich.: High/Scope.

Blalock, Hubert M. 1972. *Social Statistics.* 2d ed. New York: McGraw-Hill.

Blumstein, Alfred, and Jacqueline Cohen. 1979. "Estimation of Individual Crime Rates from Arrest Records." *Journal of Criminal Law and Criminology* 70:561–85.

Blumstein, Alfred, Jacqueline Cohen, and Paul Hsieh. 1982. *The Duration of Adult Criminal Careers.* Final Report to the National Institute of Justice. Washington, D.C.: National Institute of Justice.

Blumstein, Alfred, Jacqueline Cohen, and Harold D. Miller. 1980. "Demographically Disaggregated Projections of Prison Populations." *Journal of Criminal Justice* 8:1–26.

Blumstein, Alfred, David P. Farrington, and Soumyo Moitra. 1985. "Delinquency Careers: Innocents, Desisters, and Persisters." In *Crime and Justice: An Annual Review of Research,* vol. 6, edited by Michael Tonry and Norval Morris. Chicago: University of Chicago Press.

Blumstein, Alfred, and Elizabeth Graddy. 1982. "Prevalence and Recidivism in Index Arrests: A Feedback Model." *Law and Society Review* 16:265–90.

Bursik, Robert J. 1980. "The Dynamics of Specialization in Juvenile Offenses." *Social Forces* 58:581–64.

Carr-Hill, Roy A., Keith Hope, and Nick H. Stern. 1972. "Delinquent Generations Revisited." *Quality and Quantity* 2:327–52.

Christensen, Ronald. 1967. "Projected Percentage of U.S. Population with Criminal Arrest and Conviction Records." In *President's Commission on Law Enforcement and Administration of Justice: Task Force Report: Science and Technology.* Washington, D.C.: U.S. Government Printing Office.

Christiansen, Karl O. 1964. "Delinquent Generations in Denmark." *British Journal of Criminology* 4:259–64.

Christiansen, Karl O., and S. Gram Jensen. 1972. "Crime in Denmark—a Statistical History." *Journal of Criminal Law, Criminology, and Police Science* 63:82–92.

Cline, Hugh F. 1980. "Criminal Behavior over the Life Span." In *Constancy and Change in Human Development,* edited by Orville G. Brim and Jerome Kagan. Cambridge, Mass.: Harvard University Press.

Cloward, Richard A., and Lloyd E. Ohlin. 1960. *Delinquency and Opportunity.* New York: Free Press.

Cohen, Albert K. 1955. *Delinquent Boys.* Glencoe, Ill.: Free Press.

Cohen, Jacqueline. 1983. "Incapacitation as a Strategy for Crime Control: Possibilities and Pitfalls." In *Crime and Justice: An Annual Review of Research,* vol. 5, edited by Michael Tonry and Norval Morris. Chicago: University of Chicago Press.

Collins, James J. 1981. "Alcohol Careers and Criminal Careers." In *Drinking and Crime,* edited by James J. Collins. New York: Guilford Press.

Cook, Thomas D., and Donald T. Campbell. 1979. *Quasi-Experimentation*. Chicago: Rand McNally.

Elliott, Delbert S. 1966. "Delinquency, School Attendance, and Dropout." *Social Problems* 13:307–14.

Elliott, Delbert S., Suzanne S. Ageton, David Huizinga, Brian A. Knowles, and Rachelle J. Canter. 1983. *The Prevalence and Incidence of Delinquent Behavior: 1976–1980*. National Youth Survey Report, no. 26. Boulder, Colo.: Behavioral Research Institute.

Elliott, Delbert S., and David Huizinga. 1984. *The Relationship between Delinquent Behavior and ADM Problems*. National Youth Survey Report, no. 28. Boulder, Colo.: Behavioral Research Institute.

Elliott, Delbert S., David Huizinga, and Suzanne Ageton. 1985. *Explaining Delinquency and Drug Use*. Beverly Hills, Calif.: Sage.

Elliott, Delbert S., and Harwin L. Voss. 1974. *Delinquency and Dropout*. Lexington, Mass.: Heath.

Farrington, David P. 1977. "The Effects of Public Labeling." *British Journal of Criminology* 17:112–25.

———. 1979*a*. "Delinquent Behavior Modification in the Natural Environment." *British Journal of Criminology* 19:353–72.

———. 1979*b*. "Longitudinal Research on Crime and Delinquency." In *Crime and Justice: An Annual Review of Research*, vol. 1, edited by Norval Morris and Michael Tonry. Chicago: University of Chicago Press.

———. 1981. "The Prevalence of Convictions." *British Journal of Criminology* 21:173–75.

———. 1983. "Offending from 10 to 25 Years of Age." In *Prospective Studies of Crime and Delinquency*, edited by Katherine T. Van Dusen and Sarnoff A. Mednick. Boston: Kluwer-Nijhoff.

———. 1986. "Stepping Stones to Adult Criminal Careers." In *Development of Antisocial and Prosocial Behavior*, edited by Dan Olweus, Jack Block, and Marian R. Yarrow. New York: Academic Press.

Farrington, David P., and Trevor Bennett. 1981. "Police Cautioning of Juveniles in London." *British Journal of Criminology* 21:123–35.

Farrington, David P., Lloyd E. Ohlin, and James Q. Wilson. 1986. *Understanding and Controlling Crime: Toward a New Research Strategy*. New York: Springer-Verlag.

Federal Bureau of Investigation. 1983. *Uniform Crime Reports, 1982*. Washington, D.C.: U.S. Government Printing Office.

Feldman, Ronald A., Timothy E. Caplinger, and John S. Wodarski. 1983. *The St. Louis Conundrum*. Englewood Cliffs, N.J.: Prentice-Hall.

Fienberg, Stephen E. 1980. *The Analysis of Cross-classified Categorical Data*. 2d ed. Cambridge, Mass.: MIT Press.

Fienberg, Stephen E., and William M. Mason. 1979. "Identification and Estimation of Age-Period-Cohort Models in the Analysis of Discrete Archival Data." In *Sociological Methodology, 1979*, edited by Karl F. Schuessler. San Francisco: Jossey-Bass.

Flanagan, Timothy J. 1983. "Correlates of Institutional Misconduct among State Prisoners: A Research Note." *Criminology* 21:29–39.

Fry, Lincoln J. 1985. "Drug Abuse and Crime in a Swedish Birth Cohort." *British Journal of Criminology* 25:46–59.

Gibbens, Trevor C. N. 1984. "Borstal Boys after 25 Years." *British Journal of Criminology* 24:49–62.

Gibbens, Trevor C. N., and Joyce Prince. 1962. *Shoplifting.* London: Institute for the Study and Treatment of Delinquency.

Glaser, Daniel, and Kent Rice. 1959. "Crime, Age, and Unemployment." *American Sociological Review* 24:679–86.

Glenn, Norval D. 1977. *Cohort Analysis.* Beverly Hills, Calif.: Sage.

Glueck, Sheldon, and Eleanor T. Glueck. 1940. *Juvenile Delinquents Grown Up.* New York: Commonwealth Fund.

———. 1943. *Criminal Careers in Retrospect.* New York: Commonwealth Fund.

———. 1950. *Unraveling Juvenile Delinquency.* Cambridge, Mass.: Harvard University Press.

———. 1968. *Delinquents and Non-delinquents in Perspective.* Cambridge, Mass.: Harvard University Press.

Gold, Martin, and David J. Reimer. 1975. "Changing Patterns of Delinquent Behavior among Americans 13 through 16 Years Old: 1967–72." *Crime and Delinquency Literature* 7:483–517.

Gordon, Robert A. 1976. "Prevalence: The Rare Datum in Delinquency Measurement and Its Implications for the Theory of Delinquency." In *The Juvenile Justice System*, edited by Malcolm W. Klein. Beverly Hills, Calif.: Sage.

Gordon, Robert A., and Leon J. Gleser. 1974. "The Estimation of the Prevalence of Delinquency: Two Approaches and a Correction of the Literature." *Journal of Mathematical Sociology* 3:275–91.

Gove, Walter R. 1985. "The Effect of Age and Gender on Deviant Behavior: A Biopsychosocial Perspective." In *Gender and the Life Course*, edited by Alice S. Rossi. Hawthorne, N.Y.: Aldine.

Greenberg, David F. 1979a. "Delinquency and the Age Structure of Society." In *Criminology Review Yearbook*, edited by Sheldon Messinger and Egon Bittner. Beverly Hills, Calif.: Sage.

———. 1979b. *Mathematical Criminology.* New Brunswick, N.J.: Rutgers University Press.

———. 1983. "Age and Crime." In *Encyclopaedia of Crime and Justice*, edited by Sanford H. Kadish. New York: Free Press.

———. 1985. "Age, Crime, and Social Explanation." *American Journal of Sociology* 91:1–21.

Greenwood, Peter W., Allan Abrahamse, and Franklin E. Zimring. 1984. *Factors Affecting Sentence Severity for Young Adult Offenders.* Santa Monica, Calif.: Rand.

Greenwood, Peter W., Joan Petersilia, and Franklin E. Zimring. 1980. *Age, Crime, and Sanctions.* Santa Monica, Calif.: Rand.

Hamparian, Donna M., Richard Schuster, Simon Dinitz, and John P. Conrad. 1978. *The Violent Few.* Lexington, Mass.: Heath.

Hindelang, Michael J. 1981. "Variations in Sex-Race-Age-specific Incidence Rates of Offending." *American Sociological Review* 46:461–74.

Hirschi, Travis. 1969. *Causes of Delinquency*. Berkeley: University of California Press.

Hirschi, Travis, and Michael Gottfredson. 1983. "Age and the Explanation of Crime." *American Journal of Sociology* 89:552–84.

———. 1985a. "All Wise after the Fact Learning Theory, Again: Reply to Baldwin." *American Journal of Sociology* 90:1330–33.

———. 1985b. "The Distinction between Crime and Criminality." In *Critique and Explanation*, edited by Timothy F. Hartnagel and Robert A. Silverman. New Brunswick, N.J.: Transaction.

Hoffman, Peter B., and James L. Beck. 1984. "Burnout—Age at Release from Prison and Recidivism." *Journal of Criminal Justice* 12:617–23.

Home Office. 1940. *Criminal Statistics, England and Wales, 1938*. Command 6167. London: H.M. Stationery Office.

———. 1962. *Criminal Statistics, England and Wales, 1961*. Command 1779. London: H.M. Stationery Office.

———. 1984. *Criminal Statistics, England and Wales, 1983*. Command 9349. London: H.M. Stationery Office.

———. 1985. *Criminal Careers of Those Born in 1953, 1958, and 1963*. Home Office Statistical Bulletin 7/85. London: Home Office.

Jasinski, Jerzy. 1966. "Delinquent Generations in Poland." *British Journal of Criminology* 6:170–82.

Kean, A. W. G. 1937. "The History of the Criminal Liability of Children." *Law Quarterly Review* 211:364–70.

Keasey, Charles B., and Bruce D. Sales. 1977a. "Children's Conception of Intentionality and the Criminal Law." In *Psychology in the Legal Process*, edited by Bruce D. Sales. New York: Spectrum.

———. 1977b. "An Empirical Investigation of Young Children's Awareness and Usage of Intentionality in Criminal Situations." *Law and Human Behavior* 1:45–61.

Kitchener, Howard, Annesley K. Schmidt, and Daniel Glaser. 1977. "How Persistent Is Post-prison Success?" *Federal Probation* 41(1):9–15.

Kohlberg, Lawrence. 1976. "Moral Stages and Moralization: The Cognitive-Developmental Approach." In *Moral Development and Behavior*, edited by Thomas Lickona. New York: Holt, Rinehart & Winston.

Kurtines, William, and Esther B. Grief. 1974. "The Development of Moral Thought: Review and Evaluation of Kohlberg's Approach." *Psychological Bulletin* 81:453–70.

Langan, Patrick A., and David P. Farrington. 1983. "Two-Track or One-Track Justice? Some Evidence from an English Longitudinal Survey." *Journal of Criminal Law and Criminology* 74:519–46.

Langan, Patrick A., and Christopher A. Innes. 1985. *The Risk of Violent Crime*. Special report. Washington, D.C.: Bureau of Justice Statistics.

Loeber, Rolf, and Thomas Dishion. 1983. "Early Predictors of Male Delinquency: A Review." *Psychological Bulletin* 94:68–99.

McClintock, Frederick H., and N. Howard Avison. 1968. *Crime in England and Wales*. London: Heinemann.

McCord, Joan. 1980. "Patterns of Deviance." In *Human Functioning in Longitu-*

dinal Perspective, edited by S. B. Sells, Rick Crandall, Merrill Roff, John S. Strauss, and William Pollin. Baltimore: Williams & Wilkins.

McKissack, Ian J. 1967. "The Peak Age for Property Crimes." *British Journal of Criminology* 7:184–94.

———. 1973. "The Peak Age for Property Crimes: Further Data." *British Journal of Criminology* 13:253–61.

———. 1974. "A Less Delinquent Cohort." *British Journal of Criminology* 14:158–64.

Maxim, Paul S. 1985. "Cohort Size and Juvenile Delinquency: A Test of the Easterlin Hypothesis." *Social Forces* 63:661–81.

Miller, Stuart J., Simon Dinitz, and John P. Conrad. 1982. *Careers of the Violent*. Lexington, Mass.: Heath.

Monahan, Thomas P. 1960. "On the Incidence of Delinquency." *Social Forces* 39:66–72.

Petersilia, Joan, Peter W. Greenwood, and Marvin Lavin. 1978. *Criminal Careers of Habitual Felons*. Washington, D.C.: National Institute of Justice.

Peterson, Mark A., Harriet B. Braiker, and Suzanne M. Polich. 1981. *Who Commits Crimes?* Cambridge, Mass.: Oelgeschlager, Gunn, & Hain.

Phillpotts, Gregory J. O., and Leslie B. Lancucki. 1979. *Previous Convictions, Sentence, and Reconviction*. London: H.M. Stationery Office.

Piaget, Jean. 1932. *The Moral Judgment of the Child*. London: Routledge & Kegan Paul.

Polk, Kenneth, C. Alder, G. Bazemore, G. Blake, S. Cordray, G. Coventry, J. Galvin, and M. Temple. 1981. *Becoming Adult*. Final Report to the National Institute of Mental Health. Washington, D.C.: National Institute of Mental Health.

Porporino, Frank, and Edward Zamble. 1984. "Coping with Imprisonment." *Canadian Journal of Criminology* 26:403–21.

Rankin, Joseph H., and L. Edward Wells. 1985. "From Status to Delinquent Offenses: Escalation?" *Journal of Criminal Justice* 13:171–80.

Rodgers, Willard L. 1982. "Estimable Functions of Age, Period, and Cohort Effects." *American Sociological Review* 47:774–87.

Rojek, Dean G., and Maynard L. Erickson. 1982. "Delinquent Careers: A Test of the Career Escalation Model." *Criminology* 20:5–28.

Rose, Gerald N. G. 1968. "The Artificial Delinquent Generation." *Journal of Criminal Law, Criminology, and Police Science* 59:370–85.

Rowe, Alan R., and Charles R. Tittle. 1977. "Life Cycle Changes and Criminal Propensity." *Sociological Quarterly* 18:223–36.

Ruhland, David J., Martin Gold, and Randall J. Hekman. 1982. "Deterring Juvenile Crime: Age of Jurisdiction." *Youth and Society* 13:353–76.

Sarnecki, Jerzy, and Stefan Sollenhag. 1985. *Predicting Social Maladjustment*. Report no. 17. Stockholm: National Council for Crime Prevention.

Scharf, Peter, and Joseph Hickey. 1976. "The Prison and the Inmate's Conception of Legal Justice: An Experiment in Democratic Education." *Criminal Justice and Behavior* 3:107–22.

Sellin, Thorsten, and Marvin E. Wolfgang. 1964. *The Measurement of Delinquency*. New York: Wiley.

Shannon, Lyle W. 1981. *Assessing the Relationship of Adult Criminal Careers to Juvenile Careers.* Final report. Washington, D.C.: National Institute of Juvenile Justice and Delinquency Prevention.

————. 1985. "Risk Assessment vs. Real Prediction: The Prediction Problem and Public Trust." *Journal of Quantitative Criminology* 1:159–89.

Shover, Neal. 1983. *Age and the Changing Criminal Involvement of Ordinary Property Offenders.* Final Report to the National Institute of Justice. Washington, D.C.: National Institute of Justice.

Siegel, Sidney. 1956. *Nonparametric Statistics for the Behavioral Sciences.* New York: McGraw-Hill.

Slater, S. W., J. H. Darwin, and Wendy L. Richie. 1966. "Delinquent Generations in New Zealand." *Journal of Research in Crime and Delinquency* 3:140–46.

Sutherland, Edwin H., and Donald R. Cressey. 1974. *Criminology.* 9th ed. Philadelphia: Lippincott.

Sveri, Knut. 1965. "Group Activity." In *Scandinavian Studies in Criminology,* vol. 1, edited by Karl O. Christiansen. London: Tavistock.

Thornberry, Terence P., and Margaret Farnworth. 1982. "Social Correlates of Criminal Involvement: Further Evidence on the Relationship between Social Status and Criminal Behavior." *American Sociological Review* 47:505–18.

Tittle, Charles R. 1980. *Sanctions and Social Deviance.* New York: Praeger.

Trasler, Gordon B. 1979. "Delinquency, Recidivism, and Desistance." *British Journal of Criminology* 19:314–22.

Van Dusen, Katherine T., and Sarnoff A. Mednick. 1983. *A Comparison of Delinquency in Copenhagen and Philadelphia.* Final Report to the National Institute of Justice. Washington, D.C.: National Institute of Justice.

Wadsworth, Michael E. J. 1975. "Delinquency in a National Sample of Children." *British Journal of Criminology* 15:167–74.

Walters, A. A. 1963. "Delinquent Generations?" *British Journal of Criminology* 3:391–95.

Wellford, Charles F. 1973. "Age Composition and the Increase in Recorded Crime." *Criminology* 11:61–70.

West, Donald J. 1982. *Delinquency: Its Roots, Careers, and Prospects.* London: Heinemann.

West, Donald J., and David P. Farrington. 1973. *Who Becomes Delinquent?* London: Heinemann.

————. 1977. *The Delinquent Way of Life.* London: Heinemann.

Wikstrom, Per-Olof H. 1985. *Everyday Violence in Contemporary Sweden.* Report no. 15. Stockholm: National Council for Crime Prevention.

Wilkins, Leslie T. 1960. *Delinquent Generations.* London: H.M. Stationery Office.

Williams, Jay R., and Martin Gold. 1972. "From Delinquent Behavior to Official Delinquency." *Social Problems* 20:209–29.

Wilson, James Q., and Richard J. Herrnstein. 1985. *Crime and Human Nature.* New York: Simon & Schuster.

Wolf, Preben. 1984. "Delinquent Boys and Family Relations." In *Sequential Research,* vol. 1, edited by Preben Wolf. Micro Publications Social Science Series. Copenhagen: University of Copenhagen, Department of Sociology.

Wolfgang, Marvin E. 1980. "Some New Findings from the Longitudinal Study of Crime." *Australian Journal of Forensic Science* 13:12–29.

———. 1983. "Delinquency in Two Birth Cohorts." In *Prospective Studies of Crime and Delinquency*, edited by Katherine T. Van Dusen and Sarnoff A. Mednick. Boston: Kluwer-Nijhoff.

Wolfgang, Marvin E., Robert M. Figlio, and Thorsten Sellin. 1972. *Delinquency in a Birth Cohort*. Chicago: University of Chicago Press.

Wolfgang, Marvin E., and Paul E. Tracy. 1982. "The 1945 and 1958 Birth Cohorts: A Comparison of the Prevalence, Incidence, and Severity of Delinquent Behavior." Paper presented at a conference on "Public Danger, Dangerous Offenders, and the Criminal Justice System" sponsored by the National Institute of Justice at Harvard University.

Michael R. Gottfredson

Substantive Contributions of Victimization Surveys

ABSTRACT

Two decades of victimization research have contributed substantially to the criminological research base. Among the core findings of the National Crime Survey (NCS) are that the bulk of events uncovered by the surveys are relatively trivial, that criminal victimization of the types measured is relatively rare, and that there is a large amount of repeat victimization. Despite methodological differences between the NCS and the Uniform Crime Reports (UCR), comparisons can be made about the basic correlates of crime—differences among groups, times, and places. Both data sources show that the likelihood of crime occurring is not uniformly distributed by time or place. The NCS data indicate that robbery and assault occur disproportionately during the evening and at nighttime. Robbery happens more often on the streets or in other public places than at home. Rates of violent personal crime and household crime are generally highest in the central city. In addition, the city-level NCS data show that the majority of personal victimizations involve strangers as offenders. Rates of personal victimization are not evenly distributed throughout the population. They are generally higher for males than for females and higher for the young than for the elderly. Nonwhites have higher rates of robbery and personal larceny with contact than do whites, regardless of age. The victimization of married persons is less than that for persons who have never been married or who are divorced or separated. Victim reports about offenders closely parallel official reports with respect to age, sex, and race. For example, both data sources are in agreement that young males, particularly black males, have the highest rates of offending. Differences between NCS and UCR counts occur for some offenses, particularly assault, and in some crime rate trends. The data indicate that the rates of most crimes measured by the NCS

Michael R. Gottfredson is Associate Professor in the Department of Management and Policy at the University of Arizona.

remained relatively stable between the early 1970s and the early 1980s, while UCR data indicate substantial increases during the 1970s and a decline about 1980. People's routine daily activities, or life-styles, may be strongly related to their risks of criminal victimization. Some life-styles seem to provide more opportunity for victimization.

Sample surveys of the general population designed to discover the extent, nature, and consequences of criminal victimization have existed now for nearly two decades. Beginning with the pilot studies done on behalf of the 1967 President's Crime Commission (Ennis 1967; Reiss 1967) and now routinized by the Bureau of Justice Statistics in the annual National Crime Survey (NCS), victimization surveys today rival official data for the attention of criminological researchers. The expenditure of research funds for victimization surveys is substantial, and methodological work thrives. Victimization survey data now command their own chapters in the leading textbooks (e.g., Empey 1983; Nettler 1984). Because victimization research methods are more flexible than official data, and because the methods have the potential of unleashing the power of sociological survey techniques, victimization surveys will undoubtedly continue to be a popular method of gathering basic data. It is important to ask, therefore, after nearly two decades of research, what the major substantive contributions of victimization survey work have been and in what directions future work might head.[1]

Although this essay proposes answers to those questions, such a task is not an easy one. There now exists a vast body of high-quality research studies touching an immense range of subfields in criminology. Thus the scope of this review must necessarily be narrowed. Because good, comprehensive reviews of methodological work are widely avail-

[1] The most extensive series of victimization surveys is the NCS, undertaken on behalf of the U.S. Department of Justice, Bureau of Justice Statistics, by the U.S. Bureau of the Census. In addition to the ongoing national household probability sample that produces estimates annually, the Census Bureau has undertaken substantial surveys in major American cities for samples of both households and commercial establishments. A good general introduction to the NCS is provided by Garofalo and Hindelang (1977). These data are available in a variety of forms. Some selected tables are published in a large number of reports available from the Bureau of Justice Statistics through the National Criminal Justice Reference Service (Box 600, Rockville, Md. 20850). Annual tabulations and selected time series are published in the annual *Sourcebook of Criminal Justice Statistics*, also available from the National Criminal Justice Reference Service. Public-use data tapes and relevant documentation are provided through the Inter-university Consortium for Political and Social Research, University of Michigan. Extensive bibliographies of NCS research reports and methodological papers may be found in Gottfredson and Hindelang (1981); Lehnen and Skogan (1981); and Sparks (1981, 1982).

able, such research is not addressed except insofar as it critically addresses important substantive issues.[2] The primary focus is on the American national crime surveys, although occasional reference is made to important work in other countries.[3] In Section I, the characteristics of the national crime surveys are described. Attention is restricted to two generic issues in Sections II and III. Patterns of victimization and offending, including the social and demographic distribution of these behaviors and their trends and how such patterns compare with those revealed by official data, are considered in Section II. Recent efforts to understand the causes of crime using victimization data to study how the risk of crime varies across the population are detailed in Section III.[4] Some general conclusions about the NCS are drawn in Section IV.

I. Characteristics of the NCS

This section describes the NCS and some of its central features, compares crime estimates derived from NCS data with those based on official statistics, and summarizes research on why victims do or do not report crime to the police. It concludes by presenting three of the NCS's most important general findings—that most crime reported by victims is not especially serious, that victimization is a relatively rare event for most people, and that the likelihood of victimization varies substantially for different groups of people.

[2] Substantial reviews of this methodological work include Hindelang (1976), Penick and Owens (1976), Sparks, Genn, and Dodd (1977), Hindelang, Gottfredson, and Garofalo (1978), Fienberg (1980), Fienberg and Reiss (1980), Gottfredson and Hindelang (1981), Schneider (1981), Skogan (1981), and Sparks (1981). Unfortunately, much of the important work in this area has not been made widely available but rather exists in the form of intra-agency memoranda. Probably the most comprehensive bibliography of these papers, along with an excellent discussion, is provided in Skogan (1981). The papers by Schneider (1981) and Sparks (1982) are particularly valuable for their attention to the substantive implications of methodological aspects of the NCS.

[3] In February 1984, a "victim-risk" instrument was added to the NCS for a trial period. Results are not available as of this writing, although the questions used largely follow those used by the British Crime Survey (Hough and Mayhew 1983) and those found in the Dutch and Canadian surveys (Ministry of the Solicitor General 1983; van Dijk and Steinmetz 1984).

[4] Necessarily excluded from this review, therefore, are a number of issues for which researchers have found use for victimization data. Examples include gun control (Cook 1976), school crime (Toby 1983), general deterrence (Goldberg and Nold 1978; Zedlewski 1983), and fear of crime (Hindelang et al. 1978; Garofalo 1981; Skogan and Maxfield 1981; Maxfield 1984).

A. Features of the NCS Methodology

Not all crimes are measured, or measured well, in victimization surveys.[5] Two broad groups of offenses are typically defined among the survey-measured offenses: crimes of theft and interpersonal violence in which there is a personal confrontation between the victim and the offender (such as robbery) and crimes of theft of property in which there is no such confrontation and for which the object of theft can be construed as belonging to a housing unit rather than to an individual (such as burglary). For the former offenses the NCS uses persons as the base for crime rates, and for the latter it uses households. Some offenses, like theft of personal property from offices or restaurants and theft of automobiles or theft from automobiles, do not fall neatly into this categorization, but the former are usually treated as personal crimes and the latter as household crimes.

The classification and counting rules adopted by the NCS were designed to make the data as comparable as possible with the data routinely reported by the Uniform Crime Reports (UCR). This decision may be questioned because it does not exploit the vast potential of the individual level nature of the NCS data (although individual researchers may do so if they wish) and because it fosters comparisons between the UCR and the NCS in the measurement of the *level* of crime (an elusive concept at best).

The NCS now uses a design in which a sample, when properly weighted, is meant to be representative of the nation. Earlier, some special surveys were done in selected large cities (hereafter referred to as "city surveys"), although these are no longer done. The design and the instrument for these surveys result from a combination of cost and validity concerns and how these concerns interact with the effort to get respondents to reveal to strangers statistically rare events that vary enormously in physical and emotional consequence to the respondents.

---

[5] This essay discusses the existing NCS data, with all their faults. Excluded from the NCS are crimes that involve commercial establishments as victims (although the early city surveys did not exclude them), crimes involving the consumption, purchase, or sales of illegal commodities, substances, or acts, crimes perpetrated by formal organizations, and other so-called white-collar and victimless crimes. Also excluded are crimes in the Uniform Crime Report, Part II categories (except simple assault). These omissions, some but not all by virtue of methodology, have important consequences in relation to some purposes for which the data may be employed, such as questions of the seriousness of crime or the consequences of crime to individuals. On this point, see esp. Reiss (1982). These surveys have some trouble measuring nonstranger interpersonal violence (Hindelang 1976), and there is reason to believe that they do not measure well continuous states of victimization, as opposed to discrete events (Skogan 1981).

The sample results in about 65,000 eligible households with about 130,000 persons eligible to be interviewed in every six-month period. Of these, the Bureau of the Census reports interviews with 96 percent of the eligible households and 99 percent of the occupants of those households (an extraordinarily high response rate).[6] The NCS distinguishes between self-respondents and household respondents. The former are persons twelve years old and older who are asked a series of questions about their personal characteristics and about the details of crimes they have suffered in the previous six months (twelve- and thirteen-year-olds are interviewed by proxy). Household respondents do this also, but in addition they answer questions about the household (e.g., family income, whether they rent or own their accommodations) and about crimes that the household may have suffered. The design of the survey calls for reinterviews of households for seven six-month periods, but, unfortunately, locations rather than individuals are the sampling unit, and it is the location that is revisited for interviews. Since many respondents move during the interval, this procedure causes serious problems for interpretation of rates and for analyses over time of individuals (Lehnen and Reiss 1978). So too do the effects of repeated interviews on the likelihood that respondents will report crimes to the interviewers (Skogan 1981). (For a comprehensive discussion of methodological issues in victimization surveys, see Sparks [1981].)

B. *The Comparison of Survey Estimates with the UCR*

From the very beginning, victimization researchers were interested in how the data would compare with official data (Block and Block 1984). For example, in the first national estimates of victimization produced by Ennis (1967), the relative rank ordering of offenses by frequency as shown by the victimization method and by the UCR was shown to be similar. At least two academic traditions may have inspired such concern. First, criminologists have traditionally been interested in measurement. This interest was fostered by the knowledge that only a portion of all offenses ever made their way into official statistics. The second tradition is the enduring concern of criminologists that much selection goes on between acts and records of those acts

[6] The NCS sample probably undercounts some segments of the population considerably, although unintentionally (including young, single, black males), and other segments (including the very young) intentionally. The weighting procedures are complex and controversial (Fienberg 1980).

with the implication that the selection process itself may generate the "facts" about crime rather than reflect them.

Public policy concerns also shaped the generation of victimization data. Whereas the academic community was concerned that selectivity in recording alleged crimes jeopardized all knowledge about crime, those in charge of doing something about crime had an analogous problem. If crime statistics measured the behavior of officials and not crime, then conclusions about the effects of programs to reduce crime were necessarily suspect. What both groups wanted was a statistical series independent of the putative biases that stem from the collection of official records. These concerns have dominated these surveys from the beginning and have major implications for the type of data that have resulted.

From the earliest surveys, it has been evident that comparability between the domains tapped by official data and by victimization surveys has been only partially achieved. To some degree, survey-generated crime statistics differ in content from official statistics. The sources and nature of the differences between the UCR and the NCS present problems of different magnitudes, depending on the comparisons one wants to make.

For some issues, the overlap is sufficiently great and the correlates of interest are sufficiently robust that the method-linked differences are of little consequence. For other purposes, however, the two domains are not comparable, and the results they generate are not comparable, reminding us of the measurement maxim that the validity of any data series depends fundamentally on the purposes to which the data are put. For different uses, the data have different validities. Because offenses of the types measured by the NCS come to the attention of the police primarily through victim reporting (Gottfredson and Hindelang 1981), to understand something of the similarities and differences between official and victimization crime data it is necessary to review briefly some of the research bearing on the decision by victims to call the police when victimized.

C. Correlates of Reporting to the Police

Victims of crime are the first, and proportionately the greatest, screeners of events that enter the criminal justice decision-making process. How they exercise their discretion is thus critical not only for an understanding of crime statistics but for any assessment of the quality of operation of the criminal justice system. Victimization data permit the study of which events defined by respondents, and the survey instrument, as crimes are said by the respondents to be reported to the police.

The research on nonreporting suggests that the major dimension along which victim discretion operates is the seriousness of their victimization. Studies of victim decisions to call the police have generally taken one of two approaches. The first is to ask victims directly why they did or did not call the police; the second is to attempt to infer why victims did or did not report victimizations from information on victim, offender, and situational factors.

When asked why they do not report a crime to the police, survey respondents are likely to answer that "nothing could be done about it anyway" or that it "was not important enough." Victims of crimes of interpersonal violence are more likely than others to respond that "it was a private matter"; many victims of rape have a "fear of reprisal"; and many interpersonal victimizations (especially those taking place in schools) are "reported to someone else" (Ennis 1967; Hindelang 1976; Sparks et al. 1977). Victimization data reveal that the reasons for not calling the police have much more to do with the nature of the crime than with characteristics of the victim. The exception is that the victim-offender relationship to some extent conditions the reasons for failing to report—persons victimized by acquaintances rather than strangers are more likely to view the matter as private (Hindelang 1976).

When characteristics of incidents, victims, and offenders are studied, it is clear that what matters most is the gravity of the harm suffered by the victim. This is found regardless of whether events are distinguished according to legalistic classifications (such as the ranking used by the UCR), according to elements of offenses (such as attempted vs. completed, injury vs. no injury, weapon vs. no weapon), or according to common attitudinal measures of seriousness (Ennis 1967; Skogan 1977; Sparks et al. 1977; Gottfredson and Hindelang 1979). The seriousness effect is much stronger than race (Skogan 1977), attitude toward the police (Garofalo 1977), the victim's recent experience with the police (Garofalo 1977), the victim's social class or income (Sparks et al. 1977; Gottfredson and Hindelang 1979), the degree of urbanization characterizing the victim's community (Gottfredson and Hindelang 1979), or even the victim's self-reported criminality (Sparks et al. 1977). Any selection that does occur within these categories is more likely to occur when the victimizations under consideration are less serious.

Some people seem more likely than others to report their victimizations. Although associations between demographic factors and a tendency to call the police are slight when contrasted to the effect of offense seriousness (Hindelang 1976; Skogan 1977; Sparks et al. 1977), the data suggest that females are more likely to report than males, blacks than whites, younger persons than older persons, married persons than the never married, the better educated than the less well educated, and those victimized by strangers than those victimized by nonstrangers. The calculus of personal utility plays a significant role, judging by the high reporting rates for automobile theft and the reporting relation between police notification and the presence of theft insurance.

As indicated by a plot of nonreporting rates over time (McGarrell and Flanagan 1985, p. 276), there have been no large or substantial fluctuations in the proportions of victimizations not reported to the police over the years covered by the NCS. This suggests, but does not prove, that the processes generating the proportion reported are also quite stable.

D. Essential Features of NCS Crime Statistics

Three important features of NCS-generated crime statistics set the context for any discussion of victimization findings. First, the vast bulk of the events uncovered by such surveys are relatively trivial events. Second, criminal victimization is relatively rare. Third, victimization is not evenly distributed among the population; some categories of people suffer much more from crime than do others.

Whether measured by physical harm or financial loss (Reiss 1982) or by the victim's own judgments (Hindelang 1976), most victimization in the NCS is not particularly serious. For example, while about one-third of households in the NCS annually report that they are victimized, only 5–6 percent of all households have a member victimized by violent crime. Most victims of violent crime do not suffer bodily injury, and of those that do, most receive only brief medical attention (Reiss 1982). The majority of victimizations do not involve a direct confrontation, and the violent crimes such as assault, robbery, and rape are the least common. Furthermore, the most probable victim of either burglary or robbery is not a person or a household but a business (Hindelang 1976; Rand, Klaus, and Taylor 1983). That the bulk of victimization reported by the NCS is not particularly serious does not mean that the consequences of crime to society are slight, that there is too much concern with crime, or that individual victims do not suffer from crime. Rather, it suggests the immense variability of acts counted as crime by NCS crime estimates.

Criminal victimization of the types measured is relatively rare. Although this point is frequently made (e.g., Skogan 1981; Sparks 1982), it merits repeating because it is the essential feature of the empirical distribution of victimization. In any given reference period, the vast majority of respondents do not report any victimizations. In 1982, the rate per 1,000 persons twelve years old and older for rape was 0.8, for personal robbery 7.1, and for aggravated assault 9.3. Theft offenses have higher rates, generally. These findings have implications for the design and analysis of victimization surveys (e.g., very large general population samples are required for reliable estimates, and detailed subgroup analyses are problematic). These findings are easily forgotten in discussions about crime trends or changes in crime rates.

The NCS data show that there is considerable repeat victimization and evidence of victim proneness. That is, although serious victimization is relatively rare in the general population, some subgroups and certain individuals suffer disproportionately. Organizations are at considerably greater risk than are individuals (Reiss 1982). Statistical models based on the assumption that multiple victimization is randomly distributed are not supported by the data for property, violent, and household offenses (Sparks et al. 1977; Hindelang et al. 1978; Nelson 1980; Skogan 1981). Furthermore, the data on multiple victimization can be analyzed in such a way as to establish a link between personal and household victimization beyond that expected on the basis of demographic correlates of victimization, thus implying an environmental risk dimension (Hindelang et al. 1978; Reiss 1980; Gottfredson 1984). Reiss (1980) showed that, among the repeat victims in the NCS, there was a proneness to repeat victimization by the same type of crime and that, the more probable any given type of crime in general, the more likely it is to occur in repeat victimization.

Thus exposure to crime is not random. This finding emerges also from official data. For example, Skogan (1979) reports that two-thirds of the reported robberies in the United States in 1970 were concentrated in thirty-two cities that housed only 16 percent of the nation's population. The importance of such data is apparent whenever discussions of the "nation's crime problem" take place or whenever cross-national comparisons are made, but they are also germane to comparisons of survey-generated statistics with official measures.[7]

II. Correlates of Crime in the NCS and the UCR

When victimization surveys began, most attention focused on the much higher level of crime they revealed than was revealed in the UCR. Although understandable, such a focus is unfortunate. For etiological purposes, the central comparative question that arises is whether the patterns of correlations depicted by the NCS and the UCR are similar (Hindelang, Hirschi, and Weis 1981).

Theories of crime causation are built largely on the differences in offending or victimization among groups. All such theories are premised on differences that exist, that are nonartifactual, and that are generally stable. Differences of this sort have been apparent for some time in official data but began to be questioned by self-report findings (Hindelang, Hirschi, and Weis 1979, 1981). Of course the self-report method as generally applied has been less general in focus than victimization surveys with respect to the number of crime characteristics available for study. Spatial and temporal aspects of crime, the characteristics of victims, and the victim-offender relationship have, for example, not typically been studied with self-reports. One significant contribution of the victimization survey method therefore has been to make possible comparisons with official data in the basic correlates of crime—the differences among groups, times, and places. They thus give us some notion of how valid the differences shown in official data are for testing and constructing theories of crime causation.

Considerable research has assessed the patterns of correlates in victim survey and official data. For convenience, these correlates may be

---

[7] Although these three features pertain to victimization data, it will be noted that similar features characterize distributions of offenders, whether measured by self-reports or by official data. Thus offending distributions are markedly skewed (i.e., are characterized by a small number of persons disproportionately committing criminal acts), the bulk of the population commits few criminal acts, and most such acts are not particularly serious. The similarity of the statistical distribution invites analogies to concepts used to typologize the offending population for etiological and prevention purposes (such as "career criminals"). The lack of theoretical and empirical success such efforts have achieved on the offending side suggests that theories designed to explain "career victims" (i.e., multiple victims) would be better off attending instead to the continuous nature of the distribution of victimization. There are other features of the patterns of offending that are similar to the patterns of victimization, such as the general age, sex, race, and residence correlates. These are discussed in later sections.

reviewed under several broad headings: spatial and temporal, urbanization and neighborhood, demographic and social characteristics of victims, and offender characteristics. Although the following discussion emphasizes official/victim survey comparisons, some data unique to the victim survey method are also described. Unless otherwise noted, the discussion is restricted to the offenses covered in the NCS. Some efforts to offer explanations for the patterns reviewed below are discussed in a later section. Here the emphasis is on the descriptive data.

A. Spatial and Temporal Correlates

The likelihood of a crime occurring is not uniformly distributed by time or place. Crimes of personal violence, such as rape, assault, and robbery, occur disproportionately in the late evening and early morning hours, according to both police data and city-level victimization survey estimates (Hindelang et al. 1978). The national NCS data indicate that robbery, assault, and motor vehicle theft occur disproportionately during the evening and nighttime, whereas personal larceny tends to happen during the daytime. Burglary occurs about half the time during the day and half at night (Rand et al. 1983). Violent crimes generally take place outside the home (Hindelang et al. 1978; Rand et al. 1983). For example, in the city-level data, 70 percent of the robberies and 50 percent of the assaults occurred on the street and in other public places (Hindelang 1976). A large number of studies using official data for robbery, assault, and rape also indicate that risks are greatest away from the home, particularly on the street (Hindelang et al. 1978). Since victimization estimates may undercount nonstranger assaults, and since these may tend to occur disproportionately within the home, the victimization assault figures may overestimate the proportion taking place outside the home.

In both official and victimization survey data, most violent crimes (except homicide) are committed by strangers and only very rarely by relatives (7 percent of nonhomicide violent crime). In the city-level NCS data, 80 percent of the personal victimizations involved strangers as offenders (Hindelang 1976). For theft offenses, the proportion is higher yet. Official data tend to indicate lower proportions of assault and rape offenders being strangers to their victims than do victimization survey data, although both sources agree about the infrequency of relatives as offenders in rape and assault offenses (Hindelang et al. 1978).

B. Urbanization and Neighborhood Correlates

The NCS and other victimization survey data consistently reveal a large association between crime rates and urbanization. In general, rates of violent personal crime and of household crime are substantially higher in metropolitan areas than in smaller towns and rural areas and are higher in central cities than in suburban areas (Gibbs 1977; Sparks 1982). For robbery, which has the strongest pattern, the rates per 1,000 persons twelve years old and older for 1981 were fifteen for the central city, six for suburbs, and three for rural communities. For burglary the corresponding rates per 1,000 households were 120, 80, and 68 (Rand et al. 1983). This pattern holds generally, regardless of age, sex, major activity, family income, and whether juvenile or adult victimization is at issue (Gibbs 1977; Laub and Hindelang 1981).[8]

In a series of studies, Sampson (1983, 1985; Sampson, Castellano, and Laub 1981) has investigated how NCS rates vary according to "neighborhood" characteristics. The neighborhoods were formed by combining households into aggregates on the basis of similarity with respect to features like unemployment, income concentration, and residential mobility. Sampson discovered that neighborhood characteristics predict personal victimization risk independent of individual characteristics. Although the patterns are complex, some interesting conclusions emerge: "structural density" (high proportion of multiple dwelling unit structures) is positively related to personal victimization, holding constant not only age, sex, and race of victim but extent of urbanization as well. In addition, he showed through multivariate analyses that ecological-level social integration factors (family structure and mobility) are substantially related to personal victimization. And, at the bivariate level, poverty and income inequality are positively related to victimization.[9] But of particular relevance to this review is that Sampson cites an impressive body of research documenting the similar

---

[8] Similar patterns have been identified in England and Wales (Hough and Mayhew 1983; Gottfredson 1984) and in the Netherlands (van Dijk and Steinmetz 1984). Laub and Hindelang (1981) present an extensive discussion of variations in victimization and elements of victimization by area.

[9] Sampson (1983, p. 14) argues that the findings of some intercity NCS correlations with poverty are anomalies (cf. Shichor, Decker, and O'Brien 1979; O'Brien 1983). For a methodological discussion of this issue, see Skogan (1981, pp. 2–4). Sparks (1982, p. 84) observes that NCS victimization rates are constructed according to the area of residence of the respondent rather than the area of victimization, a feature that might inflate suburban rates for property crimes. Such an artifact would attenuate the urbanization correlation, but Sampson (1983) controlled for victims' reports of place of occurrence, with results consistent with those reported in the text.

findings from official data, leading him to conclude: "Thus, despite vastly different methods of data collection and units of analysis, the UCR and NCS seem to be in general agreement regarding the bivariate relationships of neighborhood characteristics and crime" (1983, p. 32). Sparks (1982), Rand et al. (1983), and Nettler (1984) all confirm the general agreement between the NCS and official counts of spatial patterns of crime.

C. Demographic Correlates

Although in a general population sample serious victimization is relatively rare, the risks of personal victimization are not distributed evenly throughout society. Figures 1–3 depict some of the differences from the 1982 data; these patterns have been remarkably consistent over the years covered by the NCS. In general, rates are much higher for males than for females (with the exceptions of rape and personal larceny with contact). They are higher for the young than for the elderly—indeed, rates of personal victimization decrease steadily with age from a peak in late adolescence. Regardless of age, nonwhites have higher risks of robbery and personal larceny with contact than do whites, although the reverse seems to be true for personal larceny without contact. Family income is generally inversely associated with personal victimization, and this seems to hold regardless of race, but not among juveniles (McDermott and Hindelang 1981). The rates of victimization for never married and divorced or separated persons exceed those of married

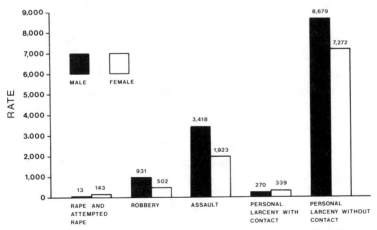

FIG. 1.—Estimated rate (per 100,000 persons twelve years of age or older) of personal victimization, by type of victimization and sex of victim, United States, 1982.

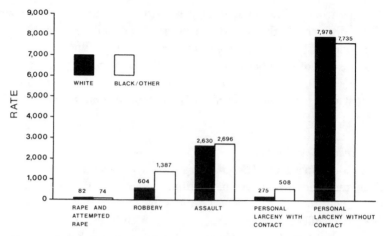

FIG. 2.—Estimated rate (per 100,000 persons twelve years of age or older) of personal victimization, by type of victimization and race of victim, United States, 1982.

persons, regardless of age (see, generally, Weis and Henney 1980; Gottfredson and Hindelang 1981; Klaus, Rand, and Taylor 1983).

Rates of household victimization decrease consistently as the age of the head of household increases. They tend to be higher for households headed by persons from minority races than for those headed by whites (with the possible exception of household larceny). Burglary rates vary with income, but somewhat differently for whites than for minority races: for whites there is a steady decrease in the rate from low to high income, with an exception of an upturn at the highest income levels. For minority races the rate is curvilinear, peaking in the middle income categories (Weis and Henney 1980; Gottfredson and Hindelang 1981).

One anomaly in the NCS data has to do with the relation between educational attainment and victimization. All the surveys show a positive correlation—for example, the higher the educational attainment, the greater the likelihood of assaultive victimization (Skogan 1981). Most analysts have regarded this as a response artifact, with the more highly educated being thought to be more "productive" respondents rather than more likely victims. If so, the question arises as to whether this bias could upset other correlations depicted by the victimization data and, in particular, the relation to other measures of social class.

Taylor (1983) considers some multivariate relations in the NCS data with special concern for the interpretation of socioeconomic status and education. He finds that increased occupational status is negatively

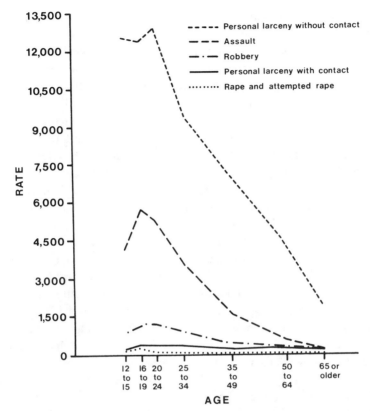

Fig. 3.—Estimated rate (per 100,000 persons twelve years of age or older) of personal victimization, by type of victimization and age of victim, United States, 1982.

correlated with violent personal victimization, with education, race, age, and school attendance held constant, but that education and violent victimization are positively correlated. He argues that "the most plausible explanation of this education effect is that it is a reporting effect associated with higher levels of cognitive ability" (1983, p. 11). Skogan (1981) notes that the response-bias interpretation for the education effect would lead to the prediction that the education-assault relation would be stronger for more trivial events where the range for interpretation by respondents may be greater. However, he found that it is not, nor does the expected negative relation between assault and family income appear to be upset by the educational effect. Gottfredson (1984) has shown that in the British Crime Survey the education effect is much like it is in the NCS but that, when education is controlled, the other major patterns in the data (e.g., age, major activity) generally persist. It may be that the education effect itself is a response artifact but does not substantially alter conclusions that may be reached about other important patterns of criminal victimization.

Not only is major activity (working, homemaker, in school, etc.) related substantially to personal victimization, but Block and Block (1984) cite work done by Dodge and Lentzner (1978), who concluded that some occupations are especially prone to repeat victimizations, especially those that involve considerable contact with strangers, including (not surprisingly) police and guards. Essentially similar findings have been reported by Hough (1983) on the basis of the British Crime Survey. Recently, Block, Felson, and Block (1985) have used NCS data to demonstrate marked differences in victimization risks according to occupation.

Although most of the demographic and social correlates of victimization depicted by the surveys are essentially consistent with the findings from official statistics, much of the victimization survey–generated assault data does not correspond well to official data on differential vulnerability to interpersonal violence. Victimization data indicate too little interpersonal violence among nonstrangers, judging by police data (Skogan 1981), and blacks report proportionately fewer minor assaults than do whites. Skogan reasons that a plausible hypothesis for this is that blacks report fewer of their less threatening encounters, while whites dredge up more—that is, that whites are more "productive" interviewees than are blacks, on the average. If true, this would account for a large number of incongruous correlates between NCS assault rates and city characteristics, such as poverty, quality of housing, and population density as these features correlate with proportion nonwhite in the United States (Skogan 1981).

The general demographic portrait of victimization painted by the NCS has been found to maintain essentially in England (Hough and Mayhew 1983), the Netherlands (van Dijk and Steinmetz 1984), Australia (Braithwaite and Biles 1984), and Canada (Ministry of the Solicitor General 1983).

D. Offender Correlates

Many of the criticisms advanced about the use of official statistics for etiological purposes center on selectivity in the recording of events in official records. Before victimization survey estimates became available, there was no empirical basis for evaluating selection, and because the possible biases that could affect selection practices are numerous, the validity of official records with respect to the demographic and social correlates of offending has often been questioned. Self-report studies initially produced results that were widely interpreted as being inconsistent with the official statistics and thus served to further question the validity of official data. Recent research on the self-report method (Hindelang et al. 1981) has provided good reasons for the discrepancies and suggests that problems in the self-report method may explain the observed differences.

Data from victimization surveys have been critical to efforts to judge the relative validity of the demographic portrait of offending shown by official data. Because the surveys ask victims to report on the age, sex, race, and number of offenders involved in their victimization, and because such reports are unaffected by any putative selection biases of the official processing system, they are critical evidence concerning the accuracy of official data. This is not to say that such victim reports are not subject to some logically possible forms of bias themselves—after all, they depend on the interpretation and reporting to interviewers by victims. But they do allow the best *empirical* test of the relative validity of the data about a few offender characteristics. Research has attended to three topics with respect to offender data in victimization surveys— the demographic profile of offending, the relation between offending and victimization, and the group nature of criminal offending.

Victim reports of the correlates of offending parallel official data with respect to sex, race, and age (Hindelang 1978, 1981; Skogan 1979). For example, Hindelang (1978, 1981) computed rates of offending from NCS data by age, race, and sex and discovered, consistent with UCR arrest data, that young males, and in particular young black males, have the highest rates. Skogan (1979) compared the proportion of arrestees in the UCR with the NCS reports by victims on the race of the offender for robbery, rape, and assault and found that 64 percent of the robbery offenders and 41 percent of the rape offenders in the NCS were reported to be black, whereas in the UCR the corresponding percentages of arrestees were 63 and 47. For serious assault, the UCR percentage was 10 percent higher than the NCS. McDermott and Hindelang (1981) have shown that, in the NCS data, males have an offending rate ranging from four to fifteen times that of females (depending on age), blacks have a rate of offending about five times that of whites, and the rate of offending is the greatest in the eighteen- to twenty-year-old group. They also showed that victimizations committed by juveniles tend to be less serious, in the sense of weapon use, financial loss, and rate of injury, than those committed by adults.

Such findings should not be interpreted as showing that there is no selection bias according to race, age, or sex in the official processing system. On the contrary, this research indicates that there may be significant amounts (Hindelang 1978). But the data indicate that the general pattern of correlates with regard to demographic characteristics between the two data sources is largely consistent, thus generating some confidence in the use of such data for theory testing and evaluation.

Victimization data strongly suggest that people tend to victimize people like themselves. Young people tend to be victimized by other young people (McDermott and Hindelang 1981), victimizations suffered by males are committed by males, and the vast majority of victimizations suffered by minority group members are committed by minority group members (Hindelang et al. 1978). Also offenders are more likely to victimize those with the same demographic characteristics than to victimize those with other characteristics (Hindelang et al. 1978). Most victimization tends to be "intraresidential" in the sense that offenders tend to commit their crimes within a short distance of their residence (for reviews, see Hindelang et al. [1978] and Reiss [1982]).

There is also considerable overlap between the offending and victim populations. Gottfredson (1984) has shown that in the British Crime Survey the likelihood of personal victimization was related to self-reported offending for a wide variety of acts, even with age and urbanization taken into account (see also Sparks et al. 1977). For example, among those reporting at least one self-reported violence offense in the British Crime Survey, the likelihood of also reporting personal victimization during the same reference period was seven times the likelihood of personal victimization for persons without a self-reported violence offense. Singer (1981) found that those most likely to be victims of violence in the Philadelphia sample he studied also had high rates of self-reported offending.

Reiss (1982) draws on NCS data to document the proposition that a substantial proportion of all victimizations are committed by more than one offender. Arguing that the NCS provides the best available data to study the extent of group offending, he shows that only 30 percent of the offenders in major personal crime incidents were lone offenders, 25 percent were in groups of two or three, and the rest were groups of four or more offenders. Groups of offenders are generally found much more often among victimizations committed by juveniles than among those committed by adults (McDermott and Hindelang 1981). Group offenders tend to be on the average younger than lone offenders, according to NCS estimates (Reiss 1982). Certainly the finding that much offending, especially by juveniles, takes place in groups is consistent with a large body of official and self-report research.

E. Crime Rate Trends

Considerable controversy has surrounded the differences in the national crime rate trends shown by the NCS and the UCR. The general crime trend generated by the NCS has been a good deal more stable than has the trend in the UCR (Sparks 1981). Sparks (1982) gives one example in which the UCR suggested an increase of nearly 17 percent between 1973 and 1974, whereas the NCS indicated no such increase. Using the measure "households touched by crime," the NCS indicates that between 1975 and 1984 there was essentially no change in the proportion of households victimized (about 30 percent). The trend in households touched by crime is presented in table 1. The small differences that exist (the series "peaked" in 1975 at 32 percent before declining to 26 percent in 1984) seem to be attributable to changes in personal larceny without contact (the offense that contributes the greatest number to this measure) rather than in the more serious offenses of burglary and violence (Rand 1983; Rand et al. 1983).

Between 1973 and 1982, the NCS paints an overall picture of stability (Paez and Shenk 1983). For example, Fienberg (1980) examined the trend data from 1973 to 1977 and concluded that the trends in crime victimization rates over that period are most notable by their absence.[10] No change in the rate of violent crime can be detected within that period, either overall or for any of the component categories of violent crime, except perhaps assault, which was lower in 1973 than more recently. (The NCS trend data are presented in table 2.) In 1982 there appeared to be something of a downturn in the overall rate of criminal victimization, attributed largely to a decline in residential burglary (Paez and Shenk 1983). However, the UCR indicated general increases in all Index crimes reported by police throughout the decade of the

---

[10] As Fienberg (1980) has noted, the simple calculation and presentation of significance levels for differences in relative changes is not an adequate way to assess change because it avoids the substantive question.

TABLE 1
Number and Percent Distribution of Households Touched by Crime, by Type of Crime, 1975–84

	1975	1976	1977	1978	1979	1980	1981	1982	1983	1984
Households touched by:										
Any NCS crimes (%)	32.0	31.5	31.3	31.3	31.3	30.0	30.0	29.3	27.4	26.0
Violent crime (%)	5.8	5.6	5.7	5.7	5.9	5.5	5.9	5.6	5.1	4.9
Rape (%)	.2	.2	.2	.2	.2	.2	.2	.2	.1	.2
Robbery (%)	1.4	1.2	1.2	1.1	1.2	1.2	1.3	1.4	1.1	1.0
Assault (%)	4.5	4.4	4.7	4.6	4.8	4.4	4.7	4.5	4.2	4.1
Personal larceny (%)	16.4	16.2	16.3	16.2	15.4	14.2	13.9	13.9	13.0	12.3
Burglary (%)	7.7	7.4	7.2	7.2	7.1	7.0	7.4	6.9	6.1	5.5
Household larceny (%)	10.2	10.3	10.2	9.9	10.8	10.4	10.2	9.6	8.9	8.5
Motor vehicle theft (%)	1.8	1.6	1.5	1.7	1.6	1.6	1.6	1.6	1.4	1.4
Households touched by crime (thousands) (N)	23,377	23,504	23,741	24,277	24,730	24,222	24,863	24,989	23,621	22,786
Households in United States (thousands) (N)	73,123	74,528	75,904	77,578	78,964	80,622	82,797	85,178	86,146	87,693

SOURCE.—Bureau of Justice Statistics (1985).
NOTE.—Detail does not add to total because of overlap in households touched by various crimes.

1970s, with the exception of motor vehicle theft (Rand et al. 1983). A number of these increases were quite substantial—from 1971 to 1981 the rate per 100,000 total population increased 39 percent for the total index, 46 percent for larceny-theft, 57 percent for aggravated assault, and 74 percent for rape (Rand et al. 1983). The homicide trend as indicated by the National Center for Health Statistics and reported by Rand et al. (1983) indicates general increases in rates per 100,000 through about 1933, general decreases through about 1958, and general increases subsequently. Although the homicide data are generally thought to be more reliable than UCR Index figures, in part because of the greater relative chances of homicide becoming known to the police, homicide may not be representative of the trends in other forms of criminal behavior. Apart from obvious differences in relative seriousness, the circumstances of homicide are often different from other crimes (e.g., the pattern of victim-offender relationships is different from most other forms of interpersonal violence).

There are, of course, many important differences between the UCR and the NCS data that must be taken into account when trend comparisons are made—the UCR only counts crimes coming to the attention of the police and recorded by them; the UCR counts crimes against businesses, whereas the NCS does not; the NCS counts only crimes against persons twelve years old and older in the personal category; and the two series use different population bases in computing rates. The series is really a very brief one: only something over a decade of experience is available.

But researchers seem fascinated with the comparison. One analysis of the discrepancies between the UCR and the NCS national trend data (Biderman, Lynch, and Peterson 1982) used the data between 1973 and 1979 to assess the extent to which the differences in reported trends were due to the differences in the crimes covered by each series and to differences in population counts in the denominators of the two series (to assess whether demographic changes that occurred during the time period and that were included differently in the two could account for some of the observed differences). The analysts discovered that, when the two data sets were adjusted to cover as well as possible the same domain of events and when the population bases were made comparable, the two series had the same directional changes, both in trend and in year-to-year fluctuations.

Probably the most crucial question that can be asked of the NCS time-series data is whether *patterns* seem to change with time. The data

TABLE 2

Number and Rate (per 1,000 Units of Each Respective Category) of Personal and Household Victimization, by Type of Victimization, United States, 1973–82

Type of Victimization	1973	1974	1975	1976	1977	1978	1979	1980	1981	1982
	Rate per 1,000 Persons Twelve Years of Age or Older									
Personal victimization:										
Crimes of violence:										
Number	5,351,000	5,510,000	5,573,000	5,599,000	5,902,000	5,941,000	6,159,000	6,130,000	6,582,000	6,459,000
(Rate)	(32.6)	(33.0)	(32.8)	(32.6)	(33.9)	(33.7)	(34.5)	(33.3)	(35.3)	(34.3)
Rape:										
Number	156,000	163,000	154,000	145,000	154,000	171,000	192,000	174,000	178,000	153,000
(Rate)	(1.0)	(1.0)	(.9)	(.8)	(.9)	(1.0)	(1.1)	(.9)	(1.0)	(.8)
Robbery:										
Number	1,108,000	1,199,000	1,147,000	1,111,000	1,083,000	1,038,000	1,116,000	1,209,000	1,381,000	1,334,000
(Rate)	(6.7)	(7.2)	(6.8)	(6.5)	(6.2)	(5.9)	(6.3)	(6.6)	(7.4)	(7.1)
Assault:										
Number	4,087,000	4,148,000	4,272,000	4,344,000	4,664,000	4,732,000	4,851,000	4,747,000	5,024,000	4,973,000
(Rate)	(24.9)	(24.8)	(25.2)	(25.3)	(26.8)	(26.9)	(27.2)	(25.8)	(27.0)	(26.4)
Aggravated assault:										
Number	1,655,000	1,735,000	1,631,000	1,695,000	1,738,000	1,708,000	1,769,000	1,707,000	1,796,000	1,754,000
(Rate)	(10.1)	(10.4)	(9.6)	(9.9)	(10.0)	(9.7)	(9.9)	(9.3)	(9.6)	(9.3)
Simple assault:										
Number	2,432,000	2,413,000	2,641,000	2,648,000	2,926,000	3,024,000	3,082,000	3,041,000	3,288,000	3,219,000
(Rate)	(14.8)	(14.4)	(15.6)	(15.4)	(16.8)	(17.2)	(17.3)	(16.5)	(17.3)	(17.1)

Crimes of theft:										
Number	14,971,000	15,889,000	16,294,000	16,519,000	16,933,000	17,050,000	16,382,000	15,300,000	15,863,000	15,553,000
(Rate)	(91.1)	(95.1)	(96.0)	(96.1)	(97.3)	(96.8)	(91.9)	(83.0)	(85.1)	(82.5)
Personal larceny with contact:										
Number	504,000	520,000	524,000	497,000	461,000	549,000	511,000	558,000	605,000	577,000
(Rate)	(3.1)	(3.1)	(3.1)	(2.9)	(2.7)	(3.1)	(2.9)	(3.0)	(3.3)	(3.1)
Personal larceny without contact:										
Number	14,466,000	15,369,000	15,770,000	16,022,000	16,472,000	16,501,000	15,871,000	14,742,000	15,258,000	14,976,000
(Rate)	(88.0)	(92.0)	(92.9)	(93.2)	(94.6)	(93.6)	(89.0)	(80.0)	(81.9)	(79.5)
Total population age twelve and older	164,363,000	167,058,000	169,671,000	171,901,000	174,093,000	176,215,000	178,284,000	184,324,000	186,336,000	188,497,000
					Rate per 1,000 Households					
Household victimization:										
Household burglary:										
Number	6,458,700	6,720,600	6,743,700	6,663,400	6,764,900	6,704,000	6,685,400	6,973,000	7,394,000	6,663,000
(Rate)	(91.7)	(93.1)	(91.7)	(88.9)	(88.5)	(86.0)	(84.1)	(84.3)	(87.9)	(78.2)
Household larceny:										
Number	7,537,300	8,933,100	9,223,000	9,300,900	9,418,300	9,351,900	10,630,100	10,468,000	10,176,000	9,705,000
(Rate)	(107.0)	(123.8)	(125.4)	(124.1)	(123.3)	(119.9)	(133.7)	(126.5)	(121.0)	(113.9)
Motor vehicle theft:										
Number	1,343,900	1,358,400	1,433,000	1,234,600	1,296,800	1,365,100	1,329,800	1,381,000	1,439,000	1,377,000
(Rate)	(19.1)	(18.8)	(19.5)	(16.5)	(17.0)	(17.5)	(17.5)	(16.7)	(17.1)	(16.2)
Total households (N)	70,442,400	72,162,900	73,559,600	74,956,100	76,412,300	77,980,400	79,498,600	82,753,000	84,095,000	85,211,000

SOURCE.—McGarrell and Flanagan (1985, p. 316).
NOTE.—Detail may not add to total because of rounding.

273

suggest that the basic correlates of household and personal victimization as revealed by the NCS have changed very little over time. For example, drawing on the NCS data from the "households touched by crime" measure, the chances of victimization have consistently related to race (black households are more likely to have members who were victims of robbery or aggravated assault), family income (positively related to theft without violence and negatively related to burglary), and urbanization (households within urban areas have substantially higher rates [Rand 1983]).

Laub (1983) has studied how the patterns of victimization involving juveniles have changed over the period 1973–81 in the NCS data, finding that the rates of juvenile offending for crimes against the person were essentially stable over that period, that there was little change in juvenile/adult offense patterns, and that the use of weapons remained unchanged (including the use of guns). All this led him to conclude that the seriousness of juvenile crime showed little systematic or substantial variation over the time period studied.

We need not become overly concerned with these time trend data. Change, or the appearance of change, is a relative judgment that largely depends on the scope of time one uses to make the judgment. Like any statistics, change data have no meaning outside a context or purpose for their evaluation. This is perhaps nowhere better demonstrated than in recent analyses of historical trends in crime in which the abscissa for the series is extended for many years (Gurr 1981). Although there is clearly considerable public interest in year-to-year crime rates, it is less clear what questions such data can answer. As Sparks (1982) argues, it is difficult to think of any contemporary theory of crime causation that could be validly evaluated on year-to-year fluctuations in crime rates.

A focus on the levels of crime and their fluctuations directs too much attention away from comparisons relevant to the scientific study of crime and may even be damaging to the longer-run interests in the valid measurement of crime for academic purposes. Of far greater importance to scientific criminology is the extent to which the correlates of crime are similar or different in alternative methods of measurement despite the different absolute levels depicted by each.

The appropriate questions about validity for etiological purposes do not concern the absolute count of crime. Hindelang et al. (1981) have shown how the use of official statistics for etiological purposes can be distinguished from their use as "social indicators" and the consequence of this distinction for common criticisms of official measures. Again, not all criticisms of crime data with respect to their inability to measure validly the absolute level of crime are pertinent to the question of whether they reliably and validly depict differences in offending, spatial and temporal patterns, et cetera. To the extent that the social indicator use of crime statistics (the level question) is confused with their etiological value (the correlate question), their validity for the latter purpose may erroneously be questioned on the grounds that they have difficulty addressing the former purpose. The history of the interpretation of crime statistics is replete with examples of this logical fallacy (see Hindelang et al. 1981).

III. Explanations of Crime Based on Victimization Surveys

Explanations of crime emerging from victimization research have focused on the large between-group differences in risk indicated by the NCS. Being essentially simple tallies by population aggregates, the UCR has not generally permitted fine calibrations of risk measures. Thus one of the most significant contributions of the NCS has been the flexibility it allows in the construction of risk measures.

Any risk statistic, or crime rate, requires two measurements. The first, of course, is the frequency of occurrence of criminal offenses. The second is a measurement of the population at risk, which forms the denominator of the rate. There are, however, both conceptual and measurement issues involved in the construction of such risk measures for crime.

The conceptual issues involve the determination of what should be counted in the first instance as "crime" and therefore included in the numerator of the risk rate (e.g., are cars taken for a "joyride" by neighborhood youths but returned before the car owner returns from work to be considered as auto thefts?). But an equally important problem is how the "population at risk" should be defined (Reiss 1967, 1982; Mayhew, Clarke, and Hough 1976; Gottfredson 1981; Clarke 1984). The closer the measurement of the population is to the units truly "at risk," the better; yet the crime statistics available prior to victimization surveys have permitted only restricted opportunities to concentrate on units at risk.

The measurement issues have received considerably more attention. Controversy has always surrounded the counting of crimes. Although the existence of the "dark figure" of unrecorded crime has never been much disputed, its nature has remained largely unknown. For constructing risk measures, the dark figure presents formidable problems. If the processes by which some offenses are added to the official measures while others are left out systematically weed out some types of victims or some types of offenses, then risk measures constructed on the basis of official statistics may not give an accurate portrait of the relative risks faced by different people.[11]

Thus risk analyses for crime have been aided greatly by the arrival of the victimization survey, which, among other things, permits more refined measurements for the numerator of crime rates. Once demographically disaggregated crime rates were possible, very large differences in victimization probabilities became apparent. At the same time, criminologists began to give serious attention to the question of opportunity and how the idea of exposure to crime should figure into calculations of risk (Reiss 1967; Gould 1969; Mayhew et al. 1976; Cohen and Felson 1979; Sparks 1982). One consequence of this has been an increase in the perceived relevance of people's routine daily activities, or life-styles, to the risk of criminal victimization.

Life-Style and Criminal Victimization.   As Cohen and Felson (1979) have argued, for a crime to occur there must first be a target (something to steal, to vandalize, or to break into or somebody to rob or to assault), a person motivated to offend, and an opportunity for the offense (the confluence in time and space of the target and offender in the absence of effective deterrents). Each of these logical and commonsensical requirements for criminal victimization has considerable implications for understanding the relative risks that different people or households may have for victimization. A substantial body of evidence suggests that *opportunities* for becoming the victim of personal crime, such as rape, robbery, and personal theft, vary directly with the extent of out-of-the-home activities, particularly at night. Felson notes in a review of past research on victimization that the "evidence indicate[s] that a far greater risk of both personal and property victimization was incurred by engaging in activities away from family and household settings: even an automobile was found to be much more exposed to theft when it belonged to persons who were often away from home. Any social

---

[11] There are a number of other critically important measurement questions in the construction of risk measures that cannot be addressed here. These include how criminal events should be counted when more than one occurs or when more than one victim is victimized in an incident, whether and to what extent multiply victimized persons or places should be multiply counted, the appropriate time unit to study, and so forth (see Sparks 1982).

trends that draw people away from home thus became important for crime rate analysis" (1983, p. 667). Research showing that the population of offenders is not evenly distributed throughout society, but that young males are unusually likely to offend in personal crimes, suggests that life-styles likely to involve extensive contact with young people lead to greater risks of victimization.

Recent theory has therefore focused attention on individual life-styles—how the routine daily activities of people, in the sense of where they go, when they go there, with whom they are likely to be in contact, and where they live and work—are likely to alter the chances of becoming the victim of crime. As examples, Hindelang et al. (1978) argue that the chances of becoming the victim of personal crime vary quite substantially according to social and demographic characteristics, which in turn are related to various routine daily activities that serve to increase the opportunity for victimization. Cohen and Felson (1979) argue that shifts in routine activity patterns over time have produced changes in property crime rates. Taking a measure of the dispersion of activities away from the home as an indicator of routine activity, their predictions about crime rate changes were consistent with the data about homicide, rape, assault, robbery, and burglary in a time-series study of UCR data from 1947 to 1974.

There have now been several major studies of life-style theory using victimization data. These studies may be grouped according to whether they use indirect measures of life-style (e.g., employment status) or direct measures (e.g., number of nights out of the home). The former use NCS data; the latter come mainly from surveys done in other countries.

Cohen, Cantor, and Kluegel (1981) examined the combined effects of demographic and life-style characteristics on the risk of personal robbery using NCS data from 1973 to 1977, specifically, the race, age, income, household size, and major activity patterns of the respondents. They discovered that, when these effects were considered simultaneously, age had a sizable relation to robbery victimization (the young had especially high risks), as did major activity (the unemployed had especially high risks, whereas home-centered persons had low risks), income (the risk of robbery decreased with increasing income), race (nonwhites had the higher risks), and living arrangements (living alone was associated with the greater risks). Cohen et al. interpret these results as being consistent with the life-style expectations. People spending much of their time at home indoors have less opportunity to become robbery victims, whereas those whose activity patterns and living circumstances place them in proximity to likely offenders have substantially higher risks. Their model produced considerable variation in risks of victimization—the highest rate group (young, unemployed, low income, black, living alone) had a risk nearly ten times higher than the average risk.

In a further analysis of personal victimization by Cohen and Cantor (1980), this time for personal larceny, the results were essentially similar. When considered in a multivariate model, larceny risks were shown to be higher for the young, those living alone, and those whose life-styles included considerable out-of-the-home activities. There did not appear to be a race effect, and the risks increased with increased income. As Garofalo (1983) has noted, such patterns are consistent with the life-style expectations, given that the personal larcenies studied were confined to those occurring outside the home and that the targets of personal larceny are primarily visible and attractive consumer goods that may be expected to belong disproportionately to those of greater income.

Innes and Gressett (1982) use the NCS and life-style concepts to help explain patterns in the victimization of women. They reason that life-style theory would lead to a prediction that rising female labor force participation and changes in family structure would expose women to greater risks of victimization, a prediction largely supported by their NCS data.

Canadian victimization surveys have used direct life-style indicators and also have found life-style to be related in important ways to the risk of victimization. The number of evenings spent outside the home each month had a strong relation to assault, robbery, personal theft, household theft, and vandalism (Corrado et al. 1980). Similar relations between victimization and direct measures of life-style have been reported in the Netherlands by van Dijk and Steinmetz (1984), who also found that, holding constant age, urbanization, social class, and former victimization experiences, going out frequently in the evening was predictive of victimization. Smith (1982) undertook a victimization survey in England and found that age and a measure of social class were related to victimization, but so too was a measure of the relative frequency of spare-time activities. Those measures that indicated greater contact with strangers in public places were especially predictive of victimization. Gottfredson (1984) analyzed data from the British Crime Survey on direct indicators of life-style and found that out-of-the-home activities (especially at night), drinking heavily, self-reported offending, and certain daytime activities that placed the respondents out of the home were substantially related to personal victimization even when age, sex, and urbanization were sequentially held constant. Widom and Maxfield (1984) have explored the victimization of women and Clarke et al. (1985) the victimization of the elderly, using the life-style indicators in the British Crime Survey.

Household offenses too seem amenable to a life-style interpretation. For example, recently Cohen and Cantor (1980) have shown how the risks of household crime (e.g., burglary) can be affected by the out-of-the-home activities of the residents. And Cohen and Felson's (1979) conclusions about changes in the opportunities for burglary were recently supported by a comparison of Dutch and American burglary rates by Block (1984). Finding that burglary and larceny rates are highest among those with the least and with the most family income, Sparks (1982) invokes the life-style concepts of target attractiveness and vulnerability—the high rate for the wealthy is because the wealthy have more to steal, while the high rate for the poor is attributable to their closer proximity to burglars or to the fact that they are less able to protect their property (cf. Hindelang et al. 1978).

It should be stressed that in all extant life-style research the basic demographic and structural correlates of criminal victimization are still strong despite controls for these life-style dimensions. Age in particular is a powerful correlate of the chances of criminal victimization, and it remains so even after the variables typically used to measure life-style are taken into consideration (Corrado et al. 1980; Gottfredson 1984). Of course the tests of the life-style perspective that are possible with the available data are limited. Going out in the evening, particularly at night, is a central life-style construct, but it is clearly only one such construct (Hindelang et al. 1978). That this variable and the situational and areal variables do seem to matter so much in accounting for victimization rates is encouraging for the viability of the life-style perspective. So too is the variability in victimization risks associated with the common measures of daytime activities used in research thus far. Although the existing research is only preliminary and the "theory" is as yet quite primitive, there is ample reason to suggest that the approach is a promising one.

To a considerable extent the life-style approach can be distinguished from other approaches to the explanation of crime by its focus on crime targets instead of offenders. Much criminological research seeks to understand crime and its social and demographic distribution by seeking to understand the motivation for offending. In contrast, the life-style approach assumes motivation to offend; the task for life-style theorists is to explicate the situations in which such motivation is least likely to be restrained. That is, differences that exist in the opportunity to offend, rather than in the desire or impetus to offend, are seen as being important in explanations of crime rates.

Life-style variables seem important because they help to predict which people and what property are likely to come into contact with likely offenders in situations in which the restraints against offending are reduced. Available data suggest strongly that variations in opportunities to offend differ for different people and over time. For example, there have been dramatic increases in the last thirty years or so in the quantity of personal disposable property available to be stolen. Sparks (1982) shows that a burglar in 1950 had one chance in ten of finding a television set within a randomly chosen household, a figure that increased to 94 percent by 1974. Felson and Cohen (1980, pp. 403–4) provide a thought-provoking list of social trends plausibly related to changed opportunity structures for crime and point to the irony that

> the very factors which increase the opportunity to enjoy the benefits of life may also increase the opportunity for predatory violations. For example, automobiles provide freedom of movement to offenders as well as average citizens and provide targets for theft. College enrollment, female labor force participation, urbanization, suburbanization, vacations, and new consumer goods provide various opportunities to escape the confines of the household while they increase the risk of predatory victimization. Indeed, the opportunity for predatory crime appears to be enmeshed in the opportunity structure for legitimate activities to such an extent that it might be very difficult to root out substantial amounts of crime without modifying much of our way of life.

IV. Conclusions

When systematic victimization surveys were first undertaken only twenty years ago, they had the potential to set criminology rocking. The statistical foundation for criminological knowledge was in trouble.

Although official data painted a consistent portrait of a core set of characteristics about crime, the portrait was vulnerable. Having essentially only one method of measurement, all logical threats to its validity were taken seriously because they were empirically nonfalsifiable. As a result, a familiar list of potential biases in official data grew (and grew) to the point that many criminologists regarded the basic data about crime as purely artifacts of the method of measurement. Self-report methods were new (Short and Nye 1957, 1958), they had logical weaknesses of their own (e.g., Nettler 1974), and early self-report results intimated that the list of problems marring the use of official data might not be long enough. Early reviews of the victimization survey method fed this impression and promised that the new method might at last prove what some theory in criminology has long been telling us—that our facts were in error: "[The UCR] are a function not only of crime, but also of the working of the system of social control: They thus confound the relationships that theorists have wished to isolate for study. Victimization surveys, which can provide separate measures of crime and of societal response to it, can overcome this limitation. A continuing national survey would thus open the way to . . . a reexamination of many received truths" (Penick and Owens 1976, p. 163).

What may we conclude about survey-generated estimates of crime in comparison with official measures? First, with respect to the etiological value of victimization data the results described above are very encouraging. Most, but not all, of the important social, demographic, and spatial/temporal differences shown by the NCS are also repeatedly found in official data, suggesting considerable convergent validity. Weis (1983, p. 391), subsequent to a review of the evidence on crime statistics, has stated this conclusion succinctly: "The . . . important purpose of crime statistics is the measurement of the distribution of crime by a variety of social, demographic, and geographic characteristics. Fortunately, the major sources of crime data—crimes known to the police, victimization surveys, and self-report surveys—generate similar distributions and correlates of crime, pointing to convergence rather than discrepancy among the measures of the basic characteristics of crime and criminals. The problems associated with each of the data sources remain, but they diminish in significance because these imperfect measures produce similar perspectives of crime."

There are certainly some differences between the patterns shown by the UCR and the NCS, particularly surrounding assault and the correlation of education with victimization.[12] But in the main the patterns revealed by the two on the vast majority of the facts of concern to contemporary criminology are similar. The result is that empirical criminology is in better shape today than ever before with respect to the confidence generated by its statistical base. The basic facts about crime cannot now be dismissed simply as artifacts of the system of crime control or as being completely dependent on the method of measurement. This development in what most fields take for granted could easily prove to be the most lasting and important contribution of the victimization method. It is somewhat ironic that a method that set out to show how big the "dark figure" of crime really was, and by so doing to suggest how faulty the measurement of crime really was, should contribute so substantially to the credibility of so many of the "received truths" it had the potential to destroy.

REFERENCES

Biderman, A., J. Lynch, and J. Peterson. 1982. "Why NCS Diverges from UCR Index Trends." Paper presented at the annual meeting of the American Society of Criminology, Denver, 1983. Mimeographed. Washington, D.C.: Bureau of Social Science Research.

Block, Carolyn B., and Richard L. Block. 1984. "Crime Definition, Crime Measurement and Victim Surveys." *Journal of Social Issues* 40:137–60.

Block, Richard L. 1984. "The Impact of Victimization, Rates and Patterns: A Comparison of the Netherlands and the United States." In *Victimization and Fear of Crime: World Perspectives*, edited by Richard Block. Washington, D.C.: U.S. Government Printing Office.

Block, Richard L., Marcus Felson, and Carolyn Block. 1985. "Crime Victimization Rates for Incumbents of 246 Occupations." *Sociology and Social Research* 69:442–51.

Braithwaite, John, and David Biles. 1984. "Victims and Offenders: The Australian Experience." In *Victimization and Fear of Crime: World Perspectives*, edited by Richard Block. Washington, D.C.: U.S. Government Printing Office.

Bureau of Justice Statistics. 1985. "Households Touched by Crime, 1984." Washington, D.C.: U.S. Department of Justice.

[12] The principal difficulties encountered by the NCS may well have a common source. Like surveys designed to assess self-reported offending there is good reason to believe that the groups with the highest rates are the least amenable to the demands of surveys, such as "getting into" the sample to begin with and "producing" at the appropriate level during the interview. (See Hindelang et al. [1981].)

Clarke, Ronald V. G. 1984. "Opportunity-based Crime Rates." *British Journal of Criminology* 24:74–83.

Clarke, Ronald V. G., Paul Ekblom, Mike Hough, and Pat Mayhew. 1985. "Elderly Victims of Crime and Exposure to Risk." *Howard Journal* 24:1–9.

Cohen, L. E., and D. Cantor. 1980. "The Determinants of Larceny." *Journal of Research in Crime and Delinquency* 17:140–59.

Cohen, L. E., D. Cantor, and J. Kluegel. 1981. "Robbery Victimization in the United States." *Social Science Quarterly* 66:644–57.

Cohen, L. E., and Marcus Felson. 1979. "Social Change and Crime Rate Trends: A Routine Activity Approach." *American Sociological Review* 44:588–608.

———. 1981. "Modeling Crime Trends: A Criminal Opportunity Perspective." *Journal of Research in Crime and Delinquency* 18(January):138–64.

Cook, Philip. 1976. "A Strategic Choice Analysis of Robbery." In *Sample Surveys of the Victims of Crime*, edited by Wesley Skogan. Cambridge, Mass.: Ballinger.

Corrado, R. R., R. Roesch, W. Glackman, J. L. Evans, and G. J. Leger. 1980. "Lifestyles and Personal Victimization: A Test of the Model with Canadian Survey Data." *Journal of Crime and Justice* 3:129–39.

Dodge, R., and H. Lentzner. 1978. "Patterns of Personal Series Incidents in the National Crime Survey." Paper presented at the annual meeting of the American Statistical Association, San Diego, California.

Empey, Lamar. 1983. *American Delinquency: Its Meaning and Construction.* Homewood, Ill.: Dorsey.

Ennis, P. H. 1967. *Criminal Victimization in the United States: A Report of a National Survey.* President's Commission on Law Enforcement and Administration of Justice. Field Surveys 2. Washington, D.C.: U.S. Government Printing Office.

Felson, Marcus. 1983. "Ecology and Crime." In *Encyclopedia of Crime and Justice*, edited by Sanford Kadish. New York: Free Press.

Felson, Marcus, and L. Cohen. 1980. "Human Ecology and Crime: A Routine Activity Approach." *Human Ecology* 8:389–406.

Fienberg, Steven. 1980. "The Measurement of Crime Victimization: Prospects for Panel Analysis of a Panel Survey." *Statistician* 29:313–50.

Fienberg, Steven, and Albert J. Reiss, Jr., eds. 1980. *Indicators of Crime and Criminal Justice: Quantitative Studies.* Washington, D.C.: U.S. Government Printing Office.

Garofalo, James. 1977. *The Police and Public Opinion.* Washington, D.C.: U.S. Government Printing Office.

———. 1981. "The Fear of Crime: Causes and Consequences." *Journal of Criminal Law and Criminology* 72:839–57.

———. 1983. "Lifestyles and Victimization: An Update." Paper presented at the Thirty-third International Course in Criminology, Vancouver, British Columbia, March.

Garofalo, James, and Michael J. Hindelang. 1977. *An Introduction to the National Crime Survey.* National Criminal Justice Information and Statistics Service. Washington, D.C.: U.S. Government Printing Office.

Gibbs, J. J. 1977. *Crime against Victims in Urban, Suburban, and Rural Areas.* Washington, D.C.: U.S. Government Printing Office.

Goldberg, I., and F. Nold. 1978. "Does Reporting Deter Burglars: An Empirical Analysis of Risk and Return in Crime." Technical Report CERDCR-4–78. Stanford, Calif.: Stanford University, Hoover Institution, Center for Econometric Studies of the Justice System.

Gottfredson, Michael R. 1984. *Victims of Crime: The Dimensions of Risk.* London: H.M. Stationery Office.

Gottfredson, Michael R., and Michael J. Hindelang. 1979. "A Study of the Behavior of Law." *American Sociological Review* 44:3–18.

———. 1981. "Sociological Aspects of Criminal Victimization." *Annual Review of Sociology* 7:107–28.

Gould, L. C. 1969. "The Changing Structure of Property Crime in an Affluent Society." *Social Forces* 48:50–59.

Gurr, Ted Robert. 1981. "Historical Trends in Violent Crimes: A Critical Review of the Evidence." In *Crime and Justice: An Annual Review of Research,* vol. 3, edited by Michael Tonry and Norval Morris. Chicago: University of Chicago Press.

Hindelang, Michael. 1976. *Criminal Victimization in Eight American Cities: A Descriptive Analysis of Common Theft and Assault.* Cambridge, Mass.: Ballinger.

———. 1978. "Race and Involvement in Common Law Personal Crimes." *American Sociological Review* 43:93–109.

———. 1981. "Variations in Sex-Race-Age-specific Incidence Rates of Offending." *American Sociological Review* 46:461–74.

Hindelang, Michael J., Michael R. Gottfredson, and James Garofalo. 1978. *Victims of Personal Crime: An Empirical Foundation for a Theory of Personal Victimization.* Cambridge, Mass.: Ballinger.

Hindelang, Michael J., Travis Hirschi, and Joseph Weis. 1979. "Correlates of Delinquency: The Illusion of Discrepancy between Self-Report and Official Measures." *American Sociological Review* 44:995–1014.

———. 1981. *Measuring Delinquency.* Beverly Hills, Calif.: Sage.

Hough, M. 1983. "Victims of Violent Crime." Paper presented at the Thirty-third International Course in Criminology, Vancouver, British Columbia, March.

Hough, M., and Pat Mayhew. 1983. *The British Crime Survey: First Report.* Home Office Research Study, no. 76. London: H.M. Stationery Office.

Innes, Christopher, and Lynne Gressett. 1982. "Patterns in the Criminal Victimization of Women, 1974–1978." Mimeographed. Ann Arbor, Mich.: Inter-University Consortium for Political and Social Research.

Klaus, P., M. Rand, and B. Taylor. 1983. "The Victim." In *Bureau of Justice Statistics Report to the Nation on Crime and Justice.* Washington, D.C.: U.S. Department of Justice.

Laub, J. 1983. *Trends in Juvenile Criminal Behavior in the United States: 1973–1981.* Working Paper 24. Albany, N.Y.: Criminal Justice Research Center.

Laub, J., and M. Hindelang. 1981. *Analysis of the National Crime Survey Data to Study Serious Delinquent Behavior.* Monograph 3. Albany, N.Y.: Criminal Justice Research Center.

Lehnen, R., and Albert J. Reiss, Jr. 1978. "Response Effects in the National Crime Survey." *Victimology* 3:110–24.

Lehnen, Robert, and Wesley Skogan. 1981. "The National Crime Survey: Working Papers." In *Current and Historical Perspectives*, vol. 1, edited by Robert Lehnen and Wesley Skogan. Washington, D.C.: U.S. Government Printing Office.

McDermott, John, and Michael Hindelang. 1981. *Analysis of National Crime Survey Data to Study Serious Delinquent Behavior.* Monograph 1. Albany, N.Y.: Criminal Justice Research Center.

McGarrell, E. F., and Timothy J. Flanagan, eds. 1985. *Sourcebook of Criminal Justice Statistics—1984.* U.S. Department of Justice, Bureau of Justice Statistics. Washington, D.C.: U.S. Government Printing Office.

Maxfield, Michael. 1984. *Fear of Crime in England and Wales.* London: H.M. Stationery Office.

Mayhew, Pat, Ronald V. G. Clarke, and J. M. Hough. 1976. *Crime as Opportunity.* Home Office Research Study, no. 34. London: H.M. Stationery Office.

Ministry of the Solicitor General. 1983. *Victims of Crime: Preliminary Finding of the Canadian Urban Victimization Survey.* Bulletin no. 1. Ottawa: Ministry of the Solicitor General, Research and Statistics Group, Programs Branch.

Nelson, J. 1980. "Multiple Victimization: A Statistical Analysis of Rare Events." *American Journal of Sociology* 4:870–91.

Nettler, G. 1974. *Explaining Crime.* New York: McGraw-Hill.

———. 1984. *Explaining Crime.* 3d rev. ed. New York: McGraw-Hill.

O'Brien, R. 1983. "Metropolitan Structure and Violent Crime: Which Measure of Crime?" *American Sociological Review* 48:434–37.

Paez, A., and F. Shenk. 1983. *Criminal Victimization in the United States: 1973–82 Trends.* Bureau of Justice Statistics Special Report. Washington, D.C.: U.S. Government Printing Office.

Penick, B. K. E., and M. E. B. Owens. 1976. *Surveying Crime.* Final Report of the Panel for the Evaluation of Crime Surveys. National Research Council, Committee on National Statistics. Washington, D.C.: National Academy of Sciences.

Rand, M. 1983. *Households Touched by Crime, 1982.* Bureau of Justice Statistics Bulletin. Washington, D.C.: U.S. Government Printing Office.

Rand, M., P. L. Klaus, and B. Taylor. 1983. "The Criminal Event." *Report to the Nation on Crime and Justice.* U.S. Department of Justice, Bureau of Justice Statistics. Washington, D.C.: U.S. Government Printing Office.

Reiss, Albert J., Jr. 1967. *Studies in Crime and Law Enforcement in Major Metropolitan Areas.* President's Commission on Law Enforcement and Administration of Justice. Field Surveys 3, vol. 1. Washington, D.C.: U.S. Government Printing Office.

———. 1980. "Victim Proneness in Repeat Victimization by Type of Crime." In *Indicators of Crime and Criminal Justice: Quantitative Studies*, edited by Steven Fienberg and Albert J. Reiss, Jr. Washington, D.C.: U.S. Government Printing Office.

———. 1982. "How Serious Is Serious Crime?" *Vanderbilt Law Review* 35:541–85.

Sampson, Robert J. 1983. "Structural Density and Criminal Victimization." *Criminology* 21:276–93.

———. 1985. "Neighborhood and Crime: The Structural Determinants of Personal Victimization." *Journal of Research in Crime and Delinquency* 22:7–40.

Sampson, Robert J., T. Castellano, and J. Laub. 1981. "Analysis of National Crime Survey Data to Study Serious Delinquent Behavior." In *Juvenile Criminal Behavior and Its Relation to Neighborhood Characteristics*, vol. 5, edited by Robert J. Sampson, T. Castellano, and J. Laub. Washington, D.C.: U.S. Government Printing Office.

Schneider, A. L. 1981. "Methodological Problems in Victim Surveys and Their Implications for Research in Victimology." *Journal of Criminal Law and Criminology* 72:818–38.

Shichor, D., D. Decker, and R. O'Brien. 1979. "Population Density and Criminal Victimization." *Criminology* 17:184–93.

Short, James, and F. Nye. 1957. "Reported Behavior as a Criterion of Deviant Behavior." *Social Problems* 5:207–13.

———. 1958. "Extent of Unrecorded Juvenile Delinquency: Tentative Conclusions." *Journal of Criminal Law and Criminology* 49:296–302.

Skogan, Wesley G. 1977. "Dimensions of the 'Dark Figure' of Unreported Crime." *Crime and Delinquency* 23:41–50.

———. 1979. "Crime in Contemporary America." In *Violence in America*, edited by H. Graham and Ted Robert Gurr. Beverly Hills, Calif.: Sage.

———. 1981. *Issues in the Measurement of Victimization*. U.S. Department of Justice, Bureau of Justice Statistics. Washington, D.C.: U.S. Government Printing Office.

Skogan, Wesley, and Michael Maxfield. 1981. *Coping with Crime: Individual and Neighborhood Reactions*. Beverly Hills, Calif.: Sage.

Smith, S. 1982. "Victimization in the Inner City: A British Case Study." *British Journal of Criminology* 22:386–402.

Sparks, Richard F. 1981. "Surveys of Victimization—an Optimistic Assessment." In *Crime and Justice: An Annual Review of Research*, vol. 3, edited by Michael Tonry and Norval Morris. Chicago: University of Chicago Press.

———. 1982. *Research on Victims of Crime*. Washington, D.C.: U.S. Government Printing Office.

Sparks, Richard F., H. Genn, and D. J. Dodd. 1977. *Surveying Victims*. London: Wiley.

Taylor, B. 1983. "Does Higher Socioeconomic Status Increase Risk of Violent Victimization or Simply Its Reporting in Crime Surveys?" Paper presented at the annual meeting of the American Society of Criminology, Denver.

Toby, Jackson. 1983. "Violence in School." In *Crime and Justice: An Annual Review of Research*, vol. 4, edited by Michael Tonry and Norval Morris. Chicago: University of Chicago Press.

van Dijk, J. J. M., and C. Steinmetz. 1984. "The Burden of Crime in Dutch Society, 1973–1979." In *Victimization and Fear of Crime: World Perspectives*, edited by Richard Block. Washington, D.C.: U.S. Government Printing Office.

Weis, Joseph. 1983. "Crime Statistics: Reporting Systems and Methods." In *Encyclopedia of Crime and Justice*, edited by Sanford Kadish. New York: Free Press.

Weis, Joseph, and J. Henney. 1980. "Crime and Criminals in the United States." In *Criminology Review Yearbook*, vol. 2, edited by E. Bittner and Sheldon Messinger. Beverly Hills, Calif.: Sage.

Widom, Cathy Spatz, and Michael G. Maxfield. 1984. "Sex Roles and the Victimization of Women: Evidence from the British Crime Survey." Paper read at the annual meeting of the American Society of Criminology, Cincinnati, November.

Zedlewski, Edward. 1983. "Deterrence Findings and Data Sources: A Comparison of the Uniform Crime Reports and the National Crime Surveys." *Journal of Research in Crime and Delinquency* 20:262–76.

Peter Reuter and Mark A. R. Kleiman

Risks and Prices: An Economic Analysis of Drug Enforcement

ABSTRACT

Marijuana and cocaine, two mass-market drugs, have been the object of a major campaign by the federal government over the past five years. That campaign apparently has not led to a significant tightening in the availability of the two drugs, though the relatively high prices of these drugs historically are a consequence of enforcement. The reason for this lack of response to recent law enforcement pressures may lie in structural characteristics of these markets rather than in a failure of tactics or of coordination of law enforcement efforts. The federal effort aims at importation and high-level distribution, which account for a modest share of the retail prices of these drugs. Increasing the risks to importers or high-level distributors is thus likely to have modest effects on the retail price and is unlikely to have any other effect on the conditions of use. Street-level enforcement is hindered by the sheer scale of the two markets and because so few of the final purchases occur in public settings. Many of the risks associated with drug trafficking come from the actions of other participants in the trades themselves, and this also limits the ability of law enforcement agencies to act in ways that will cause prices to increase or alter market conditions. Law enforcement efforts directed at heroin have been much more effective at restricting drug use.

Marijuana and cocaine are used by large numbers of Americans on a regular basis. The most recent national estimates (Miller et al. 1982) put

Peter Reuter is a Senior Economist at the Rand Corporation in Washington, D.C. Mark A. R. Kleiman is Research Associate at the John F. Kennedy School of Government, Harvard University. A different version of this essay will appear in J. M. Polich, R. K. Ellickson, P. H. Reuter, and J. Kahn, *Controlling Drug Abuse* (in press).

the numbers using these drugs at least once per month at 20 million for marijuana and 5 million for cocaine. It is generally, though not universally, thought that this is a significant social problem. The primary response to the problem has been, particularly since 1981, greatly to increase efforts at reducing the supply of these two drugs.

Despite the increased enforcement effort, which has yielded substantial results in terms of drug and asset seizures, arrests, and lengthy prison sentences, it appears that both marijuana and cocaine are still readily available. Indeed, the street price of cocaine, the best single short-run indicator of the efficacy of enforcement, has declined since the enforcement effort intensified. Cocaine consumption may have increased. Marijuana prices have risen slightly in real dollars, and there is some evidence of decreased consumption; however, that decline is more plausibly accounted for by changes in adolescent attitudes toward the health consequences of marijuana use than to intensified enforcement.

This essay attempts to account for the apparent lack of response of cocaine and marijuana consumption to the increased federal enforcement effort. We make frequent comparisons between these trades and the heroin trade, in which enforcement has led to dramatically tighter market conditions. Heroin is an appropriate comparison drug because, like the others, it starts as an agricultural product overseas, a fact which is of considerable significance for enforcement strategies. The essay also considers, albeit more briefly, the consequences of possible increases in local law enforcement efforts against retail markets in marijuana and cocaine.

Our results are simply stated. Federal enforcement efforts have great difficulty in imposing significant costs on mass-market drugs. The sheer size of the markets forces a concentration on crops in the field, export-import transactions, and high-level domestic dealing. However, these components of the production-distribution process account for a modest share of the final retail price of the drugs; about one-quarter for marijuana and one-tenth for cocaine. Thus, even if the federal effort were to succeed in raising the kilogram-level price of cocaine or the ton-level price of marijuana (those being roughly the units in which the drugs are sold in their first domestic transaction), this would have limited effect on the retail price. Since the federal efforts can do little except change prices, that is, they cannot much alter the other social and cultural conditions that affect use, they can only modestly reduce total consumption.

Intensified enforcement by local police against retail markets for cocaine and marijuana is not likely to be much more effective than the federal enforcement effort. Again, it is the already massive scale of these markets, together with the middle-class character of so many of the users, that lowers the efficacy of such enforcement. For heroin, by contrast, with a much smaller and more exposed consumer base, there is evidence that increased stringency might be effective in still further reducing consumption.

Some caveats to this analysis should be mentioned. We focus on the consequences of enforcement for price because that is the only element of the markets that is much affected by most of the enforcement activities with which we are concerned. It may well be that there are other general effects, particularly in terms of the display of social disapprobation coming from arrests, seizures, trials, and so on, which operate to lower use or keep levels of use from increasing. We do not deal with these, simply because there is no empirical basis for doing so. That is not to say that they do not exist.

We do not claim to have a complete model of the marijuana and cocaine markets. Our explanations of historic changes in the price of cocaine are tentative and point to important gaps in the research on these markets. We try to ensure that these limits in our model are made clear to the reader.

Given the length of this essay, we venture two other introductory comments. First, we believe that the specific policy conclusions are less important than is the framework that is provided for considering the evaluation of enforcement against illegal markets generally. To that extent the essay can be viewed as an exercise in industrial organization, focusing on the impact of external changes imposed through the actions of agencies. We work with even more than the average number of assumptions used in economics because the available data on illicit drug markets are so meager.

Second, our pessimistic conclusions about the effect of cocaine and marijuana enforcement on street-level prices are not condemnations of drug enforcement generally. Indeed, one purpose of providing contrasts with heroin is to suggest the conditions under which enforcement can be highly effective. Even if we are correct in our estimate of the relative ineffectiveness of additional federal expenditures on cocaine and marijuana enforcement, that does not imply either that less should be spent for such enforcement or that legalization is appropriate. It simply points to the limits of what can be achieved with certain instruments aimed at these two markets.

Section I presents certain statistical data that are important to the analysis and is followed in Section II by discussions of how drug enforcement affects illegal markets and the appropriateness of using price as an indicator of the efficacy of supply reduction efforts. Sections III and IV then consider the four instruments of enforcement or supply reduction: source-country control, interdiction, law enforcement aimed at high-level dealers, and law enforcement aimed at low-level dealers. The final section presents some policy conclusions.

I. Markets: Organization and Scale

Heroin, cocaine, and marijuana are all imported, though approximately one-eighth of the marijuana market is supplied from domestic sources. The distribution chain is long and typically involves sales between independent buyers and sellers. Each importer sells to a small number of high-level domestic dealers, each of whom in turn sells to a slightly larger number of middle-level dealers. The length of the chain is a matter of conjecture. For heroin there may be as many as five dealers between the importer and the final user and for marijuana as few as two. The length of the chain is probably variable, even for any one drug. Some importers bring in large shipments; others bring in smaller shipments. It is the size of the initial importation relative to the size of the typical consumer purchase that determines the length of the chain.

The distribution system is affected by the physical characteristics of the drug involved. For example, marijuana is far bulkier per unit value than cocaine. This requires that it be imported in relatively large, dedicated vessels. These are more easily subject to interception than are the vessels used for smuggling the very compact cocaine. Heroin is so compact per unit value that it can be concealed on passengers or in freight. The enforcement environment also makes a difference; the higher penalties levied on convicted heroin dealers make them more discreet than their cocaine and marijuana counterparts and less willing to deal with a large number of intermediate dealers.

A. Prices and Scale

These differences are also reflected in the price structure of the three drugs in 1980, the most recent year for which source-country price data have been published. Table 1 presents official data on the prices for the drugs at different points in the distribution system. Three aspects of

TABLE 1

Structure of Drug Prices, 1980* (per Pure Kilogram)

	Heroin	Cocaine	Marijuana[†]
Farmgate	$350–$1,000[‡]	$1,300–$10,000	$7–$18
Processed	$6,000–$10,000	$3,000–$10,000	$55
Export	$95,000	$7,000–$20,000	$90–$180
Import[§]	$220,000–$240,000	$50,000	$365–$720
Retail	$1.6–$2.2 million	$650,000[‖]	$1,250–$2,090

SOURCE.—Adapted from National Narcotics Intelligence Consumers Committee (1982).

* No more recent data are available for source-country prices. It is not likely that there have been significant changes in the relationship of prices at different points in the distribution system.

† Prices are for Colombian-origin marijuana, estimated to account for 75 percent of total U.S. consumption in 1980.

‡ The price of the 10 kg of opium required to manufacture 1 kg of heroin.

§ The import price refers to price at first transaction within the United States. Marijuana is purchased roughly in ton lots, cocaine in multikilo lots, and heroin in kilo lots.

‖ The original data source reported a retail price of $800,000. Other DEA data, such as those reported in U.S. General Accounting Office (1983), consistently indicate prices in the range $600–$650,000 in 1980.

the table deserve mention. First, most of the value added comes in the domestic distribution of the drug, not in its production or export. Second, the price rise within the United States is proportionately much greater for heroin than for marijuana. Third, only for marijuana does the export-import sector account for a significant share of final price.

The estimation of the scale of drug markets has attracted considerable attention. Few newspaper stories or political speeches on drug enforcement fail to mention the official 1980 estimate of $80 billion in gross sales generated by illicit drugs (National Narcotics Intelligence Consumers Committee 1982). Yet the data are so poor that estimates of revenue can vary threefold (*Miami Herald* [June 17, 1985]). Even fewer data are available for estimating the sizes of the dealer populations and the distribution of incomes among dealers.

Table 2 presents some rough estimates of total income and dealer numbers for 1982, the most recent year for which data are available from the National Household Survey (Miller et al. 1982). Details of these calculations are contained in Kleiman (1985) and Reuter (1984*b*). Here we state only the basic principles and sources underlying the calculations. Both income and dealer numbers are based on the user estimates.

TABLE 2

Drug Market Income and Dealer Estimates, 1982

	Marijuana	Cocaine	Heroin
Regular users	20,000,000	4,500,000	450,000
Users per dealer	40	25	10
Dealers	500,000	180,000	45,000
Total consumption (kg)	6,400,000	23,000	4,000
Expenditure ($ million)	4,800	7,800	8,000
Official expenditure estimates ($ million), 1980*	15,480–21,930	19,500–24,180	7,960–9,500

* No more recent data are available.

The number of drug dealers is estimated by dividing the number of users by a very rough estimate of the number of customers with whom a retailer will be willing to transact. Moore (1977) suggests that ten is the right number for heroin retailers, not including "jugglers" or addicts who sell to a small number of addict friends in order to support their own habit. We certainly expect the number to be higher for cocaine than for heroin, given the higher risk that each customer poses to the heroin dealer relative to the cocaine dealer. Simon and Witte (1982) suggest that the number for cocaine is twenty; no source is given for this. We use twenty-five. This produces a smaller number of dealers and thus will raise our estimates of the effect of a given level of enforcement.

Marijuana retailing is still less risky than cocaine or heroin selling. We assume that the average number of customers per seller is consequently even higher. Carlson et al. (1983) used a figure of fifteen. Arbitrarily, we select the number forty. While no data are available, the former number seems too low in light of the modest risks that additional customers pose to a marijuana dealer.

Retailers are not the only participants in the supply network. Others include importers, wholesalers, and their employees. However, given the sharp pyramiding in the distribution system for marijuana and cocaine, where first-level wholesalers might sell to ten or fifteen retailers, higher-level dealers constitute a small fraction of the total number of participants. High-level heroin dealers, precisely because they deal in small physical volumes, need few employees.

Our marijuana and cocaine income estimates are very imprecise.

They are lower than the published official estimates for two principal reasons. First, the official estimates assume all final sales occur at retail price. In fact, as the National Narcotics Intelligence Consumers Committee (1983a) now concedes, a significant fraction of total sales is in larger units (e.g., half ounces of cocaine) at prices far below the retail level. Second, the official consumption estimates reflect unrealistic assumptions about frequency of use by regular users and dosage units. The heroin addict estimate, developed without survey data, is probably considerably too high (Reuter 1984a) and also raises the consumption and expenditure estimates. No data are available for an alternative estimate, so we use the official figures. If they are upwardly biased, this will exaggerate the differences between heroin and the other two markets.

B. Enforcement and Its Consequences: Some Data

A short version of this essay was prepared in mid-1983 (and appeared as chap. 3 in Polich et al. [1984]) using 1982 data. It asserted that very substantial increases in enforcement activity would have little effect on consumption of cocaine and marijuana. Now that 1984 data are available on the levels of enforcement and on prices (though not on quantities), we can see that there has been at least rough confirmation of this conclusion. The following figures appear to show that a dramatic increase in the level of enforcement activities has not affected the availability of the drugs.

Table 3 provides data on drug arrests by state and local agencies for 1980–84. The majority of these arrests are for simple possession of marijuana. The total number has risen modestly over the period. How-

TABLE 3

Drug Arrests (in Thousands), 1980–84

	1980	1981	1982	1983	1984
Heroin and cocaine (totals)	68	72	113	149	181
Possession	46	49	78	109	133
Sale/distribution	22	23	35	40	48
Marijuana (totals)	406	400	456	407	419
Possession	342	344	388	337	345
Sale/distribution	64	56	68	70	74

SOURCE.—Federal Bureau of Investigation (1981–84).

ever, that modest rise masks very large changes in the composition of arrests, particularly, a substantial increase in the risks faced by dealers as opposed to users. Total heroin and cocaine arrests have risen by more than 150 percent, while arrests for sale or distribution have more than doubled. The number of persons arrested on charges of sale, distribution, or production of marijuana has also risen, though only by 16 percent. Unfortunately, we lack any national data on the disposition of these arrests, but some fragments from California and New York are presented below.

Table 4 gives some data on the federal drug enforcement effort. Federal expenditures on drug enforcement have risen dramatically over the period 1980–84. The rise is even more striking in the context of declining budgets for treatment and prevention of drug abuse (White House 1984). In current dollars, the total expenditure has risen by 70 percent. The measured output of this effort has also risen substantially. The number of persons committed to prison as a result of DEA actions increased substantially between 1980 and 1984. Drug seizures do not show the same consistent pattern year to year. However, for all three drugs, seizures are much higher in 1984 than in 1980.

Despite all this, retail prices for drugs have changed surprisingly little over the last five years, as reported in official data (table 5). The marijuana figures are hard to interpret because of the great variation in the quality of the drug, as measured by THC content. It appears that, as the share of marijuana produced domestically rises, so does the average quality, as measured by THC content. To that extent, the average price for marijuana of a given quality may have actually fallen.

In summary, we start with the following basic facts. The intensity of enforcement against the major drug markets has increased very substantially over the last five years. More people are being arrested on more serious charges and, at least at the federal level, are receiving more severe sanctions. Yet the retail price of the three drugs does not appear to have increased significantly over the same period.

II. Risks and Prices: The Theory

The major objective of drug law enforcement and source control programs is reduced drug consumption. Retail price can be used as a measure of effectiveness, for these programs can reduce use only by making drug dealing, including production and importation, so risky that dealers will require higher compensation for continued participation. Local enforcement against heroin retailers is the only significant

TABLE 4

Some Measures of Federal Drug Enforcement, 1980–84

	1980	1981	1982	1983	1984
Federal seizures:*					
Heroin	268	231	305	495	385
Cocaine	4,797	3,205	9,763	18,027	12,390
Marijuana	1,773,098	3,078,696	3,022,351	1,968,771	2,466,373
Federal incarcerations[†]	2,547	2,865	3,516	4,150	4,721[‡]
	(54.5)	(55.5)	(61.4)	(63.8)	(56.0)
Federal enforcement expenditures[§]	537	707	854	1,076	1,210

SOURCES.—For federal seizures, see U.S. Department of Justice (1984, 1985). For federal incarcerations for 1980–82, see Brown et al. (1984, p. 497), and for 1984, see Drug Enforcement Administration (1985); for federal enforcement expenditures, see White House (1984).

* Pure kilograms.

[†] The period covered is the 12 months prior to September 30 of the previous year. Average sentence length in months in parentheses.

[‡] The 1984 figure includes some persons convicted in state courts after investigations involving federal agents.

[§] Figures are for fiscal years in millions of dollars.

TABLE 5

Retail Prices (per Pure Gram), 1980–84

	1980	1981	1982	1983	1984
Heroin	2,210	2,340	2,310	2,500	2,340
Cocaine	710	790	710	330–415	330–400
Marijuana	1.30	1.66	1.10–1.75	1.40–2.25	1.40–2.25

SOURCE.—U.S. Department of Justice (1984, 1985).

exception to this statement and is considered separately below. There will always be as much of a drug physically available at the export point as U.S. customers are willing to purchase at the risk-determined retail price.[1]

There are numerous qualifications associated with use of price as an indicator of the effectiveness of drug enforcement strategies. First, price is determined by both demand and supply. A decline in price may occur either because the demand curve falls or because the supply curve rises. For purposes of evaluating the historic success of drug enforcement efforts, it is impossible to separate out the two kinds of influence. It is clear that there have been shifts in both supply and demand and that we lack a well-specified model of the drug market. However, to consider the effect of hypothetical changes in drug enforcement efforts, the major tool of this analysis, we need only consider the impact these have on price through shifts of the supply curve; we assume the direct demand effects of law enforcement to be negligible, again with the exception of heroin retailing.

The ultimate objective of drug law enforcement is to reduce consumption. Price is merely a surrogate, chosen for its notional simplicity of measurement. In fact, the available price data are poor and scarcely more reliable than consumption estimates.[2] Nonetheless, price ought to be a cheaper and more rapidly ascertainable indicator than any other. Estimates of total consumption require the cooperation of users and involve numerous sampling problems.

However, to extrapolate from price changes to consumption changes requires, at a minimum, an estimate of the price elasticity of demand,

---

[1] The inefficacy of interdiction and source-control programs in restricting the physical supply is discussed below.
[2] The problem is that federal agencies are poorly placed to collect retail price data and local police agencies are poorly motivated. For a discussion of the weakness of drug price data, see Reuter (1984a).

that is, by what percentage a 1 percent increase in price reduces demand. No such elasticity has been empirically estimated for any of the three drugs. We are forced to rely instead on impressions, reflecting knowledge of the characteristics of users and current consumption patterns.

We assume that the demand for marijuana is relatively inelastic around its current price level. The dosage price is modest compared with dosage prices for other recreational drugs, such as alcohol. Currently, it appears that a "joint" costs only about seventy-five cents and probably yields one to two hours of moderate euphoria.[3] To obtain the same effect from alcohol costs perhaps twice as much and has noticeably more unpleasant aftereffects.

Estimates of the pattern of consumption suggest that, even for heavy users, total marijuana expenditures are no more than 10 percent of total expenditures, except for the significant fraction of heavy users who are still full-time students. With the important exception of this latter group, it seems plausible to assume that a 10 percent increase in the price of marijuana would have very modest long- and short-term effects on marijuana consumption.[4]

Cocaine, by contrast, is expensive relative to other recreational drugs and to most other recreations. A session with cocaine may cost $30–$100. For many regular users, indulging three times per week, total cocaine expenditure is likely to be a significant fraction of disposable income. Moreover, cocaine apparently creates psychological dependence in some regular users. This suggests that the short-run price elasticity might be low because it is difficult for current heavy users, who account for most of the total consumption, to reduce their consumption level substantially. But the high cost of regular use suggests that the flow of users into and out of the heavy user category may be very sensitive to the current price, implying at least a modest long-term price elasticity for cocaine.

For heroin we have rather more data, though none of it sufficient for a precise estimate. It has often been assumed that the regular users of heroin, precisely because they are addicted to the drug, have very

---

[3] There is considerable variation in the potency of marijuana; the THC content, a measure of its potency, ranges from 1 to 12 percent. While high-potency marijuana is more expensive, it is not known whether the price per unit of THC is constant. Hence we can only give a very approximate measure of the cost of an hour of pleasure. See Kleiman (1985, chap. 1).

[4] Kleiman (1985, chap. 1) provides estimates of the annual expenditures by different classes of users and argues (chap. 5) for an elasticity of demand of between 0 and −0.5.

inelastic demand, that is, even very large increases in price would do little to reduce their daily consumption. However, a growing body of research (summarized in Kaplan 1983, chap. 1) suggests that quite the contrary is the case. Heroin takes such a large share of the total budget of many regular users, and they have to be so active criminally to maintain their consumption, that price increases may lead to almost proportional reductions in their intake. The elasticity of demand for heroin may be about −1 for heavy users. In addition, heroin users often cease heroin consumption, with or without medical assistance. Moreover, it is likely that the flow of novice users into the pool of heavy users is quite sensitive to retail prices. As a result, we assume the aggregate demand for heroin may have quite a high elasticity.

It is simply not possible to go beyond such broad statements at this time. We lack adequate data on price or consumption levels. The analysis will assume that the elasticity of demand is moderately high for heroin, a little lower for cocaine, and quite low for marijuana.

Throughout this analysis we assume that drug markets are competitive. The basis for this assumption is the lack of evidence for the alternative, namely, that drug markets are characterized by restrictions on entry or pricing at any level, and moderately plausible theoretical arguments that such restrictions are difficult to maintain in illegal markets without a unitary, corrupt police department (see Reuter 1983, chaps. 5, 6).[5] This assumption is critical to the analysis since the response of markets to a tax is determined by their structure.[6] It is also contrary to the official view of drug markets, though that view is enunciated in vague terms that make it difficult to determine precisely what structure officials believe these markets to have.

In part, the official view may be explained historically. It appears that there was a monopoly, in the hands of the Mafia, on heroin importation in the 1950s (see President's Commission on Law Enforcement and Administration of Justice 1967). The explanation for that monopoly may be found in any or all of three factors. First, the Mafia had considerable influence over the New York Police Department; no other criminal group had access to the corruption of that department. Second, through control of the International Longshoreman's Association,

---

[5] A ready supply of violent labor in major American cities among dealers, a lack of martial skills among the leaders, and the need to compensate agents for not attempting coups are the essential elements of the argument.

[6] Moore (1977, chap. 1) provides a good discussion of this issue with respect to the heroin market.

the Mafia had command of the docks, so it was able to protect its own shipments of heroin and increase the hazards faced by all other importers. Third, the heroin refiners were located in southern France and Italy, and there were historic and ethnic ties between them and the American Mafia members.

The point of listing these factors is to suggest how specific the circumstances were under which the Mafia was able to attain market power with respect to heroin importation. None of those conditions are any longer relevant. The New York Police Department is no longer so centrally corrupt or powerful, the docks are no longer the locus of importation since air traffic has become so large, and the refining laboratories are now located in many parts of the world. If market power still exists in the heroin importation market, then it must have some other basis.

There is, in fact, little reliable information available on the structure of drug markets at various levels. Each drug is brought in from a multitude of nations, and international collaboration among traffickers to restrict the supply and thus boost profits seems quite implausible. The relatively small share of final price received by exporters is also consistent with the claim that there is no market power at the point of export, though it is certainly not conclusive evidence. At the retail level it is apparently easy to enter the business.

That leaves intermediate distribution levels as possible locations of market power. It might be the case that the wholesale cocaine market in, say, Denver is controlled by a small number of dealers. Their power might be based on the ability to exclude other wholesalers through threats of violence. Alternatively, other Denver market participants might be unable to locate sources of wholesale quantities.

It is impossible to obtain relevant evidence on this matter. There does seem to be some violence at the higher levels of the cocaine and marijuana markets. It is estimated that a large share of all homicides in the Miami area are the result of drug trafficking activities (U.S. Senate 1980). Whether that results from efforts to monopolize or whether it represents contractual disputes or robberies cannot be determined.

A. Two Kinds of Cost

The costs imposed by enforcement on the illicit drug industry are of two kinds: costs of avoidance and costs of losses actually suffered. The first can be as readily calculated in advance, by the dealer, as any other cost of doing business. If he buys a scanner to monitor police communications, he knows in advance what the scanner costs. Losses actually suffered, on the other hand, are not known in advance.[7] From the viewpoint of enforcement agencies (or researchers), ex post, the reverse is true; incurred (imposed) costs are measurable, while the costs of avoidance can only be guessed at.

Two Meanings of "Risk."   One measure of the enforcement threat a given transaction faces is the expected value of incurred enforcement losses, that is, the sum, for each possible kind of enforcement-induced loss, of its value times its probability. If a boatload of marijuana that costs a dealer $1 million faces one chance in ten of being seized by the Coast Guard, then the expected value of incurred enforcement losses in that transaction is $100,000. That one-in-ten chance is one meaning of "risk"; tougher enforcement makes the probability of loss higher and the transaction riskier.

But "risk" can also mean the special costs that go with uncertainty. If five $200,000 transactions were involved, each with a one-in-ten chance of going wrong, rather than one $1 million transaction, the expected value of incurred enforcement losses would be the same (assuming that the only loss is the loss of the marijuana): each of the five smaller transactions would have an expected value of incurred enforcement losses of $20,000 (one-tenth of $200,000) for a total of $100,000. But the transaction would be far less risky because the chances of a catastrophic loss would be much less.

Risk in this second sense—uncertainty—is also costly. A trafficker who is willing to treat a 35 percent probability of a one-year stretch in prison as a cost of doing business, one to be measured against current consumption and the nest egg waiting on release, may find a 5 percent probability of a seven-year stretch daunting (partly because of the potential lapse of years before that nest egg can be enjoyed). Thus entrepreneurs may require larger potential profits and employees higher wages to face the same expected-value time in prison if the time is more unequally distributed.[8]

---

[7] That is, losses are not known in advance unless a dealer's business consists of so many transactions, and the possible losses on any one transaction are so small, that the enterprise represents a statistical universe. This might be true of a pimp with a string of prostitutes; fines are a stochastic but predictable cost of doing business.

[8] This assertion runs contrary to the conclusion of deterrence studies that high-probability/low-severity regimes deter more than low-probability/high-severity regimes (Cook 1980). The explanation for the difference is that drug dealers, unlike most prisoners, are probably deferring the fruits of crime while in prison; each additional year of prison defers those fruits still further. For most property crimes, the fruits are enjoyed immediately; only the punishment is deferred.

Insurance is one of the many financial services whose unavailability helps distinguish illicit from licit trades. Drug dealers must, in general, bear the financial risks that enforcement imposes (though there is some evidence of quasi-insurance relationships between exporters and importers of marijuana that help spread the risks of marijuana smuggling).

In what follows, we attempt to quantify the costs imposed by enforcement on the illicit drug industry by comparing enforcement statistics—drug and asset seizures and years in prison—with estimated participant numbers and drug volumes. For example, we compute the days spent in prison per year in the marijuana business. It should be remembered, however, that these measures are all of expected-value losses and thus ignore the "risk premiums" due to the uncertain patterns of traffickers' enforcement-related losses. To compensate for this, we assign very high values to time in prison.

B. Costs in the Illicit Drug Trade

The price of any given drug at any given distribution level has five components: cost of drugs purchased, compensation of labor, cost of capital, operational expense, and proprietors' incomes.

Cost of Drugs. The cost of drugs at any level of the trade is influenced by enforcement pressures at higher levels. In addition, an entrepreneur at any given level risks having drugs seized after he has paid for them but before he has been paid for them. If, on average, a dealer loses a fraction p of the drugs he buys as a result of enforcement action, then he will need to buy $1/(1 - p)$ the quantity he sells, and his total cost of drugs purchased will be proportionately higher.

The cost a seizure adds to the drug traffic thus depends on the stage of the traffic at which it occurs as well as the physical volume of drugs involved. Seizing or destroying marijuana in a farmer's field adds to the traffic only the cost of growing more marijuana. This is what makes "street value" calculations so meaningless and lends a false importance to the huge quantities of drugs destroyed in source-country fields.

Compensation of Labor. Employees of drug-dealing organizations need to be compensated for their alternative occupational opportunities (licit or illicit) forgone; for the expected value of the danger of imprisonment (perhaps with a risk premium added); for the dangers from other illicit-market participants, including their employers, colleagues, customers, and competitors; and for forgone leisure time. Some of these elements represent fixed costs of being in the trade, and some are costs that vary with the number and volume of transactions engaged in.

Drug-market participants whose annual incomes, divided by the number of hours actively engaged in dealing drugs, suggest very high hourly wages may not in fact demand very much money to give up an additional hour of leisure because most of their current earnings are compensation simply for the risks of being dealers.[9]

Current employees of a firm are more valuable to the firm than otherwise equivalent new employees because the risks of employing them appear to be less; they are presumably less likely to be informants than are novices. Also, the disadvantages to them of persisting in the trade—in particular, the marginal imprisonment risk—are likely to be less than the costs faced by new entrants because the seasoned employees know that their associates are (relatively) trustworthy. This may allow most drug-market employees and entrepreneurs to reap inframarginal returns (i.e., to be better off than they would be at their best alternative employment), as long as the marginal transaction involves new participants, a likely condition in periods of rapid growth. This may explain why cocaine prices in 1978–82 seemed to be at levels far above those justified by the risks involved and why they subsequently fell, despite increased enforcement pressure; the high returns in the cocaine trade eventually attracted enough new entrants to force prices down.

Raising the level of enforcement pressure increases the risks faced by the employees of dealing firms. In turn this increases the compensation required to attract and keep employees since they now face higher risks from three sources—imprisonment, violence from their employing organization, and violence from other participants.

The increased imprisonment risk is straightforward. The increased risk from the organization is slightly more complicated to analyze. Organizations will vary from each other and over time in the willingness of their proprietors to use violence to silence potential or suspected employee informants and witnesses. Employees will have to be compensated for this risk as for any other. The optimal level of violence from the firm's viewpoint depends on the level of enforcement pressure. When pressure is low, the extra wages paid by high violence firms will put them at a competitive disadvantage. But as the pressure rises, less violent firms will feel it more severely since cases against them will be easier to make. This will force them either to leave the trade or to become more violent.

[9] Of course, there is an income effect: leisure is worth more to a wealthy individual than to a poor individual, even if the wage rate per hour is the same for the two.

Thus increased enforcement pressure will tend to increase the capacities for violence of drug-dealing firms. This increase in firms' violence capacities will in turn increase the risks to all employees from interfirm violence. Drug-market firms can use violence against each other to settle business disputes and enforce contracts in the absence of recourse to courts, to steal drugs or money, or to eliminate competition. The capacities that firms develop for internal violence in response to enforcement pressure will also be available for interfirm warfare and piracy.

Cost of Capital. The cost of capital for drug dealers depends on the capital requirements of the business (determined by turnover rates, wholesale prices, and credit terms), the availability and cost of loan capital on the loan-shark market (or the equivalent), and the danger of capital loss. The higher the risk of loss, the higher the interest rate. Drug dealing may be largely internally financed once an enterprise is under way, but the cost of external capital, like the cost of new labor, may determine market prices if the market is expanding.[10]

As the price of drugs at higher levels rises, the capital cost of being a lower-level drug dealer rises as well, for the lower-level dealer must lay out more money per unit purchased. If, as we shall assume, it takes three months for marijuana to move from initial import to final sale, and if the annual cost of capital is 50 percent, then the added capital cost is 12.5 percent of the price increase. That is, a $1.00 increase in the imported price will lead to a $1.125 increase at the retail level.

Nondrug Supplies. A drug dealer needs to buy, rent, or steal vehicles to transport drugs; buy or rent warehousing space; pay the costs of travel for himself and his employees; buy equipment (e.g., communications and communications-interception gear); and pay lawyers' fees, bribes to police, and other expenses of dealing with the criminal justice system.

There will be trade-offs between some of these expenditures and the dangers of enforcement losses. The higher the level of enforcement pressure, the more organizations will choose to invest in evasion rather than suffer enforcement action. Since these expenses, unlike the results of successful enforcement actions, will not in general be officially ob-

---

[10] There may be little direct connection between drug markets and conventional loan-sharking. Drug dealers may lack the attributes (personal reputation for violence or knowledge about credit risks) to be loan sharks. On the other hand, drug dealers, because they have relatively high risks of incarceration or death, may face difficulties in borrowing from loan sharks.

served, our estimates of enforcement-imposed costs will not include them and will thus tend to underestimate; seizures of nondrug assets (discussed below) suggest that these items constitute a very small share of total distribution costs.

Proprietors' Incomes. Proprietors' incomes can be thought of as returns to their own labor and capital. They may be able to reap high rates of return in growing markets if there are significant barriers to entry. One effect of increasing enforcement pressure may be to make the markets differentially riskier for new players, thus creating entry barriers behind which existing entrepreneurs can pile up windfall profits.

Caveats. There are three important caveats. (1) We observe two things about drug enforcement expenditure and outputs. Neither is exactly what we need to model effects on the market since we do not know enforcement pressure as a function of enforcement expenditure and since enforcement outputs do not measure avoidance costs or risks from other criminals. (2) Enforcement risks depend in part on the ratio of enforcement activity to trafficking activity. The more traffickers there are competing for the attention of any fixed number of agents, the safer the traffickers are. This may explain why Miami was so dominant for so long in marijuana and cocaine importing. It may also create positive-feedback effects from increased enforcement pressure. If enforcement succeeds in shrinking a market, the effective enforcement pressure corresponding with any given level of enforcement expenditure will rise as the number of targets falls. Static estimates of marginal enforcement risk underestimate the total effect of marginal enforcement on costs. (3) This model applies better to high-level than to street-level markets. Street-level costs involve large real transactions costs—search times on both sides—that no one captures as income.

With this conceptual apparatus established, we now turn to the four components of the supply reduction strategy.

III. Source Control[11]

Throughout the twentieth century, the government of the United States has maintained that the solution to the American drug abuse problem lies with the foreign nations that produce the most important illicit drugs. The official tone has become slightly less accusatory over

[11] This section is adapted, with permission, from Peter Reuter, "Eternal Hope: America's Quest for Narcotics Control," *Public Interest*, vol. 79 (Spring 1985).

the years, but there has been no change in the view that cutting exports from countries such as Burma, Colombia, and Pakistan is the best method for reducing U.S. consumption of heroin, cocaine, and marijuana. As the White House stated in 1982, "elimination of illegal drugs at or near their foreign source is the most effective means to reduce the domestic supply of these substances" (Drug Abuse Policy Office 1982, p. 31).

This notion became a genuine part of American foreign policy when President Nixon, under heavy congressional pressure, initiated a series of bilateral agreements with source countries to assist them in reducing their exports. These agreements have become a standard component of battles between the State Department and Congress, with Congress generally charging that the State Department gives too little high-level attention to the drug problem. But there is no political dispute about the centrality of these international programs to American drug policy. The only dispute concerns the appropriate levels of expenditure and the intensity of pressure to be exerted on other nations.

Unfortunately, there is ample evidence that U.S. foreign drug control efforts have been unsuccessful and that the failures of U.S. international programs are not simply the result of incompetence or inadequate resources but are inherent in the structure of the problem. The producer countries jointly lack either the motivation or the means to reduce total production. Even if such reduction were possible, it is unlikely that U.S. imports from each of these countries, apart from Mexico, would be much affected. Just as important, the set of source countries is readily expandable. The international programs may serve a useful function in curbing illicit drug use in some major source countries, but they will do little to reduce drug abuse in the United States.

A. U.S. Control Efforts

Efforts by the United States to suppress foreign production of illicit drugs go back at least to the Shanghai Treaty of 1909. Believing that the instability of China was very much bound up with the widespread use of opium, supplied through much of the nineteenth century from India by British merchants, the United States sought a treaty system that would require all nations to control the production of opium and its derivatives. Other nations were a great deal less enthusiastic, but in 1913 thirty-four nations signed a fairly comprehensive agreement that was later extended, again at the urging of the United States, to cocaine and marijuana. In that more innocent era there was enough faith in treaties per se that no program of assistance for enforcement was established.

The growth of heroin use in the late 1960s changed U.S. policy markedly. No longer content to work through the international treaty system, the United States for the first time began to seek bilateral agreements, involving the use of U.S. resources and personnel, to strike at production in nations deemed particularly important to the American heroin problem. These efforts have been expanded since 1979 to include cocaine and marijuana.

The United States has tried a number of approaches. Some efforts focus on production itself. Resources are provided to help local law enforcement agencies eradicate crops, either through the spraying of a herbicide (as was done in Mexico for opium poppies) or by manually uprooting plants (as is occasionally done with coca plants in Peru). A number of projects have been funded, either by the United States directly or through multilateral agencies (such as the UN Fund for Drug Abuse Control), that aim at providing alternative commercial crops for farmers growing coca (in Peru) or poppies (in Burma).

Since 1978, the State Department's Bureau of International Narcotics Matters (INM) has been responsible for foreign production control efforts through diplomatic efforts and targeted economic assistance programs. In fiscal year 1985, INM had a budget appropriation of $43 million. The DEA also assists foreign governments in law enforcement activities aimed at refining and distribution, particularly in source countries. It trains foreign police at U.S. facilities and has offices in major source and transshipment countries to help target traffickers particularly significant for the United States. Its international activities were budgeted at $38 million in fiscal year 1985.

The relatively small expenditures on the international programs have sometimes led Congress to charge that the executive branch is not taking the problem seriously enough. Indeed, in 1980 Congress forced the State Department to allocate $7 million to Colombia at a time when INM believed, correctly as it turned out, that the Colombian drug enforcement agencies would accomplish little with the money. Generally, officials in INM have been consistent in their view that the most important tools are diplomatic rather than financial, and they base their optimism on the apparent success of diplomatic efforts. They claim that there is increased interest on the part of senior U.S. officials in raising these issues with their foreign counterparts and that those counterparts are more willing to follow up on promises of action.

The recent success of the Pakistani government in greatly reducing the illicit cultivation of poppies in some areas of the country is cited as an instance of effective diplomatic pressure. Though a total national ban on opium production has not been implemented, new laws, increased police efforts, and low producer prices had reduced estimated Pakistani production levels to less than forty-five tons in 1984, compared to 800 tons in 1979.

In some countries that produce opium, local increases in heroin use may have increased the willingness of governments to implement crop reduction and traffic control programs. While estimates of the addict populations in countries such as Thailand and Pakistan are extremely unreliable, it is clear that these countries believe they have a substantial problem. While there were almost no heroin addicts in Pakistan ten years ago, INM now cites an estimate of 50,000. With a certain amount of skepticism, INM cites a figure of 400,000–600,000 Thai addicts, again an entirely new phenomenon. Domestic Colombian use of a dangerous combination of marijuana and cocaine residue is a cause of concern in that country.[12]

B. Down on the Farm

Despite the increasing concern with local drug use, there are many impediments to successful crop reduction efforts in producer countries. The first is that farmers usually do not have an easy alternative commercial crop; the high value to bulk of drugs compared to other farm products is crucial when the markets are distant and the roads bad. Currently, poppies may indeed be the only crop that can be produced in remote areas of Burma and Thailand to provide steady cash income. Everyone recognizes that increased law enforcement efforts against farmers will have little effect unless other productive opportunities are provided. This takes many years. Moreover, the coca and opium crops have important licit uses; for example, Peruvian coca leaves are used for pharmaceuticals and flavoring, and poppies provide peasant farmers in Turkey with an edible oil, fuel, and cattle feed.

The development of alternative cash crops requires, among other things, the creation of a new infrastructure (roads, in particular) to permit the efficient delivery of bulkier and more perishable crops to distant markets. Farmers must also learn how to produce crops entirely new to their regions, such as cacao in the Upper Huallaga valley of

[12] A discussion of foreign addiction problems is contained in U.S. Senate (1985).

Peru and kidney beans in the Chang Mai area of Thailand. Whether these efforts will turn out to be sufficient is a matter of speculation. Indeed, improving farmers' skills might have the perverse effect of increasing the productivity of their illicit farming. The programs in Thailand show promise but encompass a population of only a few thousand, and there are no instances in which crop substitution has actually been achieved on a large scale. Indeed, a piece of black humor from a Bolivian politician sums up the matter: "We have crop substitution; cocaine has been substituted for everything else" (State Department official, personal communication, 1983).

It should be noted that there is little talk of crop substitution for marijuana producers; enforcement alone is supposed to deal with the problem. Two arguments have been made for this policy. First, marijuana is grown solely for illicit commercial purposes, whereas poppies and coca have licit uses as well. Thus one can simply spray all marijuana fields without worrying whether one or another might in fact be legal. This would not work against coca producers in Peru, where there are some 9,000 licenses for coca production. Second, producers of marijuana are "mercenary"; they are not peasant farmers without a cash crop alternative. As one official suggested, it would scarcely be good policy to reward new marijuana source countries by granting them agricultural development assistance.

A second major obstacle to crop reduction is the generally weak control of governments in the producing areas. The Thai and Burmese governments have long been fighting insurgent movements in the hills that are home to the poppy growers. The Peruvian government has little effective control in some of the regions that produce coca leaves. Similar situations exist in Afghanistan, Pakistan, Bolivia, and Laos at least. Even where governments are in firm control, are strongly motivated, and have sensible plans, they are likely to have great difficulty implementing them. The ubiquitous corruption of source-country police adds yet another obstacle; in the case of Bolivia, at least one cabinet member was actively involved in the cocaine trade.

Third, some major source countries, notably Iran and Afghanistan, are hostile to the United States. Though they may adopt policies to reduce domestic consumption, they are unconcerned about U.S. imports. Fourth, U.S. relations with most of the other countries involved in drug production are very complex. The United States would like Pakistan to adopt certain policies with respect to Afghanistan. It seeks to retain bases in Thailand. It would like Colombia to take particular positions with respect to Central America. As a DEA official said, explaining the relatively light pressure being exerted on Jamaica, "Some analysts believe that if you came in with a severe narcotics program, you could affect the existence of the present government. . . . Drugs are a serious problem but communism is a greater problem" (Treaster 1984). Given all these considerations and the disinclination of diplomats and policymakers to concern themselves with such unseemly matters as the drug trade, it is difficult to put consistent pressure on source-country governments.

Finally, and perhaps most important, the set of producer countries is not fixed. New producers emerge all the time. Brazil is apparently witnessing a rapid growth in coca and marijuana production. Until five years ago, these crops were minor and were used only for peasant consumption; by 1983, the Brazilian authorities claimed to have destroyed or seized nearly 2,000 tons of marijuana (almost 30 percent of the best estimate of U.S. consumption). Belize, an enclave of 150,000 people in Central America, may have produced 700 tons of marijuana in 1983, all for export, where none was produced five years earlier (U.S. Department of State 1985). Pakistan produced little opium prior to 1948, the British being concerned to protect the markets of opium farmers in other parts of British India. Yet by the mid-1950s there was substantial licit and illicit opium production in the North West Frontier province. There is no reason to believe that other countries with large impoverished peasant populations and weak central governments will not become significant producers if the current producers cut back production greatly. A large or traditional local market turns out not to be essential. In the instance of marijuana, we must also note the rapid growth of production in the United States.

Lack of motivation is also a barrier to effective government action. The national governments in many of these countries believe that the political costs of reducing the cash income of farmers are very high. Indeed, in describing the recent Bolivian crackdown on coca producers in the Chapare region, which involved the moving in of troops, the *New York Times* reported: "On August 17, less than a week after the Chapare occupation, the government was forced to drop the peso's official value by more than half, from 2,000 to $1 to 5,000. And in Bolivia, the world's most politically unstable country, that is enough to start talk of a coup" (Brinkley 1984). Governments dealing with the enforced stringencies of the International Monetary Fund are likely to give pause to efforts that will add to their domestic economic worries. The extent to which foreign exchange earnings from drug exports matter is unclear: in most situations only a small share of these earnings enter the official accounts, but some amount certainly does.

C. The International Pipeline

Crop reduction is touted as a goal by the United States because it is assumed that the less each source country produces, the less will be exported to America. Clearly, if none is produced, then none can be exported. But it is also plausible that quite large reductions (or increases) in any particular country's production will have little impact on exports to the United States.

We start by observing that the price of opium in source countries is trivial relative to the price of heroin in the United States. As shown in table 1, the ten kilograms of opium in Thailand needed to make one kilogram of heroin cost at most $1,000. If that price fell to $100 or rose to $5,000, it would have little effect on the price of heroin delivered to the United States (roughly $200,000 per kilogram at the importation level). Yet the effect of crop reduction, short of elimination, is simply to raise local prices.

Moreover—and contrary to what we would expect in a smoothly working international market—it appears that quite large differences in source-country prices for particular drugs have little effect on the composition of U.S. imports from country to country. For example, in the oil market Nigeria has only to raise its price by 1 percent to lose a large share of its sales; its customers have little hesitation in shifting to other suppliers. Yet the bazaar price for opium in Burma can be half that in Pakistan without any rapid shift in the origins of American heroin imports.

One plausible explanation for this is that the U.S. price of a drug from a particular country is determined chiefly not by the source-country price but by the availability of efficient international distribution networks. This is certainly consistent with the fact that most of the export price of drugs represents payments to couriers and dealers for incurring risks. For example, Mexican-source heroin was relatively cheap not because of the price of opium in Mexico (which was very high relative to other producer countries) but because of the efficient Mexican networks for distribution. The reduction of the supply in Mexico that was achieved did cut the amount flowing through the pipeline. But if it were easy to smuggle heroin *into* Mexico, the loss of this local production would be of little consequence for the United States; the cheap distribution networks would remain. As it turns out, the Mexican government is reasonably effective at making it risky to bring heroin into that country, so the trafficking networks have been thwarted.

Similarly, the increased availability of Southwest Asian heroin in Western Europe and the United States shortly after 1979 may have had less to do with the price of opium in the local markets than with the growing density of traffic from Southwest Asia to Western Europe. Pakistan has substantial expatriate communities in Britain and West Germany. There are also large communities of Armenians and Lebanese in Europe, and Iranian immigration to the United States suddenly increased after 1977. These provide broad pipelines, so to speak, within which to hide the movement of drugs.

The international cocaine market provides some evidence consistent with this view. Most cocaine entering the United States comes from Colombia, though the raw material is produced mostly in Peru and Bolivia. The advantage of Colombia as an export source is partly that it is the largest South American source of migrants to the United States. On the other hand, most cocaine exported to Europe leaves from Brazil, which has the largest migrant population in Europe.

These broader pipelines have three important advantages for drug smuggling. First, they make it more likely that the courier will not be detected because surveillance decreases in intensity as the general traffic from a particular source country increases. If there is only one flight each day from Karachi to London, then it is possible to scrutinize every vaguely suspicious looking passenger; if there are ten per day, this becomes much more difficult and expensive. Second, the probability of finding a courier able and willing to carry the drugs increases with the size of the pipeline. When the only Pakistanis traveling to London are well-to-do tourists, it will probably be hard to find a courier. The lone peasant on a plane filled by the wealthy might well get caught. But when there is a steady flow of poor migrants, it will be easy to conceal a courier within the flow. Third, if there is a large population of immigrants from the source country in the consuming country, it is more likely that the exporter can find a local high-level distributor. The more Pakistanis resident in London, the higher the probability that a Pakistani exporter can find someone there who will know an English distributor.

If this is so, then we must ask why there are relatively sudden changes in the distribution patterns to source countries. After all, the immigrant flows and the heaviness of traffic from source to consuming countries change relatively slowly; the middle-class Iranian exodus of 1978–80 was unusual. There was not a sudden increase in the number of Pakistanis in Western Europe around 1980 to explain the great increase in the flow of heroin along that path.

The pipeline effect is likely to be nonlinear. There may be thresholds—in number and composition of travelers and in the size of the local community—that, once passed, lead to rapid changes in the efficiency of the distribution through a particular pipeline.

United States source control programs have occasionally had a noticeable impact in particular source countries. Three instances stand out: the elimination of illicit opium production in Turkey in 1972, the dramatic reduction of opium output in Mexico in the mid-1970s, and the slightly later reduction of the U.S. market for Mexican marijuana. The last instance is somewhat ambiguous. The major reason for the decline in American consumption of Mexican marijuana was not the reduction in Mexican production. Rather, it was U.S. consumers' fear that the drug might have been sprayed with paraquat, a potentially dangerous herbicide used to control Mexican production.

None of the three successes had lasting effect. Turkish-source opium was rapidly replaced by that from Mexico. Mexican marijuana was even more rapidly replaced by Colombian production. Only the decline in Mexican heroin production had more than a short-term effect; from 1975 to 1979 there appears to have been a decline in U.S. consumption that is related to availability. Changes in Southwest Asia led then to renewed growth in U.S. heroin consumption. Moreover, Mexico and Turkey represent somewhat special cases. In both countries the central government is quite strong. Equally important, illicit drugs were not very important to the national or major regional economies; the political cost of stringent enforcement was not high. This situation does not hold for many of the current and potential source countries.

The sad fact is that real long-term success stories have had nothing to do with international aid and law enforcement. Vastly more important is political and economic development. Macedonia was, prior to World War II, a significant producer of opium, mostly for domestic consumption. By the early 1970s, opium production had fallen to about 5 percent of its previous level. Some analysts plausibly attribute this to general economic progress in the producing area, which made the relatively labor-intensive crop less economically attractive (Bruun, Pan, and Rexed 1975).

On the political side, we have the success of China in its southwest provinces. Though some minority groups still produce for their own consumption, the major production areas have been eliminated since the establishment of the present regime. That is probably the result of the central government's repugnance for all symptoms of decadence in the old culture. It is hard to draw any but the most pessimistic lessons from these two examples, at least for the design of drug enforcement assistance programs.

IV. Interdiction

Interdiction aims at intercepting drug shipments just as, or just before, they enter the United States. It is expected to raise retail prices by imposing costs to replace seized shipments, by raising the risk of imprisonment for people who transport drugs, and by increasing the uncertainty of dealer supplies and income. Interdiction efforts account for about 33 percent of total federal expenditures to enforce drug laws, about $280 million out of $850 million spent in fiscal year 1982.[13] The amount and share have increased rapidly since 1977 (U.S. General Accounting Office 1983).

The Coast Guard and the Customs Service carry out most interdiction operations. The Coast Guard concentrates its interdiction efforts on sea patrols around Florida and the Caribbean, through which most of the Colombian and Jamaican marijuana passes. In the past few years, especially, it has seized enormous quantities of that marijuana, but little else. The Customs Service seizes drugs through both patrol and inspection at ports of entry. Its patrols account for the majority of all federal cocaine seizures, and its inspections at ports of entry garner significant quantities of marijuana. While nontrivial amounts of heroin are seized annually, this is largely the result of investigation rather than of random inspection; consequently, we ignore heroin in this section.

As shown in table 4, the combined efforts of Customs, the Coast Guard, and the DEA have resulted in substantial seizures of marijuana and cocaine, with a sharp upward trend for cocaine.[14] These amounts

[13] There is no breakdown of drug enforcement expenditures by function for the years after 1982. However, it should be noted that the drug enforcement budgets of the two major interdiction agencies increased from $387 million in fiscal year 1982 to $512 million in fiscal year 1984.

[14] Most DEA seizures took place as a result of investigations, not interdiction. We discuss the effectiveness of investigations later.

TABLE 6

Estimated Interdiction Rates, 1984

Item Estimated	Cocaine (1,000 kg)		Marijuana (1,000 kg)	
	Lower Bound	Upper Bound	Lower Bound	Upper Bound
Seizures:				
Reported seizures*	12.4	12.4	2,466	2,466
Less overlap in reporting†	2.5	2.5	825	825
Estimated actual seizures	9.9	9.9	1,641	1,641
Shipments:				
Total estimated consumption	34.4	23.3	15,000	6,439
Less domestic production	.0	.0	1,650	704
Estimated amount imported	34.4	23.3	13,350	5,735
Total shipments to U.S. (actual seizures plus imported amount)	44.3	33.2	14,991	7,376
Seizures as percent of shipments	22.3	29.8	10.9	22.2

SOURCES.—For total reported seizures, see Organized Crime Drug Enforcement Task Force (1985, p. 68); for adjustment in reporting overlap, see U.S. General Accounting Office (1983).

* Total seizures reported by federal agencies.

† The adjustment represents rates of double reporting found by the U.S. General Accounting Office in reviewing 1982 data.

represent a significant proportion of total shipments of drugs destined for the United States—between 10 and 30 percent by our estimates (see table 6). To make these estimates, we first reduced reported seizures to correct for the overlap between the various agencies' reports, using data from the U.S. General Accounting Office (GAO) audit (1983). Then we calculated the seizure rate as a proportion of all imports (those shipments that were successfully imported plus those that were seized). Although the range of results indicates some uncertainties, it is clear that federal interdiction efforts currently impose significant costs on drug importers. Despite this, recent studies express continued skepticism about the ultimate effects of interdiction (General Accounting Office 1983; Mitchell and Bell 1980).

A. Drug Seizures

The reason for skepticism is rooted in the drug market's price structure, which is steeply graduated for all illicit drugs. As we noted in table 1, most of the retail price goes to domestic intermediaries, not to the grower, the exporter, or the importer, despite the fact that these latter parties bear the costs of production, processing, and international transportation. The universal practice of police agencies of valuing seizures at retail price vastly exaggerates the impact of seizures. The true impact is measured by the opportunity cost of those drugs at the point of seizure since that measures what it costs the distribution system to replace them.

Interdiction, treated purely as the seizure of drugs, raises price by requiring the distribution system to begin the shipment of more than one kilo of the drug for each kilo that reaches final customers. The price effect can be captured in a simple equation:

$$P_I = \frac{P_0}{1 - I},$$

where I is the interdiction rate, P_I is the price at that interdiction rate I, and P_0 is the price that would prevail at zero interdiction rate. We have observations of 1984 import selling prices and 1984 interdiction rates, from which we can deduce P_0.

For marijuana, the 1984 figures are an interdiction rate of about 0.22 and an import price of $525 per kilo; this yields a P_0 of $410. Consequently, doubling the interdiction rate to 44 percent will raise the importer selling price to $732. Assuming the absolute price increase is 12.5 percent greater at final sale, retail price rises by $237 per kilo or 13 percent. Table 7 traces out the consequences.

For cocaine, the import price increase from raising the interdiction to 60 percent from the current 30 percent (using the lower-bound con-

TABLE 7

Effects of Increased Interdiction Seizures on Marijuana Price

Item	Current Situation	Hypothetical Situation (Increased Interdiction)
Interdiction rate (%)	22	44
Amount exported to land 100 kg in U.S. (kg)	128	178
Amount seized (kg)	28	78
Amount landed in U.S. (kg)	100	100
Replacement cost of seizures (at $410 per kg) ($)	11,480	31,980
Total retail price (100 kg) ($)	175,000	198,625
Increase in retail price (%)	. . .	13

sumption estimate) is $33,000. The final price increase of $37,000 is about 6 percent of the retail price. If we use the higher consumption figures, doubling interdiction volumes has correspondingly lower retail price effects.

The much greater impact for marijuana is a consequence of the much lower markup of prices as the drug moves from import to final sale. Our assumption that absolute price increases are marked up to the same extent in the two distribution systems may be incorrect precisely because cocaine distribution is a riskier business. Nonetheless, it seems reasonable that a 1 percent rise in import price will have a smaller retail price impact for cocaine than for marijuana.

B. Effects of Arresting Couriers

So far we have considered only how interdiction of goods affects the market. However, interdiction is also supposed to create increased risks for couriers: pilots of small aircraft carrying cocaine and crewmen on vessels carrying marijuana. These people are often captured along with the drugs during interdiction, and how they are treated, once caught, will affect their perceptions of risk. Raising their risk high enough might be expected, a priori, to affect the price of the drug.

It is very difficult to obtain data on the risks faced by couriers. Records of the disposition of interdiction arrests are incomplete, and the various agencies disagree on basic estimates, such as rates of indictment, conviction, and imprisonment (General Accounting Office 1983). Based on the very fragmentary available evidence, it seems that the probability that an arrested marijuana courier will go to prison is about 40 percent.[15] If the probability of a courier's arrest is the same as the seizure rate (22.2 percent), that would imply that a marijuana courier's risk of imprisonment per trip is approximately 9 percent. The time served by imprisoned crewmen probably averaged about one year.[16] No comparable data are available for cocaine couriers.

[15] Coast Guard information for 1981 (the most recent available) shows that, in the one district for which data are available, 68 percent of arrestees were indicted and 86 percent of indictments resulted in convictions (U.S. General Accounting Office 1983, app. X). The GAO examined records of 128 individuals who were arrested and convicted as a result of seizure operations; 67 percent of these received a prison sentence. These rates are likely to be upper bounds (since, e.g., the GAO sample was missing information for many other arrestees), but taken together they suggest a maximum rate of imprisonments per arrest equal to .39 (i.e., .68 × .86 × .67).

[16] The Coast Guard reports prison sentences in South Florida, the jurisdiction accounting for most interdiction arrests, of 1.9 years. Federal offenders serve approximately 50 percent of their sentences prior to first release.

What if the government were able to raise the marijuana courier's risk radically, say, from 9 to 18 percent? The result would probably differ between marijuana and cocaine because different types of couriers may be involved. Interdiction experience indicates that a large majority of marijuana arrives by sea, mostly in small vessels operated by unskilled Colombian or other foreign nationals (National Narcotics Intelligence Consumers Committee 1984, p. 10). A significant proportion of cocaine appears to be smuggled in dedicated airplanes by skilled pilots, though there have been a number of enormous seizures (500 kg or more) of cocaine in commercial planes (see National Narcotics Intelligence Consumers Committee 1984, p. 20). In the case of marijuana boats, few crewmen have alternative earning opportunities that pay as well as smuggling. For this reason, if the risks of the activity increase, it is likely that an increase in the compensation offered will ensure an adequate supply of Colombian crewmen.

To suggest the consequences of increasing risk we use a model based on expected value of imprisonment time. A study for the Coast Guard concerning seized marijuana boats shows that the average crew numbered about six and carried about ten metric tons (10,000 kg) of marijuana (Mitchell and Bell 1980). If interdiction and prosecution rates could be raised to make crewmen's risk of one year in prison 18 percent rather than 9 percent, and if the average crewman values his freedom at $50,000 a year, each crewman would have to get $4,500 more (.09 × $50,000) per trip to compensate him for the additional risk of prison time. For a crew of six, that would raise the cost of shipping 10,000 kg by $27,000. That change increases the cost of shipment per kilogram by only $2.70—which is 0.5 percent of the importer's selling price. This would raise retail price by only $3.00 per kilo or about 0.2 percent.

Interdiction of cocaine couriers may be another story. At least some pilots bringing in drugs receive severe sentences (U.S. Senate 1981). Pilots skilled enough to fly small planes into remote airstrips at night probably have substantial alternative earning opportunities. With a high enough interdiction rate and severe enough penalties, it might be possible to deter most or all of them. The number of skilled pilots willing to incur a high probability of a long prison sentence may be very limited indeed. Nevertheless, that constraint would last only as long as it took the cocaine trade to adapt. Planes and boats are completely interchangeable for bringing in cocaine. If flying becomes too risky, importers can always revert to shipment by sea.

C. The Possibilities for Adaptation

That consideration brings us to the last point concerning the effectiveness of interdiction, namely, the ease with which cocaine and marijuana smugglers can adapt to interdiction pressure. Even if we assume that the stringency of interdiction could be greatly intensified, we cannot assume that drug smugglers will go on using the same methods once these begin to expose them to very high risks. If the seizure rate begins to rise sharply, they might change their procedures.

At present, cocaine is brought into the United States in relatively large units, often in twenty-five-kilogram loads, on dedicated planes flown by skilled pilots who assume the risk of being apprehended as cocaine couriers. This contrasts sharply with the mode of importing heroin. That drug is brought in in small units (frequently less than 2.5 kg) on general cargo or transportation vessels (both ships and planes) and by unskilled couriers, typically crewmen or air stewards. The second mode of importation appears to be less efficient. At least it is true that the absolute price increase in the export-import transaction is higher for heroin than for cocaine.

Let us assume that interdiction efforts aimed at the specialized cocaine planes become effective enough that skilled pilots could not be found to fly in the drug. More cocaine importers could then adopt the heroin mode of importation currently used by some cocaine smugglers. To see the effect of that on the final price of the drug, we can compare the costs of the two modes. The comparison is complicated by the fact that distribution is itself expensive. By importing cocaine in much smaller units, the importers are able to eliminate one level of distribution and sell further down the chain at a higher per-unit price. Taking this into account, and assuming that the price rises by 85 percent at each transaction point,[17] we can show that the middle-level price of cocaine would rise by less than $100,000 and the final price by less than $150,000 or about 20 percent.

This is not additive with the drug seizure effect since the adaptation takes place precisely to lower that seizure rate. Our models are not sufficiently refined to permit determination of the interdiction rate at which it becomes optimal to switch importing modes; in any case, it will differ among organizations. It should also be noted that the heroin

---

[17] This is consistent with a three-level distribution chain between importer and retailer and a thirteenfold price rise. Different figures would apply for marijuana.

mode price effect estimate is an upper bound since heroin couriers are probably subject to more severe penalties than are cocaine couriers if caught; that is, heroin couriers demand more money for a given size shipment.

Marijuana importers would have more difficulty adapting to extreme enforcement pressure. The bulkiness of the drug per-unit value means that the value of much smaller units simply would not compensate for the risks of smuggling them. Moreover, marijuana has a distinctive odor that is hard to mask. The heroin importation mode is not feasible. Nonetheless, importers could shift to forms of cannabis that have less bulk for a particular quantity of THC—higher potency marijuana, hashish, or hashish oil. Under current conditions, the higher labor costs of hashish production make it unattractive to market, but that could change if the risks of transporting marijuana rose.

The optimal adaptation for modest increases in pressure may simply be scaling down the size of shipment brought in by specialized vessels. Instead of bringing up "mother" ships from Colombia with fifty tons of marijuana and then off-loading to smaller coastal vessels, much marijuana is now smuggled in small, very fast oceangoing boats, known as "cigarettes." This is reflected in the failure of quantities seized to rise along with Coast Guard expenditures.

Although this adaptation raises transportation costs, it is less feasible to stop many small, fast boats than a few large ones. Since a major portion of the cost in interdiction is a Coast Guard ship's "waiting time" between sighting and boarding a smuggling vessel and returning the smuggler's boat to port (Coast Guard, personal communication, 1983), a switch to smaller smuggling craft requires much greater resources to achieve a given interdiction ratio. Moreover, with this mode of transportation, the drug again passes through fewer distribution levels, thus avoiding the markups at those levels.

Higher interdiction could also result in higher domestic production. This is not strictly an adaptation by the import business, but it could frustrate the ultimate objective of interdiction. We have little systematic data on either current or potential domestic production, but the recent increase in apparent availability of sinsemilla, Hawaiian, and other high-THC specialty varieties of marijuana suggests a substantial expansion in domestic capacity. The most recent official estimate is that 11 percent (by weight) of U.S. marijuana consumption comes from domestic sources (National Narcotics Intelligence Consumers Committee 1984, p. 9). Since domestic marijuana is of higher potency and price than imported marijuana, the domestic share of total expenditures may be much higher.

Finally, note that the cost of achieving a doubling in the interdiction rates for cocaine and marijuana may be very high indeed. The Coast Guard more than doubled its expenditures on interdiction between fiscal years 1978 and 1982 (a real increase of about 50 percent) yet seized scarcely more marijuana (and trivial amounts of any other drug) in the latter year. The interdiction rate may actually have gone down since the market probably expanded somewhat over the same period. It appears that the interdiction rate for cocaine increased substantially in 1983; that may, however, reflect a decline in the export price induced by overplanting in producer countries. Lower export price would reduce the replacement cost of seized drugs and hence the incentives to invest in costly interdiction-avoiding expenditures.

To sum up, interdiction rates currently seem to intercept about 10–30 percent of the marijuana and cocaine shipped to this country. Our analysis suggests that, unless some unforeseen change creates a strong constraint on supply in the producing countries, even much higher interdiction rates would not raise retail prices very greatly and would be very costly to achieve. If interdiction efforts were to rise sharply, cocaine and marijuana traffickers could change transportation methods that make them vulnerable to present enforcement tactics and lower the effectiveness of these efforts.

V. Actions against High-Level Domestic Distributors

The federal government has for many years conducted investigations aimed at arresting and incarcerating high-level distributors. It has recently greatly intensified that effort, as indicated by increases in the number of arrestees (table 3) and in the numbers classified as high-level dealers (Drug Enforcement Administration 1985). The DEA now devotes most of its resources to making cases against such dealers. The Treasury Department, through the Customs Service and the Internal Revenue Service (IRS), also conducts its own investigations against major dealers. These actions take the form of undercover investigation—"sting" operations—tracing dealers' finances through Currency Transaction Reports (CTRs), asset seizures, and taxation of drug-related income (National Narcotics Intelligence Consumers Committee 1983a). They have produced very visible results in the form of large drug seizures, arrests (and long prison sentences) for tens of principals in big importing and distribution enterprises, and seizures of many millions of dollars of assets. The federal drug enforcement program now accounts for a significant share of all federal law enforcement effort. For example, drug offenses accounted for 19.7 percent of all defendants disposed of in federal court in 1982, compared with 13.8 percent in 1972.

A. *Types of Actions*

In many recent successful investigations, federal agencies have mounted sting operations that capitalize on the drug trade's need for certain services. Cocaine smugglers need to obtain planes and pilots. Marijuana importers need to off-load tons of the drug very rapidly once it comes ashore and to find safe warehouses where it can be stored until sold. And high-level dealers in both trades need financial services to protect their very large incomes from detection and to invest them profitably. In buying these services from independent entrepreneurs, dealers make themselves vulnerable to investigators. In a number of cases, DEA agents have set up transportation and financial "firms," building strong cases against dealers who sought their services. For example, a federal agent with the improbable name of Ted Weed set up what became the largest off-loading enterprise in the marijuana business, leading eventually to hundreds of arrests and the seizure of hundreds of tons of marijuana (Kleiman 1985, chap. 2). In addition, federal agencies continue their more traditional types of investigations using undercover drug purchases and informants.

It has been argued that the newer investigative approaches such as sting operations have the great virtue of producing large effects because they are targeted on organizations rather than on individuals. It takes time and money for traffickers to re-create large organizations because of the need to rebuild contacts, relationships of trust, and so forth. Thus removing fifty individuals from one organization may have a larger effect than removing fifty randomly selected individuals from many organizations.

However, despite the success of such techniques in building cases, we are skeptical that eliminating organizations has much additional effect simply because there are many successful dealers who operate on a much smaller scale. If large-scale organizations were made unprofitable because of excessive exposure to law enforcement, their place would be taken by smaller-scale ones; since many smaller-scale organizations now operate, they can apparently compete with the large ones at current prices.

Apart from undercover operations, federal agencies have also begun regularly using CTRs to make cases against high-level distributors. Federal regulations require financial institutions to file CTRs for transactions of $10,000 or more. Agents have analyzed CTRs to identify members of major dealer organizations and to locate their assets for later seizure and taxation. In addition, failure to file CTRs has served as the basis for prosecution, and bribery attempts to keep bank officials from filing have provided investigative leads.[18]

Federal agencies also have authority to seize the assets of drug dealers, including vessels, aircraft, vehicles, real estate, front businesses, cash, and bank accounts. The DEA can seize assets if they are used in the drug traffic or if they were purchased with drug-produced income. The Customs Service can confiscate vehicles, aircraft, and boats used in attempts to smuggle contraband and can also seize cash entering or leaving the country in violation of currency reporting laws (reports must be filed for all cash or bearer-negotiable instruments in excess of $5,000). In addition, the IRS has used procedures such as jeopardy assessments that also enable the government to take assets quickly to satisfy tax claims.

B. Effects of Asset Seizures

Let us consider the effects of asset seizures first because the analysis is quite straightforward. The various asset seizure programs have an obvious attraction as devices for attacking the drug trade. They are relatively speedy compared with the trials of well-defended traffickers. They immobilize assets during court proceedings, thus disrupting the cash flow of criminal organizations. They serve as a condign punishment since, given that dealers enter the drug trade because they seek large incomes, it seems appropriate that they lose the assets generated by that trade. Finally, they generate revenues that help offset the costs of enforcement.

Nonetheless, it appears that these seizure programs have little prospect of making a significant difference in the retail price of drugs. The amounts reported seized do not represent the actual financial penalty

---

[18] The strengths and weaknesses of this approach have been examined in a recent report by the President's Commission on Organized Crime (1984).

imposed on a trafficker. A two-stage procedure is involved: in the first phase (seizure), the agency freezes the assets to prevent the dealer from removing them beyond the government's reach; in the second phase (forfeiture), ownership finally passes to the government after legal proceedings. After litigation, the amount realized is likely to be much lower than the amount originally seized.[19] In fact, counting actions for all types of drugs, in 1981 the DEA actually obtained only $13 million in forfeitures from its asset removal program, though seizures totaled $161 million (National Narcotics Intelligence Consumers Committee 1983*b*). For more recent years, we have only seizure figures, which in 1984 totaled $134 million. Forfeitures probably were less than half that amount.

These amounts are not large in relation to the retail value of all drugs ($20 billion for marijuana, cocaine, and heroin together, according to our lower-bound estimates). Even if federal agencies managed to realize considerably more in the future, the effect on final retail price would be modest. For example, let us suppose that the agencies could triple the value of the dealers' assets that are forfeited or taxed and that 50 percent of that value came from marijuana dealers. Although those are improbably high figures, they would raise the retail price of marijuana by less than 1 percent, treating the seizures as a tax on marijuana imports.

C. The Possibilities for Increased Investigative Effort

The prospects for making progress through intensified enforcement are a little better. One constraint that presents a major problem for local enforcement is not present; prison space can be expanded if the federal government significantly increases the numbers of those convicted of drug offenses. Also in contrast to local drug enforcement efforts, the federal government has had little difficulty in obtaining convictions and prison sentences for those it charges with violations of drug laws.

In 1984, the DEA reported 10,939 persons convicted for drug violations resulting from federal investigations (Drug Enforcement Administration 1985). In federal court, the conviction rate has been about 80 percent in recent years. Of the 10,939 convictions in 1984, 72 percent

---

[19] For instance, if a seized house is mortgaged, the mortgage holder may successfully petition for return of the property. Claims of a wife or a family may be accepted. Valuation of real property may be overstated. Vehicles may deteriorate in storage during forfeiture proceedings. In tax proceedings, the IRS may seize large amounts of assets before closure, but the amount seized may bear no relation to the actual tax assessment. Finally, the agency may lose its claim in court.

resulted in prison sentences, and the average sentence was approximately fifty-six months.[20] Though the data series available to us are not perfectly comparable, it appears that the numbers of persons convicted and the average sentence length have risen very substantially, perhaps doubling over the period 1980–84. This increase roughly parallels the increase in resources devoted to high-level drug investigations; the principal investigative and prosecutive agencies (DEA, FBI, IRS, U.S. Attorneys, and Criminal Division of the Department of Justice) increased their expenditures on drug cases from $280 million in fiscal year 1982 to $512 million in fiscal year 1984.

The success of the increased investigative effort, in terms of persons arrested, convicted, and incarcerated, is impressive. We note, though, that there are adaptations that may reduce the long-run effectiveness of that effort. We suggest that they are likely to take some time to occur because they may come about only as a result of changes in the composition of the dealer population.

For example, the newer and more successful techniques, such as sting operations and analysis of CTRs, are defeated by relatively simple adaptations. Large smuggling or distributing organizations are vulnerable to undercover operations (e.g., selling financial or transportation services) precisely because of their scale. If these investigations present too much risk, organizations can simply scale down and handle smaller quantities of both goods and money. It is useful to note here that these investigations appear to have had little success with respect to heroin, where the relatively small import bundles are handled by much smaller organizations.

As for the analysis of CTRs, a dealer can avoid the CTR requirement by converting currency into other negotiable instruments without ever making a $10,000 transaction; it simply takes slightly smaller transactions with different financial institutions. Consequently, the effectiveness of CTR analysis may be self-limiting. Ease of entry into the marijuana and cocaine markets has meant that some people who have little education or familiarity with U.S. institutions and finances have amassed considerable wealth. Thus the CTR requirement may help to weed them out, leaving a more sophisticated dealer population. It is likely that there are enough potential dealers to keep the removal of the less competent from making a difference in the market.

---

[20] Note that drug violators, like other federal prisoners, are released after serving, on the average, less than half their sentence.

D. Price Effects of Intensified Investigations

Despite the difficulties just enumerated, it is conceivable that federal agencies could, through greatly increased efforts and resource expenditures, make many more cases against high-level dealers. Let us suppose that they achieved a very large increase, say, doubling the number of drug violators now sent to prison. What effect would that have on drug prices?

We again estimate the additional compensation that dealers would require to cover their increased risks of spending time in federal prison. From the sentencing data cited earlier, we estimate that about 29,800 years of prison time were imposed on drug dealers caught as a result of federal investigation of marijuana, cocaine, and heroin dealing. Given that dealers serve, on the average, only about 45 percent of their sentence, this implies about 13,371 actual years of imprisonment.[21] Now assume that this number were doubled, that is, that 13,371 more years were imposed on dealers. In response, dealers would require extra compensation for the added risk of imprisonment. Since these are high-level dealers, many of whom are earning very large incomes, it is reasonable to impute very high values. For highest-level dealers (class 1 violators as defined by the DEA), we use a figure of $250,000, for second-level (class 2) dealers $125,000, and for the remainder $75,000.[22] Assuming the distribution of classes of dealers remained the same under the new situation as it was in 1984, the added years of imprisonment would result in a total of $2 billion added to retail prices. Compared with the total retail value of drugs, this added cost would represent a price increase of only about 10 percent.[23]

Even this modest increase would probably not appear for a few years. There would probably be a substantial time lag between increasing expenditures and completing cases. It takes time to build a network of informants, to accumulate a pool of experienced agents, and to mount investigations. These considerations must be taken together with the possibilities of dealer adaptations and the probability of very high costs.

Of course, there are numerous uncertainties here; it may be that

---

[21] Details of these calculations are presented in Kleiman (1985, tables 2–4).

[22] In 1984, the DEA estimated that, of 10,839 total domestic drug dealers sentenced, 1,447 were class 1 dealers, 779 were class 2, and 8,613 were class 3 or 4 (Drug Enforcement Administration 1985).

[23] Most of these cases are made against persons involved in high-level domestic distribution. The markup to retail price is presumably significantly less than that which applies to rises in the import price.

dealers will not readily adapt, that the agencies could accommodate large budget increases quickly, or that further innovations in investigative techniques, such as targeting organizations, will pay off more than we expect. However, with currently available information it seems unlikely that even a dramatic expansion of investigative effort against high-level drug distributors would have a very large effect on the availability or price of drugs.

It is also important to note two possible adverse consequences from increasingly stringent enforcement. First, the price increase may raise high-level dealer incomes if the elasticity of demand is less than one, a highly plausible condition for marijuana and heroin. Second, more stringent enforcement may lead to more violent organizations, which are able to discipline agents more effectively, dominating the market.

VI. Local Law Enforcement

As shown in table 3, local police make numerous arrests for drug offenses. The figure has exceeded half a million annually since 1972, though most of these arrests are for simple possession of marijuana and result in little additional penalty beyond the confiscation of a small amount of the drug. However, local law enforcement does pose a major instrument against at least one of the markets, that for heroin.

This section is divided into two parts. The first deals with the peculiar virtues of street enforcement with respect to heroin. It also argues that street enforcement is not comparably effective for cocaine and marijuana. The second part then calculates the effect on cocaine and marijuana prices of a doubling of the efficacy of local enforcement.

A. The Virtues of Street-Level Enforcement

Enforcement activities directed at major distributors and wholesalers of drugs have most of their impact on money price. In effect, they raise the "raw materials" cost of the retail-level drug dealing business without changing other conditions. Thus if high-level enforcement succeeds in raising the wholesale price of a drug, users will have to pay more for their supplies of the drug, but their search time to find a connection will not tend to change. Whether the net result is more or fewer dollars spent on the drug depends on the price elasticity of demand.

By contrast, enforcement directed at retailers and first-level wholesalers can change the number of street dealers and the openness with which they flaunt their wares. As street-level enforcement increases, the typical user will not have to pay more for a given quantity of drugs but will have to search longer for a connection. This constitutes an increase in the nonmonetary costs of the drug.

The effects of this may be large or small, but they are unambiguously good (assuming only that drug consumption is on balance an evil). Both quantity consumed and dollars spent on drugs will decrease—and, consequently, so too will the earnings of drug merchants—as a result both of the drop in quantity (due to lower effective demand) and of the downward pressure that that drop puts on prices. In addition, insofar as heroin users commit property crimes to obtain money for drugs, an increase in search time will directly reduce their incentives to commit such crimes by making it harder to convert money into heroin.

But with street-level as with high-level enforcement, heroin is far more susceptible to the effects of increased pressure than is marijuana or cocaine. Again, a major reason is sheer size: measured by numbers of regular dealers, the heroin market is perhaps a fourth the size of the cocaine market. Imposing any given level of risk on the average cocaine dealer, therefore, requires four times as many arrests, prosecutions, convictions, and prison terms as are required to impose the same level of risk on the average heroin dealer.

Two other characteristics of retail heroin dealing make it particularly susceptible to enforcement pressure. First, heroin transactions take place largely outdoors because heroin dealers are reluctant to be alone inside with heroin consumers. Second, heroin users buy drugs daily because they find it difficult or impossible to hold onto personal inventories without consuming them all at once. By contrast, marijuana transactions are infrequent; while the conventional unit of marijuana consumption is the joint, the conventional unit of purchase is the ounce, roughly sixty joints. This suggests that marijuana consumers hold personal inventories. Consequently, it is difficult to impose substantial search-time costs on a regular marijuana user, but it is easy to impose them on a regular heroin user. Moreover, since the regular heroin user suffers some discomfort unless his consumption of the drug stays regular, a failure to connect has much more serious consequences for him than an equivalent failure for even a regular marijuana user whose personal inventory is exhausted. Increased search time for heroin users, combined with occasional failures to connect, may lead users to enter drug treatment or simply to quit unassisted as the attractiveness of the user life-style decreases.

As in any drug market, if enforcement succeeds in shrinking the number of participants, the same level of enforcement resources will impose a greater level of risk on the remaining participants. In addition, a second kind of positive feedback, one due to the behavior of search time as the number of participants shrinks, may be at work in the heroin retail market. The possibility that cruising around will lead to a successful meeting whether one is a buyer looking for a seller or a seller looking for a buyer depends on the number of buyers and sellers in the market in a given region. But the number of buyers and sellers itself depends in part on the probability of a successful meeting: the search time to "score" from the buyer's perspective, the waiting time between customers from the seller's.

Unlike a higher-level dealer, a heroin retailer facing increased risks and the need to operate more discreetly may have difficulty raising his prices. He, like his customer, spends considerable time waiting for an opportunity to do business. When a willing buyer meets a willing seller, both have substantial investments in being able to take care of business right then. The situation is one of temporary bilateral monopoly, which may account for conventional pricing in the retail heroin market; no one wants to take the risk of an unsuccessful negotiation. Increased search time due to tougher enforcement increases the sunk costs on both sides; if the dealer refuses to deal with new customers, his old customers are that much more valuable to him. Thus dealers are likely to make fewer transactions without being able to raise margins. This may cause some of them to leave the business.

If, then, increasing search time in the heroin market decreases the number of active users, the decrease in the number and aggressiveness of retail dealers may not create opportunities for new entry because the smaller number of active users tends to increase dealer search time and reduce the financial rewards of the business. This combination of positive feedbacks might, in some cases, cause a local market to drop below the minimum size at which it remains self-sustaining, establishing a new equilibrium with no active users and no sellers. This is, after all, the condition that obtains throughout most of the country and even in most neighborhoods in the cities where heroin is a problem.

There is now some empirical evidence that local enforcement initiatives against heroin dealing may be effective in reducing both drug consumption and some kinds of acquisitive crime. A recent study in Lynn, Massachusetts, found that burglaries fell 41 percent year to year after the introduction of a small heroin task force (six officers from a total force of 120 in a city of 80,000) that concentrated entirely on retail sales (Kleiman, Holland, and Hayes 1984).

That decrease in burglaries was more than four times the average declines nationally, statewide, and in other Massachusetts areas with heroin problems. During the same period, demand for heroin treatment in Lynn jumped 90 percent while remaining stable in the rest of Massachusetts. Similar results have been reported (anecdotally) on the Lower East Side of Manhattan and in Richmond, Virginia.

B. Cocaine and Marijuana

For cocaine and marijuana, the dominant effect of increased local enforcement is on dealer risk. We revert then to our earlier line of analysis and try to estimate the effect that this might have on retail prices.

Arrest is, of itself, a fairly minor sanction for most arrestees. To estimate the stringency of local law enforcement, it is also necessary to obtain data on the percentages of various kinds of drug arrests leading to jail or prison sentences. Unfortunately, we have only fragmentary data on these matters. We shall use the available data to estimate the current risks that dealers face from local police, namely, the probabilities of arrest, jail time, and at least one year in prison. As before, these calculations will require that we make many assumptions. In choosing those assumptions, we shall attempt to avoid downward bias in estimating the effectiveness of possible increases in the local police effort devoted to marijuana and cocaine. We will then consider the effect on cocaine and marijuana prices of doubling local police effort.

Table 8 presents estimates of the risk of arrest for marijuana, cocaine, and heroin dealers.[24] We assume that marijuana possession arrests do not include any dealers but that one-quarter of heroin and cocaine possession arrests are of dealers.[25]

Unfortunately, heroin and cocaine are lumped together in the FBI's annual *Uniform Crime Reports.* The sale and possession arrests for heroin and cocaine are assumed to be evenly divided between the two drugs; we would guess that the true figure is that three-quarters of the dealer arrests are of heroin dealers, but that is very impressionistic. Our assumption exaggerates the estimated efficacy of the cocaine enforcement increase.

Of the jail and prison rates resulting from arrests, we have only the following data elements. (1) On December 31, 1979, 15,500 out of

[24] Throughout this section we shall ignore risks posed by federal agencies, which eschew low-level investigations and arrests.

[25] Not including jugglers (Moore 1977), i.e., addicts supporting their habits through sales.

TABLE 8
Risks Faced by Drug Retailers, 1984

	Heroin	Cocaine	Marijuana
Dealers	45,000	180,000	500,000
Sale arrests	24,000	24,000	74,000
Dealer possession arrests	12,000	12,000	0
Total dealer arrests	36,000	36,000	74,000
Annual arrests per dealer	.8	.2	.15
Probability of jail, given arrest	.16	.16	.26
Probability of prison, given arrest	.07	.07	.02
Annual probability of jail	.32	.08	.04
Annual probability of prison	.14	.035	.001
Annual expected incarceration time (days)	131	33	4.3

175,000 inmates of state prisons were serving sentences for drug offenses (Brown et al. 1984, p. 577). For purposes of calculation we assume that this is a steady-state number, that is, that 15,500 years of prison time are allocated to drug dealers each year. (2) In California, 4,931 marijuana sales arrests in 1979 produced fifty-five prison sentences and 1,301 jail sentences. Felony arrests involving drugs other than marijuana totaled 27,005 in 1979. These led to 807 prison sentences and 6,921 jail sentences.[26] (3) In New York City in 1980, there were 11,600 nonmarijuana drug felony arrests. These produced 1,200 prison sentences and 850 jail sentences (Califano 1982).[27]

The second and third pieces of data are interesting in themselves. California felony nonmarijuana drug arrestees face a 3 percent probability of a prison term, and those in New York City face over a 10 percent probability of the same outcome. But the probability of some incarceration is higher in California (28.6 percent) than in New York City (17.7 percent).

We have no data on the length of jail sentences; we know only that they are less than one year. Califano (1982) reports that only 10 percent of those jailed following conviction on misdemeanor drug arrests received more than thirty days. Let us assume, from now on, that a jail sentence is ninety days. Again, this probably biases upward our estimate of efficacy.

[26] These figures come from unpublished Offender Based Transaction Statistics tables, provided by the California Bureau of Justice Statistics.

[27] The 850 sentences were for misdemeanor convictions following felony arrest. A very small portion may have received prison sentences of a little more than a year.

For marijuana, we shall double the frequency of California for the national imprisonment rate; 2 percent of sales arrests result in prison. Judicial attitudes in California toward marijuana dealers are probably more lenient than in most other states. The jail rate we shall leave at the California level. For heroin and cocaine, we average the California and New York prison and jail rates. The probability of state prison sentence following a felony sale or dealer arrest is 7 percent; the probability of jail is 16 percent. It should be noted that these are not much lower rates than for felony arrests generally.

Our final assumption concerns length of prison sentences. The probabilities calculated so far yield approximately 5,500 dealers going to prison each year. State prisons have 15,500 serving time for drug offenses. A significant share may be for drugs other than marijuana, cocaine, or heroin. In 1981, these other drugs accounted for 32,000 sale or manufacture arrests, nearly 30 percent of the total for sale or manufacture. If we allocate for these drugs the same percentage of drug prison time, then we have 11,000 years of prison time for our three drugs and an average sentence of two years actually served.

Use of this figure, together with our assumed ninety-day jail sentence, yields the last line of table 8. The average heroin dealer can expect to spend 35 percent of his dealing career incarcerated; marijuana dealers spend 1 percent of their time incarcerated. Let us assume now that local law enforcement agencies were able to double the present level of risk imposed on cocaine and marijuana dealers. This might well require more than doubling police expenditures on drug enforcement.

If arrest rates doubled and the probabilities of various outcomes following arrest remained unchanged, what might happen to the prices of marijuana and cocaine? We need to place a value on incarceration time and on arrest itself. Given that almost all these arrests are of retailers earning significant but not large incomes from being dealers, we place a modest value on the cost of time, $50,000 per year, or $137 per day. Since arrest is a penalty per se, we need to place a value on that. Surely $5,000 would seem a high enough value for a low-level dealer. Doubling arrest and incarceration rates then requires that cocaine dealers receive an additional $7,000 each; this raises total throughput cost for twenty-three tons of cocaine by $1.3 billion or about 16 percent. For marijuana, average dealer compensation must rise by about $1,340; this raises throughput costs by $620 million or about 14 percent.

These are extremely primitive calculations. They require the use of a very large number of quantitative assumptions. We have chosen in general to use assumptions that seem biased toward detecting large effects from the application of more resources to drug law enforcement. Even under those assumptions a dramatic increase in that enforcement seems to produce only quite modest price effects. An increase of 14 percent in the price of marijuana, from about seventy-five cents to eighty-six cents per joint, would appear to require very substantial reallocation of criminal justice system resources but would generate a decrease in consumption. At a time when there is a general concern about the system's ability to apprehend and punish offenders who commit property and violent crimes, it may be hard to justify such a diversion for such modest returns.

The apparent insensitivity of the system to increases in the stringency of local enforcement is somewhat puzzling; after all, that aims at the part of the distribution system that accounts for most of the final price. If doubling the risks of arrest and incarceration for retailers does not greatly increase the price of drugs, then we must ask why the retailers receive such large returns for their participation. We speculate that the answer lies in the discontinuities of dealer utility functions. A substantial part of their current return comes from entry into the trade and is not affected by marginal changes in the various risks associated with it. For example, the vulnerability that dealers may feel as a result of their inability to seek police protection when they are robbed is not something that changes with enforcement intensity.

Similarly, the indirect risks from other participants in the trades may not be much affected by increased enforcement intensity. For example, the measures a dealer adopts to ensure that he is fairly safe from customer robbery (such as giving his drugs to an associate while he collects the money) may be just as adequate when the price of heroin is $2.00 per milligram as when it is $2.50. Finally, we suggest that, for low-level dealers, an important part of their total compensation is the return to the investment of time. If our estimates of total marijuana income, dealer numbers, and markups are correct, then the average marijuana retailer earns only about $5,000 per year from the trade. A large part of that may simply be payment for making trips to suppliers and waiting around for customers. Enforcement will have little impact on that element of his costs.

VII. Some Policy Implications

This last section considers some implications of the foregoing four policy choices. We first present a brief summary of the major results. The second part then suggests what additional considerations should be taken into account in making decisions about the level of effort that should be devoted to supply reduction programs.

A. Pessimistic Conclusions

One obvious conclusion that might be drawn from this essay is that the enforcement-oriented strategy will not work. That is not correct, or at least not in such a simple form. We have looked only at what could be achieved by fairly large increases in the efforts, predominantly federal, aimed at the cocaine and marijuana markets. The analysis has not addressed the question of what has been accomplished by drug enforcement to date. We discuss that briefly before going to the implications of what we have done.

The most striking observation about illicit drugs in this country is their high prices. Even marijuana is vastly more expensive than it would be if legally available, mostly a consequence of illegality per se and of the enforcement of that illegality. Heroin surely represents the limits of enforcement effectiveness. A white powder, readily manufactured from poppy gum, which would cost only a few dollars if legal, instead costs about $2,000 per gram on the streets of American cities. Not only is it absurdly expensive and of extraordinarily low purity, but it can also be obtained only by incurring significant risks. One surely could ask no more of enforcement against an illegal market. Yet approximately half a million people are prepared to lead quite degraded lives in pursuit of the drug.

Enforcement against cocaine and marijuana has not accomplished as much as has heroin enforcement. It is not clear that it could, given the differences in characteristics of the drugs and, perhaps relatedly, their users. But cocaine and marijuana enforcement have certainly had significant consequences for the use of the two drugs in this nation.

The question that we have addressed is whether intensified enforcement, particularly by the federal government, can much further reduce consumption. We have concluded that this is not likely. The experience of the last five years, with its large increases in federal enforcement against these drugs and at least modest increases in the risks imposed by local agencies, does not contradict this. The cocaine market may have expanded, and price has certainly declined. Marijuana prices have increased modestly, but if there has been any significant decline in consumption, as indicated by the high school seniors survey, it is most probably explained by changed attitudes toward the health consequences of marijuana use.

Part of the problem is that so many of the enforcement resources are focused on a part of the drug distribution system that accounts for very little of the retail price of the drug. Limiting coca production in Peru, capturing Colombian crewmen on marijuana smuggling ships, or imprisoning importers of Iranian heroin produces impressive statistics but imposes relatively light costs on the drug distribution system. Even producing a lot more of these enforcement outputs will not much raise the costs of distributing drugs.

More stringent enforcement at the local level does not seem to offer better prospects, except for heroin. The scale of the markets, the significance of costs that are unrelated to enforcement, and the infrequency and privacy of individual transactions all mitigate against effective cocaine and marijuana enforcement. Only for heroin do we see much possibility for increased local enforcement to reduce the availability of the drug further.

It should be noted that our analysis makes use of very conservative estimates of the size of the cocaine and marijuana markets. That has the effect of biasing upward our estimate of the efficacy of increased enforcement. For example, if the marijuana market truly is 13,000 tons and generates revenues of $18 billion, as suggested in official publications, then the likely price effect of raising total marijuana seizures through interdiction to 4,000 tons is even smaller than we estimated.

It is useful to note again that our pessimism does not extend to drug enforcement generally. There are some markets in which increased enforcement has effectively reduced the availability of the drug. Methamphetamines and methaqualone are two recent instances. Whereas these drugs were readily available in the late 1970s, a combination of treaties with the small number of foreign producer countries, in which they were produced by pharmaceutical companies for legitimate medical purposes, and the targeting of abusive prescribers in the United States, greatly reduced their availability and use by 1984. The need for expensive centralized production facilities was probably critical in those cases.

B. Evaluating Drug Enforcement Policies

The analysis above lays the basis for evaluating drug enforcement policy choices, at least qualitatively. Those choices can be thought of as concerning (1) the overall budget; (2) its allocation between high-level (close to the source for the importer) and street-level (close to the final retail transaction) activities; and (3) its allocation among target drugs—

marijuana, cocaine, heroin, and the "dangerous drugs" (synthetics). The current federal strategy is to increase the resources available, direct attention toward high-level cases, and concentrate on marijuana and cocaine.

An evaluation ought to consider both the efficacy of a given set of enforcement activities (compared to their costs and the alternative uses of those resources) in reducing drug abuse and any unwanted side effects it may have.

The analysis above does not allow us to judge whether the increase in the overall federal drug enforcement budget is wise. The current budget of about $1.2 billion looks small in relation to either the $20–$35 billion Americans spend each year on illicit drugs or the recent $47 billion estimate of the total annual social costs of illicit drug abuse (Harwood et al. 1984). On the other hand, $1.2 billion is a healthy chunk of the total federal law enforcement budget—roughly $4 billion—and a multiple of the negligible sums spent on drug abuse prevention. One cannot say whether we should be spending more or less on drug enforcement overall without making assumptions about the alternative uses of those funds, unless it appears that some spending is either futile or likely to generate unwanted side effects of greater magnitude than its benefits.

Much of the current surge in federal drug enforcement spending may, however, be going into precisely such futile or counterproductive uses. High-level marijuana and cocaine enforcement is likely to be of very limited efficacy in reducing drug abuse both because of the limited ability of federal enforcement to increase prices and otherwise limit availability and because of the relatively inelastic demand for marijuana and cocaine. Inelastic demand—the tendency of marijuana and cocaine consumers to reduce consumption less than proportionately if prices increase—means that the total dollars paid for these drugs will tend to increase as enforcement increases prices. This creates two unwanted side effects, one on consumers' budgets and the other on illicit revenues; as consumers pay more, becoming poorer, drug market entrepreneurs earn more, becoming richer. If, in addition, toughened enforcement encourages the development of drug-dealing organizations that are more enforcement resistant because they are more violent and corrupt, the overall result of putting more pressure on the top levels of the marijuana and cocaine trades will be to give the most dangerous criminals a bigger share of a larger market.

Increasing enforcement directed against users and low-level dealers of marijuana and cocaine, though without the side effects of increasing high-level enforcement, is likely to be futile because of the sheer numbers involved. Local police already arrest 400,000 marijuana consumers per year; to make use significantly more risky would require a substantial rise in the share of scarce prison space allocated to users of the drug. Heroin, by contrast, trades in a much smaller market in which demand, we have argued, is likely to be relatively elastic to price. Both these factors boost the likely efficacy of increased enforcement pressure in reducing drug abuse, and elastic demand also means that dollars spent by addicts and earned by dealers will decrease rather than increase if enforcement tightens.

High-level heroin enforcement thus deserves a bigger share than it now receives of federal drug resources. In addition, since the size and structure of the retail heroin market make it a particularly attractive enforcement target, it might be desirable to find ways to funnel federal resources into street-level heroin enforcement. This could take the form of federal investigation and prosecution of retail-level cases—as exemplified by the DEA State-Local Task Forces (now largely moribund) or the prosecutions under Manhattan's Operation Pressure Point—or of federal funding of local agents and prosecutors.

Policy-making in a field as highly charged as drug abuse is not likely to be so rational—in the economic sense—as to make these relatively refined notions a central part of the debate. We hope, however, that the approach suggested here, and the numbers that the approach generates, will create a greater interest in determining just what will be accomplished by ever-increasing federal enforcement against the cocaine and marijuana trades.

REFERENCES

Brinkley, Joel. 1984. "Bolivia Drug Crackdown Brews Trouble." *New York Times* (September 12).
Brown, Edward, Timothy Flanagan, and Maureen McLeod. 1984. *Sourcebook of Criminal Justice Statistics, 1983*. Albany, N.Y.: Criminal Justice Research Center.
Bruun, Kettil, Lynn Pan, and Ingemar Rexed. 1975. *The Gentlemen's Club*. Chicago: University of Chicago Press.
Califano, Joseph. 1982. *The 1982 Report on Drug Abuse and Alcoholism: A Report to Hugh L. Carey, Governor, State of New York*. Albany, N.Y.

Carlson, Ken, Joan Peterson, Lindsey Stellwagen, Naomi Goldstein, and Herbert Weisberg. 1983. *Unreportable Taxable Income from Selected Illegal Activities.* Cambridge, Mass.: Abt.

Cook, Philip J. 1980. "Research in Criminal Deterrence: Laying the Groundwork for the Second Decade." In *Crime and Justice: An Annual Review of Research,* vol. 2, edited by Norval Morris and Michael Tonry. Chicago: University of Chicago Press.

Drug Abuse Policy Office. 1982. *Federal Strategy for Prevention of Drug Abuse and Drug Trafficking, 1982.* Washington, D.C.: White House.

Drug Enforcement Administration. 1985. *Statistical Report, Fiscal Year 1984.* Washington, D.C.: Drug Enforcement Administration.

Federal Bureau of Investigation. 1981–84. *Uniform Crime Reports.* Washington, D.C.: U.S. Government Printing Office.

Harwood, Henrick, Diane Napolitano, Patricia Kristiansen, and James Collins. 1984. *Economic Costs to Society of Alcohol and Drug Abuse and Mental Illness: 1980.* Research Triangle Park, N.C.: Research Triangle Institute.

Kaplan, John. 1983. *Heroin: The Hardest Drug.* Chicago: University of Chicago Press.

Kleiman, Mark. 1985. *Allocating Federal Drug Enforcement Resources: The Case of Marijuana.* Ph.D. dissertation, Harvard University.

Kleiman, Mark, William Holland, and Christopher Hayes. 1984. *Report to the District Attorney for Essex County: Evaluation of the Lynn Drug Task Force.* Cambridge, Mass.: Harvard University, John F. Kennedy School of Government, Program in Criminal Justice Policy and Management.

Miller, J. D., I. H. Cisin, H. Gardiner-Keaton, P. W. Wirtz, H. I. Abelson, and P. M. Fishburne. 1982. *National Survey on Drug Abuse: Main Findings, 1982.* Washington, D.C.: National Institute on Drug Abuse.

Mitchell, T., and R. Bell. 1980. *Drug Interdiction Operations by the Coast Guard.* Alexandria, Va.: Center for Naval Analysis.

Moore, Mark. 1977. *Buy and Bust.* Lexington, Mass.: Heath.

National Narcotics Intelligence Consumers Committee. 1982. *Narcotics Intelligence Estimate.* Washington, D.C.: Drug Enforcement Administration.

———. 1983a. *An Evaluation of the Methodologies for Producing Narcotics Intelligence Estimates.* Washington, D.C.: Drug Enforcement Administration.

———. 1983b. *Narcotics Intelligence Estimate.* Washington, D.C.: Drug Enforcement Administration.

———. 1984. *Narcotics Intelligence Estimate.* Washington, D.C.: Drug Enforcement Administration.

Polich, J. M., P. Ellickson, P. Reuter, and J. Kahan. 1984. *Strategies for Controlling Adolescent Drug Use.* Santa Monica, Calif.: Rand.

President's Commission on Law Enforcement and Administration of Justice. 1967. *Task Force Report: Organized Crime.* Washington, D.C.: President's Committee on Organized Crime, U.S. Government Printing Office.

President's Commission on Organized Crime. 1984. *The Cash Connection: Organized Crime, Financial Institutions, and Money Laundering.* Washington, D.C.: U.S. Government Printing Office.

Reuter, Peter. 1983. *Disorganized Crime: The Economics of the Visible Hand.* Cambridge, Mass.: MIT Press.

———. 1984*a*. "The (Continuing) Vitality of Mythical Numbers." *Public Interest* 78 (Spring): 135–47.

———. 1984*b*. "The Economic Significance of Illegal Markets in the United States: Some Observations." In *L'Economie non-officielle,* edited by Edith Archambault and Xavier Greffe. Paris: Maspero.

Simon, Carl, and Ann Witte. 1982. *Beating the System.* Boston: Auburn.

Treaster, Joseph. 1984. "Jamaica, Close U.S. Ally, Does Little to Halt Drugs." *New York Times* (September 10).

U.S. Department of Justice. 1984. *Organized Crime Drug Enforcement Task Force Program: Annual Report.* Washington, D.C.: U.S. Department of Justice.

———. 1985. *Organized Crime Drug Enforcement Task Force Program: Annual Report.* Washington, D.C.: U.S. Department of Justice.

U.S. Department of State. Bureau of International Narcotics Matters. 1985. *Narcotics Profile Papers.* Washington, D.C.: U.S. Government Printing Office.

U.S. General Accounting Office. 1983. *Federal Drug Interdiction Efforts Need Strong Central Oversight.* Report GGD-83-52. Washington, D.C.: U.S. Government Printing Office.

U.S. Senate. 1980. *Organized Crime and the Use of Violence.* Hearings before the Permanent Subcommittee on Investigations of the Committee on Government Affairs. Washington, D.C.: U.S. Government Printing Office.

———. 1981. *International Narcotics Trafficking.* Hearings before the Permanent Subcommittee on Investigations of the Committee on Government Affairs. Washington, D.C.: U.S. Government Printing Office.

———. 1985. *International Narcotics Control.* Hearings before the Committee on Appropriations. Washington, D.C.

White House. 1984. *1984 National Strategy for Prevention of Drug Abuse and Drug Trafficking.* Washington, D.C.: U.S. Government Printing Office.